# What the General Practitioner Should Know About Trademarks and Copyrights

# American Law Institute
# American Bar Association
# Committee on Continuing Professional Education



ALI ABA

4025 Chestnut Street, Philadelphia, Pennsylvania 19104

# What the General Practitioner Should Know About Trademarks and Copyrights

**Fifth Edition**

**Arthur H. Seidel**

of the Pennsylvania, New York,
and District of Columbia Bars

ALI ABA

AMERICAN LAW INSTITUTE-AMERICAN BAR ASSOCIATION
COMMITTEE ON CONTINUING PROFESSIONAL EDUCATION
4025 CHESTNUT STREET • PHILADELPHIA • PENNSYLVANIA 19104

Library of Congress Catalog Number: 86-070229


First Edition 1959. Fifth Edition 1986

Printed in the United States of America

ISBN: 0-8318-0517-X

J. Murray Elwood of the ALI-ABA staff
supervised the publication of this book.

# Foreword

Over the years, ALI-ABA has been privileged to publish three handbooks by Mr. Arthur Seidel dealing with the law of intellectual property—*What the General Practitioner Should Know About Patent Law and Practice; What the General Practitioner Should Know About Trade Secrets and Employment Contracts;* and *What the General Practitioner Should Know About Trademarks and Copyrights.* New editions of the first two volumes appeared in 1984; this fifth edition of *What the General Practitioner Should Know About Trademarks and Copyrights* brings the entire series up-to-date.

Although the nonspecialist may have few occasions to actually register a trademark or copyright, some general knowledge of the field may at times be required to handle such diverse matters as a divorce, the purchase of a computer, or the settlement of an estate. Hence Mr. Seidel's lucid and succinct explanations of basic intangible-property law have been among the most popular ALI-ABA publications, offering general practitioners a sound introduction to complex subject matter.

For his contributions to the continuing education of the bar, ALI-ABA, his reading public, and the legal profession are deeply in debt to Mr. Seidel.

PAUL A. WOLKIN
*Executive Director,*
The American Law Institute-
American Bar Association Committee
on Continuing Professional Education

# Foreword

# Preface

In the seven years since the Fourth Edition was published, profound changes in the law of Copyrights have taken place. Similarly, there have been significant clarifications in the law of Trademarks.

The protection of software and of chips reflects the modernization of the law of Copyrights and the totally new mask statute.

The Supreme Court has clarified the status of incontestable trademark registrations.

I wish to thank my colleague Kathleen J. Gallagher, Esq., who worked closely with me on this new edition.

January 1986 Arthur H. Seidel

# Contents

Chapter 5



Chapter 6

Chapter 7



Chapter 8



Chapter 9



Chapter 10

## Chapter 11

# 1
# Introduction

## § 1.01 ORIGIN OF TRADEMARK AND COPYRIGHT STATUTES

The American trademark system is complicated because it comprises two separate systems; namely, the federal trademark statute and the trademark statutes of each of the states. The reason for the dual nature of our trademark law arises from this fact: The Federal Constitution provides in the same clause for a patent system and for a copyright system.

> Article I, Section 8. The Congress shall have power . . .
>
> To promote the progress of science and useful arts, by securing for limited times to authors and inventors the exclusive right to their respective writings and discoveries.

At the same time, however, it is completely silent with respect to provisions for regulating trademarks.

The Federal Government, therefore, has exclusive control over the patent and copyright system,[1] and legislation directed to these systems has been included among the earliest federal statutes—enactments in 1790. But it was not until 1870 that the Congress first acted concerning the regulation of trademarks. The results of this legislation were less than pleasing and point up the reason for the dual system. The Trademark Act of 1870 was held unconstitutional in the *Trade-Mark Cases*[2] on the grounds that the federal authority to regulate trademarks was limited to trademarks used in interstate commerce, in commerce with foreign nations, or with Indian tribes and did not extend to the regulation of marks used solely in intrastate commerce. Accordingly, each of the subsequent

---

[1] Until January 1, 1978, the effective date of the new copyright act, common law copyright was governed by state law. Thus the federal statute did not apply until after a work had been published. The new copyright act, however, covers both published and unpublished works.

[2] 100 U.S. 82 (1879).

trademark statutes, including the Lanham Act,[3] has been limited to the regulation of trademarks used in that manner.

It is more than a matter of mere academic interest that the trademark law does not stem directly from the Constitution. This failing has often led to serious problems that continue to plague the law.

Differences between the federal trademark statute and the trademark statutes of the states give rise to different approaches in the trademark law. For example, as discussed later, a number of the states have statutes dealing with the concept of "trademark dilution." Trademark dilution occurs when an important trademark is used on goods different from those used by the original trademark user.

The differences between the state statutes and the federal statute, which is silent on "dilution," give rise to problems that should not be present in a field in which interstate commerce is so obviously and drastically affected.

The trademark statutes of many states provide only for the registration of true trademarks; that is, marks applied by a manufacturer or merchant to identify particular goods and to distinguish his goods from those manufactured or sold by others. Stated conversely, there is no provision in these states for the registration of service marks. The lack of a register requires that parties in any litigated matter prove their title to a given mark on an individual controversy basis. Experience has shown that this kind of system inevitably fosters problems, since unscrupulous persons soon realize that the proof of title to valuable property rights cannot be established with certainty.

Conversely, the lack of a register prevents well-meaning third parties from ascertaining the existence of earlier used and subsisting service marks within the state in which they intend to operate; and this lack of information leads to conflicts that otherwise would not have arisen.

## § 1.02 THE LAW OF UNFAIR COMPETITION AND TRADEMARKS

Unfair competition has been described as the unfair sailing in another man's wind. Historically, the law of unfair competition in the United States is derived from the old common law action of "passing off" or "palming off." This branch of the law, however, has developed far beyond causes of action based on "palming off."

---

[3] Trademark Act of 1946, 15 U.S.C. §§ 1051–1127 (1982).

The development of modern advertising techniques and the recognition of the value of goodwill, both to a business enterprise and to trademarks owned by the business enterprise, have led to the development of a law of trademarks and the enveloping body of law known as unfair competition.

Unfortunately, there is no federal statute directed to unfair competition. Although the Ninth Circuit Court of Appeals has, on occasion, viewed the Lanham Act as creating a federal unfair competition statute, the overwhelming body of law supports the contention that the law of unfair competition is governed by applicable state law under *Erie Railroad Co. v. Tompkins.*[4]

A notable bridging statutory provision is contained in Section 43(a) of the Lanham Act.[5] This statute has been interpreted far more broadly than one unfamiliar with its background would surmise. Thus the Lanham Act, because of Section 43(a), is more extensive than a mere Trademark Act; and many acts of unfair competition having little, if anything, to do with trademark infringement are actionable under Section 43(a).

Congress will hopefully enact a federal unfair competition statute achieving uniformity throughout the country at least with regard to unfair competitive acts that affect interstate commerce.

## § 1.03 CATEGORIES OF MARKS

Marks may be divided into various categories according to their different properties. They may be categorized by their *form,* for example, a word, a composite of a word and a symbol, or a symbol, such as the design of an animal or an abstract design. Moreover, marks may be divided according to their *mode of use,* as is done in the Lanham Act. Marks may also be categorized or divided according to *strength,* for example, characterizing the mark as a "technical" or "strong" mark, a "suggestive" mark, a "descriptive" mark, or, to round out the spectrum, even as a mark incapable of functioning as a trademark, such as a "generic" mark.

The Lanham Act distinguishes four kinds of marks based on use. These are as follows: (1) trademarks, sometimes referred to by the authorities as "true" trademarks; (2) service marks; (3) certification marks; and (4) collective marks.

---

[4] 304 U.S. 64 (1938).

[5] *Supra* note 3, § 1125(a).

The term *trademark* is defined as including any word, name, symbol, or device, or any combination of these adopted and used by a manufacturer or merchant to identify and distinguish his goods from those manufactured or sold by others. In order for a word, name, symbol, or device to serve as a mark used in commerce, it must be placed in some manner on the goods, containers, or displays associated with the goods or on tags or labels affixed to the goods. It follows that the use of the word, name, symbol, or device in advertising, literature, or other writings not directly connected or associated with the goods does not constitute a trademark use within the contemplation of the Lanham Act. As will be more fully developed later, this is an important consideration when the registration of a trademark is undertaken; and it is necessary to provide the first date of use to the Patent Office. Parenthetically, as of 1975 the correct name is the "Patent and Trademark Office," and the "Commissioner of Patents and Trademarks." In the interest of brevity, however, reference throughout this text will be to their former names of "Patent Office" and "Commissioner of Patents."

It is possible not only to obtain rights in marks that identify goods but also to obtain rights in what is known as a *service mark.* The Lanham Act defines a service mark as a mark used in the sale or advertising of services to identify the services of one person and distinguish them from the services of others and includes, without limitation, the marks, names, symbols, titles, designations, slogans, character names, and distinctive features of radio or other advertising used in commerce. Examples of services are those rendered by cleaning establishments and refurbishing services, as well as transportation, entertainment, and engineering and development services.

A *certification mark,* as used within the meaning of the Lanham Act, means a mark used upon, or in connection with, the products or services of one or more persons, other than the owner of the mark, to certify regional or other origin, material, mode of manufacture, quality, accuracy, or other characteristics of the goods or services or to certify that the work or labor on the goods or services was performed by members of a union or other organization. Examples of these certification marks include the various "seals of approval" conferred on goods by magazines, trade associations, professional societies, testing laboratories, and similar entities.

A *collective mark,* as defined in the Lanham Act, is a trademark or service mark used by the members of a cooperative, an association, or other collective group or organization, and includes marks used to indicate membership in a union, an association, or other organization. The distinction between a collective mark and a trademark or service mark is that the collective mark is used solely to indicate membership, as on letterheads, whereas trademarks or service marks are applied to goods or services that the association sells or performs.

Trademarks, as noted before, may also be classified by their strength. By *strength,* as used in the trademark sense, is meant the degree to which a mark is a *technical* mark, as compared with a mark that is merely descriptive or deceptively misdescriptive of the goods.

The distinction between a coined or arbitrary or fanciful trademark and one that is descriptive of the goods was noted early in the development of trademark law. The classic example of a coined, arbitrary, and fanciful trademark is "Kodak," which is a meaningless word specifically coined to serve as a trademark with no descriptive or even suggestive connotation in any language. Marks of this nature are clearly entitled to the maximum protection available under the trademark law. On the other hand, it is manifest that protection should not be granted to a mark that consists of a word or symbol closely related to, and descriptive of, the goods to which it is applied. For example, "Carbonated" as applied to an effervescent soft drink could not constitute any trademark. This mark is clearly generic to all effervescent soft drinks, and to award it to one proprietor and in effect deny it to his competitor would result in a rank injustice. Stated conversely, it is impossible for a mark such as "Carbonated" to distinguish one producer's effervescent soft drink from another's and, accordingly, this mark is a generic one incapable of serving as a trademark for soft drinks. It is, however, capable of serving as a trademark for other goods, such as clothing; and for certain goods, it may rise to the level of a very strong trademark.

Intermediate between true technical marks, such as "Kodak," and generic marks, such as "Carbonated" when applied to soft drinks, the law distinguishes between marks that are *suggestive* and those that are *descriptive.* Suggestive marks do not require "secondary meaning" to function as trademarks and, as will be brought out later, may be registered upon the Principal Register. Descriptive marks that are capable of distinguishing goods or services may have standing in the trademark law provided the mark has become distinctive in commerce. One of the most interesting and novel provisions of the Lanham Act is a criterion used as one of the methods for establishing the presence of "secondary meaning" (this term itself is not used in the Act)—namely, substantially exclusive and continuous use of a mark in commerce for five years may constitute prima facie evidence that the mark has become distinctive.[6]

Both the Lanham Act and case law set up additional areas that limited the "strength" of a mark. For example, a mark that, when applied, is primarily geographically descriptive or deceptively misdescriptive of its goods or is primarily only a surname will not be deemed registerable upon the Principal Register unless secondary meaning has been established, that is, a statutory standard of relative weakness.[7]

Other marks that are altogether nonregistrable under the Lanham Act and that will probably not be accorded protection by the federal courts in infringement litigation, even when no claim to registration is made, are marks that are immoral, deceptive, scandalous or that disparage or falsely suggest a connection with persons, institutions, beliefs, or national symbols or that would bring them into contempt or disrepute.

Marks that consist of the flag or the coat of arms or other insignia of the United States, a state, a municipality, or any foreign nation are also refused registration under the Lanham Act, as are marks consisting of a name, portrait, or signature identifying a particular living individual except when his consent has been obtained, or consisting of a name, signature, or portrait of a deceased President of the United States during the life of his widow except when the consent of the widow has been obtained.

Trademarks may also be categorized by their *nature.* Thus it is possible for a word or words to be a mark or for a symbol, such as a red dot, to be a mark. It is also possible for a mark to constitute a composite including both words and symbols. "Kodak," "Coke," and "General Electric" are examples of word marks. The familiar pictorial symbols of Golden Arches, a muscular arm clenching a hammer, or the Green Giant should awaken a recognition response in all readers as symbol marks. "Gulf" within an orange disc and "Chevrolet" within its familiar geometrical pattern are examples of composite word-and-symbol marks.

The law of trademarks, however, is not limited to word marks, symbol marks, and composites of the two. The Lanham Act recognizes that the label as a whole may constitute a mark, and, indeed, the package or the configuration of the goods may constitute a mark.

---

[6] *See* Section 2(f) of the Lanham Act, *supra* note 3, at § 1052(f).

[7] For the peculiar problems attendant on surname marks, see pp. 40–42.

The mark may also consist of numerals, letters, monograms, slogans, surnames, phrases, or geographical terms. In particular, in the area of service marks, it is no longer necessary that the mark consist of matter that may be read or that may be adequately represented pictorially. Thus the familiar musical notes that form the identifying signal for radio stations in the National Broadcasting Company network have been registered as a service mark.

The distinctions between trademarks and trade names should be understood. A "trade name" or "commercial name" includes individual names and surnames; firm names and trade names used by manufacturers, industrialists, merchants, agriculturists, and others to identify their businesses, vocations, or occupations; names or titles of persons, firms, associations, corporations, companies, unions, and any manufacturing, industrial, commercial, agricultural, or other organization engaged in trade or commerce and capable of suing and being sued in a court of law. An example of a trade name is Sun Oil Company, whereas an example of a trademark is "Sunoco."

Parenthetically, trade names are not registerable under the Lanham Act.[8] The Lanham Act specifically provides for their protection in the case of foreign nationals.[9] Under the overwhelming majority holdings of the Courts of Appeals, trade names are protected by the applicable state law of unfair competition and not by the federal law.

There is a gray area in which it is not clear whether a given symbol constitutes a trademark or a trade name usage, or both. This gray area is usually present when the corporate name or trade name includes, or is identical to, the trademark. Under circumstances of this nature it is often difficult to determine whether a given usage is a trademark usage or a trade name usage. In these cases the term or symbol should be used on the label at least twice, once devoid of any connection with a geographical entity or company or corporate indication and once accompanied by a company or corporate indication and a geographical entity. Thus if Apex, Inc., of New York, New York, is using "Apex" as its principal trademark, both registration and enforcement problems can be eliminated by placing "Apex" on the label by itself and also by placing "Apex, Inc., New York, New York" on the label. If "Apex" is a registered mark, then

---

[8] Recent decisions have leaned heavily toward permitting trade names to function as a mark when service mark registration is sought. See p. 42.

[9] *Supra* Note 3, § 1126(g).

the notice of registration, such as the symbol®, should be placed only after "Apex" and not after "Apex, Inc., New York, New York."

## § 1.04 COPYRIGHTS

The law of copyrights was initially directed solely to the protection of literary and artistic property. Expanded by both statute and case law, it now overlaps the law of design patents[10] and the law of trademarks, as in the protection of "labels."

Briefly stated, the law of copyrights protects against the unauthorized printing, reprinting, publishing, copying, selling, translating, conversion, arrangement, adaptation, delivery, or performance of a copyrighted work.

The categories of work of authorship that may be proper subject matter for copyright protection are set forth in Section 102 of Title 17 of the United States Code, Title 17 being the portion of the United States Code that comprises the copyright act. The classfication adopted in Section 102 is as follows:

(1) Literary works
(2) Musical works, including any accompanying words
(3) Dramatic works, including any accompanying music
(4) Pantomimes and choreographic works
(5) Pictorial, graphic, and sculptural works
(6) Motion pictures and other audiovisual works
(7) Sound recordings.

Although the prior listing is not comprehensive and is specifically stated to be thus in the act, it gives a reasonably complete picture of materials that may be protected by copyright.

In view of Class (5) that covers prints or labels used for articles of merchandise, a clear demarcation should be made between a trademark under the Lanham Act and a label under the copyright act. Page 10 contains a specimen of a card used to carry patented adhesive cloth picture hangers by Jiffy Enterprises, Inc., of Philadelphia. This card aptly illustrates the distinction. The card carries the trademark "Jiffy," which is a registered trademark as indicated by the ® adjacent to the mark. The card in its entirety also forms the subject matter of a suitable print and pictorial illustration, including

---

[10] *See* A. SEIDEL, WHAT THE GENERAL PRACTITIONER SHOULD KNOW ABOUT PATENT LAW AND PRACTICE (4th ed. 1984).

prints or labels used for articles of merchandise within 17 U.S.C. § 102(5). Therefore, upon a given label, such as the label of a soft drink or a cosmetic, the entire label may be the proper subject matter of a copyright registration, although the trademark portion of it may be the subject matter of a trademark registration. In appropriate cases an entire label may also prove to be a trademark within the meaning of a Supplemental Register trademark (see pp. 21–22).

It is to be stressed that, for practical business and legal reasons, prime emphasis in any marketing situation should be on the trademark, with the label as a whole and its registration under the provisions of the copyright act constituting secondary matter. Thus the entire thrust of modern advertising is an emphasis or focusing upon a trademark and not upon a label.

The basis for relief and measure of relief under the copyright law differs markedly from that under the trademark law, and the inferiorities of the former, as compared to the latter, should be clearly understood. Relief under the copyright law is available only when actual copying is present. Individual words (and, surprisingly, even book titles) are not registrable under the copyright act, although with book titles and the like, in which copying has been found to be present, relief may be accorded on common law grounds, such as unfair competition.

## § 1.05 UNFAIR COMPETITION

As a practical matter, the law of unfair competition can be divided into the law of trademarks and all else that is encompassed within the law of unfair competition. As a general rule, the law of trademarks is relatively well developed both in case law and in statute, although the remaining body of the law of unfair competition is in an unsettled state. For example, there is the detailed federal trademark statute—the Lanham Act—although the majority of the Courts of Appeals maintain that there is no federal statute relating to unfair competition except, as discussed, the provisions of the Lanham Act that accord protection against unfair competition to nationals of foreign countries having treaties with the United States and that cover false designations of origin and false descriptions.

Therefore, by and large, the law of unfair competition stems from the common law of the separate states. Inasmuch as the state decisional and statutory laws relating to unfair competition are not uniform, there is no uniform body of unfair competition law. A corollary of this is that the jurisdiction of federal courts, in circuits

following the majority view over acts of unfair competition, is dependent upon either diversity of citizenship or pendent jurisdiction under 28 U.S.C. § 1338(b),[11] which provides:

> (b) The district courts shall have original jurisdiction of any civil action asserting a claim of unfair competition when

[11] This provision is deemed by many authorities as a codification of Hurn v. Oursler, 289 U.S. 238 (1933), although the view has been expressed with increasing force that the statute extends beyond this decision. For an example of the scope of this statute, see American Foresight, Inc. v. Fine Arts Sterling Silver, Inc., 268 F. Supp. 656 (E.D. Pa 1967).

joined with a substantial and related claim under the copyright, patent or trademark laws.

It is difficult to categorize all the acts encompassed within the law of unfair competition. These may range from the dynamiting of a competitor's trucks to the simulation of the package dress of his goods. The following listing embraces, in generalities, the major aspects of the law of unfair competition.

Passing or palming off one product for another (this may be accomplished with or without trademark simulation, as by simulation of overall shape, getup, label dress, and insignia); false or misleading advertising, or both; disparagement of a competitor's goods, property, or reputation (which concept is presently extended in liberal jurisdictions far beyond the classical actions for libel and slander or even so-called trade libel); the law of trade secrets and property rights in unpatented or nonpatentable but valuable intangible information,[12] the law of trade name simulation; interference with the business growth of another (which includes the old cause of action of interference with the contractual rights of another when the contractual rights involve commercial matters); unfair use of literary property; obstruction or menacing of competitor's suppliers or customers; bribery in competition; unfair usage of imported products; unfair usage of corporate stock.

In recent years the law of unfair competition has been extended to include causes of action involving drastic means affecting public policy considerations, such as actions for boycott, price wars, unfounded patent litigation, and violent physical aggression. Frequently these last-mentioned acts may be most readily dealt with as causes of action arising under the antitrust laws, and when intent to monopolize or conspiracy elements are present, serious consideration should always be given to a treble damage recovery under the antitrust laws, coupled with, or as an alternative to, an action for unfair competition.

The law of unfair competition is, therefore, a flexible changing concept that does and should adapt itself to social and business changes.

---

[12] *See* A. SEIDEL, supra note 10, Ch. 14 at 121. *See also* A. SEIDEL, WHAT THE GENERAL PRACTITIONER SHOULD KNOW ABOUT TRADE SECRETS AND EMPLOYMENT AGREEMENTS (2nd ed. 1984).

# 2
# Trademark Statutes

## § 2.01 COMPARISON BETWEEN FEDERAL AND STATE STATUTES

The duality of the United States trademark system has been referred to in Chapter 1, in which it was seen that the constitutional failure to include trademarks has led to the development of simultaneous state and federal trademark systems.

The federal statute relating to trademarks is based upon the interstate commerce clause of the Constitution. Notwithstanding the fact that both patents and trademarks are administratively dealt with by the Patent Office in the Department of Commerce, while copyrights are dealt with by the Register of Copyrights in the Library of Congress, the law of patents and copyrights springs from an express constitutional provision that confers exclusive jurisdiction on Congress (article 1, section 8), but the law of trademarks has no constitutional antecedent. This lack of a constitutional provision has resulted in both the federal trademark statute, referred to previously, and the separate trademark statutes in each of the states.

The trademark statutes of the several states vary from state to state, although in recent years there has been a pronounced effort to secure uniform state trademark registration legislation; and a number of states have already adopted a so-called Model Act. At the present time, however, a multitude of different registration procedures are employed among the states.[1] Conventionally, the registration of trademarks within a state is handled by the Secretary of State for the state. Trademark applications are frequently examined solely for compliance with formal requirements, although some of the states have an examination system in which a comparison is made with prior registered marks of the state. A fairly large number of states follow the classification system for goods adopted by the Patent Office, and some of the states have entirely lifted the regis-

---

[1] For a compilation of the state statutes relating to the registration of trademarks, see 2 SEIDEL, DUBROFF & GONDA, TRADEMARK LAW AND PRACTICE, App. M (1963).

tration provisions of either the Act of 1905 or the Lanham Act into their registration procedures.

Many of the states provide for the cancellation of registrations, both by court proceedings and by administrative action. In some of the states cancellation may be had by virtue of a prior federal registration in a third party for the same or a similar mark.

The duration of trademark registration varies from state to state, but in many states it is ten years. In some states the duration is deemed to be perpetual. This provision has proved to be highly objectionable and in recent years has been dropped by some of these states. A register that carries trademark registrations on a perpetual basis has no way of automatically divorcing itself from deadwood—for instance, marks that are no longer being used. The requirement of renewal after a fixed period, such as ten or twenty years, has the great advantage of eliminating nonused marks from the register.

Perhaps the widest divergency in state trademark statutes arises in the area of relief accorded to the owners of state trademark registrations. In some states the infringement of trademark rights is regarded as a quasi-criminal or criminal act, bordering closely on counterfeiting; and extremely severe penalties, far more severe than even the treble damage provisions of the federal statute, are available to the victorious registrant litigant. In fact, in some states the provisions relating to trademark infringement are largely or entirely penal or punitive in nature and include imprisonment. It is to be remembered that the federal trademark act is entirely a civil act, and there are no penal provisions contained in it. In recent years, however, the relative harshness of almost all of the state trademark statutes has been mitigated.

An insight into the nature of both federal and state systems may be gained by comparing the advantages to be derived from registering a trademark under the federal act as opposed to the state act. These include the following:

(1) A federal registration, other than a federal trademark registration on the Supplemental Register, is constructive notice to the country at large of the registrant's claim of ownership and is not limited to a single state.

(2) The registrant of a federal trademark registration has the right to bring suit in the United States courts, regardless of the amount in controversy or the diversity of citizenship.

(3) A federal registration entitles the registrant to register his mark substantially as a matter of right in a large number of foreign countries. No parallel rights flow from a state trademark registration.

(4) A federal trademark registration, other than a federal trademark registration on the Supplemental Register, may be filed with the Treasury Department and used to stop importations bearing infringing marks under the provisions of 19 U.S.C. § 1526 and Section 42 of the Lanham Act.[2]

(5) The scope of marks that may be registered upon the registers provided by the Lanham Act is considerably broader than that of the marks that may be registered under any of the state registration acts.[3]

(6) Since, unlike infringement actions under the patent and copyright laws, the federal courts and the state courts have concurrent jurisdiction in respect to trademark infringement actions, a federal registration may be relied upon, even in suits brought in state courts.

(7) The rights to relief and freedom from concern conferred upon the registrant by the Lanham Act far exceed those conferred by any state statute except in the area of penalties and in the concept of dilution.[4]

It is to be noted that the intent-of-act statement contained in Section 45 of the Lanham Act[5] specifically states as one of the Act's purposes:

> The intent of this Act is . . . to protect registered marks used in such commerce from interference by State, or territorial legislation. . . .

In view of this, what are the advantages of state trademark registration? This question has meaning only if prefaced by the comment that the mark considered for registration is such as to be registerable under the Lanham Act—that the mark is used in commerce as defined by the Act, since, if the mark is used solely in intrastate commerce, the mark may be registered only upon the state

[2] 15 U.S.C. § 1124 (1982).

[3] See the comparison of federal and state registration of service marks in Ch.1, at pp. 1–2.

[4] See p. 14. An insight into the rights conferred by the Lanham Act may be gained from the comparison between the Principal Register and the Supplemental Register pp. 19–22.

[5] 15 U.S.C. § 1127 (1982).

register.[6] Assuming, however, that the mark is used in interstate commerce and is registered under the provisions of the Lanham Act, there are still some advantages to be gained from a state registration as a complement to the federal registration and not as a substitute for it.

These advantages include provisions for the registering of certain marks that are not registerable under the Lanham Act, as descriptive terms are registerable in many states. Parenthetically, however, as noted previously in terms of scope, no state has a statute as broad as the Lanham Act in terms of service marks, collective marks, and certification marks.

The statutes of some states provide for the possibility of criminal prosecution and for statutory penalties. As there is no provision for statutory penalties in the Lanham Act, these state statutes may be of value in cases in which the penalty provision will be enforced by the courts. It is to be emphasized, however, that the Lanham Act provides for treble damages, destruction of infringing labels, and even destruction of "all plates, molds, matrices, and other means of making the same. . . ."[7]

Since the force of a state trademark registration is statewide, state registrations may also prove to be of value in situations in which the identical mark is used concurrently in different parts of the country to anchor title in specific areas.

## § 2.02 BACKGROUND REGARDING FEDERAL STATUTES

Since July 5, 1947, the Lanham Act has been the sole federal trademark statute. Numerous federal registrations antedate the Lanham Act, however, and consideration of the prior trademark acts is necessary.

At the time of the adoption of the Lanham Act, there were three existing classes of registrations stemming from three prior statutes: the Acts of March 3, 1881; February 20, 1905; and March 19, 1920. Consideration of selected aspects of the Acts of 1905 and 1920 will present a sufficiently complete picture for the purposes of this book.

---

[6] Many federal courts have held that, under the provisions of the Lanham Act, it is unnecessary that infringing use be in interstate commerce; it is enough if intrastate use has substantial economic effect upon interstate use by the mark's owner. The 1964 Civil Rights Act has permitted the Patent Office to rule that services performed in one state to interstate travelers was rendering of services in interstate commerce. *Ex parte* Smith Oil Corp., 156 U.S.P.Q. 62 (TTAB, 1967).

[7] 15 U.S.C. § 1118 (1982).

The 1905 Act and its numerous amendments constituted the first really comprehensive federal trademark statute. It provided for the registration of "technical" trademarks and, by virtue of a somewhat curious provision in Section 5 of the Act, known as the ten-year clause, provided for the registration of marks, without regard to their technical nature, that were in actual and exclusive use for ten years preceding February 20, 1905.[8] As a practical matter, the absence of anything beyond the ten-year clause in the 1905 Act prevented all trademark owners of nontechnical marks who had not used their marks since at least as early as 1895 from registering their marks under the Act. Since the trademark statutes of many foreign countries required that an alien trademark owner first secure a registration in his native country, this failing of the 1905 Act seriously affected the rights of American trademark owners in foreign countries.

This particular need to protect American trademark rights abroad led to the Act of 1920 that had for its primary purpose the implementation of international commitments permitting citizens of the United States to register nontechnical trademarks in foreign countries. The Act of 1920 actually went much further and opened the floodgates insofar as the registration of trademarks in the Patent Office was concerned. Thus marks that were incapable of becoming true trademarks were registered (perpetually) under the Act of 1920.

The failure to provide for the registration of other than technical trademarks that led to the ill-drafted Act of 1920 was not the only failing in the Act of 1905. The 1905 Act was of relatively narrow scope. For example, although a 1938 amendment provided for the registration of collective marks (without an adequate definition of the nature of a collective mark), there were no provisions in the 1905 Act respecting service marks. Moreover, practice under the 1905 Act developed into a maze of conflicting law both in the area of registrations and in the area of enforcement by litigation.

In terms of presenting a reasonably current picture of trademark ownership, the 1905 Act had no provision for eliminating "deadwood." Registrations were granted for twenty years, or perpetually in the case of registrations under the Act of 1920, and no affirmative

[8] The ten-year clause did not make all marks registerable, since certain marks, such as those comprising immoral matter or public insignia, could not be registered at all under the 1905 Act.

acts were required by the registrant during the term of registrations to keep them in force for the full term.

A major failing of the 1905 Act lay in its very nature. It consisted virtually of a procedural statute. Stated conversely, the advantages of registration that the 1905 Act provided were largely or entirely procedural. For example, a 1905 Act registration, regardless of its vintage, was (and is) only prima facie evidence of ownership in a lawsuit, and this evidence of ownership could (and can) be rebutted. This led to rank injustice in many situations. At no time was it possible for anyone under the 1905 Act to be certain about his ownership of a registered mark. A paramount ownership right might reside in a party who had not registered the identical mark, and this party might assert his ownership many years after the registration. The possibilities for fraud in situations such as these are self-evident.

The injustices resulting from the rebuttable nature of the statutory presumption of ownership and the fact that a registration under the 1905 Act did not carry constructive notice of ownership were probably the prime forces resulting in the enactment of the Lanham Act.

## § 2.03 THE LANHAM ACT AND PRIOR ACT REGISTRATIONS

The Lanham Act allows registrations under the Act of 1905 (and the Act of 1881) to continue in full force for their unexpired terms and to be renewed under the provisions of the Lanham Act. Section 22 of the Act[9] confers upon these registrations the status of being constructive notice of the registrant's claim of ownership. It is to be emphasized that registrations of this type and their renewals do not receive all the advantages of the Lanham Act and, in particular, the incontestability advantages provided for in Section 15[10] unless the registrant complies with the provisions of Section 12(c).[11] Compliance with Section 12(c), more often referred to as "republication under Section 12(c) of the Act," involves submitting the registrant's affidavit setting forth those goods in the registration on which the mark is still in use in commerce and a claim for the benefits of the Lanham Act, together with a fee of $100, per class. For a suitable affidavit under Section 12(c), see Appendix B. Parenthetically, the use of declarations that do not require notarization, but have the force of an affidavit, is widespread in the Patent Office.

---

[9] 15 U.S.C. § 1072 (1982).

[10] *Id.* § 1065 (1982).

[11] *Id.* § 1062(c) (1982).

The Patent Office publishes in its weekly magazine, the *Official Gazette,*[12] a notice of the affidavit and a reproduction of the mark forming the subject matter of the prior registration. An affidavit under Section 8(b)[13] must be filed between the fifth and sixth years from the date of publication, or the registration will be canceled. By virtue of Section 15 of the Act,[14] the registrant will receive incontestable rights with respect to use of the registered mark upon the filing of a suitable affidavit after five years from the date of publication of the republished mark in the *Official Gazette.*[15]

The profound change in the status of registrations under the Acts of 1881 and 1905 conferred by Section 22 of the Lanham Act[16] bears repetition. This section expressly states that registrations of this nature, as well as registrations on the Principal Register of the Act, constitute constructive notice of the registrant's claim of ownership. The importance of this change in terms of equitable defenses is deemed obvious.

## § 2.04 EFFECT OF REGISTRATION ON PRINCIPAL REGISTER

The provisions of Section 22[17] rendering a Principal Register registration constructive notice of the registrant's claim of ownership (as well as registrations under the 1881 and 1905 Acts), have already been stated. The following attributes are also conferred upon a Principal Register registration by the Lanham Act:

(1) A Principal Register registration obviously gives the registrant all the benefits provided for in the Act. These benefits include the right to bring suit in the federal courts without diversity or statutory amount; the ability to obtain an injunction enforceable by any district court of the United States, by proceedings to punish for contempt; and the right to recover profits and damages, including treble damages, attorneys' fees, and destruction of infringing labels.

(2) A Principal Register registration is prima facie evidence of the validity of the registration, the registrant's ownership of the mark, and the registrant's exclusive right to use the mark in commerce in connection with the goods or services specified in the certificate. It

---

[12] The *Official Gazette* is now published in two parts, one for patents, the other for trademarks.

[13] 15 U.S.C. § 1058(b) (1982).

[14] *Id.* § 1065 (1982).

[15] See Appendix B for suitable affidavits under Section 8 and Section 15.

[16] 15 U.S.C. § 1072 (1982).

[17] *Id.*

is to be emphasized that the evidentiary benefits flowing from a registration certificate are directed only to the goods or services specified in the certificate and not to the Patent Office class within which the goods are classified.[18] By way of example, a certificate directed to ladies' blouses, classified in Patent Class 25 entitled Clothing, has evidentiary value only for ladies' blouses and not for all articles of clothing.

(3) The prima facie evidentiary status referred to in the preceding paragraph may rise to the status of incontestability under the provisions of Section 15 of the Act.[19] In this event, the certificate of registration becomes conclusive evidence of the registrant's exclusive right to use the registered mark in commerce on the goods or services specified in the certificate, subject to the defenses or defects set forth in Section 33(b) of the Act.[20] Section 15 of the Act constitutes a radical innovation in the law of trademarks and makes it possible for a trademark owner to be free from fear concerning his rights to a mark. Perhaps the word *free* overstates the matter in that it is possible for the owner to lose his incontestability status by virtue of certain acts, including abandonment of the mark, assignment of the mark, and misuse of it by the assignee in a manner that would misrepresent the source of goods or services covered by a mark, and misuse of the mark in violation of the antitrust laws. Yet in the vast majority of instances, the owner of a registration that has become incontestable can be assured that his rights to the mark covered by registration are as secure as a benevolent trademark statute can make them.[21]

(4) As noted before, a Principal Register registration may be used to prevent the importation of goods bearing infringing marks into this country.[22] In practice this constitutes a most satisfactory method for policing a trademark and preventing its infringement by foreign manufacturers. Two practical caveats, however, should be borne in mind by anyone seeking to take advantage of these provisions:

(a) These provisions accord relatively little protection for articles to which a trademark can be applied with ease in this country. In situations when goods are shipped into the United States and an

---

[18] See *infra* p. 44 for a discussion of Patent Office classification of goods.

[19] 15 U.S.C. § 1065 (1982).

[20] *Id.* § 1115(b) (1982).

[21] Park 'N Fly, Inc. v. Dollar Park & Fly, Inc., 105 S. Ct. 658 (1985).

[22] *See* Section 42 of the Act, 15 U.S.C. § 1124 (1982), and also 19 U.S.C. § 1526 (1982).

infringing trademark is applied to the goods in the United States, recourse may possibly be had to the provisions of 19 U.S.C. § 1337(a) if a concerted plan for effecting the trademark infringement can be established. The provisions of 19 U.S.C. § 1337(a) protect United States industries against unfair methods of competition and unfair acts in the importation of articles.

(b) In some situations the possible good that may be obtained from recording one's Principal Register trademark registrations with the Department of the Treasury may be more than offset by the interference with the shipment of goods into the United States through friendly associates that are not related companies.

## § 2.05 EFFECT OF REGISTRATION ON SUPPLEMENTAL REGISTER

The existence of the Supplemental Register has already been noted. Upon this register it is possible to register marks that are capable of distinguishing goods or services but are not registerable upon the Principal Register.

For the purposes of registration on the Supplemental Register, a very broad definition of what constitutes a mark has been adopted. The statute includes within this definition trademarks, symbols, labels, packages, configurations of goods, names, words, slogans, phrases, surnames, geographical names, numerals, devices, or any combination of the foregoing provided that they function as marks and are capable of distinguishing the goods or services. If a mark is generic, it is not registerable even on the Supplemental Register.

The most frequent question in reference to the Supplemental Register is that of its *raison d'etre;* namely, what are the advantages secured by this type of trademark registration over no registration at all? A number of advantages are present over and beyond the primary purpose for the register, which is to act as a record center in which the title to marks may be deposited. Registration upon the Supplemental Register makes it possible to accomplish the following:

(1) In many foreign countries, registration in the home country is a prerequisite to obtaining registration in the foreign country. Moreover, in many foreign countries the registration requirements differ markedly from the registration requirements of this country. It is to be emphasized that at the present time there is no international convention standardizing trademark law throughout the world, so that marks that are unregisterable upon the Principal Register

may be construed as perfectly valid technical marks in other countries.

(2) Registrations on the Supplemental Register come within the purview of Section 2(d),[23] which provides for the refusal of registration of a mark that so resembles a mark registered in the Patent Office. Thus registration of the mark upon the Supplemental Register will prevent the registration of the same or a confusingly similar mark upon the Principal Register or the Supplemental Register by a third party. Parenthetically, registration of a mark on the Supplemental Register will manifestly prevent the registration of the same or a confusingly similar mark to a third party by virtue of the secondary meaning clause contained in Section 2(f) of the Act.[24]

(3) A Supplemental Register registration may be assigned (along with goodwill) and thereby provide the focal point for trademark conveyancing.

(4) Registration upon the Supplemental Register permits the registrant to bring suit in the federal courts without diversity or statutory amount and permits the registrant to obtain the benefit of the remedies set forth in the Act.

Unlike applications for the Principal Register, a full year's use in commerce for the year preceding the filing of the trademark application is required.[25] If, however, an application is originally filed on the Principal Register and subsequently transferred by amendment to the Supplemental Register (no additional filing fee is required), the full year's use may be dated back from the date of transfer, so that a full year's use preceding the original filing is not necessary.

---

[23] 15 U.S.C. § 1052(d) (1982).

[24] *Id.* § 1052(f) (1982).

[25] This may be waived by a showing that lawful use of the mark in foreign commerce has begun and that domestic registration as a basis for foreign protection is required.

# 3
# The Selection of a Trademark

## § 3.01 BEYOND THE SCOPE OF COUNSEL'S DUTIES

Through the years the author has developed a philosophy about the selection of a trademark that he feels is worthy of repeating in a "bread-and-butter" presentation on trademarks. Stated simply, this philosophy is as follows: The selection of a trademark falls outside the scope of duties to be performed by counsel. Properly, it is a matter for advertising personnel and others having skills in consumer psychology, persons who may properly gauge (insofar as it is possible) the "appeal" features of a proposed trademark.

It is the author's opinion that the selection of a "catchy" mark having a great deal of sales appeal is of far more importance to the client than the relative legal strength of the mark. Thus if a client selects a mark that is descriptive, one he considers to be far superior in a commercial sense to all other marks available to him that are not descriptive but that lack sales appeal, the client should be advised to proceed with the mark with sales appeal, letting the legal chips fall where they may, even though registration on the Principal Register may prove difficult or even impossible.

# 4
# Trademark Searches and Source Materials

## § 4.01 INTRODUCTION

The most common fact situation involving trademark searches arises when a manufacturer or service-mark user desires to adopt a new mark and wishes to assure himself that the use of this mark will not bring him into conflict with prior users of a confusingly similar mark. Although there are collections of trademarks in a number of localities, including some private nonofficial collections that purport to be more comprehensive than the collection in the Patent Office search room,[1] the great majority of trademark searches are conducted in the Patent Office trademark search room. An examination of the arrangement of trademarks in the Patent Office will reveal the strengths and weaknesses of trademark searching.

Until recently all trademark searches conducted in the Patent Office consisted of "manual searches." Thus the search was done by hand through paper records contained in Patent Office files. The Patent Office is currently in the process of placing all of the information contained in its paper records into a computer. The ultimate goal of the Patent Office is a "paperless office" in which all communications between the applicant and the Office will be entered on-line by computer.

The Patent Office is still developing, refining, and correcting the existing data base for word marks. The data base is currently available only to the Examiners. When the data base is sufficiently tested, it will be made available to the public for a fee and the Patent Office will remove all paper records from the public search room. However, manual searching will probably be practical for many years in respect to symbols. These do not lend themselves to completely accurate computer searching.

[1] Some of the private collections claim to include all the state registrations as well as all the federal registrations and a large library of common law unregistered marks.

The Patent Office maintains in the search room copies of prior trademark registrations, both expired and subsisting (the subsisting trademark registrations including both unexpired and renewed registrations), and also copies of published marks,[2] and marks presented in pending trademark applications. It is to be noted that trademark searching differs from patent searching in that information can be secured regarding pending trademark applications, whereas pending patent applications are preserved in secrecy.

Under the present search system searches are made in two locations. The *first search location* comprises the classified registered marks. These marks are located in vertical tiers of individually labeled drawers, technically known as shoes. The registrations are classified on an alphabetical basis of words. As expected, word marks constitute the great bulk of the registrations. Nonword marks are classified as symbols in accordance with the following chart.[3]

## § 4.02 TRADEMARK SYMBOLS

The symbols are indexed in the Trademark Search Room under the several symbol classifications as follows:

Animals

Birds, mammalia, vertebrate, invertebrate & animal misc.

Articles of Manufacture

Subclass breakdown according to particular representation.

Buildings and Scenery

Pyramids, sphinx & obelisks and other types of scenes according to particular representation.

---

[2] Marks that have been published for opposition in the Patent Office *Official Gazette.* See p. 48.

[3] The author wishes to acknowledge his appreciation to the head of the Trademark Search Room, Gordon E. Mitchell, who prepared the Trademark Symbol Chart.

CHECKER DESIGNS (no breakdown)

DESIGNS

Astronomical, geometrical, circles, ovals, heraldry, diamonds, triangles, crosses, keystones, hearts, seals, colors, bars, bands, stripes, fleur-de-lis, chevrons, clubs, spades, scrolls, etc.

GROTESQUE

Animal, bird & human.

HUMAN

Fanciful, portraits, statuary & Uncle Sam.

INANIMATE DESIGNS

Nests, rainbows, spider webs & misc. (including lighting, smoke, bubbles, etc.).

MYTHOLOGY

Angels, devils, cupids, fairies, etc., as well as representation of unicorns, centaurs, Paul Bunyan, etc.

NOTATION SYSTEMS

Letters, numerals, non-Latin characters, music, punctuation, prescription marks & sterling marks.

VEGETATION

Blossoms, branches & sprays, fruit, leaves, trees, wreaths, etc.

Within each drawer (shoe) the registrations are secured together by an Acco fastener. A sheet at the top of the bundle gives the expiration date for registrations that have been culled, and they are separated as "Expired or Canceled." These "Expired or Canceled" registrations are carried on microfilm. A good search should include a look through the expired and canceled registrations, and although these registrations will not be relied upon by the Patent Office, the owners may still have common law rights in the marks. Thus when a registration has been allowed to expire or has been canceled under the provisions of Section 8 of the Lanham Act[4] because of an oversight, the owner of the mark still has common law rights.

All registrations containing a word, coined or otherwise, are included in the classification of word marks. When the registration comprises more than one word or a group of phrases, the registration is classified under each of the words and each of the phrases. Moreover, when a registration comprises a compound word made up of a number of other words, such as "GUNMASTER," the registration will be classified under both of the words—namely, "GUN" and "MASTER." In addition, an attempt has been made to classify trademark registrations by prefixes and suffixes, but the collections of prefixes and suffixes are not in all cases complete, and in many cases given prefixes and suffixes are not separately classified.

Except in the case of marks for which a large number of registrations have issued, such as "Queen," there is no breakdown into classes of goods. When a large number of registrations have been issued comprising the same mark, there is a breakdown based on the Patent Office classification system[5] in order to facilitate searching.[6]

The *second search location* comprises the collection of published and pending marks. These marks are loosely placed within tiers of drawers in strict alphabetical or other arrangement that parallels the arrangement for the registered marks. The published marks include clippings from the Patent Office *Official Gazette* mounted on cardboard backers, and the pending marks contain photostatic copies of the drawings of pending trademark applications. The published marks and pending marks are interspersed with each other.

It is readily possible to determine the reason a given published mark failed to mature into a registration, since the search, if properly followed up by an examination of the docket entries, will reveal the reason (normally an opposition). The collection of published marks, therefore, forms the best means for obtaining an insight into the

---

[4] 15 U.S.C. § 1058 (1982).

[5] See p. 44.

[6] There is a breakdown based on the Patent Office classification system for many of the symbol headings referred to in the chart.

Patent Office standards in respect to the mark being searched. For example, if the identical mark under consideration has previously been published for the same goods and successfully opposed in a contested trademark opposition, the existence of this fact (which cannot be obtained from any other literature source unless the decision in the opposition was published) may constitute the firmest possible basis for a trademark opinion. Blind reliance upon past opposition, however, may be misleading. The standards affecting oppositions have changed markedly in recent years, adversely affecting a prior trademark user's rights. Uncontested oppositions are, of course of little aid in weighing close trademark matters. They are, however, a key to the aggressive nature of a potential opponent.

The following common information about the prior user and his use may be derived from prior registrations, the abstracts of published marks, and the drawings for pending trademark applications: (a) the name and address of the prior user of the mark, (b) the nature of the mark, (c) the goods upon which the mark is used, (d) the first date of use of the mark, and (e) the first date of use of the mark in interstate commerce.

## § 4.03 WEAKNESSES IN THE TRADEMARK SEARCH SYSTEM

A number of glaring weaknesses in the trademark search system should be noted. First, the Patent Office search records, manual or computerized, are limited entirely to marks for which trademark registration has been sought or obtained. The most exhaustive search in the Patent Office trademark search room will therefore fail to uncover any trace of a formerly used mark for which registration has not been sought. Inasmuch as trademark rights are primarily based on usage, the failure of the prior user to register his mark does not deprive him of a cause of action against a subsequent user of the mark. Although the incontestability provisions of the Lanham Act have gone a long way to reduce the risk of conflict with non-registered marks, the fact that only marks registered upon the Principal Register may be made incontestable and, further, that a hiatus of five years is essential between registration and the earliest possibility for rendering a registered mark incontestable indicates that even the incontestability provisions do not entirely safeguard the rights of one who contemplates adopting and registering a mark.

Second, it must be remembered that the Patent Office classification system, in the case of word marks, is strictly an alphabetical system and not a phonetic one. Since two marks may be spelled differently and yet be confusingly similar, the Patent Office system puts the trademark searcher on his mettle to conjure up all possible phonetic variations of the mark being searched and to search the phonetic variations. Moreover, the connotative synonyms of the mark being searched must also be searched, regardless of their spelling.[7] These include words drawn from foreign languages that have the same meaning as the mark being searched. The computerized system will automatically search phonetic and foreign equivalents. It will not, however, search connotative synonyms of the mark.

An example or two will perhaps clarify these difficulties and demonstrate that trademark-searching will always be an art and will never be as exact as title-searching. Assume that a client proposes to use the mark "HEATSPOT" for a variety of electrical appliances. It is apparent that a comprehensive search for this mark should include searches through synonyms for both "Heat" and "Spot," and that therefore the familiar "HOTPOINT" is most pertinent. No suggestion of "HOTPOINT," however, could be picked up from a straight alphabetical search. The situation is further complicated when it is remembered that a comprehensive search would also include foreign equivalents, such as the French word for hot, "chaud," which, of course, bears no resemblance to the English word.

This problem is greatly accentuated in the case of coined words when even the most seasoned and astute trademark searcher cannot be sure of a comprehensive search. For example, assume the client contemplates adopting the coined word "TRELLORTI." The alphabetical search would, of course, fail to reveal prior marks such as "BRELLORTI," "ELLORTI," and "TELLORTI"[8] as well as the host of other possible variations of this coined word. Because coined word marks are entitled to broader scope than marks comprising words in usage, the seriousness of this failing is accentuated, since only a

[7] This is, of course, obviated when the mark is a true technical one, such as "KODAK," and is utterly devoid of any connotation.

[8] The most one could reasonably expect from a searcher would be a search through the numerous marks commencing with "TR—." Even this would probably be far more comprehensive than is economically justifiable. A search through all the thousands of marks commencing with "r—" could run to astronomical figures. The Patent Office does attempt to crossfile foreign word marks under both the foreign spelling and the English equivalent. The helpfulness of this cross filing is limited, as the Patent Office only cross files for registered marks and not pending applications. Further, if the mark has not been translated or if the translation does not appear on the face of the registration, it will not be cross referenced. These problems should be corrected with the advent of computerized records.

relatively narrow type of search is possible when the need for a broad search is the greatest. The computerized search system will permit the trademark searcher to frame his or her search to look for marks with the same prefix or suffix. Thus in the previous example it would be possible for the searcher to request a listing of all marks with the common suffix "ORTI." The problem inherent in computer searching is that it is not possible to search each and every possible variation of a mark. Thus even assuming the searcher discovered the marks "BRELLORTI," it is possible that the searcher using a computer could overlook "BRELLORT," although "BRELLORT" would undoubtedly have been found on a manual search. Thus there are limitations in both systems.

A corollary of the foregoing is that competent trademark searching cannot be achieved at a bargain basement price, and cautious counsel is well advised to avoid advertisements offering "searches" at absurdly low figures.

Another weakness of the trademark search system is that a normal search will not encompass trademark applications that were abandoned prior to publication in the *Official Gazette.* Information about abandoned trademark applications can be gathered by other approaches, but it is normally not obtained in a routine search. An exasperating policy of the Patent Office is the destruction of abandoned trademark applications because of storage space considerations, with only the docket entries being retained to indicate the history of the proceeding.

An inherent weakness of the trademark search system is that it often does not reflect the current actualities but is only a naked legal indicium. Thus a registrant may pass out of business, or stop using his mark, or change his mark. Yet the search materials available to the public may not reflect this, even indirectly, for as many as 15 years after the event, and, in the case of renewed registrations, for as many as 20 years after the event.

The tragedies induced by the failings of the trademark search system are twofold. Assuming that both the prior user and the adopter have the highest respect for trademark property rights and wish to avoid conflicts, the unintentional use of a conflicting mark may, nevertheless, lead the adopter into litigation and the scrapping as a total loss of an extensive advertising outlay, including funds for labels, brochures, and catalogs. To protect property rights, the prior user may likewise be subjected to litigation that need never have arisen were it not for the inadequacies of the searching system.

The trademark system offers no easy solution to the difficult problem raised by its inadequate information-gathering tools. The closest approach to a solution is the opposition system, which at least partly enables trademark owners to prevent dilution of their marks by unsuspecting and well-meaning newcomers (as well as by deliberate and calculating later adopters) and which serves to forestall litigation before extensive property rights have become involved.

## § 4.04 MISCELLANEOUS ADDITIONAL TYPES OF TRADEMARK SEARCHES

In addition to searches for marks, the Patent Office maintains assignment records through which it is possible to determine the ownership of registered marks and pending trademark applications that have been conveyed from one owner to another.[9] For example, all the trademark properties of a competitor may be determined, as may the ownership to a given registration. Mere licenses, as opposed to assignment,[10] are not recorded and thus cannot be searched.

One of the most important types of trademark searches, and perhaps the most important reason for referring trademark matters to a trademark specialist, comprises the continuing searches made in the Patent Office *Official Gazette.* All trademark registrations issue from the Patent Office on Tuesday and on no other day of the week. When issued, all trademark registrations are included there.

As will be discussed in Chapter 7, before the Patent Office issues trademark registrations, it publishes all applications on the Principal Register for opposition in the *Official Gazette.* In the case of marks on the Principal Register, the registration of marks of this kind can be opposed providing the opposer takes action within 30 days of publication in the Patent Office *Official Gazette.* Accordingly, one of the most important services rendered by a trademark specialist is the continued review through the years of marks published in the *Official Gazette.* In the case of confusingly similar marks on the Principal Register, trademark counsel can recommend opposition proceedings, and in the case of registrations issued on the Supplemental Register, trademark counsel can make the client aware of the exist-

---

[9] As noted *infra* p. 93. Section 10 of the Lanham Act, 15 U.S.C. § 1060 (1982), provides: "An assignment shall be void as against any subsequent purchaser for a valuable consideration without notice, unless it is recorded in the Patent and Trademark Office within three months after the date thereof or prior to such subsequent purchase."

[10] See *infra* pp. 90–93.

ence of these marks, so that cancellation proceedings may be instituted.

The incontestability provisions of the Lanham Act have greatly underscored the need for continuing searches. Under the Lanham Act, it is possible for a registration to become incontestable so that, if timely action is not taken, dilution of a formerly used mark will occur.[11]

The imperfect nature of the trademark searching system, the possibility of human error on the part of the examiner in the Patent Office, and the incontestability provisions of the Lanham Act all point to the fact that unless timely attention is called to the forthcoming issuance of a confusingly similar trademark registration impairment of trademark rights by dilution will occur.

## § 4.05 SHEPARDIZING THE MARK

After a search has been received or when an opinion on an infringement is requested, *Shepard's United States Citations* should be consulted.[12] In the rear portion of this *Shepard's United States Citations* will be found under the heading "Trademarks" a reference to every trademark that has been litigated in any state or federal reported decision, or even mentioned in a court opinion, or has been involved in reported proceedings before the Patent Office or other administrative bodies, or mentioned in a notice under 15 U.S.C. § 1116 in the *Official Gazette* of the Patent Office. For example, if the mark in question is "Star," reference to *Shepard's* will reveal all prior cases in which this mark was considered.

In many situations the use of *Shepard's* will give an insight into the thinking of the courts and of the Patent Office on the scope of protection to be accorded a given mark. Unfortunately, a strong caveat is in order. The courts have repeatedly stated that each trademark case is dependent upon its facts and that prior opinions count for very little unless the facts are substantially identical. Accordingly, when judging a trademark situation by earlier litigation, it is necessary to consider carefully the facts of the earlier cases in order to determine whether a significant element was present in the earlier case (for example, the presence of palming off or additional acts of

---

[11] See p. 19.

[12] Note that this is not SHEPARD'S UNITED STATES CITATIONS (for the Supreme Court) but the Shepard service for patents, copyrights, and trademarks.

unfair competition beyond trademark infringement) that distinguishes the earlier case from the subject case.

Changes in statutory law should always be considered when citing an earlier trademark case as authority. Thus the earlier case may have rested upon a peculiar provision of an earlier trademark statute, such as the Act of 1905 or the Act of 1920. The effect of recent state legislation, such as the so-called antidilution statutes or secondary meaning legislation, should not be ignored when considering the probative weight of an earlier holding.

The reported cases may provide a guide to determining the presence or absence of confusion in cases in which the marks of the first user and of the second user are identical or substantially identical, but the goods are somewhat different. For example, if one is concerned with the question of whether the use of "Star" on men's shoes is an infringement of the use of "Star" on womens raincoats, a qualitative determination may be made by consulting the vast mass of decided cases involving the question of infringement between articles of clothing. It may even be possible to find one or more cases involving the exact articles of clothing in issue. For legal research in this area, the author recommends the *United States Patents Quarterly* (U.S.P.Q.) rather than the various Supreme Court reporters, the *Federal Reporter,* and the *Federal Supplement* series. For the years included in the *U.S.P.Q.*—namely, 1929 to date—and particularly since about 1938, its coverage of trademark cases is much more complete than that of the conventional reporter systems. Thus district court decisions relating to trademarks that are not reported in the *Federal Supplement* or elsewhere may be located in the *U.S.P.Q.* Moreover, the headnote indexing of the *U.S.P.Q.* is superior in respect to trademarks to the indexing in the *Federal Digest,* particularly with the more recent *U.S.P.Q.* indexes. Moreover, the *U.S.P.Q.* is the only source for the many valuable Patent Office decisions that are not carried in either the *Federal Reporter* or the *Federal Supplement* (the *Federal Reporter* carries all the decisions of the Court of Customs and Patent Appeals, which include appeals in trademark cases from the Patent Office). *Shepard's United States Citations* includes the *U.S.P.Q.*, and *U.S.P.Q.* decisions may be "Shepardized" directly when there is no parallel citation in the *Federal Reporter* system. When, however, there is a parallel citation in the *Federal Reporter* system, "Shepardizing" of the *Federal Reporter* citation should be effected. Another useful source of trademark case materials, particularly for years prior to the advent of the *U.S.P.Q.*, is the *Trade Mark Reporter.*

The widespread availability of computer legal research (Lexis and Westlaw) permits the location of every decision dealing with a trademark. The use of data banks, such as Dialog, permits the presence of trademarks in newspapers, magazines, source books, and the like, to be located.

**BIBLIOGRAPHY**

For reference works on the trademark law, on the law of unfair competition, or on both areas, the following books should be considered:

Amdur, *Trade Mark Law and Practice* (Clark 1948).
Beer, *Federal Trade Law and Practice* (Callaghan & Co. 1942).
Calimafde, *Trademarks and Unfair Competition* (Central Book Co. 1970).
Callman, *The Law of Unfair Competition, Trademarks and Monopolies* (Callaghan & Co. 4th ed. 1985).
Derenberg, *Trade-Mark Protection and Unfair Trading* (Matthew Bender 1936).
Gilson, *Trademark Protection and Practice* (Matthew Bender 1974).
Hopkins, *The Law of Trademarks, Tradenames and Unfair Competition* (W. H. Anderson & Co. 4th ed. 1924).
McCarthy, *Trademarks and Unfair Competition* (Lawyers Cooperative Publishing Co. 2nd ed. 1984).
Nims, *The Law of Unfair Competition and Trademarks* (Baker, Boorhis & Co. 1947).
Seidel, Dubroff & Gonda, *Trademark Law and Practice* (Matthew Bender 1963).
Toulmin, *Trade-Mark Handbook* (W. H. Anderson & Co. 1957).
Vandenburgh, *Trademark Law and Procedure* (Bobbs-Merrill Co. 2d ed. 1968).

# 5

# Prosecution of Federal Trademark Applications

## § 5.01 INTRODUCTION

Assuming that the search report referred to in the preceding chapter indicates that the client may both use and register the subject mark[1] and assuming further that the client has already, in fact, used the subject mark in interstate commerce, the next step is the filing of a trademark application for a federal registration.

At the outset note that it is essential that the client did, in fact, use the mark in commerce. The definition of "in commerce" as comprehended by the Lanham Act has already been alluded to. To constitute a use in commerce, the mark must be placed on the goods, their containers, the displays associated with them or on the tags or labels affixed to the goods; and the goods must be sold or transported in commerce. In the case of service marks, the mark must be used or displayed in the sale or advertising of services rendered in commerce.

It is important to note that a trademark is an appurtenant right and not a right in gross. The law does not contemplate the protection of rights in trademarks that are selected because of their "catchiness" or for some other reason but are never used. The function of the registers maintained by the Patent Office is not to divide out for future use marks that the client feels he might have use for at some later date.

It is therefore axiomatic that rights in trademarks flow from use and not from their invention. In this respect, trademarks differ markedly from patents, since the owner of a patent may restrain others from using his patented invention, although he neither uses his

[1] The Court of Customs and Patent Appeals, now the Court of Appeals for the Federal Circuit, has repeatedly recognized a distinction between the right to use a trademark and the statutory right to register it, as in cases in which there have been prior adjudications of noninfringement. Other courts have not assiduously applied this distinction.

invention nor contemplates using it in the future. The single exception to the principle that rights in trademarks arise from use relates to U.S. trademark applications filed by foreign entities. Previously the Patent Office required applicants claiming the benefits of Section 44 to comply with all office requirements. Specifically the Patent Office required that applications based on Section 44 allege use somewhere on or before the filing date of the U.S. application and provide specimens demonstrating such a use. This worked a hardship in some cases as many countries permit the filing of trademark applications based on intended use.

The Trademark Trial and Appeal Board has recently ruled that these requirements were inconsistent with the International Convention of Paris for the Protection of Industrial Property, as implemented by Trademark Act Section 44, and need not be observed in applications based on that section. This decision results in favored treatment of foreign nationals, allowing them to register marks on the basis of intended use rather than on actual use. As a result, domestic corporations, which must use their trademark before an application can be filed, are at some disadvantage. It is conceiveable that legislation will be enacted in due course to correct this discrepancy.

## § 5.02 DATES OF FIRST USE

In every trademark application the Patent Office is interested in two dates, which may or may not coincide. These are the date of first use of the mark and the date of first use of the mark in commerce. If the date of first use of the mark in commerce was also the date of first use of the mark anywhere, then the dates will coincide. If, however, the mark was first used in intrastate commerce and then at some later date used in interstate commerce, two separate dates will necessarily appear in the trademark application.[2]

With regard to true trademarks, as opposed to service marks, what is contemplated in the previous paragraph is valid trademark usage as already defined. Use of a trademark in either advertisements or correspondence is not a valid trademark usage.

---

[2] Although the most common form of "use in commerce" constitutes interstate usage, any "use in commerce" that may be lawfully regulated by Congress will support a trademark application. This includes, in addition to interstate commerce, territorial commerce, foreign commerce, and commerce with Indian tribes. Obviously, in the normal situation, the kind of commerce will be interstate.

What constitutes a bona fide use in interstate commerce has presented numerous and varied problems. Although it will not be possible to discuss them all in this brief monograph, the most important are worthy of note.

Perhaps the most frequent problem is the degree of reliance to be had on so-called pilot sales.

Extensive case law supports the view that a single sale in commerce is sufficient to support the claim of ownership in a trademark. This has led to the adoption by many of the practice of arranging for a "friendly" sale, frequently referred to as a "pilot sale," the prime purpose of which is to establish a date that can later be relied upon for a first date of use in commerce.

This technique is a dangerous one and has led to many unfortunate consequences. The Patent Office has held isolated "pilot sales," the sole purpose of which was to establish a date to be used in a trademark application, with no true subsequent sales, as constituting nothing more than a fictitious or sham use in commerce. It would therefore appear advisable in all cases to establish a continual pattern comprising a number of sales in commerce to a number of legitimate customers, which pattern should include a valid follow-through establishing beyond doubt the intent to continue to use the mark. The use of a mark on isolated occasions without the establishment of any pattern may, in a contested matter when ownership of the mark is in issue, be interpreted as being a mere casual use and of no consequence in respect to a later user, if the later user has, in fact, made use of the mark in the pattern set forth previously.

In particular, "pilot sales" at absurdly low prices or deliveries to a dealer who had not placed an order should be either avoided or followed through with a multitude of legitimate sales.

Section 5 of the Lanham Act[3] provides that legitimate use by a related company shall inure to the benefit of the applicant and that this use shall not affect the validity of the mark or its registration provided the mark is not used in a manner that deceives the public. The essence of this provision, and the essence of the entire concept of a "related company," lies in the word *control.* The term *related company* is defined in the Lanham Act as meaning any person who legitimately controls or is controlled by the registrant or applicant for registration in respect to the nature and quality of the goods or services in connection with which the mark is used. As with the

[3] 15 U.S.C. § 1055 (1982).

licensing of trademarks, discussed later, the fundamental issue is whether or not there was such a relationship that the use by the related company was merely the carrying out of the desires (expressed in trademark concepts concerning control of quality, style, and the other aspects of the goods) of the trademark owner. This entire area of the law stems from the basic premise that it is a fraud on the public by a trademark owner to permit another to use his mark so that the public will believe that he is, in fact, responsible for the goods when he is not.

The definition of "related company" in the Lanham Act comprehends far more than a stock-control relationship, such as exists between a parent and its subsidiary. The Act also covers "related companies" whose relationship arises contractually. A caveat is necessary at this point so that the "related company" provisions of the Lanham Act shall not be deemed an invitation to the violation of the antitrust laws.[4]

The Department of Justice objected strongly to the "related company" provisions of the Act prior to its enactment, and express safeguards have been inserted into the Act. The Federal Trade Commission may cancel a trademark registration when there has been misuse by an assignee. Moreover, use of a mark to violate the antitrust laws is a defense even against an incontestable registration.

## § 5.03 PROBLEM SITUATIONS IN TRADEMARK REGISTRATIONS

Certain situations arise so frequently as to constitute focal points for the development of an appreciable body of law relating to the registration of trademarks. The most common problem situations will be dealt with here. A caveat, however, is proper regarding the too literal reliance upon the views set forth in this book, since the law of trademarks—including that portion of it relating to the registration of trademarks—is in a constant state of flux. It must be remembered that the Lanham Act is a young statute and many of its ramifications have not yet been fully explored.

### § 5.03(a) Primarily Merely a Surname

It has already been seen that the Lanham Act refuses registration on the Principal Register of a mark if it is "primarily merely a surname."[5] But what constitutes "primarily merely a surname"?

---

[4] *See* Siegel v. Chicken Delight, Inc., 448 F.2d 43 (9th Cir. 1971), *cert. denied,* 405 U.S. 955 (1972).

[5] Section 2(e)(3), 15 U.S.C. § 1052 (1982).

It is possible, by diligent search through city directories and through telephone books, such as the Manhattan telephone book, to uncover individuals having surnames identical to the most technical trademarks yet invented, including, by way of example, even "Kodak." If the statute were interpreted as excluding the registration of all marks that might possibly comprise a surname, the harshness of such a doctrine would immediately lead to the most serious repercussions. In this connection even the more common surnames may be registered upon the Principal Register under the provisions of the so-called secondary meaning section; namely, Section 2(f) of the Lanham Act.

Accordingly, the clue to the interpretation of the statute lies in the words "primarily merely."

Although the tests for "primarily merely" are subjective, certain ground rules can be laid down. Even so common a surname as "Douglas" may be registerable upon the Principal Register if it can be demonstrated, as was demonstrated in the case of "Douglas," that, in addition to being a surname, it is also a given name, a species of squirrel, a common geographical location (the name of numerous cities and towns), and the name of a Scotch clan (although, since clans are named by surname, the value of this observation is debatable).

When such evidence is scanty, as with the less common surname "Winslow," registration will be refused on the basis that the mark is primarily merely a surname.

The actualities of the matter may have an important bearing upon whether a given mark is registerable. Thus if the mark is, in fact, the surname of an individual associated with the applicant, this will weigh heavily against the registration.

The connotative meaning to the English-speaking American purchasing public is another important consideration. "Rivera" was deemed registerable as a trademark for watches, since an average member of the English-speaking public would not be likely to think of it as being a surname, although, in fact, it is among the most common of Spanish surnames.

The presence of an adornment with the surname—such as the given name, the initials, or a title—has given a great deal of trouble to the authorities. There has been a distinct backing and filling concerning whether a surname accompanied by a given name is registerable, and the reported cases have at times commented at different angles on this problem.

Certain surnames, such as "Samson," that have a wide variety of meanings, connotations, and usages are registerable, even though in the last analysis these usages are related to surname usage (historically "Samson" was interpreted as "the son of Sam" and would be accompanied by a preceding given name).

## § 5.03(b) The Registration of Trade Names

As we have seen regarding trademarks (as distinguished from service marks), trade names are not registerable. It is possible, however, for the same mark to function as both a trademark and a trade name, in which event the mark will be registerable as a trademark.

A fatal indication that a mark is a trade name, rather than a trademark (at least fatal in the vast majority of instances), is that the mark is coupled with a notation indicative of a business organization, such as "& Company," or "Inc.," or is coupled with a geographical location, such as the name of a city. For this reason, when a client's proposed mark is to be identical with his trade name, the mark should appear twice on the label, once per se and once associated with a business or a geographical notation or both. Another generally fatal coupling, insofar as registration is concerned, arises when the mark is used subsequent to the preposition *by;* or more fatally, subsequent to *manufactured by.* In connection with the preposition *by,* this preposition can give rise to difficulties in connection with the "primarily merely a surname" problem, since the preposition may be indicative, or interpreted as being indicative, of an individual.

With respect to service marks, the rule concerning trade names has been greatly relaxed. This arises from the logical reasoning that many services are identified in a service mark sense by their trade name, particularly services that constitute true services and are utterly divorced from an associated manufacturing operation, such as business services like insurance.

## § 5.03(c) The Definition of Services

It is well settled that the advertising of one's end products sold under one's mark is not the rendering of services entitling the same to be dignified by a service mark registration. Moreover, a phrase or mark indicating that services are rendered by a particular person who is, in fact, the person rendering these services is likewise not a valid basis for a service mark. When a given mark is used in only one phase of a type of service, as, for example, when a given mark is used solely upon envelopes employed for the mailing of photographic film, no valid basis for a service mark registration is present for the services of processing the photographic film.

### § 5.03(d) Mark Used on Component

Another frequently encountered problem arises when registration is sought for goods that are the component parts or the material from which the product that is actually sold or used in commerce is made. A common example lies in the attempt to establish the use of a mark on fabrics by the sale of garments made from fabrics. The converse problem is also frequently present; namely, the attempt to obtain a registration of a mark on finished goods when the mark is actually used for the fabrics. It is not possible to state any simple rule that will be determinative of all cases. Thus a mark that is clearly indicative of fabrics, as, for example, a mark that comprises the slogan stating, "It's a Dan River Fabric," may not be registerable for clothes formed from the fabric, even though the mark appears on labels or hang tags affixed to the clothes. This is particularly the case when the clothes bear the mark of the clothes manufacturer. Similarly, a mark that is clearly indicative of a component or ingredient, as, for example, a component of a toothpaste, may not be registered as the mark for the toothpaste.

### § 5.03(e) Grade Mark Usage

Still other problems arise when a mark is used as a "grade" mark or "style" mark instead of a true trademark. A classic example of unregisterable grade marks is the use of "Goose Load," "Snipe Load," and "Duck Load," for various cartridge loads in shotgun shells.

## § 5.04 THE TRADEMARK APPLICATION

The trademark application is a deceptively simple document. At first glance it appears to be a simple form. If viewed in that light, however, it is a trap for the unwary.

Within trademark applications the Patent Office distinguishes three general classifications of applicants.

The first classification is that of individual applicants, who must submit their name and trade style, if any (John Doe, doing business as Apex Company); their business address, including street, city, and state; their residence address, including street, city, and state, and information regarding their citizenship. The applicant is responsible for executing the trademark application.

The second classification concerns applicants constituting firms. In this situation the information to be provided consists of the firm name and the names of the members comprising the firm; the firm's business address, including street, city, and state; the domicile of the firm; and the citizenship of each of the members of the firm. The trademark application must be executed by a member of the firm.

The third classification is that of corporations, although the Patent Office permits other collective groups, such as an association, to be substituted for a "corporation" designation. In this event the information to be furnished is the corporate name and state or country of incorporation; resident business address, including street, city, and state; and situs of corporation (or principal place of business), including street, city, and state; and the application may be executed by any corporate officer. Thus it is not necessary for the president of the corporation to execute the trademark application; it may be executed by the corporation's vice president, secretary, or treasurer. The Patent Office will also accept the signature of the Chairman of the Board of Directors but will not accept the signature of individual directors on the Board.

When the applicant is not domiciled in the United States, a domestic representative must be appointed.

The form of the trademark application will also differ, depending on whether it is directed to a trademark, service mark, collective mark, or certification mark. Appropriate modified forms for each of these types of marks, derived from the Trademark Rules, are provided in Appendix B.

In addition to the identification of the mark, every trademark application requires the submission of the class number. This refers to the Patent Office classification system, set forth in Appendix C, that was established for the convenience of the administration of the trademark examining operation by the Patent Office and that does not limit or extend the applicant's rights. As of September 1, 1973, the Patent Office adopted the so-called International Classification System.[6] Since, however, more than 900,000 registrations

---

[6] A detailed schedule in the English language of goods and services and their classification in the international classification system is set forth in INTERNATIONAL CLASSIFICATION OF GOODS AND SERVICES TO WHICH TRADE MARKS ARE APPLIED, published in 1965 and supplemented in 1967, 1970, and 1971 by the British Patent Office.

have issued under the prior classification system, it is also included in Appendix C. It should be emphasized that a single application may recite a number of goods or a number of services within a single class if the goods or services have actually been used. For example, if the applicant has used in commerce the mark sought to be registered on men's pants, shirts, shorts, hosiery, and women's coats, all these may be included within a single application, since all the goods fall within Class 25, directed to clothing. A single application, however, may not combine both goods and services or goods or services in different classes for a single government filing fee. This is basically an economic matter, as the Patent Office refuses to do several searches for a single fee. If an attempt is made to register a mark for both goods and services or for goods or services in different classes, the registration will be refused; and the applicant will be required to restrict the application to goods or services within a single class. Since, however, as noted, the motivation for this Patent Office policy lies in a basis for equitably determining appropriate filing fees, when several applications have been filed by the same applicant for the identical mark on the same register and each of the applications has been allowed, a consolidated single certificate based on the several applications may be issued. A combined application may also be filed to register the same mark within a number of classes. A fee, however, equaling the sum of the fees for filing an application in each class is required. A single certificate of registration will be issued.

It cannot be unduly emphasized that the classification system adopted by the Patent Office is for administrative purposes only and does not expand or limit rights. The statute is explicit that the rights flowing from a registered mark (as, for example, the exclusive right to use in the case of an incontestable registered mark) are limited to "the goods or services specified in the certificate." Thus the registration of a mark in Class 25 does not confer upon the owner of the registration, and can never confer upon the owner of the registration, statutory rights encompassing every article of clothing, although Class 25 is entitled "Clothing" and is specifically mentioned in the registration as the class within which the registered mark is classified.

It is not uncommon, in the case of weak marks, to find many similar or identical marks for different specific articles belonging to different registrants within the same class. This is to be expected, since the classification system includes these kinds of broad classes as Class 25 for clothing.

A drawing must be submitted with the application. In the case of a word mark, the drawing may be typewritten. In the case of a mark comprising a symbol (any mark other than a word mark), an India ink drawing of the mark must be furnished. The Trademark Rules of Practice are very explicit with respect to the requirements for the drawing. For example, when color is a feature of a mark, specific linings are required to designate specific colors. Every trademark drawing must have a heading at its top, listing in separate lines the applicant's name, post-office address, dates of first use, and the goods or services recited in the application. This heading may be typewritten.

With the trademark application and drawing must be submitted a statutory fee of $175, per class and five specimens of the mark as actually used. In the case of trademarks the specimens should normally comprise actually used labels, tags, or containers, or the displays associated with the goods. In certain cases, for example, when the mark is applied directly to the goods and the goods are bulky or expensive (for instance, a trademark applied directly to a camera), photographs may be used instead of labels.[7]

The application may include a disclaimer of unregisterable matter forming a part of the mark. For example, a composite mark may include an element that by itself is clearly unregisterable. Under these circumstances the applicant may disclaim the element, usually by designating the disclaimer as being "apart from the mark as shown." Section 6 of the Lanham Act[8] provides that a disclaimer is without prejudice with regard to both the applicant's rights existing at the time or arising later in the disclaimed matter and his rights in a later application alleging the disclaimed matter as being distinctive.

## § 5.05 SPECIFIC LABELING PROBLEMS

The specific labeling requirements of certain products, although outside the scope of this discussion, will be mentioned briefly.

---

[7] For foreign applicants claiming ownership of a trademark application or registration in their home country, see p. 39 regarding the necessity of filing specimens to evidence use of the mark.

[8] 15 U.S.C. § 1056 (1982).

The labeling of foods, drugs and related medical devices, and cosmetics is governed by the federal Food, Drug and Cosmetic Act, as amended, and the general regulations, as amended, of the United States Department of Health, Education and Welfare, Food and Drug Administration. State laws concerning labels may also be relevant. A free copy of the Act and the regulations for its administration and enforcement may be obtained by writing to Food and Drug Administration, U.S. Department of Health, Education and Welfare, Washington, D.C. The regulations cover not only labeling as such, but certified coal-tar colors, the tolerances for poisonous ingredients in foods, the certification of drugs, and the like.[9]

The labels for meat products, including lard (but not including fish), that are subject to federal inspection must be approved by the Meat Inspection Division, Bureau of Animal Industry, Department of Agriculture. The regulations governing meat inspection and labeling are contained in Title 9, Chapter I, Subchapter A, Code of Federal Regulations, 1949 Edition, Cumulative Pocket Supplements issued to it, and amendments, including those issued January 16, 1952 (17 Fed. Reg. 465), March 28, 1952 (17 Fed. Reg. 2712), and May 28, 1952 (17 Fed. Reg. 4844). The labeling requirements constitute Part 17 of the Regulations. A copy of *Regulations Governing the Meat Inspection of the United States Department of Agriculture* may be obtained by writing to the United States Department of Agriculture, Agricultural Research Service, Meat Inspection Branch, Washington, D.C.[10]

The labels for both wines and distilled alcoholic liquors must be approved by the Alcohol Tax Unit, Bureau of Internal Revenue.[11]

## § 5.06 ADMISSION AS ATTORNEYS BEFORE THE PATENT OFFICE IN TRADEMARK CASES

Practice before the Patent Office in trademark cases does not require the practitioner to be either a patent attorney or a patent agent, and thus differs markedly from the requirements concerning practice before the Patent Office in patent cases.[12]

---

[9] *See also* 21 U.S.C. Ch. 9 (1982).

[10] *See also id* at Ch. 12 (1982).

[11] For the text of the federal Fair Packaging and Labeling Act, see 15 U.S.C. § 1451(1982).

[12] For the requirements regarding admission to a practice before the Patent Office in patent cases, see A. SEIDEL, WHAT THE GENERAL PRACTITIONER SHOULD KNOW ABOUT PATENT LAW AND PRACTICE 2-4 (4th ed. 1984).

Attorneys at law in good standing before the highest court of any state, territory, or of the District of Columbia may practice before the Patent Office in trademark cases. No application for an admission by an attorney at law is necessary; a statement in a power is adequate. Recognition of attorneys is limited to each case.

## § 5.07 PROSECUTION OF THE TRADEMARK APPLICATION

After the trademark application has been filed, it will be assigned a serial number, the attorney for the applicant receiving a filing certificate bearing the serial number and filing date from the Patent Office. The trademark application will then be examined by the appropriate Examiner of Trademarks. The Examiner of Trademarks will make a search through the existing registrations and through pending trademark applications. He will also review the trademark application for formal errors.

If after his search he decides that the application contains no formal errors and is entitled to registration, the Examiner will pass the application to publication (in the case of a Principal Register application), and the mark will be published for opposition in the *Official Gazette.* In the case of a Supplemental Register application, he will issue the registration forthwith. If he finds something objectionable from a formal point of view or if he feels that the mark is not entitled to registration on substantive grounds, he will issue an office action within which he will advise the applicant (through his attorney) why the application is not entitled to registration, setting out the formal objections. He may also ask the applicant to furnish information, including exhibits, that in his opinion are necessary for a proper examination of the application.

The applicant has six months from the date of mailing of the office action to respond. The response may take the form of an amendment to the application containing the reasons underlying the amendment. It may consist of an argument stating why the application is allowable, or it may be a combination of both an amendment and an argument. In any event, the response should be such as to advance the application toward allowance.

After the response by the applicant the Examiner of Trademarks will again examine the application. He may decide to allow the application and pass it either to publication (Principal Register application) or to issuance (Supplemental Register application), or he may again reject the application for the same reasons he advanced in his first rejection or advance other reasons. If he feels that an issue has been reached and that no benefit will be gained from the further prosecution of the application, he may render a final action. If the examiner does not render a final action but again rejects the application, the applicant again has six months in which to respond.

The procedure just set forth is repeated (sometimes as many as five times or more) until ultimately the application is allowed by the Examiner of Trademarks, or he renders a final action. Upon the rendering of a final action, the applicant is limited to an appeal, a Request for Reconsideration setting forth new evidence to persuade the Examiner of Trademarks to withdraw the final refusal, or compliance with the examiner's requirements.

If the applicant, at any stage in the proceeding, fails to respond to an office action within six months (or if the examiner requires a shorter period of time, within that shorter period of time), the trademark application will be abandoned.

With respect to amendments made during the prosecution, the following should be borne in mind:

(1) No amendments to the dates of use will be accepted unless supported by the affidavit of the applicant and, if required by the examiner, by an additional showing. In no event will the Patent Office allow an amendment to the dates of use which would claim dates of use subsequent to the filing date of the application.

(2) Additions to the specification of goods or services will not be permitted unless they were in actual use at the time the application was filed and unless the amendment is supported by additional specimens and by the supplemental affidavit of the applicant supporting the dates of use.

An amendment of the description or drawing for the mark must be supported by labels and by an affidavit of the applicant that the amended mark was in actual use prior to the filing date of the application.

As expected, amendments completely changing the nature of the mark are not permitted.

The file wrapper revealing the major portion of the prosecution of a trademark application is shown in Appendix D.

## § 5.08 APPEALS FROM THE EXAMINER OF TRADEMARKS

When a trademark application has received a final action, the applicant has six months from the date of the final action in which to file an appeal to the Trademark Trial and Appeal Board. The appeal is taken simply by filing a notice of appeal and paying the required appeal fee of $100, per class. Although it is also possible to take an appeal when there has been a second refusal on the same grounds by the Examiner of Trademarks, even though there has been no final action, this type of procedure is rare.

The appellant must submit a brief on appeal within 60 days after the date of appeal. This is normally countered by a written statement of the grounds for rejection by the Examiner of Trademarks. The appellant may then file a reply brief within 20 days from the date of the examiner's statement.

The appellant may request an oral hearing on his appeal. If no request for an oral hearing is made, the appeal will be determined on brief. If there is an oral hearing, it will be heard by the Trademark Trial and Appeal Board. Although formerly the Assistant Commissioner of Patents or an examiner-in-chief heard trademark appeals, this was changed in 1958 to provide for a Trademark Trial and Appeal Board that closely resembles the Board of Appeals in patent cases. Generally, the oral hearing will consist of an argument by counsel for the appellant and a rebuttal argument presented by the Examiner of Trademarks. In the past, the Examiner of Trademarks was not required to appear at an ex parte oral argument. This policy has been changed and the Patent Office now requires the appearance of the Examiner at the oral argument.

If the decision on appeal is adverse to the appellant, further appeal must be taken outside the Patent Office, either to the Court of Appeals for the Federal Circuit, formerly the Court of Customs and Patent Appeals, or to a United States District Court, which, for purpose of service on the Commissioner of Patents, normally would be the District Court for the District of Columbia. The procedure to be followed is identical to that used in an appeal from the Board of Appeals in patent cases.[13]

## § 5.09 CHANGES AFTER ISSUANCE

After a trademark registration has issued, it is possible to have certain things done to it in particular circumstances. For example, in the case of change of ownership, upon the request of the assignee, a new certificate of registration may be issued in the name of the assignee for the unexpired part of the original period.

---

[13] Discussed in detail in SEIDEL, *supra* note 12, at 62.

Changes in the issued mark not amounting to a material alteration of the character of the mark may be made. Thus upon the payment of a fee of $100, a portion of a registered mark may be disclaimed or the mark may be amended. Goods may be deleted but not added unless it can be shown that the failure to include the goods within the registration arose through a mistake that occurred in good faith.

# 6

# Contested Patent Office Proceedings Involving Trademarks

## § 6.01 INTRODUCTION

The various types of contested Patent Office proceedings involving trademarks include oppositions to registration, proceedings to cancel a registration, interferences, and concurrent registration proceedings.

Any discussion regarding Patent Office administrative proceedings should be prefaced by the great change wrought by the Lanham Act. Thus the Lanham Act made a marked contribution to administrative trademark law in its plain recitation in Section 19 that

> In all inter partes proceedings equitable principles of laches, estoppel, and acquiescence, where applicable may be considered and applied.[1]

This statutory fiat has resulted in a broad extension of equitable principles in contested Patent Office proceedings. Although prior to the Act, and indeed prior to relatively recent Patent Office decisions and practice, the outcome, for example, of an opposition proceeding was governed largely by rigid rules, today the behavior of the parties, their extent of use, good faith use, and the like, have a marked bearing upon the outcome of Patent Office contested proceedings.

The nature of each of the contested Patent Office proceedings will be dealt with in detail in another section. All contested Patent Office trademark proceedings, however, have certain common aspects, and these aspects are preferably dealt with jointly as they are applicable to each type of contested trademark proceeding.

[1] 15 U.S.C. § 1069 (1982).

## § 6.02 GENERAL PROCEDURE IN CONTESTED PROCEEDINGS

All opposition and cancellation proceedings and many interference and concurrent registration proceedings commence with pleadings that are generally analogous to a complaint and answer. Following the pleadings, testimony periods are assigned that correspond generally to the setting of a case for trial in court proceedings. The discovery phase of the proceeding precedes the testimony periods. In place of a trial there is substituted the taking of depositions during the assigned testimony periods. After the close of the depositions there may be an oral hearing that corresponds to the oral summation in court proceedings.

With the exception of the initial pleading (for example, the notice of opposition or petition to cancel), any paper filed by a party in any type of contested Patent Office trademark proceeding must be served upon each of the other parties to the proceeding. Service upon the party is usually affected through transmission in the mail to the attorney for the party unless there be none, in which case service is made, of course, directly on the party. In ordinary circumstances, the attorney preparing the papers merely submits his Certification of Service of his mailing of the papers. It is possible, however, to effect service by delivering a copy of the paper to the person to be served, or by leaving a copy in his usual place of business with someone in his employ, or, when the person to be served has no usual place of business, by leaving a copy at his residence, with a member of his family who is over 14 years of age and of discretion.

When communications are mailed, the date of mailing will be considered the date of service. The normal requisite mailing-transmittal-time period is compensated for by adding five days to the prescribed period after service whenever a party is required to take some action.

### § 6.02(a) Discovery Procedure

The discovery procedure in contested trademark matters provides for discovery in accordance with the provisions of the Federal Rules of Civil Procedure in all inter partes trademark cases except for certain specified provisions set forth in Trademark Rule 2.120. Thus the use of discovery depositions, depositions on written questions, interrogatories, and requests for admission are now widespread in contested trademark matters before the Patent Office.

Since Patent Office Rule 2.120 details discovery procedure, it is reproduced in Appendix A.

When books, documents, or other tangible things, not privileged, have been pleaded or otherwise asserted, they may be inspected and copied by a motion to produce, presented prior to the date for taking testimony of any party.

Upon refusal to make discovery, the Trademark Trial and Appeal Board may strike out all or any part of any pleading of the party who refuses to make discovery. The Trademark Trial and Appeal Board may also dismiss the action or proceeding or any part of it, or enter a judgment as by default, or take other appropriate action if the party in the position of plaintiff fails to take testimony or offer any other evidence during its testimony period.

### § 6.02(b) Conduct of Testimony in Testimony Periods

The testimony of witnesses during the testimony periods of contested trademark proceedings is generally taken in a manner similar to that utilized for the taking of testimony in discovery depositions in court cases before the federal courts. The Trademark Rules provide for the taking of testimony during the testimony period by written questions propounded by an officer before whom depositions may be taken as well as by depositions. The use of this technique, however, is very rare, since it eliminates all the advantages derived from confrontation, including the all important follow-through of leads, openings, and the like.[2] It is the author's opinion that this technique should never be used except, possibly, for the proof of noncontested "hard" facts. If great distances prevent counsel from taking depositions, he should either employ local counsel for that purpose (acquainting local counsel with the background by mail and by telephone) or, if possible, reach an agreement with the other side of a stipulated record. Testimony by written questions may in some cases prove more expensive than depositions, since the Trademark Rules provide for the service of cross questions—20 days from the date of service of the notice of taking depositions upon written question. Within 10 days from the date of service of the cross questions, the parties who propose to take the deposition may serve redirect questions on every adverse party. Within 10 days from the date of service of the redirect questions, any party who served cross questions may serve re-cross questions upon the party who proposes to take the deposition, with the possibility of written objections to

[2] The legal systems of many foreign countries do not provide cross-examination, and hence depositions on written questions are a compromise when taking testimony outside the United States.

questions, substitute questions, motions, and so forth, being encountered all along the line.

Generally, depositions during the testimony period are taken in the office of the lawyer whose client is being examined. The notice for taking testimony must be served upon the attorney of record (unless otherwise stipulated) or, in the rare case in which there is no attorney of record, upon the adverse party. If the name of a witness is not known, a general description sufficient to identify him or the particular class or group to which he belongs may be given. Safeguards against unfair advantage gained by scheduling depositions too close together in point of time in view of travel requirements are provided in the Trademark Rules. Similarly, specific requirements regarding proper persons before whom depositions may be taken, the manner of certification, and the filing of depositions are also set forth in the Trademark Rules.

Objections of any type, such as on the evidence presented, the conduct of any party, the qualifications of the officer taking the deposition, or the manner in which the deposition is taken, are noted by the officer taking the deposition upon the record. It is to be emphasized, however, that the Trademark Rules provide: "Evidence objected to shall be taken subject to the objections."

The form of depositions is carefully prescribed by the Trademark Rules. As with discovery depositions in federal court cases, exhibits may be offered—numbered or lettered consecutively and marked with the number and title of the case and the name of the party offering the exhibit.

The original copy of the transcript of testimony, the original exhibits, and one extra copy of the transcript of testimony must be filed as promptly as possible in the Patent Office by the party who took the testimony. In addition, this party must serve one copy of the transcript of testimony, together with copies of documentary exhibits, on each adverse party within 30 days after the completion of the taking of the testimony.

Three separate testimony periods are generally provided for by the Patent Office: the testimony period for the party in the position of plaintiff (30 days); the testimony period for the party in the position of defendant (30 days); and the rebuttal testimony period (15 days). As a general rule, the Patent Office has (1) the closing date of testimony period of the party in the position of plaintiff scheduled about four months after the receipt of the last pleading, (2) the closing date of the testimony period for the party in the position of the defendant two months later, and (3) the closing date for the rebuttal testimony period one and one-half months still later.

### § 6.02(c) Procedure After Close of Testimony Period

The brief of a party in the position of the plaintiff is due within 60 days after the closing date set for rebuttal testimony. The brief of a party in the position of defendant is due within 30 days from the due date of the first brief. If a reply brief is filed by the party in the position of the plaintiff, it is due within 15 days after the due date of the brief to which it is a reply. The rules require that an original and two legible copies of all briefs be filed. Briefs are normally typewritten. Unless leave of the Trademark Trial and Appeal Board is obtained, no brief shall contain more than 50 pages of argument, and in the case of a reply brief, the entire brief should not exceed 25 pages. Each brief is required to contain an alphabetical index of cases.

In the absence of a request for an oral hearing by one of the parties, the case will be decided on the record and on the briefs.

The determination of contested trademark proceedings is effected by the Trademark Trial and Appeal Board. When an oral argument is conducted, the Board sits as a tribunal of three members. Unless express permission is given, the oral arguments are limited to one-half hour for each party.

The Board renders a formal decision, which is usually printed in whole, or in abstracted form, by the *United States Patents Quarterly*. These decisions, plus the relatively small number of decisions of the courts having appellate jurisdiction over the Patent Office, constitute the prime body of law for contested trademark proceedings.

## § 6.03 APPELLATE PROCEDURE

The appellate procedure for taking appeals in trademark cases from the Patent Office to the courts is identical to that used in appeals from the Patent Office in patent cases.[3] For this reason, appeals to the courts are possible from each of the contested proceedings—namely, oppositions, cancellations, interferences, and concurrent registration proceedings, and also, as already noted, from ex parte attempts to secure registration, as well as, although very rarely, from the refusal of the Commissioner to enter an affidavit

[3] This appellate procedure is considered in detail in A. SEIDEL, WHAT THE GENERAL PRACTITIONER SHOULD KNOW ABOUT PATENT LAW AND PRACTICE 6 (4th ed. 1984).

under Section 8 during the sixth year following the registration of a mark. The procedure in the Patent Office with respect to the last-mentioned matter comprises first a refusal to enter the affidavit by the examiner and then a petition to the Commissioner by the dissatisfied registrant.

It is to be noted that the same time limit (60 days from the date of the decision appealed from) applies to both appeals taken to the Court of Customs and Patent Appeals and appeals to the United States district courts.

Although the appellate procedure is discussed in detail in the companion volume on patent law, one additional point is worthy of notice. In contested proceedings, such as an oppositon, when an appeal to the courts is necessary or has been taken, the party who is the first user is well advised to consider electing a civil action in the United States district courts under 35 U.S.C. Section 146, combined with a cause of action for trademark infringement. This will enable the entire bundle of relative rights between the parties to be adjudicated within a single proceeding. If a settlement is possible, this approach will exert the maximum pressure upon the adversary. Of course, this suggestion is not to be followed slavishly, since it has the disadvantage of a carryover of registration issues to infringement issues and vice versa, with a consequent muddying of the waters, but it is a definite possibility to be borne in mind when the appropriate situation arises.

## § 6.04 NATURE OF PROOFS

In contested trademark proceedings, as in litigation, proof may be established by either oral testimony or documentary evidence. Although certain authorities have held that one is as competent as the other and that if the oral testimony is sufficient to establish proof, documentary evidence is unnecessary, this opinion should be at least tempered. Testimony of use that consists merely in the unaided recollection of dates, particularly dates running back many years, will generally be held insufficient to establish either priority or continuity of use. On the other hand, the oral testimony of tradesmen, customers, and competitors about use, will comprise the most cogent evidence when supported by records showing sales, purchases of labels, containers, specimens of advertising, and expenditures for advertising.

# 7

# Opposition and Cancellation Proceedings

## § 7.01 BACKGROUND OF OPPOSITIONS

By far the most prevalent form of contested trademark proceeding comprises opposition proceedings. These proceedings are governed by Section 13 of the Lanham Act:

> Any person who believes that he could be damaged by the registration of a mark upon the Principal Register may, upon payment of the required fee, file an opposition in the Patent and Trademark Office, stating the grounds therefor, within thirty days after the publication under subsection (a) of section 12 of this Act of the mark sought to be registered. Upon written request prior to the expiration of the thirty-day period, the time for filing opposition shall be extended for an additional thirty days, and further extensions of time for filing opposition may be granted by the Commissioner for good cause when requested prior to the expiration of an extension. The Commissioner shall notify the applicant of each extension of the time for filing opposition. An opposition may be amended under such conditions as may be prescribed by the Commissioner.[1]

It is to be noted that opposition proceedings may be instituted only against marks upon the Principal Register. Opposition proceedings are not available against marks on the Supplemental Register,[2] nor are opposition proceedings available against republished

---

[1] 15 U.S.C. § 1063 (1982).

[2] Section 26 of the Lanham Act, 15 U.S.C. § 1094 (1982).

marks that were registered under the Act of 1881 or the Act of 1905 and republished under Section 12(c) of the Lanham Act.[3]

The reference to the publication under Subsection (a) of Section 12 in Section 13, just quoted, refers to the publication in the *Official Gazette* of the Patent Office after an examination has been made.

The absolute necessity for an opposition system becomes evident when the inadequacies of trademark searching are recalled. The dependence of the searching system upon alphabetical order arrangements, the complexities of the English language, and the unknown factors introduced by the use of coined words prevent the rendition of searches having the trustworthiness of land title searches. For example, conventional searching techniques would fail to uncover a prior registration for "TRELLIMF" when the mark "RELLIMF" was being searched. Conventional searches frequently fail to reveal marks having similar phonetic characteristics or similar cognative meanings. With the advent of computer searching, oversights of this type may be less common as computer searching allows for a search of roots or formulatives. Thus it would be possible to search for all marks with the common suffix "-LIMF." For truly coined words, however, it may not be possible to search and discover every possible combination of the letters that may be confusingly similar.

Even worse, as noted before, the number of registered trademarks and pending trademark applications represent but a fraction of the marks used in this country. Notwithstanding the lack of registration status of their marks, owners of common law rights in trademarks have interests that the courts will protect.

Only by according the public at large the opportunity to oppose a trademark application before it matures into a registration can unjust monopolies in trademarks be avoided. Stated conversely, the opposition system provides a monitor for the Patent Office and a system by which trademark rights may be challenged before they have flowered to full registration status.

## § 7.02 THE OFFICIAL GAZETTE

Frequent reference has already been made to the *Official Gazette,* and, as this magazine is an essential tool of the trademark practitioner, the nature of the magazine is presented here.

The *Official Gazette* is issued weekly on Tuesday of each week, even if it falls on a holiday, by the Superintendent of Documents, Gov-

[3] 15 U.S.C. § 1062(c) (1982).

ernment Printing Office, Washington, D.C., at an annual subscription rate for the patents section of $250 and $205 for the trademarks section. This subscription rate has been subject to rapid and considerable increase in recent years. The *Official Gazette* is in two discrete sections, one of which is devoted to patents and includes an abstract of each patent issued that week (all patents and trademark registrations are issued on Tuesday of each week, whether or not it is a holiday). The Trademark Section of the *Official Gazette* is of primary concern insofar as the trademark practitioner is concerned.

The Trademark Section of the *Official Gazette* contains the following:

### *(1) Notices of Suit*

Section 34 of the Lanham Act[4] requires the clerks of all federal courts to give notice in writing to the Commissioner of Patents within one month after the filing of any action, suit, or proceeding arising under the Lanham Act. This notice sets forth the names and addresses of the litigants and the number or numbers of the registrations involved in the suit. In addition, the Act requires the clerks to notify the Commissioner within one month after a decision is rendered, appeal taken, or a decree issued. The Commissioner incorporates these notices into the file wrapper of the involved trademark registrations. In addition, the notices are published in the Trademark Section of the *Official Gazette.* Review of the Trademark Section, therefore, enables one to learn of the institution of all trademark litigation throughout the United States in the federal courts, even though the litigation is never carried to a reported decision. Similarly, the outcome of all litigation of this type may be ascertained, even though the outcome is by virtue of a nonreported order or decree. As a practical matter, the notices in the *Official Gazette* are, in the main, some two months or so behind the date of the action or disposition referred to in the notice. On occasion delays greatly in excess of two months are encountered because of the neglect of a court clerk to notify the Commissioner.

### *(2) Orders and Condition of Trademark Applications*

The Trademark Section of the *Official Gazette* also carries any orders of the Commissioner of Patents or of an Assistant Commissioner of Patents affecting practice before the Patent Office. In addition, the

[4] *Id.* § 1116 (1982).

gross condition of trademark applications before the Patent Office is tabulated, including the date of the oldest new application before each of the Trademark Examining Divisions, the date of the oldest amended applications before each of the Trademark Examining Divisions, similar information for renewals, and Section 12(c) publications.

### *(3) Miscellaneous Notices*

The Trademark Section of the *Official Gazette* also carries miscellaneous notices, such as notices respecting service by publication.

### *(4) Specific Marks*

The principal portion of the Trademark Section of the *Official Gazette* is devoted to the marks published for opposition. This is required reading every week for every trademark practitioner if he is to render maximum service to his clients. The marks published for opposition are arranged in classes following the trademark classification system, and the following information is presented relative to each mark: (a) its serial number; (b) the name of the applicant and his address; (c) the filing date of the application; (d) the mark that is being published for opposition, which, in the case of a mark involving a symbol, will present the symbol and, in the case of a mark involving a word in distinctive lettering, will present the word in its distinctive lettering; (e) one or more of the following matters, if present—a statement of any related registrations owned by the applicant referred to in the applicant's application, a translation of the mark if it is a word drawn from a foreign language, the portion of the mark that has been disclaimed if, in fact, a portion of the mark is disclaimed, information relative to the person from whom the mark is derived in the case of marks involving a signature or a pictorial illustration of a specific human being; (f) the goods to which the mark is applied; and (g) the date or dates of first use. A specimen page from this portion of the Trademark Section of the *Official Gazette* is shown on page 63.

The Trademark Section of the *Official Gazette* also includes the publication of service marks, collective marks, and certification marks. Furthermore, it includes a listing by classes of the trademark registrations issued upon the Principal Register and of the trademarks registered upon the Supplemental Register. Information similar to the information furnished regarding marks published for opposition is provided with respect to the listing of registrations

JANUARY 14, 1986 U.S. PATENT AND TRADEMARK OFFICE TM 133

**CLASS 42—(Continued).**

SN 476,242. MUSKET CORPORATION, OKLAHOMA CITY, OK. FILED 4-19-1984.

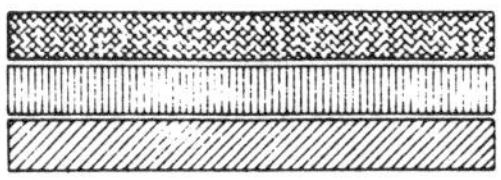

THE DRAWING IS LINED FOR THE COLORS ORANGE, RED AND BROWN.

THE MARK IS COMPRISED OF THREE PARALLEL, HORIZONTAL STRIPES OF INDETERMINATE LENGTH WHICH, FROM TOP TO BOTTOM, ARE LINED FOR THE COLORS ORANGE, RED AND BROWN, RESPECTIVELY, AND THE DESIGNATED COLORS ARE A FEATURE OF THE MARK.

SEC. 2(F).

FOR RETAIL CONVENIENCE STORE SERVICES (U.S. CL. 101).

FIRST USE 7-4-1981; IN COMMERCE 8-21-1981.

---

SN 498,057. SATAY CLUB, INC., MOBILE, AL. FILED 9-6-1984.

NO CLAIM IS MADE TO THE EXCLUSIVE RIGHT TO USE "SATAY CLUB", APART FROM THE MARK AS SHOWN.

FOR RESTAURANT SERVICES (U.S. CL. 100).

FIRST USE 9-0-1983; IN COMMERCE 9-0-1983.

---

SN 509,090. HOOK DRUGS, INC., INDIANAPOLIS, IN. FILED 11-16-1984.

**WE LIKE TO SEE YOU SMILE**

FOR RETAIL DRUG STORE AND PHARMACY SERVICES (U.S. CLS. 100 AND 101).

FIRST USE 10-16-1984; IN COMMERCE 10-16-1984.

**CLASS 42—(Continued).**

SN 516,668. CHARTER MEDICAL CORPORATION, MACON, GA. FILED 1-8-1985.

**NATIONAL RECOVERY NETWORK**

NO CLAIM IS MADE TO THE EXCLUSIVE RIGHT TO USE "NATIONAL RECOVERY", APART FROM THE MARK AS SHOWN.

FOR OUTPATIENT ADDICTIVE DISEASE TREATMENT (U.S. CL. 100).

FIRST USE 10-0-1984; IN COMMERCE 10-0-1984.

---

SN 516,884. YOON, IN S., DBA EL POLLO MEJOR, LOS ANGELES, CA. FILED 1-10-1985.

NO CLAIM IS MADE TO THE EXCLUSIVE RIGHT TO USE "EL POLLO MEJOR", "BEST CHICKEN" AND THE DEPICTION OF A CHICKEN, APART FROM THE MARK AS SHOWN.

THE ENGLISH TRANSLATION OF THE PHRASE "EL POLLO MEJOR" IN THE MARK IS "THE BEST CHICKEN".

FOR RESTAURANT SERVICES (U.S. CL. 100).

FIRST USE 10-15-1981; IN COMMERCE 10-15-1981.

---

SN 518,049. MILLER, JAMES ROBERT, NEDERLAND, CO. FILED 1-18-1985.

FOR CUSTOM DESIGN OF JEWELRY; RETAIL JEWELRY STORE SERVICES (U.S. CLS. 100 AND 101).

FIRST USE 10-1-1984; IN COMMERCE 11-7-1984.

upon the Supplemental Register. As stated before, the marks upon the Supplemental Register are not subject to opposition but are subject to cancellation proceedings and hence are not published prior to their issuance as registrations.

Furthermore, registrations that have been renewed, canceled, amended, or disclaimed are set forth, as well as registrations published under Section 12(c). An index of registrants is also provided in each issue.

An annual index relating to the Trademark Section of the *Official Gazette* is published each year in a buckram volume.

Very useful working tools for trademark lawyers are the annual computer printouts of all the subsisting trademark registrations, namely, The Trademark Register of the United States.[5]

## § 7.03 BASIS FOR OPPOSITION

The opening portion of the first sentence of Section 13 sets forth a statement that is essential with respect to the institution of an opposition but is frequently overlooked by nontrademark specialists. It is a condition precedent for the right of a person to institute an opposition that the person demonstrate the possibility of damage to him from the registration of the mark sought to be opposed. Thus the academic institution of oppositions, so as to permit a further review of the action of the trademark examiner, is not contemplated by the statute. As a general rule, if the opposer fails to show any damage not common to the general public, he cannot institute an opposition proceeding. Although in an academic and theoretical sense, every trademark registration removes a mark from the public domain and therefore damages the general public, this is not such a degree of damage as provides the basis for a trademark opposition.

As a general rule, likelihood of confusion between the published mark and a mark used by the opposer is the most common basis of damage upon which opposition proceedings are based. It is to be emphasized that the opposer need not have registered his mark to be able to institute an opposition. Ownership of a nonregistered mark or trade name is a sufficient basis to oppose the registration of a mark by another whose use is likely to lead to confusion.

---

[5] Published by The Trademark Register, 300 Washington Square, Washington, D.C. 20036, and The Compu-Mark Directory of U.S. Trademarks, published by Compu-mark U.S., 1333 F. Street, N.W., 6th Floor, Washington, D.C. 20005.

Likelihood of confusion is not the only basis of damage sufficient to entitle a party to institute an opposition. For example, it is a proper basis for the institution of an opposition when the mark sought to be opposed is a descriptive term that is unregisterable, and registration would deprive the industry, of which the opposer is a member, of a valuable common descriptive term. In this situation, the registrant would be obtaining unfair advantage over his competitors by restricting their use of a term that was the common property of the entire industry before the term was sought to be registered. Thus the registration of "Spacer" was successfully opposed, when this term was sought to be registered as a secondary meaning mark for a machine tool having a mechanism for providing relative movement between a tool holder and a work support to locate each relative to the other, on the grounds that "spacer" was nothing more than the common descriptive name of a machine tool that includes a spacing mechanism and did not perform a trademark function. The opposer was a manufacturer of a variety of mechanisms for providing relative movement between a tool holder and a work support.

The opposer may also sustain sufficient damage to justify an opposition if the issuance of a registration to the applicant violates a contract between the opposer and the applicant. Under these circumstances the Trademark Trial and Appeal Board will evaluate the relative rights of the applicant and opposer arising from the contract.

In the most common basis for opposition, namely, likelihood of confusion, the opposer alleges that he has used the mark (either in the identical form or in a closely related form) upon the identical goods or upon related goods, so that there is likelihood of confusion between the marks of the parties.

## § 7.04 MODE OF PROOF IN OPPOSITIONS

Prior to August 27, 1982, Section 13 of the Trademark Act required that every notice of opposition be verified. This requirement was amended by the Act of August 27, 1982, which deleted the requirement for a verified noticc of opposition. An opposition may now be signed either by the opposing party or by the party's attorney. An opposition signed by an attorney need not be accompanied by a written power of attorney.

A notice of opposition is not deemed a substitute for the taking of testimony and the presentation of proofs. Statements in a notice of opposition alleging dates of use and continuity of use will not, in and of themselves, support a finding that the opposer did use his mark on these dates or continuously thereafter. Evidence supporting the allegations made in the notice of opposition must be presented during the testimony phase of the opposition proceeding. Similarly, the dates of use alleged in a trademark application cannot be used as evidence that the mark was used on these dates by the applicant.

It must be remembered that the burden of going forward in an opposition proceeding is upon the opposer, and in recent years this burden has become more onerous. The Court of Appeals for the Federal Circuit, formerly the Court of Customs and Patent Appeals, has repeatedly shown in its recent decisions an intense dislike for so-called paper oppositions, which in former years were relatively prevalent. In paper oppositions the opposer relies solely on previous registrations belonging to him and presents his claim of likelihood of confusion solely on the basis of the registrations. The author does not mean to imply that it is not possible to prevail in a contested opposition without the taking of testimony, since, as noted, the Patent Office will receive in evidence and make part of the record all registrations of an opposer (or petitioner or cancellation) for which two copies are presented with the notice of opposition.

The institution of a paper opposition, however, is unwise both psychologically and tactically. Psychologically, the failure to present testimony evinces an indication that the opposer does not regard his damage as too serious, since it is not worth the expense and trouble of taking testimony; and tactically, it is unwise, since the most potent evidence can be introduced into an opposition only through the taking of testimony. In addition, Trademark Rules provide for entertaining a motion to dismiss a proceeding for failure to take testimony when the failure is by the party in the position of the plaintiff.

The proofs to be offered during the testimony period in an opposition in which the basis of damage is the likelihood of confusion or actual confusion generally resemble the proof offered in trademark litigation. Thus the opposer should demonstrate his ownership of his marks, his first dates of use and his continuous use, and the degree of goodwill behind his marks. Evidence bearing on these aspects of the opposer's case should be presented, including exhibits of goods, invoices for labels, specimens of advertising, and preferably breakdown tabulations respecting advertising. The strength and scope of opposers' marks are, of course, dependent upon the extent or duration of their use and the extent of the advertising support behind their use as well as their technical nature. If the opposer had used his marks upon a wide variety of goods, evidence of this usage should be submitted.

Of course, if the opposer knows of instances of actual confusion, testimony and evidence about the actual confusion should be presented. As with the conduct of trademark litigation, the presentation of "expert" testimony on the question of likelihood of confusion should be minimized, and the major stress should be laid upon the presentation of positive evidence. It must be remembered, both in the Patent Office and in the courts, that the trier in trademark matters does not appreciate the suggestion that he surrender his own judgment about the likelihood of confusion and substitute the "expert" judgment of others. The trier is at all times cognizant of his duty to render an opinion on this question and aware that he cannot substitute the opinion of "expert" witnesses for his own, assuming that in this area there are any true "experts," an assumption not generally supported by the decided cases.

The use of polls and psychological recognition tests as an objective mode of presentation of evidence is gradually being accepted by the Patent Office. For polls to be admitted, however, they must be fair and unbiased. The characteristics of a good poll can be found in the Chapter 9 discussion of trademark litigation.

As already noted, Section 19 of the Lanham Act[6] provides for the consideration and application in contested proceedings of the equitable principles of laches, estoppel, and acquiescence. Although constituting a profound advance in the law, this section has been conservatively construed by the Court of Appeals for the Federal Circuit, formerly the Court of Customs and Patent Appeals, in respect to its use by an applicant in an opposition proceeding. This court has determined that merely because the first user of a trademark has delayed for many years the institution of trademark litigation, he is not barred from opposing a mark when a later user seeks to register it. Specifically, the court concluded that the first user is under no duty to attack a later user's right to use a mark if he does not choose to do so on the penalty of being deprived of the right to oppose an application to register. Nevertheless, when implied or affirmative assurances are present, the applicant should seek to establish equitable defenses.

---

[6] 15 U.S.C. § 1069 (1982).

## § 7.05 PROCEDURE FOLLOWED IN OPPOSITIONS

The procedure followed in an opposition complies with the procedure prescribed for contested proceedings in general, discussed in Chapter 6.

The 30-day period for filing a notice of opposition is crucial. It is possible to request extensions to the statutory 30-day period for filing a notice of opposition. A first extension of time of not more than 30 days will be granted upon request if it is submitted within the 30-day period. Further extensions of time for filing the opposition may be granted when requested prior to the expiration of any extension of time previously granted but require a showing of good cause. Extensions of time aggregating more than 120 days from the date of publication of the mark will not be granted except upon a showing of extraordinary circumstances or the consent of the applicant.

The request for extension of time should be accompanied by a showing of good cause and the time period of extension should be specified. The notice of opposition should be accompanied by the statutory filing fee for an opposition—$200, per class.

After a notice of opposition is filed in duplicate,[7] accompanied by the statutory fee of $200,[8] it is examined by the Clerk of the Trademark Trial and Appeal Board to determine whether the notice of opposition is in order and has been properly filed. The clerk for the Board prepares a notice identifying the title and number of the proceeding and the application involved and designates a time within which an answer must be filed. Copies of this notice are forwarded to the attorneys for the parties. Along with the notice the applicant will receive the duplicate copy of the notice of opposition and exhibits.

The answer may contain any affirmative defense and may include a request for affirmative relief by way of cancellation of a registration pleaded in the notice of opposition. Unless this is done in the answer, no defense attacking the validity of a registration pleaded in the notice of opposition will be entertained.

A great degree of caution is recommended with respect to seeking the cancellation of a registration pleaded in the notice of opposition. In the case of an opposition proceeding in which the issue is like-

---

[7] Exhibits, such as copies of trademark registrations, if filed, should be in duplicate.

[8] Unless the fee has been previously paid.

lihood of confusion and it is clear that the opposers use antedates that of the applicant, the applicant's seeking to cancel an opposer's registration pleaded in his notice of opposition may create an inference of the existence of a likelihood of confusion arising from the simultaneous use by the applicant and the opposer of their marks; even worse, it may be construed as a tacit admission of the presence of the likelihood of confusion. The author, therefore, recommends that in these circumstances a request for affirmative relief by way of cancellation of opposer's registration be brought only when this relief may be bottomed upon a basis other than the likelihood of confusion. A classic example in which affirmative relief by way of cancellation would be advisable is a situation in which the opposer has abandoned the mark forming his registration or one in which the opposer's registration was obtained by fraud. The author would be inclined to handle with a great degree of care and to carefully consider the advisability of requesting affirmative relief in a situation in which the basis to be advanced is that the mark of the opposer had become generic. Unless it was clear that this attack would not reflect adversely upon the applicant's mark, because of the differences between the mark of the opposer and the mark of the applicant, it would not be advisable to launch this type of attack.

A notice of opposition may be withdrawn without prejudice before the answer is filed. After the answer is filed, the notice of opposition may not be withdrawn without prejudice except with the consent of the applicant. A determination in an opposition proceeding is res judicata in respect to a subsequent cancellation proceeding on all issues that could have been raised in the opposition proceeding.

With respect to the interesting question of whether the institution of an opposition proceeding may be construed as a charge of infringement sufficient to create a justifiable controversy under the Declaratory Judgment Act,[9] at least one court of appeals has held that a notice of opposition should not be so construed and that a notice of opposition has as its only purpose the prevention of the registration of a mark.

## § 7.06 BACKGROUND OF CANCELLATION PROCEEDINGS

The cancellation of registrations on the Principal Register, or under the Act of 1881 or the Act of 1905, is governed by Section 14 of the Lanham Act,[10] which reads as follows:

---

[9] 28 U.S.C. §§ 2201, 2202 (1982).

[10] 15 U.S.C. § 1064 (1982).

A petition to cancel a registration of a mark, stating the grounds relied upon, may, upon payment of the prescribed fee, be filed by any person who believes that he is or will be damaged by the registration of a mark on the principal register established by this Act, or under the Act of March 3, 1881, or the Act of February 20, 1905 —

(a) within five years from the date of the registration of the mark under this Act; or

(b) within five years from the date of publication under section 12(c) hereof of a mark registered under the Act of March 3, 1881, or the Act of February 20, 1905; or

(c) at any time if the registered mark becomes the common descriptive name of an article or substance, or has been abandoned, or its registration was obtained fraudulently or contrary to the provisions of section 4 or of subsection( a), (b), or (c) of section 2 of this Act or a registration hereunder, or contrary to similar prohibitory provisions of said prior Acts for a registration thereunder, or if the registered mark is being used by, or with the permission of, the registrant so as to misrepresent the source of the goods or services in connection with which the mark is used; or

(d) at any time if the mark is registered under the Act of March 3, 1881, or the Act of February 20, 1905, and has not been published under the provisions of subsection (c) of Section 12 of this Act; or

(e) at any time in the case of a certification mark on the ground that the registrant (1) does not control, or is not able legitimately to exercise control over, the use of such mark, or (2) engages in the production or marketing of any goods or services to which the certification mark is applied, or (3) permits the use of the certification mark for other purposes than to certify or (4) discriminately refuses to certify the goods or services of any person who maintains the standards or conditions which such mark certifies.

*Provided,* That the Federal Trade Commission may apply to cancel on the grounds specified in subsections (c) and (e) of this section any mark registered on the principal register established by this Act, and the prescribed fee shall not be required.

The cancellation of registrations from the Supplemental Register is governed by Section 24 of the Lanham Act[11] and may be effected at any time by any person who believes that he is or will be damaged by the registration.

The forms taken by proceedings in respect to the cancellation of registrations under Section 14 and under Section 24 are identical, and furthermore, cancellation proceedings are similar in most respects to oppositions. Thus the same issues and the same modes of proof will be encountered in both types of proceedings.

As already noted, cancellation proceedings in the Patent Office are not the only way to effect the cancellation of trademark registrations. Section 37 of the Lanham Act[12] confers complete power upon the federal courts in any action involving a registered trademark to order the cancellation of registrations, in whole or in part, to restore canceled registrations, and otherwise to rectify the Patent Office registers. The Commissioner of Patents is expressly controlled by any certified decree and order of a court in this regard. In fact, when there are co-pending infringement and Patent Office cancellation actions involving the same registration, the Patent Office will suspend the cancellation proceeding pending the outcome of the infringement litigation.[13]

Because of the foregoing, in a situation in which an infringement action is to be instituted against the owner of a trademark registration, it is inadvisable to institute, simultaneously or subsequently, a cancellation proceeding in the Patent Office. Except in rare circumstances, little, if anything, can be accomplished by a proceeding of this nature, as the Patent Office will suspend the contested proceedings before it, pending the outcome of the litigation in which the issues involved in the Patent Office proceeding can also be determined. Accordingly, as a general rule, in these situations complete relief should be sought in the courts in the infringement suit.

Substantially the same body of substantive law, namely, the legal tests and logical inquiries to be used in resolving likelihood of confusion, is applicable to cancellation proceedings as is applicable to opposition proceedings. Thus both the Court of Appeals for the Federal Circuit and the Patent Office rely upon the same decisions as precedents in both types of cases. The reader, however, should

[11] *Id.* § 1092 (1982).

[12] *Id.* § 1119 (1982).

[13] Similarly, the Patent Office will suspend co-pending opposition proceedings.

not be misled into thinking that the burden upon a petitioner for cancellation is identical to the burden upon an opposer. Though there is no clear statement in the decisions defining in practical terms the quantum of increased burden upon a petitioner for cancellation, the decisions of the Court of Appeals for the Federal Circuit clearly evince that a cancellation petitioner may, in fact, have a heavier burden to meet although there is no blanket requirement.

A comparison of Sections 13 and 14 will emphasize that the petitioner for cancellation, like an opposer, must establish "damage." An interesting exception in this regard, sometimes upheld by the Patent Office, arises in cases in which it is demonstrated that trademark registrations were obtained as a result of false and misleading statements under oath to the Patent Office. Under such circumstances the registrations are deemed void *ab initio.* Void registrations will be canceled "without regard to the rights of the parties to the cancellation proceedings."

The formal procedure in a cancellation proceeding is substantially identical to that followed in an opposition proceeding except that the petition to cancel must present the name of the respondent party to whom the notice shall be sent. A single petition may apply for the cancellation of more than one registration owned by a single party, if appropriate, but under these circumstances, the statutory cancellation fee of $200, per class must be paid in respect to each registration.

# 8

# Trademark Interferences and Concurrent Registration Proceedings

---

## § 8.01 BACKGROUND ON INTERFERENCES

An interference proceeding determines who is the first user and therefore the rightful owner of a trademark. Although in former years these proceedings were relatively common, recent changes in the Trademark Rules have made them very rare. Interference proceedings are not possible in connection with Supplemental Register registrations and applications or with registrations that have become incontestable.

An interference will not be declared between two applications or between an application and a registration except upon petition to the Commissioner. The Commissioner will, according to the current practice, declare interferences only upon a showing of extraordinary circumstances that would result in a party being unduly prejudiced without an interference. The availability of an opposition or cancellation proceeding to a party will in ordinary circumstances be deemed to remove any undue prejudice.

A condition precedent to the declaration of an interference is a finding that the marks forming the subject matter of the controversy have been established as registrable by each party, with the exception of the interfering mark.

The interference will be declared and instituted by the mailing of a notice of interference to each of the parties.

A motion period of up to 40 days after the notice of interference is mailed permits each of the parties to move to dissolve the interference on the grounds that no interference in fact exists, or that there has been such an irregularity in declaring the interference as will preclude a proper determination of the interference, or that an applicant's mark is not registrable. Either party may bring a motion to add to the interference any other conflicting application that he may own.

The motions are decided by the Examiner of Trademarks, and the interference proceedings are stayed until his decision. Provision is made for oral hearings upon the request of the parties to the Examiner of Trademarks.

An appeal may be taken from a decision granting a motion to dissolve to the Trademark Trial and Appeal Board. No appeal may be had from a decision denying a motion to dissolve, but the question may be reviewed by the Trademark Trial and Appeal Board in its final decision in the interference.

Under the present practice the issue in an interference between applications is the respective right of each of the parties to registration. The issue in an interference between an application and a registration is the same, but if the final decision is adverse to the registrant, a registration to the applicant will not be authorized so long as the interfering registration remains on the Register.

The junior party—namely, the party whose application or registration involved in the interference has the latest filing date—has the burden of proof.

Procedures are available for a party requesting affirmative relief by way of cancellation of a registration, in which case conformity must be had with Section 14 of the Lanham Act. In addition, parties may be added to the interference.

## § 8.02 CONCURRENT REGISTRATION PROCEEDINGS

The three forms of contested proceedings discussed before antedate the Lanham Act. Thus on the date on which the Lanham Act became effective, there was a large body of law with respect to opposition and cancellation proceedings and trademark interferences. The Lanham Act, however, added a new form of contested trademark proceeding that was not possible under any of the preceding trademark statutes. In fact, one of the discrepancies between the federal trademark statutes that preceded the Lanham Act and the common law was that the common law provided for the concurrent ownership of a trademark by a number of parties in situations in which there had been a good faith simultaneous usage in different parts of the country,[1] although there was no parallel provision for a concurrent registration in the federal trademark statutes preceding the Lanham Act. The Lanham Act eliminated this divergency by providing in Section 1 for applications claiming concurrent use, that is, exceptions to a claim of exclusive use:

> That in the case of every application claiming concurrent use the applicant shall state exceptions to his claim of exclusive use, in which he shall specify, to the extent of his knowledge, any concurrent use by others, the goods in connection with which and the areas in which each concurrent use exists, the periods of each use, and the goods and area for which the applicant desires registration.[2]

In Section 2(d) of the Lanham Act the Commissioner of Patents was authorized to register concurrent registrations upon a determination that confusion is not likely to result from the continued use of these concurrently used marks (under conditions and limitations that the Commissioner may prescribe):

> That when the Commissioner determines that confusion, mistake, or deception is not likely to result from the continued use by more than one person of the same or similar marks under conditions and limitations as to the mode or place of use of the marks or the goods in connection with which such marks are used, concurrent registrations may be issued to such persons when they have become entitled to use such marks as a result of their concurrent lawful use in commerce prior to (i) the earliest of the filing dates of the applications pending or of any registration issued under this Act; or (ii) July 5, 1947, in the case of registrations previously issued under the Act of March 3, 1881, or February 20, 1905, and continuing in full force and effect on that date; or (iii) July 5, 1947, in case of applications filed under the Act of February 20, 1905, and registered after July 5, 1947. Concurrent registrations may also be issued by the Commissioner when a court of competent jurisdiction has finally determined that more than one person is

---

[1] Thus in The United Drug Company v. Theodore Rectanus Company, 248 U.S. 90 (1918), the simultaneous good faith usage of "Rex" in Massachusetts and Kentucky by different parties for between 25 and 30 years gave rise to an estoppel against the first user.

[2] 15 U.S.C. § 1051 (1982).

> entitled to use the same or similar marks in commerce. In issuing concurrent registrations, the Commissioner shall prescribe conditions and limitations as to the mode or place of use of the mark or the goods in connection with which such mark is registered to the respective persons. . . .[3]

By this statutory fiat a new form of contested proceeding was created for the Patent Office, namely, concurrent registration proceedings. A wide variety of conditions and limitations may attach to the grant of a concurrent use registration. The geographical areas within which the mark may be used may be limited; the use may be limited to specific goods, or a wide variety of conditions regarding mode of use may be required.

As a practical matter, the number of concurrent registration proceedings that have resulted in concurrent registrations is relatively small. It has been repeatedly held that the issuance of concurrent registrations is an extraordinary remedy for extraordinary circumstances and that registrations of this kind should be issued only when the proofs clearly show the existence of substantial rights as a result of widespread and continued use. The Commissioner has further interpreted the statute as placing upon the Patent Office the duty to protect the public from confusion, which duty transcends an agreement between the parties to a concurrent registration proceeding consenting to concurrent registrations. Indeed, only in situations in which a substantial hardship would result from the refusal to register will the Patent Offie issue concurrent registrations.

---

[3] *Id.* § 1052(d) (1982).

# 9
# Trademark Litigation

## § 9.01 GENERAL BACKGROUND, FORUM, JURY AND NONJURY TRIALS, GOALS

The trial of trademark cases is among the most difficult branches of litigation, and it is possible to present here only the most common problems connected with trademark litigation and offer advice on how to resolve them.

As with patent litigation, a realistic appraisal of trademark litigation would not be complete without a comment about the differences in hospitality for this type of litigation exhibited by the various circuits. Since the granting of certiorari by the Supreme Court is extraordinary in trademark litigation—more so even than in patent litigation or copyright litigation, when it is rare enough—the various circuit courts of appeal act for all practical purposes as the courts of last resort in the federal system.

The choice of a forum in trademark litigation is as important, therefore, as in any other litigation; and when an infringer is capable of being sued in a number of forums, the selection of the most hospitable one is not an academic matter. A similar value judgment should be made regarding whether suit is to be brought in the state courts or in the federal courts in situations in which a marked difference in hospitality toward trademark litigation is present and in which the selection of one of a number of forums is possible.

Trademark litigation is ill-suited to trial by jury, particularly since the determination of damages is made by the jury, resulting in a trial that is both cumbersome and drawn out. The determination of damages is best left to an accounting before a master. A settlement is preferable, however, since in most cases the total cost of the accounting, considering all of its aspects, will prove to be more than the award.[1]

[1] In one suit in the Third Circuit, the accounting, including appeals to the courts, ran for almost 15 years at a total cost to the litigants of probably well over a half million dollars. The amount of the award, including interest, was under $150,000.

As with patent litigation, trademark litigation should be viewed primarily in terms of injunctive relief rather than as a potential source of money. True, under the differential costs procedure by which trademark accountings are conducted, it is possible, when the infringer fails to apportion or is unable to apportion his profit, for his entire profit to be given to the trademark owner, resulting in what Mr. Justice Frankfurter termed a "windfall." Yet in the type of trademark litigation that is most frequently encountered, the prime relief that is obtained is the enjoining of the defendant from infringing the plaintiff's trademark. Although Section 35 of the Lanham Act[2] provides for the recovery of both profits and damages and the trebling of damages in certain cases, as a general rule the award of treble damages is unusual. A practical adjunct to the award on an injunction is contained in Section 36 of the Lanham Act,[3] which provides for the destruction of all infringing labels, signs, prints, packages, wrappers, receptacles, and advertisements in the possession of the defendant and all plates, molds, and matrices. Commencing in 1975, attorneys' fees may be awarded in trademark litigations in an "exceptional case" (the same criterion provided in the patent statute relating to the award of attorney's fees).

## § 9.02 COMPLICATING FACTORS IN TRADEMARK LITIGATION

In the rare situation in which the trademark owner has an incontestable trademark registration and (1) there is no issue about his use or ownership or abandonment of the mark, and (2) the defendant is using the identical mark on somewhat different goods or a similar mark on the same goods or on closely related goods, and (3) with no other issues being present, the trial of a trademark lawsuit becomes a relatively simple matter. This is, however, normally not the case. There are often present in the lawsuit one or more of the following complicating factors:

1. The mark or goods, or both, of the defendent are far enough away from the plaintiff's trademark rights to create a question about the likelihood of confusion.

When the defendent is using the plaintiff's mark on different goods, the plaintiff should consider advancing a claim for relief founded upon the theory of dilution. The chances of success for a cause of action based on dilution will vary directly with the strength

[2] 15 U.S.C. §1117 (1982).
[3] *Id.* §1118 (1982).

of the plaintiff's mark, including both its technical nature and the degree of goodwill behind it, and the likelihood of expansion in terms of natural growth by the plaintiff toward the merchandising of the goods of the defendant. The dilution theory stems from cases in which an infringer copied a well-known mark for goods that were appreciably different from those of the plaintiff and was then enjoined. A classical application of the dilution theory constituted the enjoining of "Tiffany" as a mark for the production and distribution of motion pictures on the suit of the world-renowned jewelry corporation. A number of states have enacted antidilution statutes, having as a purpose the aiding of trademark owners in this type of situation. The antidilution statutes, however, have proved to be of relatively little value to plaintiffs, since the courts have generally applied the common law doctrines to achieve their decisions and tied in the statute as an afterthought. Accordingly, in dilution cases the plaintiff should seek to demonstrate the strength of his mark as being *sui generis* and should attempt, when the supporting facts are present, to color his case by establishing bad faith on the part of the alleged infringer.[4]

2. In most trademark situations there is at least the possibility of acts of unfair competition. Whenever possible, a cause of action for unfair competition should be joined with a cause of action for trademark infringment. When diversity is absent, reliance should be had on Title 28 of the United States Code, Section 1338(b).

3. Equitable defenses, such as laches, estoppel, and acquiescence, are frequently present in trademark litigation situations. It is to be noted, under the overwhelming weight of authority, that mere laches, without more, although barring an accounting, will not prevent the plaintiff from securing an injunction. An injunction will be barred when an estoppel situation is present—namely, acts of the trademark owner that would lead a reasonable man to believe that he was safe in continuing a given course of conduct. In one decision the Third Circuit held that plaintiff was entitled to injunctive relief despite a 40-year delay in bringing suit.

4. Since trademark litigation is normally based in equity, the defense of unclean hands is possible. Other available defenses are

---

[4] The presence of an intent to deceive on the part of the infringer is most easily demonstrated when the plaintiff's mark is a technical one. Since there is an infinite variety of these marks, it is reasonable to conclude that an infringement was deliberate. When the plaintiff's mark is suggestive, its innocent adoption by the defendant is a distinct possibility.

abandonment, as through nonuse with intent to abandon; affirmative acts of abandonment; extinguishment by virtue of faulty transfer or license; and attacks on the nature of the trademark or its scope.

Perhaps the most common instance of misuse giving rise to unclean hands is the designation of a trademark as registered in the Patent Office before it was actually registered. If this was done with intent to deceive, it may constitute this kind of unclean hands so as to deny the trademark owner access to a court of equity on the issue of trademark infringment but not necessarily on unfair competition.

5. In appropriate situations there may be a defense that the mark in issue, when applied to the goods in issue, is generic and hence incapable of supporting a claim for relief.

6. Loss of distinctiveness upon the part of plaintiff's mark may be demonstrated by showing a widespread use of the mark by third parties. A defendant's counsel may make a good start in this direction by making a comprehensive search for the mark in the Patent Office and investigating the registrations of others. Although loss of distinctiveness is not tantamount to abandonment and is not a complete defense, it serves to markedly limit the scope of the plaintiff's mark.

7. Lack of both competition and the possibility of competition, as, for example, the demonstration that the defendant's sales were made through different channels of trade to a different class of purchasers, may be a good defense, absent any issue of dilution.

An almost infinite variety of other defenses and issues may be present. These defenses, which will not be discussed here, are set forth at length in the several reference works on trademark law that have been published.[5]

## § 9.03 MODES OF PROOF IN TRADEMARK LITIGATION

In the vast majority of cases the primary issues of proof descend to the likelihood of confusion or the existence of confusion. These are among the most difficult concepts to prove. As was stated before in connection with contested trademark proceedings before the Patent Office, statements disguised as the opinion of expert witnesses on the likelihood of confusion are virtually of no value and ordinarily will not be received. The Supreme Court has gone so far as to characterize this type of testmony as "being rather the expression of the opinion of the witnesses than substantive proof of existing

[5] See p. 35 for a listing of these volumes.

facts," and not as "testimony in the proper sense of the word." Attempts to introduce this type of evidence, no matter how well disguised, only antagonize an experienced trial judge and accomplish nothing.

The existence of confusion may be demonstrated by actual examples of it. Thus the goods of the infringer may have been returned to the trademark owner for repair. Distributors may have confused the trademark owner with the infringer in their advertising copy. Mail may have been misdirected, such as requests for credits and correspondence about return. Customers may have written that they were deceived into purchasing another's goods under the impression that they were purchasing the trademark owner's goods. Tradesmen may in desperation resort to signs indicating that they are carrying the trademark owner's goods, in order to distinguish them from a similarly branded competitor's goods.

When the marks involved are associated with their user's trade names, mail may be misdelivered or telephone calls addressed to the wrong party.

All the foregoing and an infinite number of other examples evidence confusion. All of the foregoing, when present in a case, should be utilized.

No matter how many examples of confusion, however, are brought in by the trademark owner, it is always possible for the defendant to comment sneeringly that these instances of confusion constitute such an insignificant trifle when compared to the total number of transactions involving the marks of the parties as to be of no probative value. In respect to the proof of confusion, it should be borne in mind that letters, signed statements, and affidavits by persons *not available as witnesses* going to this issue are normally inadmissible. The statement of employees concerning hearsay instances of confusion are likewise of no value. In a similar "no value" category are probe letters and the like whose purpose is to "plant a bug in the ear" on this question.

Although the testimony of professional shoppers will be considered, the credibility of this testimony, particularly when the technique used borders on entrapment or provocation, may be readily attacked, more so if the shopper's compensation is contingent upon satisfactory results. Yet, in all fairness, many a trademark suit has been won upon the testimony of paid shoppers and this source of evidence, when appropriate and fair, should not be overlooked.

Under the present mode of trying trademark cases, the author cannot unduly stress the need for producing all relevant physical evidence for the court's examination, preferably simulating in the presentation the manner in which the goods in dispute are sold. The object of trial counsel should be to enable the court, after an examination of the plaintiff's and defendant's objects in their sales environment, to determine from the background of the court's own experience and from the testimony of the tradesmen and consumers whether or not there is a likelihood of confusion. This mode of presentation is infinitely preferable to a presentation before the court by each side of dozens of witnesses, each stating (often in parrot-like fashion) their knowledge on the question of likelihood of confusion.

Counsel for the trademark owner should always have his weather eye cocked for any evidence indicating deliberate infringement. The possibility of securing even a minor amount of evidence justifies protracted discovery before trial. The establishment of deliberate infringement will greatly diminish the infringer's defenses and increase markedly the possibility of the award of an accounting, treble damages, and, since January 1975, attorneys' fees. The deliberate infringement required is on the part of the infringer and not on the part of independent contractors who serve as distributors for the alleged infringer's goods. Normally, absent an agency relationship, the action of independent contractors may not be imputed to the infringer.

In this connection note that distributors and retailers, as well as manufacturers, are trademark infringers. Whether it is advisable from a business point of view for a manufacturer to sue another manufacturer's retailers is debatable. A retailer will not soon forget that he was drawn into a lawsuit by a manufacturer, and the manufacturer's customers may bear this in mind, perhaps indefinitely. Even the presence of hold harmless agreements from the retailer's supplier may not salve his feelings in this regard. For this reason, unless potent considerations concerning either forum or effect upon the trade are present, litigation should never be instituted against a retailer but only against prime suppliers.

The proof of the absence of confusion is substanially impossible other than by objective techniques such as polling. Negative evidence proves nothing, regardless of its quantity. Thus even one hundred witnesses parading before the court, each of whom testifies that he is not and was not confused, proves absolutely nothing when a trademarked item has been sold to millions of persons.

## § 9.04 POLL TECHNIQUES

Poll techniques have already been mentioned. These techniques, though expensive, offer the only solution to the present morass into which trademark litigation has descended. This discussion should not and cannot be a sounding board for the adoption of objective approaches to the trial of trademark cases. Yet if industry is willing to rely upon poll-taking techniques as superior to the informed "guesstimates" of executives who work in a given field their entire business lives, why should not these same techniques be used in court cases in which the first introduction of the judge to the matter before him comes with the commencement of the trial? Perhaps, as a matter of fairness, the poll-taking should not be conducted by either of the parties, but it should be conducted under the authority of the judge. This is not to suggest poll-taking as a substitute for judicial determinations, but merely that the courts take advantage of every developing modern and social science technique.

The history of the 1936 and 1948 presidential elections and the disastrous polls that accompanied them may bring a wry smile to the reader. The type of poll to be used in trademark cases, however, tests the state of mind of the person being polled, *a present fact,* and does not seek to determine what his future actions will be on the basis of his present statements.

The subject of polls has proved to be one of infinite fascination to the trademark bar. An enormous body of literature has been established relating to these techniques, their relationship to the rules of evidence particularly the hearsay rule, and their value in both Patent Office contested proceedings and in court cases.

The Federal Rules of Evidence support the admission of polls. Rule 803, Sections 1, 3, and 24 provide approach guidelines bearing on the admissibiilty of poll-type evidence. The notes of the advisory committee for Rule 703 indicate that this rule was intended to provide a more satisfactory basis for ruling upon the admissability of public opinion poll evidence. "Attention is directed to the validity of the techniques employed rather than to relatively fruitless inquiries whether hearsay is involved." The vast body of technique and law concerning poll-taking is beyond the scope of this book. The author, however, would like to present what he regards as the most valid form of poll-taking and the one that is most likely to be received in evidence.

Any poll that is to be used in a contested proceeding before the patent office or in a court trial should avoid being deemed "loaded." The use of suggestive or leading questions in a poll should be scrupulously avoided, and the persons being polled should at all times be unaware of the purpose of the survey. The persons being polled need only be told that the poll is a market research project. Indeed, if possible, it is advisable that even the pollsters conducting the poll in the field remain unaware about the purpose of the survey as well as the name of the ultimate party who is paying for their services.

A well-conducted poll should avoid questions directed to the opinion of the person being polled. The utmost care should be employed in making certain that those being polled represent an accurate cross-section of the consumers who are exposed to the trademarked item. Thus the poll should not be confined to one geographical area or to one class or group of consumers of the trademarked item. The poll should include a sufficient number of inquiries to permit valid statistical treatment of the results. As a rule, at least 500 inquiries should be made in any given instance.

The persons conducting the poll should be present at the trial so as to be available for cross-examination.

One of the most successful forms of poll in terms of acceptability to the courts has been conducted as follows:

I. *Q.* Are you familiar with this product? (The trademarked product of the infringer is demonstrated.)

As this question is asked of a customer who has just purchased the product, the answer is invariably in the affirmative.

II. *Q.* Does the company that made this product make any other product with which you are familiar?

This question determines whether there is a confusion about the source, which, of course, is a basic issue in likelihood of confusion situations.

If the answer to Question II is in the negative or sets out products other than those made by the trademark owner, then the following question may be put to determine whether there is a possibility of confusion from the concurrent sale of both the trademarked item and the allegedly infringing item:

III. *Q.* Does the company which makes this product also make "____________"? (The product covered by the trademark in suit is inserted into the blank.)

The results obtained from the poll may be tabulated in terms of percentages and presented as an objective determination on the issues of actual confusion and likelihood of confusion.

This polling technique has far better than an even chance of being received in evidence, notwithstanding an objection of hearsay, since the state of mind of the persons being polled has been recorded rather than hearsay comments. When received in evidence, a poll is a most persuasive evidentiary factor, since it may readily be argued that a well-conducted poll more accurately reflects the true nature of the state of things than a series of depositions or a subjective determination in the abstract by the court.

A further liberalization regarding the receipt of polls will hopefully flow from the Federal Rules of Evidence.

## § 9.05 PROBLEM SITUATIONS

Through the years a number of types of marks have offered a great deal of difficulty in litigation. For example, there are legions of cases involving the rights to marks consisting of a surname. In these cases, there must be a balancing of equities between the rights of an owner of a well-established mark that happens to be a surname—such as "Ford," "Bacardi," "Jergens," and "Baker"—and the right of every man to use his own name in his own business. One extreme includes the infringer's use of stratagems, such as bringing into the corporation an individual whose only contribution was a surname that resembled the mark the corporation was copying. At the other extreme are cases in which the relief sought comprised exclusive rights on a wide front over a mark consisting of one of the most common of surnames, such as "Johnson."

The development of the law in this area has been logical. Although a wide range of variations and modifications is present, as a rule the courts will attempt to safeguard the rights of the trademark owner. This can be done either by enjoining the infringer absolutely in the case of a flagrant infringement, particularly when the mark is a relatively uncommon surname, or by attempting to provide safeguards, such as requiring the insertion on the label of distinguishing phraseology, for instance, "Not Connected with—."[6] In these cases, the paramount consideration is to safeguard the public against confusion and fraud arising from the poaching upon the first user's goodwill. What has been said about marks in this area applies equally well to trade names and in particular to corporate names. With respect to corporate names, no good reason is seen for having a corporation bear any particular name, and the ancient right to use one's personal name is not present to the same degree, as in the case of an individual or partnership business.

Another area in which profound difficulties have developed lies in the use of color. Because practically the number of colors is decidedly limited, the protection of color within the trademark law has been confined entirely to regarding color as a secondary element. If other features pointing to infringement are present, color simulation will be a cumulative factor.

The same is more or less true in the unfair competition cases involving package dress, package configuration, and label simultion. The duplication of color viewed in combination with other elements is a factor, but not the primary consideration, upon which infringement or noninfringement is found. It is perhaps regrettable that the use of color has not been accorded much status in the trademark law, as many important trademarks depend primarily upon color, such as the familiar red and white label used on the various soups sold by the Campbell Soup Company.

A secondary element serving to distinguish trademarks, as such, is type of script. Visually, a mark printed in block letters may appear to be appreciably different from the same mark in Gothic script. The law, however, has developed along very liberal lines in this area and has taken notice of the auditory aspects of trademarks, as would arise from the advertising of trademarks upon the radio. Thus although the use of characteristic lettering or script may in some cases prove to be a critical distinguishing feature, the modern tendency is to disregard script per se.

A situation in which the courts have frequently been reluctant to recognize trademark rights, and which may result in a considerable and serious economic loss, arises when a name is given to a patented device to distinguish it as a new article from other articles of the

---

[6] A person who has adopted and used his own surname as a trade name or trademark may transfer the same with the goodwill of his business and may be prevented from using his own name in connection with his business.

same character. Under these circumstances, even during the life of the patent, the name is not properly a trademark but is the generic name for the article. Upon the expiration of the patent, the identifying name passes to the public and may be used by anyone. "Shredded Wheat" is a classical example of an important mark that passed into the public domain in this fashion.

Accordingly, the valuable patents rights, articles, machines, or compositions embodying the patent rights owned by the client should not be designated by a particular name. This doctrine can be overcome by utilizing a trademark for both patented and unpatented embodiments, so that the trademark does not particularly identify a patented invention. The skillful use of this technique has enabled the trademark "Kodak" to remain a valid and most valuable trademark, notwithstanding its use (as a true trademark) on numerous patented items.

## § 9.06 ABANDONMENT AS DEFENSE

No discussion of trademark litigation could be complete without mention of the great boon conferred by the yardstick provisions defining abandonment in Section 45 of the Lanham Act, which state:

> A mark shall be deemed to be "abandoned"—
>
> (a) When its use has been discontinued with intent not to resume. Intent not to resume may be inferred from circumstances. Nonuse for two consecutive years shall be prima facie abandonment.
>
> (b) When any course of conduct of the registrant, including acts of omission as well as commission, causes the mark to lose its significance as an indication of origin.[7]

The great combination made by this definition is the provision of a yardstick—namely, nonuse for two years—for prima facie abandonment. Prior to the Lanham Act the defense of abandonment in the nonuse situation was a very difficult one to prove. The concept of abandonment is intimately associated with intent, and, absent evidence bearing on an intent to abandon, it was repeatedly held that mere disuse did not as a matter of law destroy a trademark right. Since the defense of abandonment is an affirmative defense with the burden upon the party asserting it, the difficulties by the Lanham Act are self-evident. Of course, when nonuse is coupled

---

[7] 15 U.S.C. §1127 (1982).

with a prolonged failure to prevent others from using a mark, or other factors are present, equitable principles—such as laches, estoppel, or acquiescence—may become involved.

Paragraph (b) of the definition of abandonment covers situations in which a trademark is permitted to become generic. Many valuable trademarks have been lost to their owners in this fashion, although the decisions sometimes becloud the matter by asserting the loss of rights to be due to laches.

# 10
# Transfer of Trademark Rights

## § 10.01 INTRODUCTION

We have already seen that trademark rights develop from appropriation and use. Use of the trademark is essential, as its mere adoption without use will fail to establish legal rights.

Another quality of trademarks should be borne in mind in order to appreciate the problems connected with transfer. A trademark to a variable degree reflects the reputation of its owner. In the case of personal services the trademark may identify a particular individual, even though it is not his given name or surname. "The Babe," "The Duke," and "The King" are good examples from the world of sports and entertainment. This matter of personal reputation should be especially clear to members of the bar, who, perhaps more than any other class of persons, appreciate the reputation behind a law firm's name or the name of an individual lawyer. In view of this the origin of the common law principle that a deception upon the public may arise when a trademark is transferred from one person to another should be apparent.

Yet there are many legitimate business situations in which the transfer of rights under a trademark is either desirable or essential. For example, the sale of a business that includes among its assets valuable trademark rights. Alternatively, the situation may be modified when what is sold is but a portion of a business. In other common situations there is a parent-subsidiary relationship between separate concerns, both of which wish to operate under certain trademarks; or the owner of valuable trademark rights, such as a soft drink company, may wish to license others to bottle and distribute its product under its trademark. All of these situations involve the transfer or sharing of trademark rights. It is one of the tragedies of the law that if the transfer of trademark rights is bungled, there may be a legal extinguishment or abandonment of the trademark. This flows from the common law principle of deception of the public stated earlier.

## § 10.02 ASSIGNMENTS AND LICENSES

The assignee of a trademark becomes the complete owner of the entire right, title, and interest to the trademark. Anything less than an assignment is a license. Licenses under trademarks may be exclusive, in which case the licensee alone has the right to use the trademark (with the title and a reversion in the trademark's licensor), or the license may be nonexclusive, in which case the licensor has the right to license others than the licensee to use the trademark. Trademark licenses may be limited as to time or as to place or in other regards.

### § 10.02(a) Assignments

Assignments may be made of registered trademarks, marks for which an application to register has been filed, or for nonregistered marks for which no application to register has been filed.[1] Generally, assignments may be classified into two categories: those in which the assignment covers the transfer of the mark with the goodwill of the business in which the mark is used, and those in which the assignment covers the transfer of the mark together with the part of the goodwill of the business connected with the use of and symbolized by the mark. It is expressly stated in Section 10 of the Lanham Act[2] that in the latter situation it is not necessary to include the goodwill of the business connected with the use of and symbolized by any other mark used in the business, or by the name or style under which the business is conducted.

In both classifications the assignment of the mark is coupled with the transfer of goodwill—either the entire goodwill of the business or that part of the goodwill of the business connected with the use of and symbolized by the mark. Indeed, to be strictly accurate, the foregoing should have been stated with the emphasis upon the assignment of the goodwill and with the transfer of the trademark as an incident to the assignment of the goodwill. Technically, this is termed an "assignment appurtenant."

The naked assignment of a trademark, technically referred to as an assignment in gross, is invalid. The legal consequences of an invalid transfer are not firmly established by the cases. Whether the transferor's rights in the trademark are completely destroyed in these

---

[1] See Appendix B for specimen trademark assignments for an application for registration and for a registered mark.

[2] 15 U.S.C. § 1060 (1982).

circumstances or whether he is thereafter denied access to a court of equity by virtue of unclean hands, and is thus unable to sue for trademark infringement, or whether the assignment is merely a nullity with perhaps a form of estoppel arising between the assignor and assignee is not clear. Probably the best rule is to relate the loss of rights to the quantum of intent to deceive the public, in which case extinguishment of the trademark is avoided when the invalid assignment was innocent.

As in other areas involving the transfer of rights, the law looks to substance, rather than to form, in determining the nature of the transfer. Thus the mere fact that an agreement is termed an assignment will not prevent a court from construing the agreement as a license, if, in fact, the agreement proves to be a license. Moreover, the mere recitation of the transfer of goodwill in an agreement does not render valid an assignment that, in fact, is invalid. For example, in situations in which there is no goodwill to transfer, the mere recitation in an assignment agreement of goodwill being transferred does not raise the level of the transaction to a valid trademark assignment.

While the assignee of an invalid assignment receives nothing, he may subsequently acquire rights to the trademark by adoption. His first date of use, however, runs from his date of adoption and not from the first date of use of the assignor.

As with the unsold property of a bankrupt, when a business concern goes out of business and is not sold to anyone, its trademarks, trade name, and goodwill likewise go out of existence. The transfer of trademarks and goodwill after a concern has long been out of business accomplishes nothing. In the trademark practice one occasionally sees the buying up of old trademarks and trade names from the former owner or owners of extinct businesses in order to give rise to a colorable claim of an early date of first use. As indicated before in the case of extinct businesses, this stratagem is futile and, if anything, leaves a bad taste with the trier of facts.

### § 10.02(b) Licenses

The related company provisions of the Lanham Act have done much to clear away the cobwebs regarding both subsidiary-parent situations and the licensing of trademarks. A "related company" is defined in Section 45 of the Lanham Act as follows:

> The term "related company" means any person who legitimately controls or is controlled by the registant or appli-

> cant for registration in respect to the nature and quality of the goods or services in connection with which the mark is used.[3]

The use of a mark by related companies is regulated by Section 5 of the Lanham Act, which provides as follows:

> Where a registered mark or a mark sought to be registered is or may be used legitimately by related companies, such use shall inure to the benefit of the registrant or applicant for registration, and such use shall not affect the validity of such mark or of its registration, provided such mark is not used in such manner as to deceive the public.[4]

Accordingly, under these statutory provisions, unless the use is in such a manner as to deceive the public, there is normally no problem in the use of trademarks by related companies, such as in the normal parent and subsidiary relations.

As with assignments, a naked license under a trademark is invalid. Trademarks may not be licensed in gross, but they may be licensed if not separated from the goodwill. In the most common license situation in which the owner of a trademark licenses another to apply the trademark to articles that the licensee produces, rigorous controls relating to the production of the article must be set forth to avoid the fatal separation. Thus the licensed articles should be manufactured either under the supervision of the licensor or under his direction.

A trademark license is a difficult contract to prepare. No easy rule can be established concerning the adequacy of the control exercised by the licensor; this varies from situation to situation depending upon the nature of the goods being licensed, trade practices, and so forth. At all times it must be remembered that the trademark license is not a means for circumventing the antitrust laws so that, although quality standards must be fixed, trademark licenses may not be utilized for price-fixing conspiracies or to require tie-ins.

In addition, it is difficult, particularly in the case of exclusive licenses, to avoid having the trademark and goodwill become associated with the licensee rather than with the licensor. If the license situation is the type in which the licensor can recapture his goodwill and trademark from the licensee, there is no problem; but if the

[3] *Id.* § 1127 (1982).
[4] *Id.* § 1055 (1982).

nature of things is that the trademark and goodwill become intimately associated with the licensee, the licensor may find that his rights to the mark and goodwill have been lost.

Moreover, trademark licensing situations require policing by the licensor. If the licensee fails to conform to the standards established by the licensor and the licensor does not police him and takes no action to compel him to conform, the licensor's rights to the trademark and goodwill may be extinguished.

Because of recent developments in the law relating to products liability, licensors should seriously consider requiring the licensee to name the licensor as a coinsured in its products liability insurance policy covering the products being sold under the trademarks. The reason for this caution is that there are recent decisions holding that because a licensor's trademark is used on the goods, the public identifies these goods with the licensor and believes that he stands behind the goods. A number of decisions have held the licensor liable under the law of agency, namely that the licensee is the apparent agent of the licensor.

## § 10.03 RECORDATION OF ASSIGNMENTS

The recordation of assignments in the Patent Office is governed by the second portion of Section 10 of the Lanham Act, which reads as follows:

> A registered mark or a mark for which application to register has been filed shall be assignable with the goodwill of the business in which the mark is used, or with that part of the goodwill of the business connected with the use of and symbolized by the mark, and in any such assignment it shall not be necessary to include the goodwill of the business connected with the use of and symbolized by any other mark used in the business or by the name or style under which the business is conducted. Assignments shall be by instruments in writing duly executed. Acknowledgment shall be prima facie evidence of the execution of an assignment and when recorded in the Patent and Trademark Office the record shall be prima facie evidence of execution. An assignment shall be void as against any subsequent purchaser for a vaulable consideration without notice, unless it is recorded in the Patent and Trademark Office within 3 months after the date thereof or prior to such subsequent purchase. A separate record of assignments submitted for

> recording hereunder shall be maintained in the Patent and Trademark Office.
>
> An assignee not domiciled in the United States shall be subject to and comply with the provisions of section 1(d) hereof.[5]

There is no parallel statutory provision for the recordation of trademark licenses.

In view of Section 10, counsel should always have a search of the assignment records made prior to the purchase of a registered trademark. If he represents the assignee, in doubtful cases he should retain the consideration for the assignment in escrow for three months after the assignment is recorded so as to avoid the possibility of loss of rights to an earlier assignee.

Of course, it goes without saying that all trademark assignments should be recorded. The statutory fee for recording the assignment of a trademark registration is $100 and $20 for each additional trademark registration or application.

Furthermore, under Section 10, a registered trademark or a mark for which application to register has been filed may be assigned only by instruments in writing duly executed. If the assignment of a trademark that has been registered or is the subject of a trademark application is parol, only common law rights to the mark are transferred. Since these assignments cannot be recorded, they run the risk of being cut off by subsequent purchasers, for a valuable consideration without notice, who record their assignments. Accordingly, any parol assignment involving goodwill and a trademark, either a registered trademark or the subject of a pending trademark application, should be reduced to writing and recorded.

---

[5] *Id.* § 1060 (1982).

# 11 Copyrights

## § 11.01 INTRODUCTION

On January 1, 1978, the general revision of Title 17 U.S.C., pertaining to copyright, and replacing the Act of 1909 as the basic copyright statute, went into effect.

The revision works substantial changes, preempting common law protection for unpublished works, altering the duration of the term of protection afforded by copyright, limiting the scope of the so-called manufacturing clause, and substantially moderating the effects of publication without notice of copyright.

The revision affects works already fixed in tangible form on January 1, 1978, insofar as duration and termination of copyright are at issue, although these works are treated differently from those fixed in tangible form after the effective date of the revision.

With respect to the exclusive rights and limitations on those rights, the revision applies to all works covered by copyright. There is no indication that works existing on January 1, 1978, are to be exempted from the licensing provisions, from library photocopying provisions, or from any similar limitation on the rights of the copyright proprietor.

Other aspects of the revision do not affect works that predate January 1, 1978. Any work in the public domain on that date remains in the public domain. Thus the more generous provisions of the revision with respect to publication without notice are of no avail to the copyright claimant who, on or before December 31, 1977, distributed without restriction copies of his work bearing no notice of copyright.

Since the revision is the principal expression of copyright law with which the practitioner must hereafter be concerned, all references are to the revision except when otherwise indicated. The Act of 1909 will generally be cited only for contrast with the revision.

## § 11.02 COPYRIGHTABLE SUBJECT MATTER

The various kinds of works that may be copyrighted have already been listed.[1] Some consideration should be given to what constitutes noncopyrightable subject matter. The copyright act now provides in Section 102(b) what was implicit under the previous law: Copyright protection does not extend to naked ideas, such as ideas for ways of doing business, accounting, keeping records, and advertising. In each instance the client must be advised that a writing embodying the ideas may be protected by copyright, but that protection extends only to the writing and not to the ideas or thoughts set forth in the writing. Thus absent express restrictive covenants not to do so, any member of the public is free to take advantage of the intellectual content of any writing if copying of the writing is avoided.

For the best approach available under the law for the protection of unpatentable ideas, resort should be had, when possible, to the law of trade secrets.[2]

The Register of Copyrights has also refused to grant copyright registrations for mere forms that are devoid of an appreciable text, such as time cards, report forms, graph paper, account books, diaries, scoreboards, address books, order forms, and vouchers.

The Copyright Office Letter No. 32 relating to this problem summarizes the law as follows:

> In order to be copyrightable, a work must contain at least a certain minimum amount of authorship in the form of original literary, artistic, or musical expression. Copyright cannot be secured for names, titles, and phrases or clauses such as column headings, simple check lists, and the like. The format, arrangement, or typography of a blank form or similar work is not a copyrightable element. Furthermore, it is not possible to copyright works consisting entirely of information that is common property containing no original authorship; works of this type could include, for example: standard calendars, height and weight charts, tape measures and rulers, schedules of sporting events, and lists or tables taken from public documents or other common sources.

---

[1] See p. 8, which set forth the categories of works of authorship of Section 102 of the Copyright Act.

[2] *See* A. Seidel, What the General Practitioner Should Know About Trade Secrets and Employment Agreements (2d ed. 1984).

> It is only the particular manner in which an author expresses himself in his writings that can be protected by copyright. The ideas, plans, methods, or systems that he describes, or that are embodied in his works, are not copyrightable. Thus there would be no way to secure copyright protection for the idea or principle behind a blank form or similar work, or for any of the methods or systems involved in it.
>
> An original literary or pictorial work may be subject to copyright registration if published in conjunction with a blank form or other uncopyrightable material, provided the requirements of the copyright law have been met. However, copyright in such a case would extend protection only to the original literary or pictorial expression used by the author, as distinguished from the blank form or other uncopyrightable aspects of the work.

Accordingly, if the client wishes to copyright forms of one kind or another, the best approach is to place these forms in a book, stating in a preface or introduction an explanation of how to use them. The entire book can then be copyrighted and receive the scope of protection enumerated.

The foregoing is not to be construed as meaning that under all circumstances ideas and titles may not be protected.

Under appropriate circumstances ideas or titles, such as the titles of books or plays, may be protected under the law of unfair competition. This protection, however, does not stem from the copyright act. It should be noted that, although the Copyright Office will not accept a title, such as the title of a radio or television program, the title may be registered as a service mark if the radio or television program has been broadcast and the title functions as a service mark.

As with names and titles, the Copyright Office has refused to register "claims to exclusive rights in the names of products or organizations, pen names, stage names, titles, catch words, slogans, advertising phrases, mottos, and the like. This is true even if the name, title, phrase, or expression is novel, distinctive, or lends itself to a play on words."[3]

---

[3] Copyright Office Letter No. 19.

## § 11.03 UNPUBLISHED WORKS

Formerly for works that were unpublished, resort was had to the common law of the states for protection. This is clearly altered in the Copyright Act, Section 301(a):

> On and after January 1, 1978, all legal or equitable rights that are equivalent to any of the exclusive rights within the general scope of copyright as specified by Section 106 in works of authorship that are fixed in a tangible medium of expression and come within the subject matter of copyright as specified by Section 102 and 103, whether created before or after that date and whether published or unpublished, are governed exclusively by this title. Thereafter, no person is entitled to any such right or equivalent right in any such work under the common law or statutes of any State.

Unpublished works are protected without regard to the nationality or domicile of the author. Published works, however, are subject to protection only if one of the criteria set forth in Section 104(b) is met:

> (1) [O]n the date of first publication, one or more of the authors is a national or domiciliary of the United States, or is a national, domiciliary, or sovereign authority of a foreign nation that is a party to a copyright treaty to which the United States is also a party, or is a stateless person, wherever that person may be domiciled; or
>
> (2) [T]he work is first published in the United States or in a foreign nation that, on the date of first publication, is a party to the Universal Copyright Convention; or
>
> (3) [T]he work is first published by the United Nations or any of its specialized agencies, or by the Organization of American States; or
>
> (4) [T]he work comes within the scope of a Presidential proclamation. Whenever the President finds that a particular foreign nation extends, to works by authors who are nationals or domiciliaries of the United States, copyright protection on substantially the same basis as that on which the foreign nation extends protection to works of its own nationals and domiciliaries and works first published in that nation, the President may by proclamation extend protection under this title to works of which one or more of the

> authors is, on the date of first publication, a national, domiciliary, or sovereign authority of that nation, or which was first published in that nation. The President may revise, suspend, or revoke any such proclamation or impose any conditions or limitations on protection under a proclamation.

The time duration of common law copyright was perpetual. Now copyright protection accrues when the work is first fixed in tangible form, irrespective of when published, and endures for the life of the author plus fifty years, irrespective of when publication occurs and even if there is no publication.[4]

## § 11.04 PUBLICATION

Publication no longer begins the running of the Copyright Act, but its nature should be understood, since it affects the time when notice must be placed upon the work and the duration of copyright in works created before January 1, 1978, and not published or in the public domain on that date.

Publication is defined in Section 101 as:

> "... the distribution of copies ... of a work to the public by sale or other transfer of ownership, or by rental, lease or lending. The offering to distribute copies ... to a group of persons for purposes of further distribution, public performance, or public display, constitutes publication. A public performance or display of a work does not of itself constitute publication."

Since publication without the statutory copyright notice may constitute dedication to the public if no recourse is or can be had to the so-called savings provision, Section 405, complete loss of rights may follow an ill-advised publication without notice.[5]

## § 11.05 METHOD OF SECURING COPYRIGHT REGISTRATION

After the work is fixed in tangible form, the copyright may be registered by means of an application for registration. Application is made on forms furnished by the Copyright Office and these may be obtained by writing to the Register of Copyrights, Library of

---

[4] See pp. 105–108 for qualifications respecting duration of copyright in works in existence on January 1, 1978, the effective date of the Copyright Act.

[5] See pp. 101–104.

Congress, Washington, D.C. 20559. Copies of the most widely used forms are reproduced in Appendix E. Instructions for the execution of each of the forms are carried on the forms themselves, as well as the procedures for securing copyright registration. The statutory fee for registering a copyright is $10. It is advisable that frequent users maintain a charge account with the Register of Copyrights.

Statutory copyright in a sound recording is a new concept in United States copyright law and relates only to sound recordings fixed on or after February 15, 1972.

The sound recording must carry the following notice:

Ⓟ year name of copyright proprietor.

Note that the symbol is Ⓟ and not ©. In place of the name of the proprietor, the notice can include an abbreviation by which the name of the copyright owner is recognized or a generally known alternative designation of the owner. When the producer of the sound recording is named on the labels or containers of the copies of the sound recording, and if no other name appears in conjunction with the notice, the producer's name will be considered by the Copyright Office as a part of the notice.

The statute provides for the prompt deposit of copies in the Copyright Office after publication. A delay even of years in depositing the copies is not fatal, however, to one's cause of action for infringement, although no action can be maintained before the copies are actually deposited. Section 407 of the copyright act provides for the demand by the Register of Copyrights for the deposit of copies, and, on default, a fine of $250 to $2,500 plus the retail price of the best edition of the work.

In certain industries, such as the lithographing of prints and labels for boxes, it may prove advantageous to insert the copyright notice on all new prints and labels and deposit only those that time proves to be of commercial significance. Similarly, all architects and design engineers should apply the statutory notice to their tracings, and hence to all copies of their prints, even though they do not intend to deposit every one with the Register of Copyrights.[6] Years later,

[6] The only disadvantage to this procedure, one which could develop into a very serious situation, is if there are a large number of writings and the request is made by the Register of Copyrights that they be deposited. By way of example, assume that there were several thousand drawings that carried the statutory notice. A demand from the Register of Copyrights would lead to the necessity of depositing

the presence of this statutory notice may buttress a claim or supply a missing element to a cause of action.

The registration procedure employed for issuing certificates of registration is simplicity in the extreme. Nothing in the copyright system is comparable to the examination for registerability that includes a search through prior registrations in the trademark system. The copyright application and deposited copies are examined solely to make certain that they satisfy the statutory requirements. Unless there is some defect of form in the application or deposited copies, the application will be approved and the certificate issued within a few weeks or less. If there are any mistakes in the application, an opportunity is always given to correct them. The Copyright Office will make every effort to suggest remedial procedures to cure mistakes that can be cured. Except in the most unusual situations, the Copyright Office will accept without question any statements made to it.

Should a registrant later discover a mistake in his certificate, it can be corrected. In summary, the operation of the Copyright Office is a simple and direct type of solicitation procedure substantially devoid of the intricacies that surround both patent and trademark solicitation.

## § 11.06 NOTICE OF COPYRIGHT

The *sine qua non* of the United States law of copyrights with respect to published works is notice. The form of notice is expressly provided for by statute and should be rigorously adhered to. Section 401 of the Copyright Act reads as follows:

> Notice of Copyright: Visually perceptible copies
>
> (a) GENERAL REQUIREMENT—Whenever a work protected under this title is published in the United States or elsewhere by authority of the copyright owner, a notice of copyright as provided by this section shall be placed on all publicly distributed copies from which the work can be visually perceived, either directly or with the aid of a machine or device.
>
> (b) FORM OF NOTICE—The notice appearing on the copies shall consist of the following three elements:

all these thousands of drawings with the Register. This could be a matter of great expense and inconvenience.

> (1) the symbol © (the letter C in a circle), or the word "Copyright," or the abbreviation "Copr."; and
>
> (2) the year of first publication of the work; in the case of compilations or derivative works incorporating previously published material, the year date of first publication of the compilation or derivative work is sufficient. The year date may be omitted where a pictorial, graphic, or sculptural work, with accompanying text matter, if any, is reproduced in or on greeting cards, postcards, stationery, jewelry, dolls, toys, or any useful articles; and
>
> (3) the name of the owner of copyright in the work, or an abbreviation by which the name can be recognized, or a generally known alternative designation of the owner.
>
> (c) POSITION OF NOTICE—The notice shall be affixed to the copies in such manner and location as to give reasonable notice of the claim of copyright. The Register of Copyrights shall prescribe by regulation, as examples, specific methods of affixation and positions of the notice on various types of works that will satisfy this requirement, but these specifications shall not be considered exhaustive.

The Universal Copyright Convention became effective in the United States on September 16, 1955. This convention enables citizens of the signatory countries to receive certain reciprocal rights. The use of the notice prescribed by the Universal Copyright Convention on all copies from the time of first publication, satisfies the formalities that the domestic law of any foreign country adhering to that Convention might otherwise require as a condition of copyright in that country; this is the so-called national treatment doctrine. United States authors or authors domiciled in the United States must comply with all the formalities of the United States act to assure protection here, although they need only publish their works bearing the convention notice to be accorded in all other contracting countries the protection afforded by the laws of those countries, as qualified by the Universal Copyright Convention.

The form of notice prescribed by the Universal Copyright Convention consists of "©," the named copyright proprietor, and the year of first publication. Thus: "© The American Law Institute 1986." It is recommended that this form of notice be adopted for all occasions, including those specified in Section 401, in which another form of notice may be utilized. Although the United States statute permits other forms of notice, the benefits of the Universal Copyright Convention will not be secured unless the specified notation is employed.

A number of frequently encountered situations bear discussion. Many textbooks, maps, and the like, are either revised or rewritten as new editions. The revisions, or new editions containing an appreciable amount of new and original material, may be copyrighted by a separate copyright, following the identical procedure used for securing the original copyright. In these circumstances it is the best practice to indicate both the original copyright notice and the later copyright notice. For example, when the original copyright was secured in 1969 by John Doe for the original edition of a book and a second copyright was secured in 1986 for a new edition of the book, it is recommended that the following notice be carried: "© John Doe 1969, 1986."

A caveat about the mechanics of printing is necessary. The copyright notice must be of sufficient size to be read by the naked eye. This caveat must be remembered when the copyrighted work is one that is reduced from a larger image during manufacture or is applied to a work of art and presents a situation in which the copyright proprietor is apt to wish that the notice be as minute as possible.

Another recurring problem is the use of pseudonyms by the copyright proprietor. It is recommended that pseudonyms and pen names be avoided with respect to the copyright notice, although they may be carried as the name of the author below the title of the work. The new act provides for the duration of copyright in works by anonymous and pseudonymous authors.[7] In the case of a partnership proprietor, since the partnership is a legal entity, it is not necessary to present the names of each of the partnership proprietors. Apparently the name of a corporation is adequate without the inclusion of more information.

Before the adoption of the Universal Copyright Convention, it was relatively common for publishers to include beneath the notice an additional nonstatutory notice intended to safeguard rights in foreign countries and to provide a further warning of claim. One form of the notice reads: "All rights reserved, including the right to reproduce this book or portions thereof in any form."

---

[7] *See* Section 302(c).

The use of additional notice of this kind at the present time may be of some value under the Buenos Aires Copyright Convention of 1910. It cannot be deemed to be harmful provided the correct notice required by the Universal Copyright Convention or one of the alternatives under Section 401 is utilized. Under no circumstances can a nonstatutory notice take the place of the notice provided for by Section 401.

If the proper copyright notice is omitted from published copies of the work, Section 405 sets forth those conditions under which copyright protection is not lost:

(1) The notice is omitted from a relatively small number of the publicly distributed copies; or

(2) Copyright registration is effected within five years of the publication without notice, and a "reasonable effort" is made to add notice to all copies distributed publicly after the omission is discovered; or

(3) The notice was omitted in violation of an express requirement in writing by the copyright proprietor that distributed copies of the work bear the proper notice.

## § 11.07 PRINTS AND LABELS

The registration of labels, as opposed to the registration of trademarks, is under the copyright law administered by the Copyright Office. All the labels that are distributed, including those used prior to the filing of the copyright registration, must bear the statutory notice provided for in Section 401 and discussed previously.[8] As with other forms of notice, since the United States is a signatory to the Universal Copyright Convention, when feasible the notice should be "©" accompanied by the year, date, and full name in order to secure the benefits of the Universal Copyright Convention in adhering foreign countries.

The copyrighting of labels is not to be viewed as an alternative to trademark registration procedures but as a supplement to them. For example, the Patent Office has refused to register the mere background display for a word mark apart from the dominating word mark except in those cases in which secondary meaning is shown and registration may be had under Section 2(f) of the Lanham Act. In *Ex parte Booth Bottling Co., Inc.*[9] the Patent Office refused to register

---

[8] See pp. 101–102.

[9] 110 U.S.P.Q. 240 (1956).

the outline design of a shield-shaped label with a disc superimposed on it (the disc carrying the registered word mark "Booth's") on the grounds that the symbol sought to be registered constituted a mere background display. Whether copyright protection for the label as a whole might have improved the applicant's position in these circumstances is not certain, but this area is one in which copyright registrations for labels may prove of value. Another area in which label copyright registrations are recommended is when the entire label design is a unique one and the subject of advertisements.

Among the successful instances of label protection is *Silvers v. Russell,* which involved the infringement of phonograph record labels.[10]

It can therefore be stated that as a practical matter it is unwise to substitute the copyrighting of labels for trademark protection; the value of copyright protection as a secondary weapon to support registered trademarks is of relatively minor importance.

As noted, the duration of a copyright is the life of the author, plus 50 years. When the maximum term of copyright was 56 years, fears were expressed in the trademark bar that the inclusion of a registered trademark in a copyrighted label or advertisement might result in the extinguishment of the mark at the final expiration of the copyright, along with the remainder of the copyrighted text. These fears appear to be groundless, and the objection should not be given credence.

## § 11.08 DURATION, RENEWAL, AND TERMINATION OF COPYRIGHTS

The previous term of United States copyrights was 28 years from the date of first publication. In the twenty-eighth year, the copyright could be renewed for an additional 28 years. Upon the expiration of the second term of 28 years, the copyright passed into the public domain. Congress in its revision of the copyright laws has extended the renewal term to 47 years.

Chapter Three in the revised Copyright Act brings United States practice concerning the term of copyright into line with that of many foreign countries. It is common in foreign countries to relate the term of copyright to the life of the author to enable the copyright

---

[10] 113 F. Supp. 119 (S.D. Cal. 1953). Reproductions of the infringed and infringing labels are at 113 F. Supp. 120.

in a work to exist for the full life of its author, plus an additional number of years.

The position formerly held by the United States was advantageous because it enabled an exact determination of the date upon which rights terminated, without reference to anything other than the copyrighted work. It further avoided the difficult task of establishing the length of the author's life.

Section 302(a) of the new statute provides:

> § 302. Duration of copyright: Works created on or after January 1, 1978,
>
> (a) IN GENERAL—Copyright in a work created on or after January 1, 1978, subsists from its creation and, except as provided by the following subsections, endures for a term consisting of the life of the author and fifty years after the author's death.

Section 303 relating to works which previously would have been the subject of common law copyright, provides:

> § 303. Duration of copyright: Works created but not published or copyrighted before January 1, 1978.
>
> Copyright in a work created before January 1, 1978, but not theretofore in the public domain or copyrighted subsists from January 1, 1978, and endures for the term provided by Section 302. In no case, however, shall the term of copyright in such work expire before December 31, 2002; and if the work is published on or before December 31, 2002, the term of copyright shall not expire before December 31, 2027.

Under Section 303, the perpetual term of common law works that were in existence on January 1, 1978, terminates on December 31, 2002, unless the work is published on or before December 31, 2002. If published before December 31, 2002, the term of copyright shall not expire before December 31, 2027, and may extend longer depending on the life of the author. This means that copyright rights in enormous numbers of unpublished manuscripts, such as letters going back to antiquity, will terminate on December 31, 2002, unless published between January 1, 1978, and December 31, 2002.

Section 304 requires renewal of all statutory copyrights existing on January 1, 1978, that have not yet been renewed. The renewal term for these works shall be 47 years. If a renewal has been secured, the renewal term is extended to accord the copyright proprietor a total of 75 years of protection.

Under Section 304, renewal copyrights in any posthumous work or any periodical, cyclopedic, or other composite work or any work copyrighted by a corporate body or by an employer in the case of a work for hire may be claimed by the proprietor. Renewal copyrights in the case of any other copyrighted work may be claimed by:

a. The *author* of the work if he is still living at the time when renewal is sought.

b. If the author is not living, his *widow* (or *widower*) or *children* may claim renewal.

c. If the author, his widow (or widower), and all of his children are not living, and the author has left a will, the author's *executor* may claim renewal.

d. If the author died without leaving a will, and neither his widow (or widower) nor any of his children is living, his *next of kin* may claim renewal.

This involved act was drafted to protect authors and the families of authors who had made faulty bargains with publishers. To accomplish this purpose, control of the renewal of the works enumerated in the act is conferred upon the author or, if he is dead, upon his family. The underlying rationale is that the purpose of the copyright acts is to safeguard authors rather than publishers or other parties dealing with the author's work. Nevertheless, although the goals sought to be achieved by the state are praiseworthy, the complexity of the act has created many traps for the unwary. It is not entirely clear whether the renewal term is a continuation of the original term or the creation of a new one. This question has significant implications in the assignment of an original term by the author.

The Supreme Court has somewhat clarified this area of the law by construing the right to renew as an assignable right, at least when the author is alive at the time the renewal application is made. If the author is dead at the time the right to renew accrues, the right does not go to his assignee but goes in accordance with the act as previously analyzed.

The termination provisions embodied in Section 202 of the act fulfill essentially the same purpose as the renewal provisions. With the exception of work done for hire, either by an employee or by an independent contractor, any transfer or license of right under a copyright executed after January 1, 1978, is subject to termination by serving notice on the grantee or his successor in title during a 5-year period beginning 35 years from the time of the grant; or if the grant covers the right of publication, 35 years from date of publication; or 40 years from the time of the grant, whichever term ends first.

Termination may be effected notwithstanding any agreement to the contrary by the author or, if the author is dead, by those persons who own more than one half of that author's "termination interest." The surviving spouse takes the entire termination interest unless there are surviving children or grandchildren, in which case the spouse takes one half of the interest. The surviving children and the surviving children of any dead child divide, *per stirpes,* one half of the author's interest if there is a surviving spouse, and own the entire interest if there is no surviving spouse.

Application for renewal copyright should be filed on Form R provided by the Copyright Office. It is not necessary to transmit copies of the copyrighted work to effect renewal.

One of the principal duties of a trademark and copyright lawyer is the maintenance of calendars running years into the future for renewals and terminations. Because the 28-year term of a copyright exceeds the 20-year term of a trademark registration, as does the 35-year termination provision, the maintenance of a tickler system for copyright renewals and terminations provides the maximum strain in terms of years. Yet nowhere is the need for an efficient tickler system more important than in the renewal and termination of copyrights. Failure to renew a copyright in the twenty-eighth year constitutes a complete dedication to the public, and the copyright cannot be revived. Failure to terminate a grant during the statutory period permits the grant to continue in effect for the full term of copyright unless the grant itself provides otherwise.

## § 11.09 THE CONVEYANCING OF RIGHTS TO A COPYRIGHT

The conveyancing of rights to a copyright is similar to the licensing and assignment of rights under a patent. Licensing and assignment of rights under a patent are discussed at length in Chapter 10, of *What the General Practitioner Should Know About Patent Law and Practice.*[11]

---

[11] A. SEIDEL, WHAT THE GENERAL PRACTIONER SHOULD KNOW ABOUT PATENT LAW AND PRACTICE 103 (4th ed. 1984).

Chapter 10 applies, in large part, to copyrights, since substantially the same considerations apply to them as to patents. The same considerations affecting an exclusive and a nonexclusive license are present in the law of copyrights as in the law of patents.

The Copyright Office operates under a recording statute that is analogous to the patent recording statute. Section 205 of the copyright act provides that unless an assignment of copyright is recorded within one month after its execution in the United States (or two months after its execution outside of the United States), the assignment shall be void as against a bona fide purchaser or mortgagee for a valuable consideration, without notice, whose assignment is duly recorded earlier.

Recordation of the transfer by which copyright ownership is claimed is also a prerequisite to an infringement action under Section 205(d). Suit may be instituted, however, on a cause of action that arose before recording.

## § 11.10 COPYRIGHT SEARCHES AND RECORDS

The Copyright Office will make searches through its records for a small fee. Examples of searches that are frequently made include searches for assignments to determine the present title to a copyright, searches for certificates of registration when information relating to an allegedly copyrighted work and its author are furnished, and searches for the titles of books or songs. Under the revised law, the Copyright Office will also maintain records with respect to the status of authors of copyrighted works.

The registration certificates, assignments, record books, and indexes of the Copyright Office are open to public inspection; the public may make copies of copyright entries made in the record books.

The Register of Copyrights publishes interim catalogs to the titles of all articles deposited and registered for copyright, as well as indexes to the catalogs. In addition, there is published a consolidated catalog and index covering an entire year. The current catalog of copyright entires and its index volumes may be admitted in any court as prima facie evidence of the facts regarding any copyright registration referred to in it.

## § 11.11 LITIGATION

Chapter Five of the Copyright Act permits the following:

§ 502: An injunction restraining the infringement

§ 503: Impounding of the infringing articles during the action

§ 504: Damages and profits, with the criteria for the determination explicitly stated in the act, with the statutory penalty yardstick set forth in the act as an alternative to actual damages and profits

§ 506: Costs and attorneys fees.

Section 506 of the Copyright Act provides for criminal penalties in the case of willful infringement or fraudulent notice of copyright. Although its predecessor Sections 104 and 105 were rarely invoked, it is now a policy of the Department of Justice to criminally prosecute so-called tape pirates, who duplicate musical recordings, and so-called film pirates, who duplicate motion picture film.

The certificate of copyright registration is prima facie evidence of the facts stated in it under Section 410(c), if copyright registration is secured within five years after first publication of the work. Unless this prima facie presumption is rebutted by the infringer, it is usually not necessary to prove the validity of plaintiff's copyright. The evidentiary weight accorded a later-secured certificate of registration is within the court's discretion.

The trier of fact determines infringement by a side-by-side comparison. The courts have varied on the degree of similarity needed to establish infringement; it is largely dependent upon the precise fact situation. When similarities may be attributed to a common source, such as an historical event or natural object, a higher standard is followed than in a work of pure fiction; that is, the similarities must be greater to negate the defense of independent creation from common or public domain source material. The inclusion of the same mistakes in the copyrighted work and in the defendant's work, such as in the case of maps or directories, is, of course, the most cogent evidence of infringement.

As a general rule, the nub of the plaintiff's case will include establishing access on the part of the defendant. Access is commonly deemed to be nothing more than a reasonable opportunity to have seen the copyrighted work. Proof of lack of access on the part of the defendant is a complete defense, since the relief accorded by the Copyright Act is against copying. Of course, because Section 106 of the Copyright Act provides for the exclusive right to reproductions and derivative works as well as copies, display, and performance rights, the infringement may take forms other than direct copying.

A statute of limitations for copyright actions has been enacted. Section 507 provides for a three-year statute of limitations for copyright infringement. It should be noted that there is no federal statue of limitations governing trademark suits.

## § 11.12 FAIR USE

The demands of news, comedy, learning, and criticism have led to the development of the doctrine of fair use. Fair use of copyrighted material may be defined as the amount of copying of a copyrighted work permitted under the law that does not give rise to a cause of action.

The doctrine, developed in the courts, receives its first statutory recognition in Section 107 of the Copyright Act. This is the first section in the new act limiting the exclusive rights of the copyright proprietor.

The scope of the fair use defense varies from situation to situation. There is no safe number of bars of music, lines of poetry, or paragraphs of prose that may be quoted, burlesqued, or transformed. Section 107 itself only sets forth some of the factors to be considered:

> Notwithstanding the provisions of Section 106, the fair use of a copyrighted work, including such use by reproduction in copies or phonorecords or by any other means specified by that section, for purposes such as criticism, comment, news reporting, teaching (including multiple copies for classroom use), scholarship, or research, is not an infringement of copyright. In determining whether the use made of a work in any particular case is a fair use the factors to be considered shall include—
>
> (1) The purpose and character of the use, including whether such use is of a commercial nature or is for non-profit educational purposes
>
> (2) The nature of the copyrighted work
>
> (3) The amount and substantiality of the portion used in relation to the copyrighted works as a whole and
>
> (4) The effect of the use upon the potential market for or value of the copyrighted work.

The very thorny problem of whether the photocopying (by Xerox or other commercial photocopying equipment) of copyrighted work constitutes fair use has been, in part, resolved by statute. Section

108 expressly sanctions limited library photocopying if copies are distributed on a nonprofit basis by institutions open to the public.[12] On January 1, 1983, and at five-year intervals thereafter, the Register of Copyrights is to report to Congress on the effects of this provision and its success in balancing the rights of creators and the needs of users.

## § 11.13 COPYRIGHT PROTECTION ABROAD FOR UNITED STATES CITIZENS

Copyright protection for works of United States citizens may be obtained in the great majority of foreign countries by virtue of conventions, treaties, agreements, or the legislative provisions of these countries.

The Universal Copyright Convention has already been discussed on page 111. The basic principle of this convention is that each contracting country shall accord to works of nationals of other contracting countries and works first published in those other countries copyright protection no less effective than that accorded to works of its own nationals. This so-called national treatment is accorded with a minimum of formalities, the convention providing in effect that the use of the symbol "©" accompanied by the name of the copyright owner and the year date of publication on all copies ("© John Doe 1986") will satisfy the formalities that the domestic law of any foreign country adhering to the convention might otherwise require as a condition of copyright in that country. As noted, United States authors, or authors domiciled in the United States, must comply with all the formalities of the United States law to be protected in the United States, although they need only publish works bearing the convention notice to be accorded, in all other contracting countries, the protection afforded under the laws of those countries, as qualified by the convention. The form of the convention notice will, however, satisfy Section 401. The Universal Copyright Convention also affords protection automatically to unpublished works, without notice of other formalities.

---

[12] Photocopying that does not fall within the scope of Section 108, it may be noted, may fall within the scope of the general fair use provision, Section 107. This has been recognized by the Regulations promulgated under the statute and by the libraries themselves, as evidenced by the revision of the Interlibrary Loan Request Form employed for loans and photocopies.

Contracting countries under the convention include:

Australia
Austria
Belgium
Brazil
Canada
Cuba
Czechoslovakia
Denmark
Finland
France
Germany, W. (Federal Republic)
Greece
Hungary
India
Ireland
Israel
Italy
Japan
Lebanon
Liberia
Mexico
Netherlands
New Zealand
Nigeria
Norway
Pakistan
Portugal
Spain
Sweden
Switzerland
United Kingdom
United States of America
Venezuela
Yugoslavia

The United States had also adhered, with a number of other American republics, to the copyright convention signed at Buenos Aires, Argentina, in 1910. Since this convention is open to adherence only by Western Hemisphere republics, the nations of the Eastern Hemisphere and Canada are excluded. This convention specifies that authors of any contracting country who have secured copyright in their own country will enjoy in the other countries the rights accorded by their respective legislation provided that the work to be copyrighted contains "a statement indicating the reservation of the property right."

The countries that have adhered to the Convention on Literary and Artistic Copyright signed at the Fourth International Conference of American States, Buenos Aires, 1910, are as follows:

Argentina
Bolivia
Brazil
Chile
Colombia
Costa Rica
Dominican Republic
Ecuador
Guatemala
Haiti
Honduras
Mexico
Nicaragua
Panama
Paraguay
Peru
United States of America
Uruguay

The United States has bilateral copyright relations with a number of foreign countries that may not be parties to either the Universal Copyright Convention or the Buenos Aires Convention. In some of these foreign countries, particularly those that are not members of the Berne Union to be discussed later in the text, United States authors or proprietors who desire to secure copyright protection for their works may find it necessary to comply with the formalities required by the copyright law and administrative regulations of the particular country.

Countries with which the United States has bilateral copyright relations are as follows:

- Argentina
- Australia
- Austria
- Belgium
- Brazil
- Cambodia
- Canada
- Chile
- China
- Costa Rica
- Cuba
- Czechoslovakia
- Denmark
- El Salvador (by virtue of Mexico City Convention, 1902)
- Finland
- France
- Germany, E. (Democratic Republic)
- Germany, W. (Federal Republic
- Greece
- Hungary
- India
- Ireland
- Israel
- Italy
- Luxembourg
- Mexico
- Monico
- Netherlands
- New Zealand
- Norway
- Philippines, Republic of the
- Poland
- Portugal
- Rumania
- South Africa, Republic of
- Spain
- Sweden
- Switzerland
- Thailand (Siam)
- United Kingdom

The United States has bilateral copyright relations with each of the listed countries by virtue of proclamation or treaty. In addition, certain of these countries are members of the Universal Copyright Convention, the Buenos Aires Convention, or both, to which the United States is also a party.

The Berne Conventions are worthy of mention, although the United States is not a signatory and is not a member of the Berne

Union.[13] A large number of countries (predominantly European and excluding the United States) are members of the International Union for the Protection of Literary and Artistic Works, better known as the Berne Union, with headquarters at Berne, Switzerland. Under the provisions of the several Berne Conventions, authors of any country belonging to the Union enjoy in the other countries the rights granted by such countries to their own citizens with respect to their works, whether unpublished or first published in any country of the Union. Authors of a country not belonging to the Union (for example, the United States) may secure the rights granted by these conventions—provided they publish their works first or simultaneously in a country of the Union. The question of what constitutes a bona fide first or simultaneous publication in a particular foreign country is a difficult legal one, and the use of the services of a copyright lawyer of that country is advisable for the first experience in a given country.

The following is a recent list of contracting Berne Union countries:

Australia
Austria
Belgium
Brazil
Bulgaria
Canada
Czechoslovakia
Denmark
Finland
France
Germany, W. (Federal Republic)
Luxembourg
Monaco
Morocco
Netherlands
New Zealand
Greece
Holy See (Vatican City)
Hungary
Iceland
India
Indonesia
Ireland
Israel
Italy
Japan
Lebanon
Liechtenstein
South Africa, Republic of
Spain
Sweden
Switzerland
Syria

[13] The Berne Union is made up of countries adhering to one or more of the following: the original Berne Convention of 1886 and the successive revisions of Paris 1896, Berlin 1908, Rome 1928, Brussels 1948, Stockholm 1967, and Paris 1971. Individual countries have different relationships under one or more of the conventions, and persons interested in obtaining detailed information, including application of the different provisions to territorial areas, should consult the Bureau de l'Union, Helvetiastrasse 7, Berne, Switzerland.

Norway
Pakistan
Philippines, Republic of the
Poland
Portugal
Rumania
Thailand (Siam)
Tunisia
Turkey
United Kingdom
Yugoslavia

## § 11.14 MORAL RIGHTS AND DROIT DE SUITE

It should be noted that the United States copyright act does not provide for the protection of "moral rights," which are protected in many civil law countries. These rights protect the integrity and reputation of the artistic creator after he has parted with his work by restricting the right to alter the work. The Universal Copyright Convention also neglects to mention "moral rights." The Convention delegations clearly sought to avoid any reference to these rights. Nevertheless, a right analogous to "moral right" has been recognized both in the United States and in Great Britain on various grounds, such as libel, unfair competition, and the right of privacy. It was in *Gillian v. American Broadcasting Co.,*[14] that a United States court came the closest to applying a "moral rights" doctrine. In that case the Court of Appeals found a truncated version of the Monty Python television program by the American Broadcasting Company to be an impairment of the integrity of the author's rights, and enjoinable.

The United States common law and the United States Copyright statutes have never contained anything analogous to the civil law *droit de suite.* Under this civil law doctrine the creator of a work, such as an artist or a sculptor, may share in the increased value of that work after the work is sold by him.

A number of states, including California and New York, have enacted statues introducing rights analogous to moral rights and/or the *droit de suite.*

## § 11.15 COPYRIGHT PROTECTION FOR COMPUTER SOFTWARE

The most recent Copyright Act became effective January 1, 1978. The Act provides for protection of "original works of authorship fixed in any tangible medium of expression . . ." including "literary works." Computer programs and data bases are considered copyrightable "literary works." The copyright laws protect the "expression" adopted by the programmer in a computer program and not

[14] 538 F. 2d 14 (2d Cir. 1976).

the idea, process, or method embodied in a program. The process or method embodied in a program involves the interrelationship between software and hardware components and is properly the subject of protection under the patent laws.

A copyrightable work must be differentiated from the medium in which the work is fixed because the work may be embodied in a multitude of media. Copyright rights in a work automatically inure to the author when the work is fixed in a tangible medium. A work is considered to be fixed in a tangible medium when it is sufficiently permanent or stable to permit it to be "perceived, reproduced or otherwise communicated for a period of more than transitory duration." It is not required that the work be directly readable by a human to satisfy the "fixation" requirement. Thus computer software embodied in a tape, disk, or ROM satisfies the "fixation" requirement.[15]

Whenever a copyrightable work is published, a notice of copyright must be placed on all publicly distributed copies. A copy of a computer program would be the tape, disk, or ROM carrying the program.[16] For computer software in machine-readable copies (tape, disk, or ROM) the following alternative methods of providing notice are acceptable: (1) Notice incorporated in the software in machine-readable form of the type that the notice is displayed at the user's terminal at sign on, (2) notice that is continuously displayed at the terminal, or (3) legible notice reproduced durably on a gummed or other label secured to the copy (disk, tape, or ROM) or to a box, reel, cartridge, cassette, or other container for the copy.

At any time during the continuance of copyright in a work, the owner may obtain a certificate of registration by depositing with the Copyright Office one complete copy of an unpublished work or two complete copies of the best edition of a published work, together with the copyright application and fee. When the computer software, whether published or unpublished, is fixed in a machine-readable form only, the Copyright Office requires the deposit of the first and last twenty-five pages of one copy in visually perceptible form, that is, the printout or listing, together with the page containing the copyright notice, if any. Alternative modes of deposit may be requested under the "special relief" provisions of 37 C.F.R.

---

[15] Apple Computer, Inc. v. Franklin Computer Corp., 714 F. 2d 1240, 1249 (3d Cir. 1983).

[16] See *supra* pp. 101–104 regarding proper form of copyright notice.

§ 202.20(d)(1). The Copyright Office requests deposit of the source code version of the program but will, after an exchange of correspondence with the applicant, accept the deposit of object code under the "rule of doubt."

The owner of copyright has the following exclusive rights: (1) to reproduce the copyrighted work in copies (tape, disk, or ROM, and the like), (2) to prepare derivative works (for example, translations, abridgments, condensations) based on the copyrighted work, (3) to distribute copies to the public by sale or other transfer of ownership, or by rental, lease, or lending, (4) to perform and display the work publicly. Under the old Act, a copy had to be readable by a human to constitute an infringing copy. Under the new Act, the requirement of human readability was abandoned.

Notwithstanding the provisions of Section 106, it is not an infringement for the owner of a copy (tape, disk, or ROM) of computer software to prepare one other copy, provided that: (1) The new copy is created as an essential step in the utilization of the computer software in conjunction with a machine, or (2) the new copy is for archival purposes only.

The copyright owner, having obtained a certificate of registration, may obtain the following relief against infringers: (1) temporary and final injunctive relief, (2) actual damages, (3) infringer's profits to the extent not taken into account in computing actual damages, (4) statutory damages, in lieu of actual damages and profits, not less than $250.00 or more than $10,000.00, (5) costs and a reasonable attorneys' fee, (6) impoundment of copies (tapes, disks, ROMs, and the like) during the pendency of a lawsuit and destruction of copies as part of a final judgment or decree.

Advantages of copyright protection include: (1) easy to obtain and maintain upon satisfaction of formal requirements, (2) long term of protection, and (3) availability of timely, preliminary relief. Disadvantages include: (1) uncertainty of availability of protection against copying tape, disk, or ROM (the Supreme Court has not decided the question, although appellate cases indicate protection is available), (2) difficulty in policing copying when software has been widely disseminated, (3) no protection against independent creation, proof of copyright being required, and (4) protection against copying of expression only.

### § 11.15(a) Procedures For Obtaining Copyright Registration

The owner of a copyright or of any exclusive right in a computer program may apply for registration of the copyright claim by filing the appropriate application and fee, together with the required deposit. The form of this deposit varies depending on the type of work submitted for registration but generally consists of some type of "identifying portions" of the work. Deposit of less than the entire work is acceptable in limited instances.

When a computer program is fixed or published only in the form of machine readable copies, the deposit for registration must consist of one copy of identifying portions of the program, reproduced in a form visually perceptible without the aid of a machine or device, either on paper or in microform. For these purposes "identifying portions" means either the first and last 25 pages or equivalent units of the program if reproduced on paper, or at least the first and last 25 pages or equivalent units of the program if reproduced in microform, together with the page or equivalent unit containing the copyright notice, if any.

If the computer program is less than 50 pages in length, the entire program should be deposited. For registration of a derivative computer program, identifying portions of the new material should be included in the deposit.

The Copyright Office considers source code to be the best representation of copyrightable authorship in a computer program. Thus the identifying material deposited for a computer program should be in a source code.

When the applicant is unable or unwilling to deposit identifying material in source code, depositing only object code instead, registration for the copyright program will be made under the Rule of Doubt if the applicant confirms in writing that the work as deposited contains copyrightable material. Because object code is basically unintelligible to copyright examiners, it is not possible to examine the deposit to determine the presence of copyrightable authorship. The doubt in this instance does not concern the copyrightability of computer programs in general.

When a computer program is an unpublished work that is treated by the author as confidential information, the owner can request special relief from these deposit requirements. Special relief is a procedure which allows the Register of Copyrights to grant the applicant the option of depositing less than or other than that required under the general deposit provisions. Special relief is an option available to computer program applicants when they are unable or unwilling to deposit the usual identifying material in source code format.

### § 11.15(b) The Semiconductor Chip Protection Act of 1984

Federal statutory protection is now available for semiconductor chips and mask works fixed in semiconductor chip products. The Semiconductor Chip Protection Act enacted by Congress became effective November 18, 1984.

A "semi-conductor chip" product is defined in the Act as the final or intermediate form of any product having two or more layers of metallic, insulating, or semiconductor material, deposited or otherwise placed on or etched away or otherwise removed from a piece of semiconductor material in accordance with a predetermined pattern and intended to perform electronic circuitry functions.

Mask works are generally defined as the layered design of insulating and conductive material that causes the semiconductor chip to operate in a particular manner.

Although the Semiconductor Chip Protection Act and the Copyright Act are both administered by the Copyright Office, the provisions of the Semiconductor Chip Protection Act differ in many respects from the provisions of the Copyright Act and the type of protection provided.

# Appendixes

# Appendix A

## PATENT OFFICE RULE 2.120

***2.120 Discovery.***

(a) ***In general.*** The provisions of the Federal Rules of Civil Procedure relating to discovery shall apply in opposition, cancellation, interference and concurrent use registration proceedings except as otherwise provided in this section. The Trademark Trial and Appeal Board will specify the closing date for the taking of discovery.

(b) ***Discovery deposition within the United States.*** The deposition of a natural person shall be taken in the Federal judicial district where the person resides or is regularly employed or at any place on which the parties agree by stipulation. The responsibility rests wholly with the party taking discovery to secure the attendance of a proposed deponent other than a party or anyone who, at the time set for the taking of the deposition, is an officer, director, or managing agent of a party, or a person designated under Rule 30(b)(6) or Rule 31(a) of the Federal Rules of Civil Procedure. (See 35 U.S.C. 24.)

(c) ***Discovery deposition in foreign countries.*** (1) The discovery deposition of a natural person residing in a foreign country who is a party or who, at the time set for the taking of the deposition, is an officer, director, or managing agent of a party, or a person designated under Rule 30(b)(6) or Rule 31(a) of the Federal Rules of Civil Procedure, shall, if taken in a foreign country be taken in the manner prescribed by § 2.124 unless the Trademark Trial and Appeal Board, upon motion for good cause, orders or the parties stipulate, that the deposition be taken by oral examination.

(2) Whenever a foreign party is or will be, during a time set for discovery, present within the United States or any territory which is under the control and jurisdiction of the United States, such party may be deposed by oral examination upon notice by the party seeking discovery. Whenever a foreign party has or will have, during a time set for discovery, an officer, director, managing agent, or other person who consents to testify on its behalf, present within the United States or any territory which is under the control and jurisdiction of the United States, such officer, director, managing agent, or other person who consents to testify in its behalf may be deposed by oral examination upon notice by the party seeking discovery. The party seeking discovery may have one or more officers, directors, managing agents, or other persons who consent to testify on behalf of the adverse party, designated under Rule 30(b)(6) of the Federal Rules of Civil Procedure. The deposition of a person under this paragraph shall be taken in the Federal judicial district where the witness resides or is regularly employed, or, if the witness neither resides nor is regularly employed in a Federal judicial district, where the witness is at the time of the deposition. This paragraph does not preclude the taking of a discovery deposition of a foreign party by any other procedure provided by paragraph (c)(1) of this section.

(d) ***Request for production.*** The production of documents and things under the provisions of Rule 34 of the Federal Rules of Civil Procedure will be made at the place where the documents and things are usually kept, or where the parties agree, or where and in the manner which the Trademark Trial and Appeal Board, upon motion, orders.

(e) ***Motion for an order to compel discovery.*** If a party fails to designate a person pursuant to Rule 30(b)(6) or Rule 31 (a) of the Federal Rules of Civil Procedure, or if a party or such designated person, or an officer, director or managing agent of a party fails to attend a deposition or fails to answer any question propounded in a discovery deposition, or any interrogatory, or fails to produce and permit the inspection and copying of any document or thing, the party seeking discovery may file a motion before the Trademark Trial and Appeal Board for an order to compel a designation, or attendance at a deposition, or an answer, or production and an opportunity to inspect and copy. The motion shall include a copy of the request for designation or of the relevant portion of the discovery deposition; or a copy of the interrogatory with any answer or objection that was made; or a copy of the request for production, any proffer of production or objection to production in response to the request, and a list and brief description of the documents or things that were not produced for inspection and copying. The motion must be supported by a written statement from the moving party that such party or the attorney therefor has made a good faith effort, by conference or correspondence, to resolve with the other party or the attorney therefor the issues presented in the motion and has been unable to reach agreement. If issues raised in the motion are subsequently resolved by agreement of the parties, the moving party should inform the Board in writing of the issues in the motion which no longer require adjudication.

(f) ***Motion for a protective order.*** Upon motion by a party from whom discovery is sought, and for good cause, the Trademark Trial and Appeal Board may make any order which justice requires to protect a party from annoyance, embarrassment, oppression, of undue burden or expense, including one or more of the types or orders provided by clauses (1) through (8), inclusive, of Rule 26(c) of the Federal Rules of Civil Procedure. If the motion for a protective order is denied in whole or in part, the Board may, on such conditions (other than an award of expenses to the party prevailing on the motion) as are just, order that any party provide or permit discovery.

(g) ***Failure to comply with order.*** If a party fails to comply with an order of the Trademark Trial and Appeal Board relating to discovery, including a protective order, the Board may make any appropriate order, including any of the orders provided in Rule 37(b)(2) of the Federal Rules of Civil Procedure, except that the Board does not have authority to hold any person in contempt or to award any expenses to any party. The Board may impose against a party any of the sanctions provided by this subsection in the event that said party or any attorney, agent, or designated witness of that party fails to comply with a protective order made pursuant to Rule 26(c) of the Federal Rules of Civil Procedure.

(h) ***Request for admissions.*** Requests for admissions shall be governed by Rule 36 of the Federal Rules of Civil Procedure except that the Trademark Trial and Appeal Board does not have authority to award any expenses to any party. A motion by a party to determine the sufficiency of an answer or objection to a request made by that party for an admission shall include a copy of the request for admission and any exhibits thereto and of the answer or objection. The motion must be supported by a written statement from the moving party that such party or the attorney therefor has made a good faith effort, by conference or correspondence, to resolve with the other party or the attorney therefor the issues presented in the motion and has been unable to reach agreement. If issues raised in the motion are subsequently resolved by agreement of the parties, the moving party should inform the Board in writing of the issues in the motion which no longer require adjudication.

(i) ***Telephone and pre-trial conferences.*** (1) Whenever it appears to the Trademark Trial and Appeal Board that a motion filed in an inter partes proceeding is of such nature that its resolution by correspondence is not practical, the Board may, upon its own initiative or upon request made by one or both of the parties, resolve the motion by telephone conference.

(2) Whenever it appears to the Trademark [sic] and Appeal Board that questions or issues arising during the interlocutory phase of an inter partes proceeding have become so complex that their resolution by correspondence or telephone conference is not practical and that resolution would be likely to be facilitated by a conference in person of the parties or their attorneys with a Member or Attorney-Examiner of the Board, the Board may, upon its own initiative or upon motion made by one or both of the parties, request that the parties or their attorneys, under circumstances which will not result in undue hardship for any party, meet with the Board at its offices for a pre-trial conference.

(j) ***Use of discovery deposition, admission, or answer to interrogatory.*** (1) The discovery deposition of a party or of anyone who at the time of taking the deposition was an officer, director or managing agent of a party, or a person designated by a party pursuant to Rule 30(b)(6) or Rule 31(a) of the Federal Rules of Civil Procedure, may be offered in evidence by an adverse party.

(2) Except as provided in paragraph (j)(1) of this section, the discovery deposition of a witness, whether or not a party, shall not be offered in evidence unless the person whose deposition was taken is, during the testimony period of the party offering the deposition, dead; or out of the United States (unless it appears that the absence of the witness was procured by the party offering the deposition); or unable to testify because of age, illness, infirmity, or imprisonment; or cannot be served with a subpoena to compel attendance at a testimonial disposition; or there is a stipulation by the parties; or upon a showing that such exceptional circumstances exist as to make it desirable, in the interest of justice, to allow the deposition to be used. The use of a discovery deposition by any party under this paragraph will be allowed only by stipulation of the parties approved by the Trademark Trial and Appeal Board, or by order of the Board on motion, which shall be filed at the time of the purported offer of the deposition in evidence, unless the motion is based upon a claim that such exceptional circumstances exist as to make it desirable in the interest of justice, to allow the deposition to be used, in which case the motion shall be filed promptly after the circumstances claimed to justify use of the deposition became known.

(3) A discovery deposition, an answer to an interrogatory, or an admission to a request for admission, which may be offered in evidence under the provisions of paragraph (j) of this section may be made of record in the case by filing the deposition or any part thereof with any exhibit to the part that is filed, or a copy of the interrogatory and answer thereto with any exhibit made part of the answer, or a copy of the request for admission and any exhibit thereto and the admission

(or a statement that the party from whom an admission was requested failed to respond thereto), together with a notice of reliance. The notice of reliance and the material submitted thereunder should be filed during the testimony period of the party who files the notice of reliance. An objection made at a discovery deposition by a party answering a question subject to the objection will be considered at final hearing.

(4) If only part of a discovery deposition is submitted and made part of the record by a party, an adverse party may introduce under a notice of reliance any other part of the deposition which should in fairness be considered so as to make not misleading what was offered by the submitting party.

(5) An answer to an interrogatory, or an admission to a request for admission, may be submitted and made part of the record by only the inquiring party except that, if answers to interrogatories or fewer than all of the admissions are offered in evidence by the inquiring party, the responding party may introduce under a notice of reliance any other answers to interrogatories, or any other admissions, which should in fairness be considered so as to make not misleading what was offered by the inquiring party.

(6) Paragraph (j) of this section will not be interpreted to preclude the reading or the use of a discovery deposition, or answer to an interrogatory, or admission as part of the examination or cross-examination of any witness during the testimony period of any party.

(7) When a discovery deposition, or a part thereof, or an answer to an interrogatory, or an admission, has been made of record by one party in accordance with the provisions of paragraph (j)(3) of this section, it may be referred to by any party for any purpose permitted by the Federal Rules of Evidence.

(8) Interrogatories, requests for production, requests for admissions, and materials or depositions obtained during the discovery period should not be filed with the Board except when submitted with a motion to compel discovery, or in support of or response to a motion for summary judgment, or under a notice of reliance during a party's testimony period.

# Appendix B

## FORMS FOR TRADEMARK CASES

Over the years, the U.S. Patent and Trademark Office has developed a set of forms for trademark applications, as well as for other documents frequently required to be filed in the Patent and Trademark Office. The Trademark Office periodically revises and updates these forms. The majority of the revisions merely reflect changes in format. Less frequently, the Trademark Office will make substantive changes to documents due to revisions in the law or new interpretations of the statute.

At present, the forms are in the process of being revised and it is not possible to purchase the complete set. Application forms for individuals, corporations and partnerships can be requested from the Patent and Trademark Office. When the current version is available, a complete set can be purchased from the Superintendent of Documents, U.S. Government Printing Office, Washington, D.C. 20402.

A listing of the forms for trademark cases follows. The forms reproduced in this treatise are indicated by an asterisk (*) next to the form number.

The forms can be supplemented, as necessary, to include additional data.

Many of the documents filed in the Patent and Trademark Office must be verified by the applicant. This includes trademark applications, renewal applications, and combined declarations under Sections 8 and 15. Verification may take the form of an Affidavit under oath before a notary public or a Declaration as provided in Rule 2.20 of the Act. Both types of verification are reflected in the forms reproduced herein.

## FORMS FOR TRADEMARK CASES

| Form Number | | | Title |
|---|---|---|---|
| *PTO-FB-TM | 100 | (individual) | Trademark Application, Principal Register, with Oath |
| *PTO- | 1476 | (individual) | Trademark Application, Principal Register, with Declaration |
| *PTO-FB-TM | 102 | (partnership) | Trademark Application, Principal Register, with Oath |
| *PTO- | 1477 | (partnership) | Trademark Application, Principal Register, with Declaration |
| *PTO-FB-TM | 104 | (corporation) | Trademark Application, Principal Register, with Oath |
| *PTO- | 1478 | (corporation) | Trademark Application, Principal Register, with Declaration |
| *PTO-FB-TM | 106 | (individual) | Service Mark Application, Principal Register, with Oath |
| *PTO-FB-TM | 107 | (individual) | Service Mark Application, Principal Register, with Declaration |
| *PTO-FB-TM | 108 | (partnership) | Service Mark Application, Principal Register, with Oath |
| *PTO-FB-TM | 109 | (partnership) | Service Mark Application, Principal Register, with Declaration |
| *PTO-FB-TM | 110 | (corporation) | Service Mark Application, Principal Register, with Oath |
| *PTO-FB-TM | 111 | (corporation) | Service Mark Application, Principal Register, with Declaration |
| *PTO-FB-TM | 112 | (corporation) | Collective Trademark or Collective Service Mark Application, Principal Register, with Oath |
| *PTO-FB-TM | 113 | (corporation) | Collective Trademark or Collective Service Mark Application, Principal Register, with Declartion |
| *PTO-FB-TM | 114 | (corporation) | Collective Membership Mark Application, Principal Register, with Oath |
| PTO-FB-TM | 115 | (corporation) | Collective Membership Mark Application, Principal Register, with Declaration |

| Form Number | | | Title |
|---|---|---|---|
| PTO-FB-TM | 116 | (individual) | Certification Mark Application, Principal Register, with Oath |
| PTO-FB-TM | 117 | (individual) | Certification Mark Application, Principal Register, with Declaration |
| PTO-FB-TM | 118 | (partnership) | Certification Mark Application, Principal Register, with Oath |
| PTO-FB-TM | 119 | (partnership) | Certification Mark Application, Principal Register, with Declaration |
| PTO-FB-TM | 120 | (corporation) | Certification Mark Application, Principal Register, with Oath |
| PTO-FB-TM | 121 | (corporation) | Certification Mark Application, Principal Register, with Declaration |
| PTO-FB-TM | 122 | (individual) | Trademark or Service Mark Application Based on Concurrent Use, Principal Register, with Oath |
| PTO-FB-TM | 123 | (individual) | Trademark or Service Mark Application Based on Concurrent Use, Principal Register, with Declaration |
| PTO-FB-TM | 124 | (partnership) | Trademark or Service Mark Application Based on Concurrent Use, Principal Register, with Oath |
| PTO-FB-TM | 125 | (partnership) | Trademark or Service Mark Application Based on Concurrent Use, Principal Register, with Declaration |
| PTO-FB-TM | 126 | (corporation) | Trademark or Service Mark Application Based on Concurrent Use, Principal Register, with Oath |
| PTO-FB-TM | 127 | (corporation) | Trademark or Service Mark Application Based on Concurrent Use, Principal Register, with Declaration |
| PTO-FB-TM | 128 | (individual) | Trademark Application, Supplemental Register, with Oath |

| Form Number | | | Title |
|---|---|---|---|
| PTO-FB-TM | 129 | (individual) | Trademark Application, Supplemental Register, with Declaration |
| *PTO-FB-TM | 130 | (partnership) | Trademark Application, Supplemental Register, with Oath |
| *PTO-FB-TM | 131 | (partnership) | Trademark Application, Supplemental Register, with Declaration |
| *PTO-FB-TM | 132 | (corporation) | Trademark Application, Supplemental Register, with Oath |
| *PTO-FB-TM | 133 | (corporation) | Trademark Application, Supplemental Register, with Declaration |
| *PTO-FB-TM | 134 | (individual) | Service Mark Application, Supplemental Register, with Oath |
| *PTO-FB-TM | 135 | (individual) | Service Mark Application, Supplemental Register, with Declaration |
| *PTO-FB-TM | 136 | (partnership) | Service Mark Application, Supplemental Register, with Oath |
| *PTO-FB-TM | 137 | (partnership) | Service Mark Application, Supplemental Register, with Declaration |
| *PTO-FB-TM | 138 | (corporation) | Service Mark Application, Supplemental Register, with Oath |
| *PTO-FB-TM | 139 | (corporation) | Service Mark Application, Supplemental Register, with Declaration |
| *PTO-FB-TM | 140 | (corporation) | Collective Trademark or Collective Service Mark Application, Supplemental Register, with Oath |

| Form Number | | | Title |
|---|---|---|---|
| *PTO-FB-TM | 141 | (corporation) | Collective Trademark or Collective Service Mark Application, Supplemental Register, with Declaration |
| *PTO-FB-TM | 142 | (corporation) | Collective Membership Mark Application, Supplemental Register, with Oath |
| *PTO-FB-TM | 143 | (corporation) | Collective Membership Mark Application, Supplemental Register, with Declaration |
| *PTO-FB-TM | 144 | (individual) | Certification Mark Application, Supplemental Register, with Oath |
| *PTO-FB-TM | 145 | (individual) | Certification Mark Application, Supplemental Register, with Declaration |
| *PTO-FB-TM | 146 | (partnership) | Certification Mark Application, Supplemental Register, with Oath |
| *PTO-FB-TM | 147 | (partnership) | Certification Mark Application, Supplemental Register, with Declaration |
| *PTO-FB-TM | 148 | (corporation) | Certification Mark Application, Supplemental Register, with Oath |
| *PTO-FB-TM | 149 | (corporation) | Certification Mark Application, Supplemental Register, with Declaration |
| *PTO-FB-TM | 150 | | Power of Attorney at Law |
| *PTO-FB-TM | 151 | | Designation of Domestic Representative |
| *PTO-FB-TM | 152 | | Claim of Priority based on 15 USC 1126(d) |
| *PTO-FB-TM | 153 | | Claim of Foreign registration based on 15 USC 1126(e) |
| *PTO-FB-TM | 200 | | Application for Renewal of Registration of a Mark, with Oath |
| *PTO-FB-TM | 201 | | Application for Renewal of Registration of a Mark, with Declaration |

| Form Number | | Title |
|---|---|---|
| *PTO-FB-TM | 202 | Affidavit for Publication of a Mark under Section 12(c), with Oath |
| *PTO-FB-TM | 203 | "Affidavit" for Publication of a Mark under Section 12(c), with Declaration |
| *PTO-FB-TM | 204 | Affidavit of Use of a Mark Required by Section 8, with Oath |
| *PTO-FB-TM | 205 | "Affidavit" of Use of a Mark Required by Section 8, with Declaration |
| *PTO-FB-TM | 206 | Affidavit of Incontestability of a Mark under Section 15, with Oath |
| *PTO-FB-TM | 207 | "Affidavit" of Incontestability of a Mark under Section 15, with Declaration |
| *PTO-FB-TM | 208 | Combined Affidavit of Use and Incontestability of a Mark under Sections 8 and 15, with Oath |
| *PTO-FB-TM | 209 | Combined "Affidavit" of Use and Incontestability of a Mark under Sections 8 and 15, with Declaration |
| *PTO-FB-TM | 300 | Opposition to the Registration of a Mark |
| *PTO-FB-TM | 301 | Petition to Cancel a Registration of a Mark |
| *PTO-FB-TM | 302 | Ex Parte Appeal from Examiner of Trademarks to Trademark Trial and Appeal Board |
| *PTO-FB-TM | 400 | Assignment of Application for Registration of a Mark |
| *PTO-FB-TM | 401 | Assignment of Registration of a Mark |
| *PTO-FB-TM | 402 | Certificate of Mailing under—37 CFR 1.8(a) |
| *PTO-FB-TM | 403 | Certificate of Express Mail under 37 CFR 1.10 |

| **TRADEMARK APPLICATION, PRINCIPAL REGISTER, WITH OATH** (Individual) | MARK *(identify the mark)* |
|---|---|
| | CLASS NO. *(if known)* |

TO THE COMMISSIONER OF PATENTS AND TRADEMARKS:

NAME OF APPLICANT, AND BUSINESS TRADE NAME. IF ANY

BUSINESS ADDRESS

RESIDENCE ADDRESS

CITIZENSHIP OF APPLICANT

The above identified applicant has adopted and is using the trademark shown in the accompanying drawing [1] for the following goods: ______________________________

______________________________,

and requests that said mark be registered in the United States Patent and Trademark Office on the Principal Register established by the Act of July 5, 1946.

The trademark was first used on the goods [2] on ____________ *(date)*; was first used on the goods [2] in ______________________ *(type of commerce)* commerce [3] on ____________ *(date)*; and is now in use in such commerce.

[4]

The mark is used by applying it to[5] ______________________________

______________________________

and five specimens showing the mark as actually used are presented herewith.

[6]

State of ____________________ )
) ss.
County of ____________________ )

______________________________
*(name of applicant)*

states that he/she believes himself/herself to be the owner of the trademark sought to be registered; to the best of his/her knowledge and belief no other person, firm, corporation or association has the right to use said mark in commerce, either in the identical form or in such near resemblance thereto as to be likely, when applied to the goods of such other person, to cause confusion, or to cause mistake, or to deceive; and the facts set forth in this application are true.

______________________________
*(signature of applicant)*

JURAT:

Subscribed and sworn to before me, this ________ day of ________________, ______.

______________________________
*(notary public)*

PTO-FB-TM 100 (Trademark) (Individual) (Rev. 12-83) Patent and Trademark Office - U.S. DEPT. OF COMMERCE

*(over)*

PTO–FB–TM 138 (Trademark) (Individual) (Rev. 12-83)

## REPRESENTATION

If the applicant is not domiciled in the United States, a domestic representative must be designated. See Form PTO–FB–TM 151.

If applicant wishes to furnish a power of attorney, see Form PTO–FB–TM 150. An attorney at law is not required to furnish a power.

## JURAT

The person who signs the jurat must be authorized to administer oaths by the law of the jurisdiction where executed, and the seal or stamp of the notary, or other evidence of authority in the jurisdiction of execution, must be affixed.

## FOOTNOTES

1 If applicant is an association or other similar type of juristic entity, change "corporation" throughout to an appropriate designation.

2 If registration is sought for a word or numeral mark not depicted in any special form, the drawing may be the mark typed in capital letters on letter-size bond paper; otherwise, the drawing should be made with india ink on a good grade of bond paper or on bristol board.

3 If more than one item of goods in a class is set forth and the dates given for that class apply to only one of the items listed, insert the name of the item to which the dates apply.

4 Type of commerce should be specified as "interstate," "territorial," "foreign," or other type of commerce which may lawfully be regulated by Congress. Foreign applicants relying upon use must specify commerce which Congress may regulate, using wording such as commerce with the United States or commerce between the United States and a foreign country.

5 If the mark is other than a coined, arbitrary or fanciful mark, and the mark is believed to have acquired a secondary meaning, insert whichever of the following paragraphs is applicable:

a) The mark has become distinctive of applicant's goods as a result of substantially exclusive and continuous use in ____________________ *(type of commerce)* commerce for the five years next preceding the date of filing of this application.

b) The mark has become distinctive of applicant's goods as evidenced by the showing submitted separately.

6 Insert the manner or method of using the mark with the goods, i.e., "the goods," "the containers for the goods," "displays associated with the goods," "tags or labels affixed to the goods," or other method which may be in use.

7 The required fee of $175.00 for each class must be submitted. (An application to register the same mark for goods and/or services in more than one class may be filed; however, goods and/or services, and dates of use, by class, must be set out separately, and specimens and a fee for each class are required.)

Patent and Trademark Office - U.S. DEPT. OF COMMERCE

| **TRADEMARK APPLICATION, PRINCIPAL REGISTER, WITH DECLARATION** (Individual) | MARK *(identify the mark)* |
|---|---|
| | CLASS NO. *(if known)* |

TO THE COMMISSIONER OF PATENTS AND TRADEMARKS:

NAME OF APPLICANT, AND BUSINESS TRADE NAME, IF ANY

BUSINESS ADDRESS

RESIDENCE ADDRESS

CITIZENSHIP OF APPLICANT

The above identified applicant has adopted and is using the trademark shown in the accompanying drawing [1] for the following goods: ______________________________

______________________________,

and requests that said mark be registered in the United States Patent and Trademark Office on the Principal Register established by the Act of July 5, 1946.

The trademark was first used on the goods [2] on ____________ *(date)* ; was first used on the goods [2] in ______________________ *(type of commerce)* commerce [3] on ____________ *(date)* ;

and is now in use in such commerce.

4

The mark is used by applying it to[5]) ______________________________

______________________________

and five specimens showing the mark as actually used are presented herewith.

6

______________________________
*(name of applicant)*

being hereby warned that willful false statements and the like so made are punishable by fine or imprisonment, or both, under Section 1001 of Title 18 of the United States Code and that such willful false statements may jeopardize the validity of the application or any registration resulting therefrom, declares that he/she believes himself/herself to be the owner of the trademark sought to be registered; to the best of his/her knowledge and belief no other person, firm, corporation, or association has the right to use said mark in commerce, either in the identical form or in such near resemblance thereto as may be likely, when applied to the goods of such other person, to cause confusion, or to cause mistake, or to deceive; the facts set forth in this application are true; and all statements made of his/her own knowledge are true and all statements made on information and belief are believed to be true.

______________________________
*(signature of applicant)*

______________________________
*(date)*

PTO-1476 (Trademark) (Individual) (Rev. 12-83) Patent and Trademark Office - U.S. DEPT. OF COMMERCE

*(over)*

PTO–1476 (Trademark) (Individual) (Rev. 12-83)

REPRESENTATION

If the applicant is not domiciled in the United States, a domestic representative must be designated. See Form PTO–FB–TM 151.

If applicant wishes to furnish a power of attorney, see Form PTO–FB–TM 150. An attorney at law is not required to furnish a power.

FOOTNOTES

1 If registration is sought for a word or numeral mark not depicted in any special form, the drawing may be the mark typed in capital letters on letter-size bond paper; otherwise, the drawing should be made with india ink on a good grade of bond paper or on bristol board.

2 If more than one item of goods in a class is set forth and the dates given for that class apply to only one of the items listed, insert the name of the item to which the dates apply.

3 Type of commerce should be specified as "interstate," "territorial," "foreign," or other type of commerce which may lawfully be regulated by Congress. Foreign applicants relying upon use must specify commerce which Congress may regulate, using wording such as commerce with the United States or commerce between the United States and a foreign country.

4 If the mark is other than a coined, arbitrary or fanciful mark, and the mark is believed to have acquired a secondary meaning, insert whichever of the following paragraphs is applicable:

a) The mark has become distinctive of applicant's goods as a result of substantially exclusive and continuous use in ______________________ commerce for the five years next preceding the date
*(type of commerce)*
of filing of this application.

b) The mark has become distinctive of applicant's goods as evidenced by the showing submitted separately.

5 Insert the manner or method of using the mark with the goods, i.e., "the goods," "the containers for the goods," "displays associated with the goods," "tags or labels affixed to the goods," or other method which may be in use.

6 The required fee of $175.00 for each class must be submitted. (An application to register the same mark for goods and/or services in more than one class may be filed; however, goods and/or services, and dates of use, by class, must be set out separately, and specimens and a fee for each class are required.)

Patent and Trademark Office - U.S. DEPT of COMMERCE

| **TRADEMARK APPLICATION, PRINCIPAL REGISTER, WITH OATH** (Partnership) | MARK *(identify the mark)*<br>CLASS NO. *(if known)* |
|---|---|

TO THE COMMISSIONER OF PATENTS AND TRADEMARKS:

NAME OF PARTNERSHIP

NAMES OF PARTNERS

BUSINESS ADDRESS OF PARTNERSHIP

CITIZENSHIP OF PARTNERS

The above identified applicant has adopted and is using the trademark shown in the accompanying drawing [1] for the following goods:
and requests that said mark be registered in the United States Patent and Trademark Office on the Principal Register established by the Act of July 5, 1946.

The trademark was first used on the goods [2] on ______________ *(date)* ; was first used on the goods [2] in ______________________________ *(type of commerce)* commerce [3] on ______________ *(date)* ;
and is now in use in such commerce.
[4]

The mark is used by applying it to[5] ______________________________

______________________________

and five specimens showing the mark as actually used are presented herewith.
[6]

State of ______________ )
) ss.
County of ______________ )

______________________________
*(name of partner)*

states that he/she is a partner of applicant partnership; he/she believes said partnership to be the owner of the trademark sought to be registered; to the best of his/her knowledge and belief no other person, firm, corporation or association has the right to use said mark in commerce, either in the identical form or in such near resemblance thereto as to be likely, when applied to the goods of such other person, to cause confusion, or to cause mistake, or to deceive; and the facts set forth in this application are true.

______________________________
*(signature of partner)*

JURAT:

Subscribed and sworn to before me, this __________ day of ______________ , ______.

______________________________
*(notary public)*

PTO-FB-TM 102 (Trademark) (Partnership) (Rev. 12-83) Patent and Trademark Office - U.S. DEPT. of COMMERCE

*(over)*

PTO–FB–TM 102 (Trademark) (Partnership) (Rev. 12-83)

## REPRESENTATION

If the applicant is not domiciled in the United States, a domestic representative must be designated. See Form PTO–FB–TM 151.

If applicant wishes to furnish a power of attorney, see Form PTO–FB–TM 150. An attorney at law is not required to furnish a power.

## JURAT

The person who signs the jurat must be authorized to administer oaths by the law of the jurisdiction where executed, and the seal or stamp of the notary, or other evidence of authority in the jurisdiction of execution, must be affixed.

## FOOTNOTES

1 If registration is sought for a word or numeral mark not depicted in any special form, the drawing may be the mark typed in capital letters on letter-size bond paper; otherwise, the drawing should be made with india ink on a good grade of bond paper or on bristol board.

2 If more than one item of goods in a class is set forth and the dates given for that class apply to only one of the items listed, insert the name of the item to which the dates apply.

3 Type of commerce should be specified as "interstate," "territorial," "foreign," or other type of commerce which may lawfully be regulated by Congress. Foreign applicants relying upon use must specify commerce which Congress may regulate, using wording such as commerce with the United States or commerce between the United States and a foreign country.

4 If the mark is other than a coined, arbitrary or fanciful mark, and the mark is believed to have acquired a secondary meaning, insert whichever of the following paragraphs is applicable:

a) The mark has become distinctive of applicant's goods as a result of substantially exclusive and continuous use in ______________________ (*type of commerce*) commerce for the five years next preceding the date of filing of this application.

b) The mark has become distinctive of applicant's goods as evidenced by the showing submitted separately.

5 Insert the manner or method of using the mark with the goods, i.e., "the goods," "the containers for the goods," "displays associated with the goods," "tags or labels affixed to the goods," or other method which may be in use.

6 The required fee of $175.00 for each class must be submitted. (An application to register the same mark for goods and/or services in more than one class may be filed; however, goods and/or services, and dates of use, by class, must be set out separately, and specimens and a fee for each class are required.)

Patent and Trademark Office • U.S. DEPT of COMMERCE

| TRADEMARK APPLICATION, PRINCIPAL REGISTER, WITH DECLARATION (Partnership) | MARK *(identify the mark)*<br><br>CLASS NO. *(if known)* |
|---|---|

TO THE COMMISSIONER OF PATENTS AND TRADEMARKS:

NAME OF PARTNERSHIP

NAMES OF PARTNERS

BUSINESS ADDRESS OF PARTNERSHIP

CITIZENSHIP OF PARTNERS

The above identified applicant has adopted and is using the trademark shown in the accompanying drawing [1] for the following goods: ______________________________

______________________________,

and requests that said mark be registered in the United States Patent and Trademark Office on the Principal Register established by the Act of July 5, 1946.

The trademark was first used on the goods [2] on ______________ *(date)*; was first used on the goods [2] in ______________ *(type of commerce)* commerce [3] on ______________ *(date)*; and is now in use in such commerce.

4

The mark is used by applying it to[5] ______________________________
and five specimens showing the mark as actually used are presented herewith.

6

______________________________
*(name of partner)*

being hereby warned that willful false statements and the like so made are punishable by fine or imprisonment, or both, under Section 1001 of Title 18 of the United States Code and that such willful false statements may jeopardize the validity of the application or any registration resulting therefrom, declares that he/she is a partner of applicant partnership; he/she believes said partnership to be the owner of the trademark sought to be registered; to the best of his/her knowledge and belief no other person, firm, corporation, or association has the right to use said mark in commerce, either in the identical form or in such near resemblance thereto as may be likely, when applied to the goods of such other person, to cause confusion, or to cause mistake, or to deceive; the facts set forth in this application are true; and all statements made of his/her own knowledge are true and all statements made on information and belief are believed to be true.

______________________________
*(signature of partner)*

______________________________
*(date)*

PTO-1477 (Trademark) (Partnership) (Rev. 12-83)

Patent and Trademark Office - U.S. DEPT. of COMMERCE

*(over)*

PTO–1477 (Trademark) (Partnership) (Rev. 12-83)

## REPRESENTATION

If the applicant is not domiciled in the United States, a domestic representative must be designated. See Form PTO–FB–TM 151.

If applicant wishes to furnish a power of attorney, see Form PTO–FB–TM 150. An attorney at law is not required to furnish a power.

## FOOTNOTES

1 If registration is sought for a word or numeral mark not depicted in any special form, the drawing may be the mark typed in capital letters on letter-size bond paper; otherwise, the drawing should be made with india ink on a good grade of bond paper or on bristol board.

2 If more than one item of goods in a class is set forth and the dates given for that class apply to only one of the items listed, insert the name of the item to which the dates apply.

3 Type of commerce should be specified as "interstate," "territorial," "foreign," or other type of commerce which may lawfully be regulated by Congress. Foreign applicants relying upon use must specify commerce which Congress may regulate, using wording such as commerce with the United States or commerce between the United States and a foreign country.

4 If the mark is other than a coined, arbitrary or fanciful mark, and the mark is believed to have acquired a secondary meaning, insert whichever of the following paragraphs is applicable:

a) The mark has become distinctive of applicant's goods as a result of substantially exclusive and continuous use in ______________ (*type of commerce*) commerce for the five years next preceding the date of filing of this application.

b) The mark has become distinctive of applicant's goods as evidenced by the showing submitted separately.

5 Insert the manner or method of using the mark with the goods, i.e., "the goods," "the containers for the goods," "displays associated with the goods," "tags or labels affixed to the goods," or other method which may be in use.

6 The required fee of $175.00 for each class must be submitted. (An application to register the same mark for goods and/or services in more than one class may be filed; however, goods and/or services, and dates of use, by class, must be set out separately, and specimens and a fee for each class are required.)

Patent and Trademark Office - U.S. DEPT of COMMERCE

*(Instructions on reverse side)*

| **TRADEMARK APPLICATION, PRINCIPAL REGISTER, WITH OATH** (Corporation) | MARK *(identify the mark)* |
|---|---|
| | CLASS NO. *(if known)* |

TO THE COMMISSIONER OF PATENTS AND TRADEMARKS:

NAME OF CORPORATION [1]

STATE OR COUNTRY OF INCORPORATION

BUSINESS ADDRESS OF CORPORATION

The above identified applicant has adopted and is using the trademark shown in the accompanying drawing [2] for the following goods: ______________________________

______________________________,

and requests that said mark be registered in the United States Patent and Trademark Office on the Principal Register established by the Act of July 5, 1946.

The trademark was first used on the goods [3] on ____________ *(date)*; was first used on the goods [3] in ____________ *(type of commerce)* commerce [4] on ____________ *(date)*; and is now in use in such commerce.

5

The mark is used by applying it to [6] ______________________________

______________________________

and five specimens showing the mark as actually used are presented herewith.

7

State of ____________ )
) ss.
County of ____________ )

______________________________
*(name of officer of corporation)*

states that he/she is ____________ *(official title)* of applicant corporation and is authorized to execute this instrument on behalf of said corporation; he/she believes said corporation to be owner of the trademark sought to be registered; to the best of his/her knowledge and belief no other person, firm, corporation or association has the right to use said mark in commerce, either in the identical form or in such near resemblance thereto as to be likely, when applied to the goods of such other person, to cause confusion, or to cause mistake, or to deceive; and the facts set forth in this application are true.

______________________________
*(name of corporation)*

By ______________________________
*(signature of officer of corporation, and official title of officer)*

JURAT:

Subscribed and sworn to before me, this ____________ day of ____________, ______.

______________________________
*(notary public)*

PTO-FB-TM 104 (Trademark) (Corporation) (Rev. 12-83) Patent and Trademark Office - U.S. DEPT of COMMERCE

*(over)*

PTO–FB–TM 104 (Trademark) (Corporation) (Rev. 12-83)

## REPRESENTATION

If the applicant is not domiciled in the United States, a domestic representative must be designated. See Form PTO–FB–TM 151.

If applicant wishes to furnish a power of attorney, see Form PTO–FB–TM 150. An attorney at law is not required to furnish a power.

## JURAT

The person who signs the jurat must be authorized to administer oaths by the law of the jurisdiction where executed, and the seal or stamp of the notary, or other evidence of authority in the jurisdiction of execution, must be affixed.

## FOOTNOTES

1 If applicant is an association or other similar type of juristic entity, change "corporation" throughout to an appropriate designation.

2 If registration is sought for a word or numeral mark not depicted in any special form, the drawing may be the mark typed in capital letters on letter-size bond paper; otherwise, the drawing should be made with india ink on a good grade of bond paper or on bristol board.

3 If more than one item of goods in a class is set forth and the dates given for that class apply to only one of the items listed, insert the name of the item to which the dates apply.

4 Type of commerce should be specified as "interstate," "territorial," "foreign," or other type of commerce which may lawfully be regulated by Congress. Foreign applicants relying upon use must specify commerce which Congress may regulate, using wording such as commerce with the United States or commerce between the United States and a foreign country.

5 If the mark is other than a coined, arbitrary or fanciful mark, and the mark is believed to have acquired a secondary meaning, insert whichever of the following paragraphs is applicable:

a) The mark has become distinctive of applicant's goods as a result of substantially exclusive and continuous use in ______________________ commerce for the five years next preceding the date
(type of commerce)
of filing of this application.

b) The mark has become distinctive of applicant's goods as evidenced by the showing submitted separately.

6 Insert the manner or method of using the mark with the goods, i.e., "the goods," "the containers for the goods," "displays associated with the goods," "tags or labels affixed to the goods," or other method which may be in use.

7 The required fee of $175.00 for each class must be submitted. (An application to register the same mark for goods and/or services in more than one class may be filed; however, goods and/or services, and dates of use, by class, must be set out separately, and specimens and a fee for each class are required.)

Patent and Trademark Office - U.S. DEPT. OF COMMERCE

| **TRADEMARK APPLICATION, PRINCIPAL REGISTER, WITH DECLARATION** (Corporation) | MARK *(identify the mark)* |
|---|---|
| | CLASS NO. *(if known)* |

TO THE COMMISSIONER OF PATENTS AND TRADEMARKS:

NAME OF CORPORATION [1]

STATE OR COUNTRY OF INCORPORATION

BUSINESS ADDRESS OF CORPORATION

The above identified applicant has adopted and is using the trademark shown in the accompanying drawing [2] for the following goods: ______________________________

______________________________,

and requests that said mark be registered in the United States Patent and Trademark Office on the Principal Register established by the Act of July 5, 1946.

The trademark was first used on the goods [3] on ____________ *(date)*; was first used on the goods [3] in ______________ *(type of commerce)* commerce [4] on ______________ *(date)*; and is now in use in such commerce.

5

The mark is used by applying it to [6] ______________________________

and five specimens showing the mark as actually used are presented herewith.

7

______________________________
*(name of officer of corporation)*

being hereby warned that willful false statements and the like so made are punishable by fine or imprisonment, or both, under Section 1001 of Title 18 of the United States Code and that such willful false statements may jeopardize the validity of the application or any registration resulting therefrom, declares that he/she is ______________________________ *(official title)*

of applicant corporation and is authorized to execute this instrument on behalf of said corporation; he/she believes said corporation to be the owner of the trademark sought to be registered; to the best of his/her knowledge and belief no other person, firm, corporation, or association has the right to use said mark in commerce, either in the identical form or in such near resemblance thereto as may be likely, when applied to the goods of such other person, to cause confusion, or to cause mistake, or to deceive; the facts set forth in this application are true; and all statements made of his/her own knowledge are true and all statements made on information and belief are believed to be true.

______________________________
*(name of corporation)*

By ______________________________,
*(signature of officer of corporation, and official title of officer)*

______________________________
*(date)*

PTO-1478 (Trademark) (Corporation) (Rev. 12-83) Patent and Trademark Office - U.S. DEPT. of COMMERCE

*(over)*

PTO–1478 (Trademark) (Corporation) (Rev. 12-83)

REPRESENTATION

If the applicant is not domiciled in the United States, a domestic representative must be designated. See Form PTO–FB–TM 151.

If applicant wishes to furnish a power of attorney, see Form PTO–FB–TM 150. An attorney at law is not required to furnish a power.

FOOTNOTES

1 If applicant is an association or other similar type of juristic entity, change "corporation" throughout to an appropriate designation.

2 If registration is sought for a word or numeral mark not depicted in any special form, the drawing may be the mark typed in capital letters on letter-size bond paper; otherwise, the drawing should be made with india ink on a good grade of bond paper or on bristol board.

3 If more than one item of goods in a class is set forth and the dates given for that class apply to only one of the items listed, insert the name of the item to which the dates apply.

4 Type of commerce should be specified as "interstate," "territorial," "foreign," or other type of commerce which may lawfully be regulated by Congress. Foreign applicants relying upon use must specify commerce which Congress may regulate, using wording such as commerce with the United States or commerce between the United States and a foreign country.

5 If the mark is other than a coined, arbitrary or fanciful mark, and the mark is believed to have acquired a secondary meaning, insert whichever of the following paragraphs is applicable:

a) The mark has become distinctive of applicant's goods as a result of substantially exclusive and continuous use in ______________________ commerce for the five years next preceding the date
(type of commerce)
of filing of this application.

b) The mark has become distinctive of applicant's goods as evidenced by the showing submitted separately.

6 Insert the manner or method of using the mark with the goods, i.e., "the goods," "the containers for the goods," "displays associated with the goods," "tags or labels affixed to the goods," or other method which may be in use.

7 The required fee of $175.00 for each class must be submitted. (An application to register the same mark for goods and/or services in more than one class may be filed; however, goods and/or services, and dates of use, by class, must be set out separately, and specimens and a fee for each class are required.)

Patent and Trademark Office - U.S. DEPT of COMMERCE

| **SERVICE MARK APPLICATION, PRINCIPAL REGISTER, WITH OATH** (Individual) | MARK *(identify the mark)* |
|---|---|
| | CLASS NO. *(if known)* |

TO THE COMMISSIONER OF PATENTS AND TRADEMARKS:

NAME OF APPLICANT, AND BUSINESS TRADE NAME, IF ANY

BUSINESS ADDRESS

RESIDENCE ADDRESS

CITIZENSHIP OF APPLICANT

The above identified applicant has adopted and is using the service mark shown in the accompanying drawing [1] for the following services ______________________________

______________________________________________________________,
and requests that said mark be registered in the United States Patent and Trademark Office on the Principal Register established by the Act of July 5, 1946.

The service mark was first used in connection with the services [2] on ______________ *(date)* ; was first used in connection with the services [2] rendered in ______________________ *(type of commerce)* commerce [3] on ______________________ *(date)* ; and is now in use in such commerce.

4

The mark is used by [5] ______________________________________________

______________________________________________________________

and five specimens showing the mark as actually used are presented herewith.

6

State of ______________________________ )
 ) ss.
County of ______________________________ )

______________________________
*(name of applicant)*

states that he/she believes himself/herself to be the owner of the service mark sought to be registered; to the best of his/her knowledge and belief no other person, firm, corporation or association has the right to use said mark in commerce, either in the identical form or in such near resemblance thereto as to be likely, when applied to the services of such other person, to cause confusion, or to cause mistake, or to deceive; and the facts set forth in this application are true.

______________________________
*(signature of applicant)*

JURAT:

Subscribed and sworn to before me, this ______________ day of ______________ , ____.

______________________________
*(notary public)*

PTO-FB-TM 106 (Service Mark) (Individual) (Rev. 12-83) Patent and Trademark Office - U.S. DEPT. of COMMERCE

*(over)*

PTO–FB–TM 106 (Service Mark) (Individual) (Rev. 12-83)

## REPRESENTATION

If the applicant is not domiciled in the United States, a domestic representative must be designated. See Form PTO–FB–TM 151.

If applicant wishes to furnish a power of attorney, see Form PTO–FB–TM 150. An attorney at law is not required to furnish a power.

## JURAT

The person who signs the jurat must be authorized to administer oaths by the law of the jurisdiction where executed, and the seal or stamp of the notary, or other evidence of authority in the jurisdiction of execution, must be affixed.

## FOOTNOTES

1 If registration is sought for a word or numeral mark not depicted in any special form, the drawing may be the mark typed in capital letters on letter-size bond paper; otherwise, the drawing should be made with india ink on a good grade of bond paper or on bristol board. If the mark is of a nature that a drawing is not practicable, insert a description of the mark instead of reference to the drawing.

2 If more than one item of services in a class is set forth and the dates given for that class apply to only one of the items listed, insert the name of the item to which the dates apply.

3 Type of commerce should be specified as "interstate," "territorial," "foreign," or other type of commerce which may lawfully be regulated by Congress. Foreign applicants relying upon use must specify commerce which Congress may regulate, using wording such as commerce with the United States or commerce between the United States and a foreign country.

4 If the mark is other than a coined, arbitrary or fanciful mark, and the mark is believed to have acquired a secondary meaning, insert whichever of the following paragraphs is applicable:

a) The mark has become distinctive of applicant's services as a result of substantially exclusive continuous use in ______________________ commerce for the five years next preceding the date
(type of commerce)
of filing of this application.

b) The mark has become distinctive of applicant's services as evidenced by the showing submitted separately.

5 State the manner or method of using the mark in the sale or advertising of the services.

6 The required fee of $175.00 for each class must be submitted. (An application to register the same mark for goods and/or services in more than one class may be filed; however, goods and/or services, and dates of use, by class, must be set out separately, and specimens and a fee for each class are required.)

Patent and Trademark Office - U.S. DEPT of COMMERCE

| **SERVICE MARK APPLICATION, PRINCIPAL REGISTER, WITH DECLARATION** (Individual) | MARK *(identify the mark)* |
|---|---|
| | CLASS NO. *(if known)* |

TO THE COMMISSIONER OF PATENTS AND TRADEMARKS:

NAME OF APPLICANT, AND BUSINESS TRADE NAME, IF ANY

BUSINESS ADDRESS

RESIDENCE ADDRESS

CITIZENSHIP OF APPLICANT

The above identified applicant has adopted and is using the service mark shown in the accompanying drawing [1] for the following services: ____________________

____________________,

and requests that said mark be registered in the United States Patent and Trademark Office on the Principal Register established by the Act of July 5, 1946.

The service mark was first used in connection with the services [2] on ____________ *(date)* ; was first used in connection with the services [2] rendered in ____________ *(type of commerce)* commerce [3] on ____________ *(date)* ; and is now in use in such commerce.

4

The mark is used by [5] ____________________

____________________

and five specimens showing the mark as actually used are presented herewith.

6

____________________
*(name of applicant)*

being hereby warned that willful false statements and the like so made are punishable by fine or imprisonment, or both, under Section 1001 of Title 18 of the United States Code and that such willful false statements may jeopardize the validity of the application or any registration resulting therefrom, declares that he/she believes himself/herself to be the owner of the service mark sought to be registered; to the best of his/her knowledge and belief no other person, firm, corporation, or association has the right to use said mark in commerce, either in the identical form or in such near resemblance thereto as may be likely, when applied to the services of such other person, to cause confusion, or to cause mistake or to deceive; the facts set forth in this application are true; and all statements made of his/her own knowledge are true and all statements made on information and belief are believed to be true.

____________________
*(signature of applicant)*

____________________
*(date)*

PTO-FB-TM 107 (Service Mark) (Individual) (Rev. 12-83) Patent and Trademark Office - U.S. DEPT. of COMMERCE

*(over)*

PTO–FB–TM 107 (Service Mark) (Individual) (Rev. 12-83)

## REPRESENTATION

If the applicant is not domiciled in the United States, a domestic representative must be designated. See Form PTO–FB–TM 151.

If applicant wishes to furnish a power of attorney, see Form PTO–FB–TM 150. An attorney at law is not required to furnish a power.

## FOOTNOTES

1 If registration is sought for a word or numeral mark not depicted in any special form, the drawing may be the mark typed in capital letters on letter-size bond paper; otherwise, the drawing should be made with india ink on a good grade of bond paper or on bristol board. If the mark is of a nature that a drawing is not practicable, insert a description of the mark instead of reference to the drawing.

2 If more than one item of services in a class is set forth and the dates given for that class apply to only one of the items listed, insert the name of the item to which the dates apply.

3 Type of commerce should be specified as "interstate," "territorial," "foreign," or other type of commerce which may lawfully be regulated by Congress. Foreign applicants relying upon use must specify commerce which Congress may regulate, using wording such as commerce with the United States or commerce between the United States and a foreign country.

4 If the mark is other than a coined, arbitrary or fanciful mark, and the mark is believed to have acquired a secondary meaning, insert whichever of the following paragraphs is applicable:

a) The mark has become distinctive of applicant's services as a result of substantially exclusive and continuous use in ______________________ *(type of commerce)* commerce for the five years next preceding the date of filing of this application.

b) The mark has become distinctive of applicant's services as evidenced by the showing submitted separately.

5 State the manner or method of using the mark in the sale or advertising of the services.

6 The required fee of $175.00 for each class must be submitted. (An application to register the same mark for goods and/or services in more than one class may be filed; however, goods and/or services, and dates of use, by class, must be set out separately, and specimens and a fee for each class are required.)

Patent and Trademark Office - U.S. DEPT. of COMMERCE

| **SERVICE MARK APPLICATION, PRINCIPAL REGISTER, WITH OATH** (Partnership) | MARK *(identify the mark)* |
|---|---|
| | CLASS NO. *(if known)* |

TO THE COMMISSIONER OF PATENTS AND TRADEMARKS:

NAME OF PARTNERSHIP

NAMES OF PARTNERS

BUSINESS ADDRESS OF PARTNERSHIP

CITIZENSHIP OF PARTNERS

The above identified applicant has adopted and is using the service mark shown in the accompanying drawing [1] for the following services: ______________________________

______________________________,

and requests that said mark be registered in the United States Patent and Trademark Office on the Principal Register established by the Act of July 5, 1946.

The service mark was first used in connection with the services [2] on ______________ *(date)* ; was first used in connection with the services [2] rendered in ______________ *(type of commerce)* commerce [3] on ______________ *(date)* ; and is now in use in such commerce.

4

The mark is used by [5] ______________________________

______________________________

and five specimens showing the mark as actually used are presented herewith.

6

State of ______________________ )
) ss.
County of ______________________ )

______________________
*(name of partner)*

states that he/she is a partner of applicant partnership, he/she believes said partnership to be the owner of the service mark sought to be registered; to the best of his/her knowledge and belief no other person, firm, corporation or association has the right to use said mark in commerce, either in the identical form or in such near resemblance thereto as to be likely, when applied to the services of such other person, to cause confusion, or to cause mistake, or to deceive; and the facts set forth in this application are true.

______________________
*(signature of partner)*

JURAT:

Subscribed and sworn to before me, this ________ day of ______________, ______.

______________________
*(notary public)*

PTO-FB-TM 108 (Service Mark) (Partnership) (Rev. 12-83) Patent and Trademark Office - U.S. DEPT. of COMMERCE

*(over)*

PTO–FB–TM 108 (Service Mark) (Partnership) (Rev. 12-83)

REPRESENTATION

If the applicant is not domiciled in the United States, a domestic representative must be designated. See Form PTO–FB–TM 151.

If applicant wishes tof urnish a power of attorney, see Form PTO–FB–TM 150. An attorney at law is not required to furnish a power.

JURAT

The person who signs the jurat must be authorized to administer oaths by the law of the jurisdiction where executed, and the seal or stamp of the notary, or other evidence of authority in the jurisdiction of execution, must be affixed.

FOOTNOTES

1 If registration is sought for a word or numeral mark not depicted in any special form, the drawing may be the mark typed in capital letters on letter-size bond paper; otherwise, the drawing should be made with india ink on a good grade of bond paper or on bristol board. If the mark is of a nature that a drawing is not practicable, insert a description of the mark instead of reference to the drawing.

2 If more than one item of services in a class is set forth and the dates given for that class apply to only one of the items listed, insert the name of the item to which the dates apply.

3 Type of commerce should be specified as "interstate," "territorial," "foreign," or other type of commerce which may lawfully be regulated by Congress. Foreign applicants relying upon use must specify commerce which Congress may regulate, using wording such as commerce with the United States or commerce between the United States and a foreign country.

4 If the mark is other than a coined, arbitrary or fanciful mark, and the mark is believed to have acquired a secondary meaning, insert whichever of the following paragraphs is applicable:

a) The mark has become distinctive of applicant's services as a result of substantially exclusive and continuous use in ______________________ commerce for the five years next preceding the
*(type of commerce)*
date of filing of this application.

b) The mark has become distinctive of applicant's services as evidenced by the showing submitted separately.

5 State the manner or method of using the mark in the sale or advertising of the services.

6 The required fee of $175.00 for each class must be submitted. (An application to register the same mark for goods and/or services in more than one class may be filed; however, goods and/or services, and dates of use, by class, must be set out separately, and specimens and a fee for each class are required.)

Patent and Trademark Office - U.S. DEPT. OF COMMERCE

| **SERVICE MARK APPLICATION, PRINCIPAL REGISTER, WITH DECLARATION** (Partnership) | MARK *(identify the mark)* |
|---|---|
| | CLASS NO. *(if known)* |

TO THE COMMISSIONER OF PATENTS AND TRADEMARKS:

NAME OF PARTNERSHIP

NAMES OF PARTNERS

BUSINESS ADDRESS OF PARTNERSHIP

CITIZENSHIP OF PARTNERS

The above identified applicant has adopted and is using the service mark shown in the accompanying drawing [1] for the following services: ______________________________

______________________________,
and requests that said mark be registered in the United States Patent and Trademark Office on the Principal Register established by the Act of July 5, 1946.

The service mark was first used in connection with the services [2] on ______________ *(date)* ; was first used in connection with the services [2] rendered in ______________ *(type of commerce)* commerce [3] on ______________ *(date)* ; and is now in use in such commerce.

4

The mark is used by [5] ______________________________

______________________________
and five specimens showing the mark as actually used are presented herewith.

6

______________________________
*(name of partner)*

being hereby warned that willful false statements and the like so made are punishable by fine or imprisonment, or both, under Section 1001 of Title 18 of the United States Code and that such willful false statements may jeopardize the validity of the application or any registration resulting therefrom, declares that he/she is a partner of applicant partnership; he/she believes said partnership to be the owner of the service mark sought to be registered; to the best of his/her knowledge and belief no other person, firm, corporation, or association has the right to use said mark in commerce, either in the identical form or in such near resemblance thereto as may be likely, when applied to the services of such other person, to cause confusion, or to cause mistake, or to deceive; the facts set forth in this application are true; and all statements made of his/her own knowledge are true and all statements made on information and belief are believed to be true.

______________________________
*(signature of partner)*

______________________________
*(date)*

PTO-FB-TM 109 (Service Mark) (Partnership )(Rev. 12-83) Patent and Trademark Office - U.S. DEPT. of COMMERCE

*(over)*

PTO–FB–TM 109 (Service Mark) (Partnership) (Rev. 12-83)

## REPRESENTATION

If the applicant is not domiciled in the United States, a domestic representative must be designated. See Form PTO–FB–TM 151.

If applicant wishes to furnish a power of attorney, see Form PTO–FB–TM 150. An attorney at law is not required to furnish a power.

## FOOTNOTES

1 If registration is sought for a word or numeral mark not depicted in any special form, the drawing may be the mark typed in capital letters on letter-size bond paper; otherwise, the drawing should be made with india ink on a good grade of bond paper or on bristol board. If the mark is of a nature that a drawing is not practicable, insert a description of the mark instead of reference to the drawing.

2 If more than one item of services in a class is set forth and the dates given for that class apply to only one of the items listed, insert the name of the item to which the dates apply.

3 Type of commerce should be specified as "interstate," "territorial," "foreign," or other type of commerce which may lawfully be regulated by Congress. Foreign applicants relying upon use must specify commerce which Congress may regulate, using wording such as commerce with the United States or commerce between the United States and a foreign country.

4 If the mark is other than a coined, arbitrary or fanciful mark, and the mark is believed to have acquired a secondary meaning, insert whichever of the following paragraphs is applicable:

a) The mark has become distinctive of applicant's services as a result of substantially exclusive and continuous use in ______________________ commerce for the five years next preceding the
*(type of commerce)*
date of filing of this application.

b) The mark has become distinctive of applicant's services as evidenced by the showing submitted separately.

5 State the manner or method of using the mark in the sale or advertising of the services.

6 The required fee of $175.00 for each class must be submitted. (An application to register the same mark for goods and/or services in more than one class may be filed; however, goods and/or services, and dates of use, by class, must be set out separately, and specimens and a fee for each class are required.)

*(Instructions on reverse side)*

| **SERVICE MARK APPLICATION, PRINCIPAL REGISTER, WITH OATH** (Corporation) | MARK *(identify the mark)* |
|---|---|
| | CLASS NO. *(if known)* |

TO THE COMMISSIONER OF PATENTS AND TRADEMARKS:

NAME OF CORPORATION [1]

STATE OR COUNTRY OF INCORPORATION

BUSINESS ADDRESS OF CORPORATION

The above identified applicant has adopted and is using the trademark shown in the accompanying drawing [2] for the following services: ______________________________

______________________________,

and requests that said mark be registered in the United States Patent and Trademark Office on the Principal Register established by the Act of July 5, 1946.

The service mark was first used in connection with the services [3] on ____________ *(date)*; was first used in connection with the services [3] rendered in ____________ *(type of commerce)* commerce [4] on ____________ *(date)*; and is now in use in such commerce.

5

The mark is used by [6] ______________________________

______________________________

and five specimens showing the mark as actually used are presented herewith.

7

State of ____________ )
) ss.
County of ____________ )

______________________________
*(name of officer of corporation)*

states that he/she is ______________________________
*(official title)*

of applicant corporation and is authorized to execute this instrument on behalf of said corporation; he/she believes said corporation to be the owner of the service mark sought to be registered; to the best of his/her knowledge and belief no other person, firm, corporation or association has the right to use said mark in commerce, either in the identical form or in such near resemblance thereto as to be likely, when applied to the services of such other person, to cause confusion, or to cause mistake, or to deceive; and the facts set forth in this application are true.

______________________________
*(name of corporation)*

By ______________________________
*(signature of officer of corporation, and official title of officer)*

JURAT:

Subscribed and sworn to before me, this ________ day of ____________, ____.

______________________________
*(notary public)*

PTO-FB-TM 110 (Service Mark) (Corporation) (Rev. 12-83) Patent and Trademark Office - U.S. DEPT. of COMMERCE

*(over)*

PTO–FB–TM 110 (Service Mark) (Corporation) (Rev. 12-83)

## REPRESENTATION

If the applicant is not domiciled in the United States, a domestic representative must be designated. See Form PTO–FB–TM 151.

If applicant wishes to furnish a power of attorney, see Form PTO–FB–TM 150. An attorney at law is not required to furnish a power.

## JURAT

The person who signs the jurat must be authorized to administer oaths by the law of the jurisdiction where executed, and the seal or stamp of the notary, or other evidence of authority in the jurisdiction of execution, must be affixed.

## FOOTNOTES

1 If applicant is an association or other similar type of juristic entity, change "corporation" throughout to an appropriate designation.

2 If registration is sought for a word or numeral mark not depicted in any special form, the drawing may be the mark typed in capital letters on letter-size bond paper; otherwise, the drawing should be made with india ink on a good grade of bond paper or on bristol board. If the mark is of a nature that a drawing is not practicable, insert a description of the mark instead of reference to the drawing.

3 If more than one item of services in a class is set forth and the dates given for that class apply to only one of the items listed, insert the name of the item to which the dates apply.

4 Type of commerce should be specified as "interstate," "territorial," "foreign," or other type of commerce which may lawfully be regulated by Congress. Foreign applicants relying upon use must specify commerce which Congress may regulate, using wording such as commerce with the United States or commerce between the United States and a foreign country.

5 If the mark is other than a coined, arbitrary or fanciful mark, and the mark is believed to have acquired a secondary meaning, insert whichever of the following paragraphs is applicable:

a) The mark has become distinctive of applicant's services as a result of substantially exclusive and continuous use in ______________________ commerce for the five years next preceding the date
*(type of commerce)*
of filing of this application.

b) The mark has become distinctive of applicant's services as evidenced by the showing submitted separately.

6 State the manner or method of using the mark in the sale or advertising of the services.

7 The required fee of $175.00 for each class must be submitted. (An application to register the same mark for goods and/or services in more than one class may be filed, however, goods and/or services, and dates of use, by class, must be set out separately, and specimens and a fee for each class are required.)

Patent and Trademark Office - U.S. DEPT. of COMMERCE

| **SERVICE MARK APPLICATION, PRINCIPAL REGISTER, WITH DECLARATION** (Corporation) | MARK *(identify the mark)* |
|---|---|
| | CLASS NO. *(if known)* |

TO THE COMMISSIONER OF PATENTS AND TRADEMARKS:

NAME OF PARTNERSHIP

NAMES OF PARTNERS

BUSINESS ADDRESS OF PARTNERSHIP

CITIZENSHIP OF PARTNERS

The above identified applicant has adopted and is using the service mark shown in the accompanying drawing [2] for the following services: ______

______,

and requests that said mark be registered in the United States Patent and Trademark Office on the Principal Register established by the Act of July 5, 1946.

The service mark was first used in connection with the services [3] on ______ *(date)* ; was first used in connection with the services [3] rendered in ______ *(type of commerce)* commerce [4] on ______ *(date)* ; and is now in use in such commerce.

5

The mark is used by [6] ______

______

and five specimens showing the mark as actually used are presented herewith.

7

______
*(name of officer of corporation)*

being hereby warned that willful false statements and the like so made are punishable by fine or imprisonment, or both, under Section 1001 of Title 18 of the United States Code and that such willful false statements may jeopardize the validity of the application or any registration resulting therefrom, declares that he/she is ______ *(official title)*

of applicant corporation and is authorized to execute this instrument on behalf of said corporation; he/she believes said corporation to be the owner of the service mark sought to be registered; to the best of his/her knowledge and belief no other person, firm, corporation, or association has the right to use said mark in commerce, either in the identical form or in such near resemblance thereto as may be likely, when applied to the services of such other person, to cause confusion, or to cause mistake, or to deceive; the facts set forth in this application are true; and all statements made of his/her own knowledge are true and all statements made on information and belief are believed to be true.

______
*(name of corporation)*

By ______
*(signature of officer of corporation, and official title of officer)*

______
*(date)*

PTO-FB-TM 111 (Service Mark) (Corporation) (Rev. 12-83) Patent and Trademark Office - U.S. DEPT. of COMMERCE

*(over)*

PTO–FB–TM 111 (Service Mark) (Corporation) (Rev. 12-83)

## REPRESENTATION

If the applicant is not domiciled in the United States, a domestic representative must be designated. See Form PTO–FB–TM 151.

If applicant wishes to furnish a power of attorney, see Form PTO–FB–TM 150. An attorney at law is not required to furnish a power.

## FOOTNOTES

1 If applicant is an association or other similar type of juristic entity, change "corporation" throughout to an appropriate designation.

2 If registration is sought for a word or numeral mark not depicted in any special form, the drawing may be the mark typed in capital letters on letter-size bond paper; otherwise, the drawing should be made with india ink on a good grade of bond paper or on bristol board. If the mark is of a nature that a drawing is not practicable, insert a description of the mark instead of reference to the drawing.

3 If more than one item of services in a class is set forth and the dates given for that class apply to only one of the items listed, insert the name of the item to which the dates apply.

4 Type of commerce should be specified as "interstate," "territorial," "foreign," or other type of commerce which may lawfully be regulated by Congress. Foreign applicants relying upon use must specify commerce which Congress may regulate, using wording such as commerce with the United States or commerce between the United States and a foreign country.

5 If the mark is other than a coined, arbitrary or fanciful mark, and the mark is believed to have acquired a secondary meaning, insert whichever of the following paragraphs is applicable:

a) The mark has become distinctive of applicant's services as a result of substantially exclusive and continuous use in ______________________ commerce for the five years next preceding the date
*(type of commerce)*
of filing of this application.

b) The mark has become distinctive of applicant's services as evidenced by the showing submitted separately.

6 State the manner or method of using the mark in the sale or advertising of the services.

7 The required fee of $175.00 for each class must be submitted. (An application to register the same mark for goods and/or services in more than one class may be filed; however, goods and/or services, and dates of use, by class, must be set out separately, and specimens and a fee for each class are required.)

Patent and Trademark Office - U.S. DEPT. of COMMERCE

| **COLLECTIVE TRADEMARK OR COLLECTIVE SERVICE MARK APPLICATION, PRINCIPAL REGISTER, WITH OATH** (Corporation) | MARK *(identify the mark)* |
|---|---|
| | CLASS NO. *(if known)* |

TO THE COMMISSIONER OF PATENTS AND TRADEMARKS:

NAME OF PARTNERSHIP

NAMES OF PARTNERS

BUSINESS ADDRESS OF PARTNERSHIP

CITIZENSHIP OF PARTNERS

The above identified applicant has adopted and is exercising legitimate control over the use of the collective mark shown in the accompanying drawing [2] for the following goods (services)[3]: ____________

________________________________________________________________,
and requests that said mark be registered in the United States Patent and Trademark Office on the Principal Register established by the Act of July 5, 1946.

The collective mark was first used on the goods (services)[3, 4] by members of applicant on ______ *(date)*; was first used by said members on the goods (services) [4] in __________________ *(type of commerce)* commerce [5] on ______________________ *(date)*; and is now in use in such commerce.

6

The mark is used by applying it to [7] ______________________________________

______________________________________________________________
and five specimens showing the mark as actually used are presented herewith.

8

State of ____________________________ )
) ss.
County of ___________________________ )

______________________________________________________________
*(name of officer of corporation)*

states that he/she is ___________________________________________
*(official title)*

of applicant corporation and is authorized to execute this instrument on behalf of said corporation; he/she believes said corporation to be the owner of the collective mark sought to be registered; to the best of his/her knowledge and belief no other person, firm, corporation or association has the right to use said mark in commerce, either in the identical form or in such near resemblance thereto as to be likely, when applied to the goods (services)[3] of such other person, to cause confusion, or to cause mistake, or to deceive; and the facts set forth in this application are true.

______________________________
*(name of corporation)*

By ______________________________

______________________________
*(signature of officer of corporation, and official title of officer)*

JURAT:

Subscribed and sworn to before me this ________ day of __________________, ____.

______________________________
*(notary public)*

PTO-FB-TM 112 (Collective Mark) (Corporation) (Rev. 12-83) Patent and Trademark Office - U.S. DEPT. of COMMERCE

(over)

PTO–FB–TM 112 (Collective Mark) (Corporation) (Rev. 12-83)

## REPRESENTATION

If the applicant is not domiciled in the United States, a domestic representative must be designated. See Form PTO–FB–TM 151.
If applicant wishes to furnish a power of attorney, see Form PTO–FB–TM 150. An attorney at law is not required to furnish a power.

## JURAT

The person who signs the jurat must be authorized to administer oaths by the law of the jurisdiction where executed, and the seal or stamp of the notary, or other evidence of authority in the jurisdiction of execution, must be affixed.

## FOOTNOTES

1 If applicant is an association or other similar type of juristic entity, change "corporation" throughout to an appropriate designation.

2 If registration is sought for a word or numeral mark not depicted in any special form, the drawing may be the mark typed in capital letters on letter-size bond paper; otherwise, the drawing should be made with india ink on a good grade of bond paper or on bristol board.

3 Delete the word "goods" or the word "services," as appropriate. (An application to register the same mark for goods and/or services in more than one class may be filed; however, goods and/or services, and dates of use, by class, must be set out separately, and specimens and a fee for each class are required.)

4 If more than one item of goods (or services) in a class is set forth and the dates given for that class apply to only one of the items listed in that class, insert the name of the item to which the dates apply for that class.

5 Type of commerce should be specified as "interstate," "territorial," "foreign," or other type of commerce which may lawfully be regulated by Congress. Foreign applicants relying upon use must specify commerce which Congress may regulate, using wording such as commerce with the United States or commerce between the United States and a foreign country.

6 If the mark is other than a coined, arbitrary or fanciful mark, and the mark is believed to have acquired a secondary meaning, insert whichever of the following paragraphs is applicable:

a) The mark has become distinctive of the goods (or services) as a result of substantially exclusive and continuous use in ________________________ commerce for the five years next preceding the
*(type of commerce)*
date of filing of this application.

b) The mark has become distinctive of the goods (or services) as evidenced by the showing submitted separately.

7 Insert the manner or method of using the mark with the goods, i.e., "the goods," "the containers for the goods," "displays associated with the goods," "tags or labels affixed to the goods," or other method which may be in use; or state the manner or method of using the mark in the sale or advertising of the services.

8 The required fee of $175.00 for each class must be submitted.

Patent and Trademark Office - U.S. DEPT. of COMMERCE

| COLLECTIVE TRADEMARK OR COLLECTIVE SERVICE MARK APPLICATION, PRINCIPAL REGISTER, WITH DECLARATION (Corporation) | MARK *(identify the mark)*<br><br>CLASS NO. *(if known, using the class numbers for goods and services)* |
|---|---|

TO THE COMMISSIONER OF PATENTS AND TRADEMARKS:

NAME OF CORPORATION [1]

STATE OR COUNTRY OF INCORPORATION

BUSINESS ADDRESS OF CORPORATION

The above identified applicant has adopted and is exercising legitimate control over the use of the collective mark shown in the accompanying drawing [2] for the following goods (services)[3]: ___________

_______________________________________________,

and requests that said mark be registered in the United States Patent and Trademark Office on the Principal Register established by the Act of July 5, 1946.

The collective mark was first used on the goods (services)[3, 4] by members of applicant on _______ *(date)*; was first used by said members on the goods (services) [4] in ____________ *(type of commerce)* commerce [5] on ______________ *(date)*; and is now in use in such commerce.

6

The mark is used by applying it to [7] _______________________________

_______________________________________________

and five specimens showing the mark as actually used are presented herewith.

8

_______________________________
*(name of officer of corporation)*

being hereby warned that willful false statements and the like so made are punishable by fine or imprisonment, or both, under Section 1001 of Title 18 of the United States Code and that such willful false statements may jeopardize the validity of the application or any registration resulting therefrom, declares that he/she is ______________________ *(official title)*

of applicant corporation and is authorized to execute this instrument on behalf of said corporation; he/she believes said corporation to be the owner of the collective mark sought to be registered; to the best of his/her knowledge and belief no other person, firm, corporation or association has the right to use said mark in commerce, either in the identical form or in such near resemblance thereto as may be likely, when applied to the goods (services)[3] of such other person, to cause confusion, or to cause mistake, or to deceive; the facts set forth in this application are true; and all statements made of his/her own knowledge are true and all statements made on information and belief are believed to be true.

_______________________________
*(name of corporation)*

By _______________________________
*(signature of officer of corporation, and official title of officer)*

_______________________________
*(date)*

PTO-FB-TM 113 (Collective Mark) (Corporation) (Rev. 12-83) Patent and Trademark Office - U.S. DEPT. of COMMERCE

*(over)*

PTO–FB–TM 113 (Collective Mark) (Corporation) (Rev. 12-83)

## REPRESENTATION

If the applicant is not domiciled in the United States, a domestic representative must be designated. See Form PTO–FB–TM 151.

If applicant wishes to furnish a power of attorney, see Form PTO–FB–TM 150. An attorney at law is not required to furnish a power.

## FOOTNOTES

1 If applicant is an association or other similar type of juristic entity, change "corporation" throughout to an appropriate designation.

2 If registration is sought for a word or numeral mark not depicted in any special form, the drawing may be the mark typed in capital letters on letter-size bond paper; otherwise, the drawing should be made with india ink on a good grade of bond paper or on bristol board.

3 Delete the word "goods" or the word "services," as appropriate. (An application to register the same mark for goods and/or services in more than one class may be filed; however, goods and/or services, and dates of use, by class, must be set out separately, and specimens and a fee for each class are required.)

4 If more than one item of goods (or services) in a class is set forth and the dates given for that class apply to only one of the items listed in that class, insert the name of the item to which the dates apply for that class.

5 Type of commerce should be specified as "interstate," "territorial," "foreign," or other type of commerce which may lawfully be regulated by Congress. Foreign applicants relying upon use must specify commerce which Congress may regulate, using wording such as commerce with the United States or commerce between the United States and a foreign country.

6 If the mark is other than a coined, arbitrary or fanciful mark, and the mark is believed to have acquired a secondary meaning, insert whichever of the following paragraphs is applicable:

a) The mark has become distinctive of the goods (or services) as a result of substantially exclusive and continuous use in ______________________ commerce for the five years next preceding the date of filing of this application.
*(type of commerce)*

b) The mark has become distinctive of the goods (or services) as evidenced by the showing submitted separately.

7 Insert the manner or method of using the mark with the goods, i.e., "the goods," "the containers for the goods," "displays associated with the goods," "tags or labels affixed to the goods," or other method which may be in use; or state the manner or method of using the mark in the sale or advertising of the services.

8 The required fee of $175.00 for each class must be submitted.

Patent and Trademark Office - U.S. DEPT. of COMMERCE

| COLLECTIVE MEMERSHIP MARK APPLICATION, PRINCIPAL REGISTER, WITH OATH (Corporation) | MARK *(identify the mark)* |
|---|---|
| | CLASS NO. 200 |

TO THE COMMISSIONER OF PATENTS AND TRADEMARKS:

NAME OF CORPORATION [1]

STATE OR COUNTRY OF INCORPORATION

BUSINESS ADDRESS OF CORPORATION

The above identified applicant has adopted and is exercising legitimate control over the use of the collective membership mark shown in the accompanying drawing [2] to indicate membership in applicant organization which is a [3]____________________________________________________________, and requests that said mark be registered in the United States Patent and Trademark Office on the Principal Register established by the Act of July 5, 1946.

The collective membership mark was first used by a member of applicant on ______________ *(date)*; was first used by a member of applicant in ________________ *(type of commerce)* commerce [4] on ________________ *(date)* and is now in use in such commerce.

[5]

The mark is used by applying it to [6] ________________________________________________________

__________________________________________________________________________

and five specimens showing the mark as actually used are presented herewith.

[7]

State of __________________________ )<br>
) ss.<br>
County of __________________________ )

________________________________________________
*(name of officer of corporation)*

states that he/she is ____________________________________________________________
*(official title)*

of applicant corporation and is authorized to execute this instrument on behalf of said corporation; he/she believes said corporation to be the owner of the collective membership mark sought to be registered; to the best of his/her knowledge and belief no other person, firm, corporation or association has the right to use said mark in commerce, either in the identical form or in such near resemblance thereto as to be likely, when used, to cause confusion, or to cause mistake, or to deceive; and the facts set forth in this application are true.

________________________________________
*(name of corporation)*

By ________________________________________,
*(signature of officer of corporation, and official title of officer)*

JURAT:

Subscribed and sworn to before me, this ___________ day of _______________, ____.

________________________________________
*(notary public)*

PTO-FB-TM 114 (Membership) (Corporation) (Rev. 12-83) Patent and Trademark Office - U.S. DEPT. of COMMERCE

*(over)*

PTO–FB–TM 114 (Membership) (Corporation) (Rev. 12-83)

## REPRESENTATION

If the applicant is not domiciled in the United States, a domestic representative must be designated. See Form PTO–FB–TM 151.

If applicant wishes to furnish a power of attorney, see Form PTO–FB–TM 150. An attorney at law is not required to furnish a power.

## JURAT

The person who signs the jurat must be authorized to administer oaths by the law of the jurisdiction where executed, and the seal or stamp of the notary, or other evidence of authority in the jurisdiction of execution, must be affixed.

## FOOTNOTES

1 If applicant is an association or other similar type of juristic entity, change "corporation" throughout to an appropriate designation.

2 If registration is sought for a word or numeral mark not depicted in any special form, the drawing may be the mark typed in capital letters on letter-size bond paper; otherwise, the drawing should be made with india ink on a good grade of bond paper or on bristol board.

3 State the general nature of the applicant organization, such as social club, chemical manufacturers' trade association, milk producers' association, political society, labor union, as may be appropriate.

4 Type of commerce should be specified as "interstate," "territorial," "foreign," or other type of commerce which may lawfully be regulated by Congress. Foreign applicants relying upon use must specify commerce which Congress may regulate, using wording such as commerce with the United States or commerce between the United States and a foreign country.

5 If the mark is other than a coined, arbitrary or fanciful mark, and the mark is believed to have acquired a secondary meaning, insert whichever of the following paragraphs is applicable:

a) The mark has become distinctive of membership as a result of substantially exclusive and continuous use in ______________________ commerce for the five years next preceding the date
*(type of commerce)*
of filing of this application.

b) The mark has become distinctive of membership as evidenced by the showing submitted separately.

6 Insert the manner or method of using the mark to indicate membership, such as membership cards or certificates, window decals, or other method which may be in use.

7 The required fee of $175.00 for the class must be submitted.

| TRADEMARK APPLICATION, SUPPLEMENTAL REGISTER, WITH OATH (Partnership) | MARK *(identify the mark)* |
|---|---|
| | CLASS NO. *(if known)* |

TO THE COMMISSIONER OF PATENTS AND TRADEMARKS:

NAME OF PARTNERSHIP

NAMES OF PARTNERS

BUSINESS ADDRESS OF PARTNERSHIP

CITIZENSHIP OF PARTNERS

The above identified applicant has adopted and is using the trademark shown in the accompanying drawing [1] for the following goods: ______________________________

______________________________,

and requests that said mark be registered in the United States Patent and Trademark Office on the Supplemental Register established by the Act of July 5, 1946.

The trademark was first used on the goods [2] on ____________ *(date)*; was first used on the goods [2] in ______________________ *(type of commerce)* commerce [3] on ______________ *(date)*; and is now in use in such commerce.

*(check one box)*

☐ The mark has been in lawful use in commerce on or in connection with the goods for the year preceding the filing of this application.

☐ The mark has not been in use in commerce for the full year preceding the filing of this application, but applicant requires domestic registration as a basis for foreign protection of the mark. (Applicant must submit a separate showing that domestic registration is in fact necessary for foreign protection of the mark before the full year's use will be waived.)

The mark is used by applying it to [4] ______________________________

______________________________

and five specimens showing the mark as actually used are presented herewith.

[5]

State of ______________________ )
) ss.
County of ______________________ )

______________________________
*(name of partner)*

states that he/she is a partner of applicant partnership; he/she believes said partnership to be the owner the trademark sought to be registered; to the best of his/her knowledge and belief no other person, firm, corporation or association has the right to use said mark in commerce, either in the identical form or in such near resemblance thereto as to be likely, when applied to the goods of such other person, to cause confusion, or to cause mistake, or to deceive; and the facts set forth in this application are true.

______________________________
*(signature of partner)*

JURAT:

Subscribed and sworn to before me, this ____________ day of ______________ , ____ .

______________________________
*(notary public)*

PTO-FB-TM 130 (TM, Supp. Reg.) (Partnership) (Rev. 12-83) Patent and Trademark Office - U.S. DEPT. of COMMERCE

*(over)*

PTO–FB–TM 130 (TM, Supp. Reg.) (Partnership) (Rev. 12-83)

## REPRESENTATION

If the applicant is not domiciled in the United States, a domestic representative must be designated. See Form PTO–FB–TM 151.

If applicant wishes to furnish a power of attorney, see Form PTO–FB–TM 150. An attorney at law is not required to furnish a power.

## JURAT

The person who signs the jurat must be authorized to administer oaths by the law of the jurisdiction where executed, and the seal or stamp of the notary, or other evidence of authority in the jurisdiction of execution, must be affixed.

## FOOTNOTES

1 If registration is sought for a word or numeral mark not depicted in any special form, the drawing may be the mark typed in capital letters on letter-size bond paper; otherwise, the drawing should be made with india ink on a good grade of bond paper or on bristol board.

2 If more than one item of goods in a class is set forth and the dates given for that class apply to only one of the items listed, insert the name of the item to which the dates apply.

3 Type of commerce should be specified as "interstate," "territorial," "foreign," or other type of commerce which may lawfully be regulated by Congress. Foreign applicants relying upon use must specify commerce which Congress may regulate, using wording such as commerce with the United States or commerce between the United States and a foreign country.

4 Insert the manner or method of using the mark with the goods, i.e., "the goods," "the containers for the goods," "displays associated with the goods," "tags or labels affixed to the goods," or other method which may be in use.

5 The required fee of $175.00 for each class must be submitted. (An application to register the same mark for goods and/or services in more than one class may be filed; however, goods and/or services, and dates of use, by class, must be set out separately, and specimens and a fee for each class are required.)

Patent and Trademark Office - U.S. DEPT. of COMMERCE

| **TRADEMARK APPLICATION, SUPPLEMENTAL REGISTER, WITH DECLARATION** (Partnership) | MARK *(identify the mark)* |
|---|---|
| | CLASS NO. *(if known)* |

TO THE COMMISSIONER OF PATENTS AND TRADEMARKS:

NAME OF PARTNERSHIP

NAMES OF PARTNERS

BUSINESS ADDRESS OF PARTNERSHIP

CITIZENSHIP OF PARTNERS

The above identified applicant has adopted and is using the trademark shown in the accompanying drawing [1] for the following goods: ______________________________

______________________________,

and requests that said mark be registered in the United States Patent and Trademark Office on the Supplemental Register established by the Act of July 5, 1946.

The trademark was first used on the goods [2] on ____________ *(date)* ; was first used on the goods [2] in ______________________ *(type of commerce)* commerce [3] on ____________ *(date)* ; and is now in use in such commerce.

*(check one box)*

☐ The mark has been in lawful use in commerce on or in connection with the goods for the year preceding the filing of this application.

☐ The mark has not been in use in commerce for the full year preceding the filing of this application, but applicant requires domestic registration as a basis for foreign protection of the mark. (Applicant must submit a separate showing that domestic registration is in fact necessary for foreign protection of the mark before the full year's use will be waived.)

The mark is used by applying it to [4] ______________________________

______________________________

and five specimens showing the mark as actually used are presented herewith.

[5]

______________________________
*(name of partner)*

being hereby warned that willful false statements and the like so made are punishable by fine or imprisonment, or both, under Section 1001 of Title 18 of the United States Code and that such willful false statements may jeopardize the validity of the application or any registration resulting therefrom, declares that he/she is a partner of applicant partnership; that he/she believes said partnership to be the owner of the trademark sought to be registered; to the best of his/her knowledge and belief no other person, firm, corporation, or association has the right to use said mark in commerce, either in the identical form or in such near resemblance thereto as may be likely, when applied to the goods of such other person, to cause confusion, or to cause mistake, or to deceive; the facts set forth in this application are true; and all statements made of his/her own knowledge are true and all statements made on information and belief are believed to be true.

______________________________
*(signature of partner)*

______________________________
*(date)*

PTO-FB-TM 131 (TM, Supp. Reg.) (Partnership) (Rev. 12-83) Patent and Trademark Office - U.S. DEPT. of COMMERCE

*(over)*

PTO–FB–TM 131 (TM, Supp. Reg.) (Partnership) (Rev. 12-83)

REPRESENTATION

If the applicant is not domiciled in the United States, a domestic representative must be designated. See Form PTO–FB–TM 151.

If applicant wishes to furnish a power of attorney, see Form PTO–FB–TM 150. An attorney at law is not required to furnish a power.

FOOTNOTES

1 If registration is sought for a word or numeral mark not depicted in any special form, the drawing may be the mark typed in capital letters on letter-size bond paper; otherwise, the drawing should be made with india ink on a good grade of bond paper or on bristol board.

2 If more than one item of goods in a class is set forth and the dates given for that class apply to only one of the items listed, insert the name of the item to which the dates apply.

3 Type of commerce should be specified as "interstate," "territorial," "foreign," or other type of commerce which may lawfully be regulated by Congress. Foreign applicants relying upon use must specify commerce which Congress may regulate, using wording such as commerce with the United States or commerce between the United States and a foreign country.

4 Insert the manner or method of using the mark with the goods, i.e., "the goods," "the containers for the goods," "displays associated with the goods," "tags or labels affixed to the goods," or other method which may be in use.

5 The required fee of $175.00 for each class must be submitted. (An application to register the same mark for goods and/or services in more than one class may be filed; however, goods and/or services, and dates of use, by class, must be set out separately, and specimens and a fee for each class are required.)

Patent and Trademark Office - U.S. DEPT. of COMMERCE

| **TRADEMARK APPLICATION, SUPPLEMENTAL REGISTER, WITH OATH** (Corporation) | MARK *(identify the mark)*<br><br>CLASS NO. *(if known)* |
|---|---|

TO THE COMMISSIONER OF PATENTS AND TRADEMARKS:

NAME OF CORPORATION [1]

STATE OR COUNTRY OF INCORPORATION

BUSINESS ADDRESS OF CORPORATION

The above identified applicant has adopted and is using the trademark shown in the accompanying drawing [2] for the following goods: ______________________________

______________________________, and requests that said mark be registered in the United States Patent and Trademark Office on the Supplemental Register established by the Act of July 5, 1946.

The trademark was first used on the goods [3] on ____________ *(date)* ; was first used on the goods [3] in ______________________ *(type of commerce)* commerce [4] on ______________ *(date)* ; and is now in use in such commerce.

*(check one box)*

☐ The mark has been in lawful use in commerce on or in connection with the goods for the year preceding the filing of this application.

☐ The mark has not been in use in commerce for the full year preceding the filing of this application, but applicant requires domestic registration as a basis for foreign protection of the mark. (Applicant must submit a separate showing that domestic registration is in fact necessary for foreign protection of the mark before the full year's use will be waived.)

The mark is used by applying it to [5] ______________________________

______________________________

and five specimens showing the mark as actually used are presented herewith.

[6]

State of ______________________ )
) ss.
County of ______________________ )

______________________________
*(name of officer of corporation)*

states that he/she is ______________________________
*(official title)*

of applicant corporation and is authorized to execute this instrument on behalf of said corporation; he/she believes said corporation to be the owner of the trademark sought to be registered; to the best of his/her knowledge and belief no other person, firm, corporation or association has the right to use said mark in commerce, either in the identical form or in such near resemblance thereto as to be likely, when applied to the goods of such other person, to cause confusion, or to cause mistake, or to deceive; and the facts set forth in this application are true.

______________________________
*(name of corporation)*

By ______________________________
*(signature of officer of corporation, and official title of officer)*

JURAT:

Subscribed and sworn to before me, this ____________ day of ____________ , ____ .

______________________________
*(notary public)*

PTO-FB-TM 132 (TM, Supp. Reg.) (Corporation) (Rev. 12-83) — Patent and Trademark Office - U.S. DEPT. of COMMERCE

*(over)*

## REPRESENTATION

If the applicant is not domiciled in the United States, a domestic representative must be designated. See Form PTO–FB–TM 151.

If applicant wishes to furnish a power of attorney, see Form PTO–FB–TM 150. An attorney at law is not required to furnish a power.

## JURAT

The person who signs the jurat must be authorized to administer oaths by the law of the jurisdiction where executed, and the seal or stamp of the notary, or other evidence of authority in the jurisdiction of execution, must be affixed.

## FOOTNOTES

1 If applicant is an association or other similar type of juristic entity, change "corporation" throughout to an appropriate designation.

2 If registration is sought for a word or numeral mark not depicted in any special form, the drawing may be the mark typed in capital letters on letter-size bond paper; otherwise, the drawing should be made with india ink on a good grade of bond paper or on bristol board.

3 If more than one item of goods in a class is set forth and the dates given for that class apply to only one of the items listed, insert the name of the item to which the dates apply.

4 Type of commerce should be specified as "interstate," "territorial," "foreign," or other type of commerce which may lawfully be regulated by Congress. Foreign applicants relying upon use must specify commerce which Congress may regulate, using wording such as commerce with the United States or commerce between the United States and a foreign country.

5 Insert the manner or method of using the mark with the goods, i.e., "the goods," "the containers for the goods," "displays associated with the goods," "tags or labels affixed to the goods," or other method which may be in use.

6 The required fee of $175.00 for each class must be submitted. (An application to register the same mark for goods and/or services in more than one class may be filed; however, goods and/or services, and dates of use, by class, must be set out separately, and specimens and a fee for each class are required.)

Patent and Trademark Office - U.S. DEPT. of COMMERCE

| TRADEMARK APPLICATION, SUPPLEMENTAL REGISTER, WITH DECLARATION (Corporation) | MARK *(identify the mark)* |
|---|---|
| | CLASS NO. *(if known)* |

TO THE COMMISSIONER OF PATENTS AND TRADEMARKS:

NAME OF CORPORATION [1]

STATE OR COUNTRY OF INCORPORATION

BUSINESS ADDRESS OF CORPORATION

The above identified applicant has adopted and is using the trademark shown in the accompanying drawing [2] for the following goods: ______________________________

______________________________,

and requests that said mark be registered in the United States Patent and Trademark Office on the Supplemental Register established by the Act of July 5, 1946.

The trademark was first used on the goods [3] on __________ *(date)* ; was first used on the goods [3] in ______________ *(type of commerce)* commerce [4] on ______________ *(date)* ; and is now in use in such commerce.

*(check one box)*

☐ The mark has been in lawful use in commerce on or in connection with the goods for the year preceding the filing of this application.

☐ The mark has not been in use in commerce for the full year preceding the filing of this application, but application requires domestic registration as a basis for foreign protection of the mark. (Applicant must submit a separate showing that domestic registration is in fact necessary for foreign protection of the mark before the full year's use will be waived.)

The mark is used by applying it to [5] ______________________________

______________________________

and five specimens showing the mark as actually used are presented herewith.

6

______________________________
*(name of officer of corporation)*

being hereby warned that willful false statements and the like so made are punishable by fine or imprisonment, or both, under Section 1001 of Title 18 of the United States Code and that such willful false statements may jeopardize the validity of the application or any registration resulting therefrom, declares that he/she is ______________ *(official title)* of applicant corporation and is authorized to execute this instrument on behalf of said corporation; he/she believes said corporation to be the owner of the trademark sought to be registered; to the best of his/her knowledge and belief no other person, firm, corporation, or association has the right to use said mark in commerce, either in the identical form or in such near resemblance thereto as may be likely, when applied to the goods of such other person, to cause confusion, or to cause mistake, or to deceive; the facts set forth in this application are true; and all statements made of his/her own knowledge are true and all statements on information and belief are believed to be true.

______________________________
*(name of corporation)*

By ______________________________
*(signature of officer of corporation, and official title of officer)*

______________________________
*(date)*

PTO-FB-TM 133 (TM, Supp. Reg.) (Corporation) (Rev. 12-83) — Patent and Trademark Office - U.S. DEPT. of COMMERCE

*(over)*

PTO–FB–TM 133 (TM, Supp. Reg.) (Corporation) (Rev. 12-83)

REPRESENTATION

If the applicant is not domiciled in the United States, a domestic representative must be designated. See Form PTO–FB–TM 151.

If applicant wishes to furnish a power of attorney, see Form PTO–FB–TM 150. An attorney at law is not required to furnish a power.

FOOTNOTES

1 If applicant is an association or other similar type of juristic entity, change "corporation" throughout to an appropriate designation.

2 If registration is sought for a word or numeral mark not depicted in any special form, the drawing may be the mark typed in capital letters on letter-size bond paper; otherwise, the drawing should be made with india ink on a grade of bond paper or on bristol board.

3 If more than one item of goods in a class is set forth and the dates given for that class apply to only one of the items listed, insert the name of the item to which the dates apply.

4 Type of commerce should be specified as "interstate," "territorial," "foreign," or other type of commerce which may lawfully be regulated by Congress. Foreign applicants relying upon use must specify commerce which Congress may regulate, using wording such as commerce with the United States or commerce between the United States and a foreign country.

5 Insert the manner or method of using the mark with the goods, i.e., "the goods," "the containers for the goods," "displays associated with the goods," "tags or labels affixed to the goods," or other method which may be in use.

6 The required fee of $175.00 for each class must be submitted. (An application to register the same mark for goods and/or services in more than one class may be filed; however, goods and/or services, and dates of use, by class, must be set out separately, and specimens and a fee for each class are required.)

Patent and Trademark Office - U.S. DEPT. of COMMERCE

| SERVICE MARK APPLICATION, SUPPLEMENTREGISTER, WITH OATH (Individual) | MARK *(identify the mark)* |
|---|---|
| | CLASS NO. *(If known)* |

TO THE COMMISSIONER OF PATENTS AND TRADEMARKS:

NAME OF APPLICANT, AND BUSINESS TRADE NAME, IF ANY

BUSINESS ADDRESS

RESIDENCE ADDRESS

CITIZENSHIP OF APPLICANT

The above identified applicant has adopted and is using the service mark shown in the accompanying drawing [1] for the following services: ______________________________

______________________________,
and requests that said mark be registered in the United States Patent and Trademark Office on the Supplemental Register established by the Act of July 5, 1946.

The service mark was first used in connection with the services [2] on ______________ *(date)* ; was first used in connection with the services [2] rendered in ______________ *(type of commerce)* commerce [3] on ______________ *(date)* ; and is now in use in such commerce.

*(Check one box)*

☐ The mark has been in lawful use in commerce on or in connection with the services for the year preceding the filing of this application.

☐ The mark has not been in use in commerce for the full year preceding the filing of this application, but applicant requires domestic registration as a basis for foreign protection of the mark. (Applicant must submit a separate showing that domestic registration is in fact necessary for foreign protection of the mark before the full year's use will be waived.)

The mark is used by [4] ______________________________

______________________________
and five specimens showing the mark as actually used are presented herewith.
[5]

State of ______________ )
) ss.
County of ______________ )

______________________________
*(name of applicant)*

states that he/she believes himself/herself to be the owner of the service mark sought to be registered; to the best of his/her knowledge and belief no other person, firm, corporation or association has the right to use said mark in commerce, either in the identical form or in such near resemblance thereto as to be likely, when applied to the services of such other person, to cause confusion, or to cause mistake, or to deceive; and the facts set forth in this application are true.

______________________________
*(signature of applicant)*

JURAT:

Subscribed and sworn to before me this ______ day of ______________ , ____ .

______________________________
*(notary public)*

PTO-FB-TM 134 (SM, Supp. Reg.) (Individual) (Rev. 12-83) Patent and Trademark Office - U.S. DEPT. of COMMERCE

*(over)*

PTO–FB–TM 134 (SM, Supp. Reg.) (Individual) (Rev. 12-83)

## REPRESENTATION

If the applicant is not domiciled in the United States, a domestic representative must be designated. See Form PTO–FB–TM 151.

If applicant wishes to furnish a power of attorney, see Form PTO–FB–TM 150. An attorney at law is not required to furnish a power.

## JURAT

The person who signs the jurat must be authorized to administer oaths by the law of the jurisdiction where executed, and the seal or stamp of the notary, or other evidence of authority in the jurisdiction of execution, must be affixed.

## FOOTNOTES

1 If registration is sought for a word or numeral mark not depicted in any special form, the drawing may be the mark typed in capital letters on letter-size bond paper; otherwise, the drawing should be made with india ink on a good grade of bond paper or on bristol board. If the mark is of a nature that a drawing is not practicable, insert a description of the mark instead of reference to the drawing.

2 If more than one item of services in a class is set forth and the dates given for that class apply to only one of the items listed, insert the name of the item to which the dates apply.

3 Type of commerce should be specified as "interstate," "territorial," "foreign," or other type of commerce which may lawfully be regulated by Congress. Foreign applicants relying upon use must specify commerce which Congress may regulate, using wording such as commerce with the United States or commerce between the United States and a foreign country.

4 State the manner or method of using the mark in the sale or advertising of the services.

5 The required fee of $175.00 for each class must be submitted. (An application to register the same mark for goods and/or services in more than one class may be filed; however, goods and/or services, and dates of use, by class, must be set out separately, and specimens and a fee for each class are required.)

Patent and Trademark Office - U.S. DEPT. of COMMERCE

(Instructions on reverse side)

| SERVICE MARK APPLICATION, SUPPLEMENTAL REGISTER, WITH DECLARATION (Individual) | MARK *(identify the mark)* |
|---|---|
| | CLASS NO. *(if known)* |

TO THE COMMISSIONER OF PATENTS AND TRADEMARKS:

NAME OF APPLICANT, AND BUSINESS TRADE NAME, IF ANY

BUSINESS ADDRESS

RESIDENCE ADDRESS

CITIZENSHIP OF APPLICANT

The above identified applicant has adopted and is using the service mark shown in the accompanying drawing [1] for the following services: ______________________________________________

______________________________________________________________________,

and requests that said mark be registered in the United States Patent and Trademark Office on the Supplemental Register established by the Act of July 5, 1946.

The service mark was first used in connection with the services [2] on ________________ *(date)*; was first used in connection with the services [2] rendered in ________________ *(type of commerce)* commerce [3] on ________________ *(date)*; and is now in use in such commerce.

*(Check one box)*

☐ The mark has been in lawful use in commerce on or in connection with the services for the year preceding the filing of this application.

☐ The mark has not been in use in commerce for the full year preceding the filing of this application, but applicant requires domestic registration as a basis for foreign protection of the mark. (Applicant must submit a separate showing that domestic registration is in fact necessary for foreign protection of the mark before the full year's use will be waived.)

The mark is used by [4] ______________________________________________

______________________________________________________________________

and five specimens showing the mark as actually used are presented herewith.

5

______________________________________________________________________
*(name of applicant)*

being hereby warned that willful false statements and the like so made are punishable by fine or imprisonment, or both, under Section 1001 of Title 18 of the United States Code and that such willful false statements may jeopardize the validity of the application or any registration resulting therefrom, declares that he/she believes himself/herself to be the owner of the service mark sought to be registered; to the best of his/her knowledge and belief no other person, firm, corporation, or association has the right to use said mark in commerce, either in the identical form or in such near resemblance thereto as may be likely, when applied to the services of such other person, to cause confusion, or to cause mistake, or to deceive; the facts set forth in this application are true; and all statements made of his/her own knowledge are true and all statements made on information and belief are believed to be true.

______________________________
*(signature of applicant)*

______________________________
*(date)*

PTO FB-TM 135 (SM, Supp. Reg.) (Individual) (Rev. 12-83) — Patent and Trademark Office - U.S. DEPT. of COMMERCE

*(over)*

PTO–FB–TM 135 (SM, Supp. Reg.) (Individual) (Rev. 12-83)

REPRESENTATION

If the applicant is not domiciled in the United States, a domestic representative must be designated. See Form PTO–FB–TM 151.

If applicant wishes to furnish a power of attorney, see Form PTO–FB–TM 150. An attorney at law is not required to furnish a power.

FOOTNOTES

1 If registration is sought for a word or numeral mark not depicted in any special form, the drawing may be the mark typed in capital letters on letter-size bond paper; otherwise, the drawing should be made with india ink on a good grade of bond paper or on bristol board. If the mark is of a nature that a drawing is not practicable, insert a description of the mark instead of reference to the drawing.

2 If more than one item of services in a class is set forth and the dates given for that class apply to only one of the items listed, insert the name of the item to which the dates apply.

3 Type of commerce should be specified as "interstate," "territorial," "foreign," or other type of commerce which may lawfully be regulated by Congress. Foreign applicants relying upon use must specify commerce which Congress may regulate, using wording such as commerce with the United States or commerce between the United States and a foreign country.

4 State the manner or method of using the mark in the sale or advertising of the services.

5 The required fee of $175.00 for each class must be submitted. (An application to register the same mark for goods and/or services in more than one class may be filed; however, goods and/or services, and dates of use, by class, must be set out separately, and specimens and a fee for each class are required.)

Patent and Trademark Office - U.S. DEPT. of COMMERCE

| **SERVICE MARK APPLICATION, SUPPLEMENTAL REGISTER, WITH DECLARATION** (Partnership) | MARK *(identify the mark)* |
|---|---|
| | CLASS NO. *(if known)* |

TO THE COMMISSIONER OF PATENTS AND TRADEMARKS:

NAME OF CORPORATION [1]

STATE OR COUNTRY OF INCORPORATION

BUSINESS ADDRESS OF CORPORATION

CITIZENSHIP OF PARTNERS

The above identified applicant has adopted and is using the service mark shown in the accompanying drawing [1] for the following services: ______________________________

______________________________,

and requests that said mark be registered in the United States Patent and Trademark Office on the Supplemental Register established by the Act of July 5, 1946.

The service mark was first used in connection with the services [2] on ______________ *(date)*; was first used in connection with the services [2] rendered in ______________ *(type of commerce)* commerce [3] on ______________ *(date)*; and is now in use in such commerce.

*(Check one box)*

☐ The mark has been in lawful use in commerce on or in connection with the services for the year preceding the filing of this application.

☐ The mark has not been in use in commerce for the full year preceding the filing of this application, but applicant requires domestic registration as a basis for foreign protection of the mark. (Applicant must submit a separate showing that domestic registration is in fact necessary for foreign protection of the mark before the full year's use will be waived.)

The mark is used by [4] ______________________________

______________________________

and five specimens showing the mark as actually used are presented herewith.

5

State of ______________________ )
) ss.
County of ______________________ )

______________________________
*(name of partner)*

states that he/she is a partner of applicant partnership; he/she believes said partnership to be the owner of the service mark sought to be registered; to the best of his/her knowledge and belief no other person, firm, corporation or association has the right to use said mark in commerce, either in the identical form or in such near resemblance thereto as to be likely, when applied to the services of such other person, to cause confusion, or to cause mistake, or to deceive; and the facts set forth in this application are true.

______________________________
*(signature of partner)*

JURAT:

Subscribed and sworn to before me this ____________ day of ______________ , ____ .

______________________________
*(notary public)*

PTO-FB-TM 136 (SM, Supp. Reg.) (Partnership) (Rev. 12-83) Patent and Trademark Office - U.S. DEPT. of COMMERCE

*(over)*

PTO–FB–TM 136 (SM, Supp. Reg.) (Partnership) (Rev. 12-83)

## REPRESENTATION

If the applicant is not domiciled in the United States, a domestic representative must be designated. See Form PTO–FB–TM 151.

If applicant wishes to furnish a power of attorney, see Form PTO–FB–TM 150. An attorney at law is not required to furnish a power.

## JURAT

The person who signs the jurat must be authorized to administer oaths by the law of the jurisdiction where executed, and the seal or stamp of the notary, or other evidence of authority in the jurisdiction of execution, must be affixed.

## FOOTNOTES

1 If registration is sought for a word or numeral mark not depicted in any special form, the drawing may be the mark typed in capital letters on letter-size bond paper; otherwise, the drawing should be made with india ink on a good grade of bond paper or on bristol board. If the mark is of a nature that a drawing is not practicable, insert a description of the mark instead of reference to the drawing.

2 If more than one item of services in a class is set forth and the dates given for that class apply to only one of the items listed, insert the name of the item to which the dates apply.

3 Type of commerce should be specified as "interstate," "territorial," "foreign," or other type of commerce which may lawfully be regulated by Congress. Foreign applicants relying upon use must specify commerce which Congress may regulate, using wording such as commerce with the United States or commerce between the United States and a foreign country.

4 State the manner or method of using the mark in the sale or advertising of the services.

5 The required fee of $175.00 for each class must be submitted. (An application to register the same mark for goods and/or services in more than one class may be filed; however, goods and/or services, and dates of use, by class, must be set out separately, and specimens and a fee for each class are required.)

Patent and Trademark Office - U.S. DEPT. of COMMERCE

| SERVICE MARK APPLICATION, SUPPLEMENTAL REGISTER, WITH DECLARATION (Partnership) | MARK *(identify the mark)* |
|---|---|
| | CLASS NO. *(if known)* |

TO THE COMMISSIONER OF PATENTS AND TRADEMARKS:

NAME OF PARTNERSHIP

NAMES OF PARTNERS

BUSINESS ADDRESS OF PARTNERSHIP

CITIZENSHIP OF PARTNERS

The above identified applicant has adopted and is using the service mark shown in the accompanying drawing [1] for the following services: ______________________________

______________________________,

and requests that said mark be registered in the United States Patent and Trademark Office on the Supplemental Register established by the Act of July 5, 1946.

The service mark was first used in connection with the services [2] on ____________ *(date)* ; was first used in connection with the services [2] rendered in ____________ *(type of commerce)* commerce [3] on ____________ *(date)* ; and is now in use in such commerce.

*(Check one box)*

☐ The mark has been in lawful use in commerce on or in connection with the services for the year preceding the filing of this application.

☐ The mark has not been in use in commerce for the full year preceding the filing of this application, but applicant requires domestic registration as a basis for foreign protection of the mark. (Applicant must submit a separate showing that domestic registration is in fact necessary for foreign protection of the mark before the full year's use will be waived.)

The mark is used by [4] ______________________________

______________________________

and five specimens showing the mark as actually used are presented herewith.

5

______________________________
*(name of partnership)*

being hereby warned that willful false statements and the like so made are punishable by fine or imprisonment, or both, under Section 1001 of Title 18 of the United States Code and that such willful false statements may jeopardize the validity of the application or any registration resulting therefrom, declares that he/she is a partner of applicant partnership; he/she believes said partnership to be the owner of the service mark sought to be registered; to the best of his/her knowledge and belief no other person, firm, corporation, or association has the right to use said mark in commerce, either in the identical form or in such near resemblance thereto as may be likely, when applied to the services of such other person, to cause confusion, or to cause mistake, or to deceive; the facts set forth in this application are true; and all statements made of his/her own knowledge are true and all statements made on information and belief are believed to be true.

______________________________
*(signature of partner)*

______________________________
*(date)*

PTO-FB-TM 137 (SM, Supp. Reg.) (Partnership) (Rev. 12-83) Patent and Trademark Office - U.S. DEPT. of COMMERCE

*(over)*

PTO–FB–TM 137 (SM, Supp. (Reg.) (**Partnership**) (Rev. 12-83)

REPRESENTATION

If the applicant is not domiciled in the United States, a domestic representative must be designated. See Form PTO–FB–TM 151.

If applicant wishes to furnish a power of attorney, see Form PTO–FB–TM 150. An attorney at law is not required to furnish a power.

FOOTNOTES

1 If registration is sought for a word or numeral mark not depicted in any special form, the drawing may be the mark typed in capital letters on letter-size bond paper; otherwise, the drawing should be made with india ink on a good grade of bond paper or on bristol board. If the mark is of a nature that a drawing is not practicable, insert a description of the mark instead of reference to the drawing.

2 If more than one item of services in a class is set forth and the dates given for that class apply to only one of the items listed, insert the name of the item to which the dates apply.

3 Type of commerce should be specified as "interstate," "territorial," "foreign," or other type of commerce which may lawfully be regulated by Congress. Foreign applicants relying upon use must specify commerce which Congress may regulate, using wording such as commerce with the United States or commerce between the United States and a foreign country.

4 State the manner or method of using the mark in the sale or advertising of the services.

5 The required fee of $175.00 for each class must be submitted. (An application to register the same mark for goods and/or services in more than one class may be filed; however, goods and/or services, and dates of use, by class, must be set out separately, and specimens and a fee for each class are required.)

Patent and Trademark Office - U.S. DEPT. of COMMERCE

| **SERVICE MARK APPLICATION, SUPPLEMENTAL REGISTER, WITH OATH** (Corporation) | MARK *(identify the mark)*<br><br>CLASS NO. *(if known)* |
|---|---|

TO THE COMMISSIONER OF PATENTS AND TRADEMARKS:

NAME OF CORPORATION [1]

STATE OR COUNTRY OF INCORPORATION

BUSINESS ADDRESS OF CORPORATION

The above identified applicant has adopted and is using the service mark shown in the accompanying drawing [2] for the following services: ______________________________

______________________________________________________,

and requests that said mark be registered in the United States Patent and Trademark Office on the Supplemental Register established by the Act of July 5, 1946.

The service mark was first used in connection with the services [3] on ____________ *(date)* ; was first used in connection with the services [3] rendered in ____________ *(type of commerce)* commerce [4] on ____________ *(date)* ; and is now in use in such commerce.

*(Check one box)*

☐ The mark has been in lawful use in commerce on or in connection with the services for the year preceding the filing of this application.

☐ The mark has not been in use in commerce for the full year preceding the filing of this application, but applicant requires domestic registration as a basis for foreign protection of the mark. (Applicant must submit a separate showing that domestic registration is in fact necessary for foreign protection of the mark before the full year's use will be waived.)

The mark is used by [5] ______________________________

______________________________________________________

and five specimens showing the mark as actually used are presented herewith.
[6]

State of ______________________ )
 ) ss.
County of ______________________ )

______________________________
*(name of officer of corporation)*

states that he/she is ______________________ *(official title)* of applicant corporation

and is authorized to execute this instrument on behalf of said corporation; he/she believes said corporation to be the owner of the service mark sought to be registered, to the best of his/her knowledge and belief no other person, firm, corporation or association has the right to use said mark in commerce, either in the identical form or in such near resemblance thereto as to be likely, when applied to the services of such other person, to cause confusion, or to cause mistake, or to deceive; and the facts set forth in this application are true.

______________________________
*(name of corporation)*

By ______________________________
*(signature of officer of corporation, and official title of officer)*

JURAT:

Subscribed and sworn to before me this ________ day of ____________ , ____ .

______________________________
*(notary public)*

PTO-FB-TM 138 (SM, Supp. Reg.) (Corporation) (Rev. 12-83) Patent and Trademark Office - U.S. DEPT. of COMMERCE

PTO–FB–TM 138 (SM. Supp. Reg.) (Corporation) (Rev. 12-83)

REPRESENTATION

If the applicant is not domiciled in the United States, a domestic representative must be designated. See Form PTO–FB–TM 151.

If applicant wishes to furnish a power of attorney, see Form PTO–FB–TM 150. An attorney at law is not required to furnish a power.

JURAT

The person who signs the jurat must be authorized to administer oaths by the law of the jurisdiction where executed, and the seal or stamp of the notary, or other evidence of authority in the jurisdiction of execution, must be affixed.

FOOTNOTES

1 If applicant is an association or other similar type of juristic entity, change "corporation" throughout to an appropriate designation.

2 If registration is sought for a word or numeral mark not depicted in any special form, the drawing may be the mark typed in capital letters on letter-size bond paper; otherwise, the drawing should be made with india ink on a good grade of bond paper or on bristol board.

3 If more than one item of goods in a class is set forth and the dates given for that class apply to only one of the items listed, insert the name of the item to which the dates apply.

4 Type of commerce should be specified as "interstate," "territorial," "foreign," or other type of commerce which may lawfully be regulated by Congress. Foreign applicants relying upon use must specify commerce which Congress may regulate, using wording such as commerce with the United States or commerce between the United States and a foreign country.

5 If the mark is other than a coined, arbitrary or fanciful mark, and the mark is believed to have acquired a secondary meaning, insert whichever of the following paragraphs is applicable:

a) The mark has become distinctive of applicant's goods as a result of substantially exclusive and continuous use in ______________________ commerce for the five years next preceding the date
*(type of commerce)*
of filing of this application.

b) The mark has become distinctive of applicant's goods as evidenced by the showing submitted separately.

6 Insert the manner or method of using the mark with the goods, i.e., "the goods," "the containers for the goods," "displays associated with the goods," "tags or labels affixed to the goods," or other method which may be in use.

7 The required fee of $175.00 for each class must be submitted. (An application to register the same mark for goods and/or services in more than one class may be filed; however, goods and/or services, and dates of use, by class, must be set out separately, and specimens and a fee for each class are required.)

Patent and Trademark Office - U.S. DEPT. OF COMMERCE

| **SERVICE MARK APPLICATION, SUPPLEMENTAL REGISTER, WITH DECLARATION** (Corporation) | MARK *(identify the mark)* |
|---|---|
| | CLASS NO. *(if known)* |

TO THE COMMISSIONER OF PATENTS AND TRADEMARKS:

NAME OF CORPORATION [1]

STATE OR COUNTRY OF INCORPORATION

BUSINESS ADDRESS OF CORPORATION

The above identified applicant has adopted and is using the service mark shown in the accompanying drawing [2] for the following services: ______________________________

______________________________,

and requests that said mark be registered in the United States Patent and Trademark Office on the Supplemental Register established by the Act of July 5, 1946.

The service mark was first used in connection with the services [3] on ______________ *(date)* ; was first used in connection with the services [3] rendered in ______________ *(type of commerce)* commerce [4] on ______________ *(date)* ; and is now in use in such commerce.

*(Check one box)*

☐ The mark has been in lawful use in commerce on or in connection with the services for the year preceding the filing of this application.

☐ The mark has not been in use in commerce for the full year preceding the filing of this application, but applicant requires domestic registration as a basis for foreign protection of the mark. (Applicant must submit a separate showing that domestic registration is in fact necessary for foreign protection of the mark before the full year's use will be waived.)

The mark is used by [5] ______________________________

______________________________

and five specimens showing the mark as actually used are presented herewith.

6

______________________________
*(name of officer of corporation)*

being hereby warned that willful false statements and the like so made are punishable by fine or imprisonment, or both, under section 1001 of Title 18 of the United States Code and that such willful false statements may jeopardize the validity of the application or any registration resulting therefrom, declares that he/she is ______________ *(official title)* of applicant corporation and is authorized to execute this instrument on behalf of said corporation; he/she believes said corporation to be the owner of the service mark sought to be registered; to the best of his/her knowledge and belief no other person, firm, corporation, or association has the right to use said mark in commerce, either in the identical form or in such near resemblance thereto as may be likely, when applied to the services of such other person, to cause confusion, or to cause mistake, or to deceive; the facts set forth in this application are true; and all statements made of his/her own knowledge are true and all statements made on information and belief are believed to be true.

______________________________
*(name of corporation)*

By ______________________________
*(signature of officer of corporation, and official title of officer)*

______________________________
*(date)*

PTO-FB-TM 139 (SM, Supp. Reg.) (Corporation) (Rev. 12-83) — Patent and Trademark Office - U.S. DEPT. of COMMERCE

*(over)*

PTO–FB–TM 139 (SM, Supp. Reg.) (Corporation) (Rev. 12-83)

REPRESENTATION

If the applicant is not domiciled in the United States, a domestic representative must be designated. See Form PTO–FB–TM 151.

If applicant wishes to furnish a power of attorney, see Form PTO–FB–TM 150. An attorney at law is not required to furnish a power.

FOOTNOTES

1 If applicant is an association or other similar type of juristic entity, change "corporation" throughout to an appropriate designation.

2 If registration is sought for a word or numeral mark not depicted in any special form, the drawing may be the mark typed in capital letters on letter-size bond paper; otherwise, the drawing should be made with india ink on a good grade of bond paper or on bristol board. If the mark is of a nature that a drawing is not practicable, insert a description of the mark instead of reference to the drawing.

3 If more than one item of services in a class is set forth and the dates given for that class apply to only one of the items listed, insert the name of the item to which the dates apply.

4 Type of commerce should be specified as "interstate," "territorial," "foreign," or other type of commerce which may lawfully be regulated by Congress. Foreign applicants relying upon use must specify commerce which Congress may regulate, using wording such as commerce with the United States or commerce between the United States and a foreign country.

5 State the manner or method of using the mark in the sale or advertising of the services.

6 The required fee of $175.00 for each class must be submitted. (An application to register the same mark for goods and/or services in more than one class may be filed; however, goods and/or services, and dates of use, by class, must be set out separately, and specimens and a fee for each class are required.)

Patent and Trademark Office - U.S. DEPT. of COMMERCE

| **COLLECTIVE TRADEMARK OR COLLECTIVE SERVICE MARK APPLICATION, SUPPLEMENTAL REGISTER, WITH OATH** (Corporation) | MARK *(identify the mark)*<br><br>CLASS NO. *(If known, using the class numbers for goods and services)* |
|---|---|

TO THE COMMISSIONER OF PATENTS AND TRADEMARKS:

NAME OF CORPORATION [1]

STATE OR COUNTRY OF INCORPORATION

BUSINESS ADDRESS OF CORPORATION

The above identified applicant has adopted and is exercising legitimate control over the use of the collective mark shown in the accompanying drawing [2] for the following goods (services): [3]

______________________________

______________________________

and requests that said mark be registered in the United States Patent and Trademark Office on the Supplemental Register established by the Act of July 5, 1946.

The collective mark was first used on the goods (services) [3 4] by members of applicant on _________ *(date)*; was first used by said members on the goods (services) [3 4] in ____________ *(type of commerce)* commerce [5] on ____________ *(date)*; and is now in use in such commerce.

*(Check one box)*

☐ The mark has been in lawful use in commerce on or in connection with the goods or services for the year preceding the filing of this application.

☐ The mark has not been in use in commerce for the full year preceding the filing of this application, but applicant requires domestic registration as a basis for foreign protection of the mark. (Applicant must submit a separate showing that domestic registration is in fact necessary for foreign protection of the mark before the full year's use will be waived.)

The mark is used by applying it to [6] ______________________________

______________________________

and five specimens showing the mark as actually used are presented herewith. [7]

State of ____________ )
) ss.
County of ____________ )

______________________________ *(name of officer of corporation)*

states that he/she is ____________ *(official title)* of applicant corporation and is authorized to execute this instrument on behalf of said corporation; he/she believes said corporation to be the owner of the collective mark sought to be registered, to the best of his/her knowledge and belief no other person, firm, corporation or association has the right to use said mark in commerce, either in the identical form or in such near resemblance thereto as to be likely, when applied to the goods (services)[3] of such other person, to cause confusion, or to cause mistake, or to deceive; and the facts set forth in this application are true.

______________________________ *(name of corporation)*

By ______________________________ *(signature of officer of corporation, and official title of officer)*

JURAT:

Subscribed and sworn to before me, this ________ day of ____________ , ______ .

______________________________ *(notary public)*

PTO-FB-TM 140 (Collective, Supp. Reg.) (Corporation) (Rev. 12-83) Patent and Trademark Office - U.S. DEPT. of COMMERCE

PTO-FB-TM 140 (Collective, Supp. Reg.) (Corporation) (Rev. 12-83)

## REPRESENTATION

If the applicant is not domiciled in the United States, a domestic representative must be designated. See Form PTO-FB-TM 151.

If applicant wishes to furnish a power of attorney, see Form PTO-FB-TM 150. An attorney at law is not required to furnish a power.

## JURAT

The person who signs the jurat must be authorized to administer oaths by the law of the jurisdiction where executed, and the seal or stamp of the notary, or other evidence of authority in the jurisdiction of execution, must be affixed.

## FOOTNOTES

1 If applicant is an association or other similar type of juristic entity, change "corporation" throughout to an appropriate designation.

2 If registration is sought for a word or numeral mark not depicted in any special form, the drawing may be the mark typed in capital letters on letter-size bond paper; otherwise, the drawing should be made with india ink on a good grade of bond paper or on bristol board.

3 Delete the word "goods" or the word "services," as appropriate. (An application to register the same mark for goods and/or services in more than one class may be filed; however, goods and/or services, and dates of use, by class, must be set out separately, and specimens and a fee for each class are required.)

4 If more than one item of goods (or services) in a class is set forth and the dates given for that class apply to only one of the items listed, insert the name of the item to which the dates apply.

5 Type of commerce should be specified as "interstate," "territorial," "foreign," or other type of commerce which may lawfully be regulated by Congress. Foreign applicants relying upon use must specify commerce which Congress may regulate, using wording such as commerce with the United States or commerce between the United States and a foreign country.

6 Insert the manner or method of using the mark with the goods, i.e., "the goods," "the containers for the goods," "displays associated with the goods," "tags or labels affixed to the goods," or other method which may be in use; or state the manner or method of using the mark in the sale or advertising of the services.

7 The required fee of $175.00 for each class must be submitted.

*(Instructions on reverse side)*

| **COLLECTIVE TRADEMARK OR COLLECTIVE SERVICE MARK APPLICATION, SUPPLEMENTAL REGISTER, WITH DECLARATION** (Corporation) | MARK *(identify the mark)* |
|---|---|
| | CLASS NO. *(if known, using the class numbers for goods and services)* |

TO THE COMMISSIONER OF PATENTS AND TRADEMARKS:

NAME OF CORPORATION [1]

STATE OR COUNTRY OF INCORPORATION

BUSINESS ADDRESS OF CORPORATION

The above identified applicant has adopted and is exercising legitimate control over the use of the collective mark shown in the accompanying drawing [2] for the following goods (services): [3]

________________________________________

________________________________________

and requests that said mark be registered in the United States Patent and Trademark Office on the Supplemental Register established by the Act of July 5, 1946.

The collective mark was first used on the goods (services) [3 4] by members of applicant on ________ *(date)*; was first used by said members on the goods (services) [3 4] in ____________ *(type of commerce)* commerce [5] on ____________ *(date)*; and is now in use in such commerce.

*(Check one box)*

- ☐ The mark has been in lawful use in commerce on or in connection with the goods or services for the year preceding the filing of this application.
- ☐ The mark has not been in use in commerce for the full year preceding the filing of this application, but applicant requires domestic registration as a basis for foreign protection of the mark. (Applicant must submit a separate showing that domestic registration is in fact necessary for foreign protection of the mark before the full year's use will be waived.)

The mark is used by applying it to [6] ____________________________

________________________________________

and five specimens showing the mark as actually used are presented herewith.

[7] ____________________________
*(name of officer of corporation)*

being hereby warned that willful false statements and the like so made are punishable by fine or imprisonment, or both, under section 1001 of Title 18 of the United States Code and that such willful false statements may jeopardize the validity of the application or any registration resulting therefrom, declares that he/she is ____________ *(official title)* of applicant corporation and is authorized to execute this statement on behalf of said corporation; he/she believes said corporation to be the owner of the collective mark sought to be registered; to the best of his/her knowledge and belief no other person, firm, corporation, or association has the right to use said mark in commerce, either in the identical form or in such near resemblance thereto as may be likely, when applied to the goods (services)[3] of such other person, to cause confusion, or to cause mistake, or to deceive; the facts set forth in this application are true and all statements made of his/her own knowledge are true and all statements made on information and belief are believed to be true.

____________________________
*(name of corporation)*

By ____________________________

____________________________
*(signature of officer of corporation, and official title of officer)*

____________________________
*(date)*

PTO-FB-TM 141 (Collective, Supp. Reg.) (Corporation) (Rev. 12-83) Patent and Trademark Office - U.S. DEPT. of COMMERCE

*(over)*

PTO–FB–TM 141 (Collective, Supp. Reg.) (Corporation) (Rev. 12-83)

REPRESENTATION

If the applicant is not domiciled in the United States, a domestic representative must be designated. See Form PTO-FB-TM 151.

If applicant wishes to furnish a power of attorney, see Form PTO-FB-TM 150. An attorney at law is not required to furnish a power.

FOOTNOTES

1 If applicant is an association or other similar type of juristic entity, change "corporation" throughout to an appropriate designation.

2 If registration is sought for a word or numeral mark not depicted in any special form, the drawing may be the mark typed in capital letters on letter-size bond paper; otherwise, the drawing should be made with india ink on a good grade of bond paper or on bristol board.

3 Delete the word "goods" or the word "services," as appropriate. (An application to register the same mark for goods and/or services in more than one class may be filed; however, goods and/or services, and dates of use, by class, must be set out separately, and specimens and a fee for each class are required.)

4 If more than one item of goods (or services) in a class is set forth and the dates given for that class apply to only one of the items listed, insert the name of the item to which the dates apply.

5 Type of commerce should be specified as "interstate," "territorial," "foreign," or other type of commerce which may lawfully be regulated by Congress. Foreign applicants relying upon use must specify commerce which Congress may regulate, using wording such as commerce with the United States or commerce between the United States and a foreign country.

6 Insert the manner or method of using the mark with the goods, i.e., "the goods," "the containers for the goods," "displays associated with the goods," "tags or labels affixed to the goods," or other method which may be in use; or state the manner or method of using the mark in the sale or advertising of the services.

7 The required fee of $175.00 for each class must be submitted.

Patent and Trademark Office - U.S. DEPT. of COMMERCE

| CORPORATION COLLECTIVE MEMBERSHIP MARK APPLICATION, SUPPLEMENTAL REGISTER, WITH OATH (Corporation) | MARK *(identify the mark)* |
|---|---|
| | CLASS NO. **200** |

TO THE COMMISSIONER OF PATENTS AND TRADEMARKS:

NAME OF CORPORATION[1]

STATE OR COUNTRY OF INCORPORATION

BUSINESS ADDRESS OF CORPORATION

The above identified applicant has adopted and is exercising legitimate control over the use of the collective membership mark shown in the accompanying drawing[2] to indicate membership in applicant organization which is a [3] ______________________________,
and requests that said mark be registered in the United States Patent and Trademark Office on the Supplemental Register established by the Act of July 5, 1946.

The collective membership mark was first used by a member of applicant on ______________ *(date)*; was first used by a member of applicant in ______________ *(type of commerce)* commerce[4] on ______________ *(date)*; and is now in use in such commerce.

*(Check one box)*

☐ The mark has been in lawful use in commerce for the year preceding the filing of this application.

☐ The mark has not been in use in commerce for the full year preceding the filing of this application, but applicant requires domestic registration as a basis for foreign protection of the mark. (Applicant must submit a separate showing that domestic registration is in fact necessary for foreign protection of the mark before the full year's use will be waived.)

The mark is used by applying it to [5] ______________________________

______________________________

and five specimens showing the mark as actually used are presented herewith.

6

State of ______________ )
) ss.
County of ______________ )

______________________________ *(name of officer of corporation)* states that he/she ______________________________ *(official title)* of applicant corporation and is authorized to execute this instrument on behalf of said corporation; he/she believes said corporation to be the owner of the collective membership mark sought to be registered; to the best of his/her knowledge and belief no other person, firm, corporation or association has the right to use said mark in commerce, either in the identical form or in such near resemblance thereto as to be likely, when used, to cause confusion, or to cause mistake or to deceive; and the facts set forth in this application are true.

______________________________
*(name of corporation)*

______________________________
*(signature of officer of corporation, and official title of officer)*

JURAT:

Subscribed and sworn to before me this ______________ day of ______________, ____ .

______________________________
*(notary public)*

PTO-FB-TM 142 (Membership, Supp. Reg.) (Corporation) (Rev. 12-83) *(over)* Patent and Trademark Office - U.S. DEPT. of COMMERCE

**PTO–FB–TM 142 (Membership, Supp. Reg.) (Corporation) (Rev. 12-83)**

REPRESENTATION

If the applicant is not domiciled in the United States, a domestic representative must be designated. See Form PTO–FB–TM 151.

If the applicant wishes to furnish a power of attorney, see Form PTO-FB-TM 150. An attorney at law is not required to furnish a power.

JURAT

The person who signs the jurat must be authorized to administer oaths by the law of the jurisdiction where executed, and the seal or stamp of the notary, or other evidence of authority in the jurisdiction of execution, must be affixed.

FOOTNOTES

1 If applicant is an association or other similar type of juristic entity, change "corporation" throughout to an appropriate designation.

2 If registration is sought for a word or numeral mark not depicted in any special form, the drawing may be the mark typed in capital letters on letter-size bond paper; otherwise, the drawing should be made with india ink on a good grade of bond paper or on bristol board.

3 State the general nature of the applicant organization, such as social club, chemical manufacturers' trade association, milk producers' association, political society, labor union, as may be appropriate.

4 Type of commerce should be specified as "interstate," "territorial," "foreign," or other type of commerce which may lawfully be regulated by Congress. Foreign applicants relying upon use must specify commerce which Congress may regulate, using wording such as commerce with the United States or commerce between the United States and a foreign country.

5 Insert the manner or method of using the mark to indicate membership, such as membership cards or certificates, window decals, or other method which may be in use.

6 The required fee of $175.00 for the class must be submitted.

Patent and Trademark Office - U.S. DEPT. of COMMERCE

| **COLLECTIVE MEMBERSHIP MARK APPLICATION, SUPPLEMENTAL REGISTER, WITH DECLARATION** (Corporation) | MARK *(identify the mark)* |
|---|---|
| | CLASS NO. **200** |

TO THE COMMISSIONER OF PATENTS AND TRADEMARKS:

NAME OF CORPORATION [1]

STATE OR COUNTRY OF INCORPORATION

BUSINESS ADDRESS OF CORPORATION

The above identified applicant has adopted and is exercising legitimate control over the use of the collective membership mark shown in the accompanying drawing [2] to indicate membership in applicant organization which is a [3] ______________________________

and requests that said mark be registered in the United States Patent and Trademark Office on the Supplemental Register established by the Act of July 5, 1946.

The collective membership mark was first used by a member of applicant on ______________ *(date)*; was first used by a member of applicant in ______________ *(type of commerce)* commerce [4] on ______________ *(date)*; and is now in use in such commerce.

*(Check one box)*

☐ The mark has been in lawful use in commerce for the year preceding the filing of this application.

☐ The mark has not been in use in commerce for the full year preceding the filing of this application, but applicant requires domestic registration as a basis for foreign protection of the mark. (Applicant must submit a separate showing that domestic registration is in fact necessary for foreign protection of the mark before the full year's use will be waived.)

The mark is used by applying it to [5] ______________________________

______________________________

and five specimens showing the mark as actually used are presented herewith.

[6]

______________________________ *(name of officer of corporation)*, being hereby warned that willful false statements and the like so made are punishable by fine or imprisonment, or both, under Section 1001 of Title 18 of the United States Code and that such willful false statements may jeopardize the validity of the application or any registration resulting therefrom, declares that he/she is ______________________________ *(official title)* of applicant corporation and is authorized to execute this instrument on behalf of said corporation; he/she believes said corporation to be the owner of the collective membership mark sought to be registered; to the best of his/her knowledge and belief no other person, firm, corporation or association has the right to use said mark in commerce, either in the identical form or in such near resemblance thereto as to be likely, when used, to cause confusion, or to cause mistake, or to deceive; the facts set forth in this application are true; and all statements made of his/her own knowledge are true and all statements made on information and belief are believed to be true.

______________________________
*(name of corporation)*

By ______________________________
*(signature of officer of corporation, and official title of officer)*

______________________________
*(date)*

PTO-FB-TM 143 (Membership, Supp. Reg.) (Corporation) (Rev. 12-83) *(over)* Patent and Trademark Office - U.S. DEPT. of COMMERCE

PTO–FB–TM 143 (Membership, Supp. Reg.) (Corporation) (Rev. 12-83)

## REPRESENTATION

If the applicant is not domiciled in the United States, a domestic representative must be designated. See Form PTO-FB-TM 151.

If the applicant wishes to furnish a power of attorney, see Form PTO-FB-TM 150. An attorney at law is not required to furnish a power.

## FOOTNOTES

1 If applicant is an association or other similar type of juristic entity, change "corporation" throughout to an appropriate designation.

2 If registration is sought for a word or numeral mark not depicted in any special form, the drawing may be the mark typed in capital letters on letter-size bond paper; otherwise, the drawing should be made with india ink on a good grade of bond paper or on bristol board.

3 State the general nature of the applicant organization, such as social club, chemical manufacturers' trade association, milk producers' association, political society, labor union, as may be appropriate.

4 Type of commerce should be specified as "interstate," "territorial," "foreign," or other type of commerce which may lawfully be regulated by Congress. Foreign applicants relying upon use must specify commerce which Congress may regulate, using wording such as commerce with the United States or commerce between the United States and a foreign country.

5 Insert the manner or method of using the mark to indicate membership, such as membership cards or certificates, window decals, or other method which may be in use.

6 The required fee of $175.00 for the class must be submitted.

Patent and Trademark Office - U.S. DEPT. of COMMERCE

*(Instructions on reverse side)*

| **CERTIFICATION MARK APPLICATION, SUPPLEMENTAL REGISTER, WITH OATH** (Individual) | MARK *(identify the mark)* |
|---|---|
| | CLASS ☐ A. GOODS ☐ B. SERVICES |

TO THE COMMISSIONER OF PATENTS AND TRADEMARKS:

NAME OF APPLICANT, AND BUSINESS TRADE NAME, IF ANY

BUSINESS ADDRESS

RESIDENCE ADDRESS

CITIZENSHIP OF APPLICANT

The above identified applicant has adopted and is exercising legitimate control over the use of the certification mark shown in the accompanying drawing [2] for the following goods (services)[3]: ______________________________ ,

and requests that said mark be registered in the United States Patent and Trademark Office on the Supplemental Register established by the Act of July 5, 1946.

The certification mark, as used by persons authorized by applicant, certifies [4] ______________________________ ;

said mark was first used on the goods (services)[3] by a person authorized by applicant on __________ *(date)*

was first used by a person authorized by applicant on the goods (services)[3] in __________ *(type of commerce)* commerce [5] on __________ *(date)* ; and is now in use in such commerce.

*(Check one box)*

☐ The mark has been in lawful use in commerce on or in connection with the goods or services for the year preceding the filing of this application.

☐ The mark has not been in use in commerce for the full year preceding the filing of this application, but applicant requires domestic registration as a basis for foreign protection of the mark. (Applicant must submit a separate showing that domestic registration is in fact necessary for foreign protection of the mark before the full year's use will be waived.)

The mark is used by applying it to [6] ______________________________

and five specimens showing the mark as actually used are presented herewith.

Applicant is not engaged in the production or marketing of any goods or services to which the mark is applied.

7 8

State of __________ )
) ss.
County of __________ )

__________
*(name of applicant)*

states that he/she believes himself/herself to be the owner of the certification mark sought to be registered; to the best of his/her knowledge and belief no other person, firm, corporation or association has the right to use said mark in commerce, either in the identical form or in such near resemblance thereto as to be likely, when applied to the goods (services)[3] of such other person, to cause confusion, or to cause mistake, or to deceive; and the facts set forth in this application are true.

__________
*(signature of applicant)*

JURAT:

Subscribed and sworn to before me this __________ day of __________ , ____ .

__________
*(notary public)*

PTO-FB-TM 144 (Certification, Supp. Reg.) (Individual) (Rev. 12-83) Patent and Trademark Office - U.S. DEPT. of COMMERCE

*(over)*

PTO–FB–TM 144 (Certification, Supp. Reg.) (Individual) (Rev. 12-83)

## REPRESENTATION

If the applicant is not domiciled in the United States, a domestic representative must be designated. See Form PTO-FB-TM 151.

If applicant wishes to furnish a power of attorney, see Form PTO-FB-TM 150. An attorney at law is not required to furnish a power.

## JURAT

The person who signs the jurat must be authorized to administer oaths by the law of the jurisdiction where executed, and the seal or stamp of the notary, or other evidence of authority in the jurisdiction of execution, must be affixed.

## FOOTNOTES

1 Check A or B for a single application for a single fee. (An application to register the same certification mark in Class A and in Class B may be filed, but the goods and services, and dates of use, by class, must be set out separately, and specimens and a fee for each class are required.)

2 If registration is sought for a word or numeral mark not depicted in any special form, the drawing may be the mark typed in capital letters on letter-size bond paper; otherwise, the drawing should be made with india ink on a good grade of bond paper or on bristol board.

3 Delete the word "goods" or the word "services" as appropriate.

4 Insert a statement indicating what it is that the mark certifies. The mark may, for instance, certify a particular regional origin of the goods; or the mark may certify a characteristic of material, of mode of manufacture, of quality, or accuracy, or other characteristic of the goods or services; or the mark may certify that the work (or labor) used in rendering the services, was work performed by members of applicant.

5 Type of commerce should be specified as "interstate," "territorial," "foreign," or other type of commerce which may lawfully be regulated by Congress. Foreign applicants relying upon use must specify commerce which Congress may regulate, using wording such as commerce with the United States or commerce between the United States and a foreign country.

6 Insert the manner or method of using the mark with the goods, i.e., "the goods," "the containers for the goods," "displays associated with the goods," "tags or labels affixed to the goods," or other method which may be in use; or state the manner or method of using the mark in the sale or advertising of the services.

7 This form should not be used for geographical terms as indications of regional origin because they are eligible for registration on the Principal Register (sec. 2(e)(2) of the act).

8 The required fee of $175.00 for each class must be submitted.

Patent and Trademark Office - U.S. DEPT. of COMMERCE

*(Instructions on reverse side)*

| **CERTIFICATION MARK APPLICATION, SUPPLEMENTAL REGISTER, WITH DECLARATION** (Individual) | MARK *(identify the mark)* |
|---|---|
| | CLASS [1]: ☐ A. GOODS ☐ B. SERVICES |

TO THE COMMISSIONER OF PATENTS AND TRADEMARKS:

NAME OF APPLICANT, AND BUSINESS TRADE NAME, IF ANY

BUSINESS ADDRESS

RESIDENCE ADDRESS

CITIZENSHIP OF APPLICANT

The above identified applicant has adopted and is exercising legitimate control over the use of the certification mark shown in the accompanying drawing [2] for the following goods (services)[3]:

______________________________________________

______________________________________________,

and requests that said mark be registered in the United States Patent and Trademark Office on the Supplemental Register established by the Act of July 5, 1946.

The certification mark, as used by persons authorized by applicant, certifies [4] ______________

______________________________________________;

said mark was first used on the goods (services)[3] by a person authorized by applicant on ________ *(date)*

was first used by a person authorized by applicant on the goods (services)[3] in ______________ *(type of commerce)* commerce [5] on ________ *(date)*; and is now in use in such commerce.

*(Check one box)*

☐ The mark has been in lawful use in commerce on or in connection with the goods or services for the year preceding the filing of this application.

☐ The mark has not been in use in commerce for the full year preceding the filing of this application, but applicant requires domestic registration as a basis for foreign protection of the mark. (Applicant must submit a separate showing that domestic registration is in fact necessary for foreign protection of the mark before the full year's use will be waived.)

The mark is used by applying it to [6] ______________________________

______________________________________________

and five specimens showing the mark as actually used are presented herewith.

Applicant is not engaged in the production or marketing of any goods or services to which the mark is applied.

7 8

______________________________
*(name of applicant)*

being hereby warned that willful false statements and the like so made are punishable by fine or imprisonment, or both, under Section 1001 of Title 18 of the United States Code and that such willful false statements may jeopardize the validity of the application or any registration resulting therefrom, declares that he/she believes himself/herself to be the owner of the certification mark sought to be registered; to the best of his/her knowledge and belief no other person, firm, corporation or association has the right to use said mark in commerce, either in the identical form or in such near resemblance thereto as may be likely, when applied to the goods (services)[3] of such other person, to cause confusion, or to cause mistake, or to deceive; the facts set forth in this application are true; and all statements made of his/her own knowledge are true and all statements made on information and belief are believed to be true.

______________________________
*(signature of applicant)*

______________________________
*(date)*

PTO-FB-TM 145 (Certification, Supp. Reg.) (Individual) (Rev. 12-83) Patent and Trademark Office - U.S. DEPT. of COMMERCE

(over)

PTO-FB-TM 145 (Certification, Supp. Reg.) (Individual) (Rev. 12-83)

REPRESENTATION

If the applicant is not domiciled in the United States, a domestic representative must be designated. See Form PTO-FB-TM 151.

If applicant wishes to furnish a power of attorney, see Form PTO-FB-TM 150. An attorney at law is not required to furnish a power.

FOOTNOTES

1 Check A or B for a single application for a single fee. (An application to register the same certification mark in Class A and in Class B may be filed, but the goods and services, and dates of use, by class, must be set out separately, and specimens and a fee for each class are required.)

2 If registration is sought for a word or numeral mark not depicted in any special form, the drawing may be the mark typed in capital letters on letter-size bond paper; otherwise, the drawing should be made with india ink on a good grade of bond paper or on bristol board.

3 Delete the word "goods" or the word "services" as appropriate.

4 Insert a statement indicating what it is that the mark certifies. The mark may, for instance, certify a particular regional origin of the goods; or the mark may certify a characteristic of material, of mode of manufacture, of quality, or accuracy, or other characteristic of the goods or services; or the mark may certify that the work (or labor) used in manufacturing or producing the goods or the work (or labor) used in rendering the services, was work performed by members of applicant.

5 Type of commerce should be specified as "interstate," "territorial," "foreign," or other type of commerce which may lawfully be regulated by Congress. Foreign applicants relying upon use must specify commerce which Congress may regulate, using wording such as commerce with the United States or commerce between the United States and a foreign country.

6 Insert the manner or method of using the mark with the goods, i.e., "the goods," "the containers for the goods," "displays associated with the goods," "tags or labels affixed to the goods," or other method which may be in use; or state the manner or method of using the mark in the sale or advertising of the services.

7 This form should not be used for geographical terms as indications of regional origin because they are eligible for registration on the Principal Register (sec. 2(e)(2) of the act).

8 The required fee of $175.00 for each class must be submitted.

Patent and Trademark Office - U.S. DEPT. of COMMERCE

| **CERTIFICATION MARK APPLICATION, SUPPLEMENTAL REGISTER, WITH OATH** (Partnership) | MARK *(identify the mark)*<br>CLASS [1]: ☐ A. GOODS ☐ B. SERVICES |
|---|---|

TO THE COMMISSIONER OF PATENTS AND TRADEMARKS:

NAME OF PARTNERSHIP

NAMES OF PARTNERS

BUSINESS ADDRESS OF PARTNERSHIP

CITIZENSHIP OF PARTNERS

The above identified applicant has adopted and is exercising legitimate control over the use of the certification mark shown in the accompanying drawing [2] for the following goods (services)[3]: ______________________________ ______________________________, and requests that said mark be registered in the United States Patent and Trademark Office on the Supplemental Register established by the Act of July 5, 1946.

The certification mark, as used by persons authorized by applicant, certifies [4] ______________________________ ______________________________; said mark was first used on the goods (services)[3] by a person authorized by applicant on ________ *(date)*; was first used by a person authorized by applicant on the goods (services)[3] in ______________ *(type of commerce)* commerce [5] on __________ *(date)*; and is now in use in such commerce.

*(Check one box)*

☐ The mark has been in lawful use in commerce on or in connection with the goods or services for the year preceding the filing of this application.

☐ The mark has not been in use in commerce for the full year preceding the filing of this application, but applicant requires domestic registration as a basis for foreign protection of the mark. (Applicant must submit a separate showing that domestic registration is in fact necessary for foreign protection of the mark before the full year's use will be waived.)

The mark is used by applying it to [6] ______________________________ ______________________________ and five specimens showing the mark as actually used are presented herewith.

Applicant is not engaged in the production or marketing of any goods or services to which the mark is applied.

7 8

State of ______________________ )
) ss.
County of ______________________ )

______________________________ *(name of partner)*

states that he/she is a partner of applicant partnership; he/she believes said partnership to be the owner of the certification mark sought to be registered; to the best of his/her knowledge and belief no other person, firm, corporation or association has the right to use said mark in commerce, either in the identical form or in such near resemblance thereto as to be likely, when applied to the goods (services)[3] of such other person, to cause confusion, or to cause mistake, or to deceive; and the facts set forth in this application are true.

______________________________ *(signature of partner)*

JURAT:

Subscribed and sworn to before me this __________ day of ______________, ____ .

______________________________ *(notary public)*

PTO-FB-TM 146 (Certification, Supp. Reg.) (Partnership) (Rev. 12-83) Patent and Trademark Office - U.S. DEPT. of COMMERCE

*(over)*

PTO–FB–TM 146 (Certification, Supp. Reg.) (Partnership) (Rev. 12-83)

## REPRESENTATION

If the applicant is not domiciled in the United States, a domestic representative must be designated. See Form PTO-FB-TM 151.

If applicant wishes to furnish a power of attorney, see Form PTO-FB-TM 150. An attorney at law is not required to furnish a power.

## JURAT

The person who signs the jurat must be authorized to administer oaths by the law of the jurisdiction where executed, and the seal or stamp of the notary, or other evidence of authority in the jurisdiction of execution, must be affixed.

## FOOTNOTES

1 Check A or B for a single application for a single fee. (An application to register the same certification mark in Class A and in Class B may be filed, but the goods and services, and dates of use, by class, must be set out separately, and specimens and a fee for each class are required.)

2 If registration is sought for a word or numeral mark not depicted in any special form, the drawing may be the mark typed in capital letters on letter-size bond paper; otherwise, the drawing should be made with india ink on a good grade of bond paper or on bristol board.

3 Delete the word "goods" or the word "services" as appropriate.

4 Insert a statement indicating what it is that the mark certifies. The mark may, for instance, certify a particular regional origin of the goods; or the mark may certify a characteristic of material, of mode of manufacture, of quality, or accuracy, or other characteristic of the goods or services; or the mark may certify that the work (or labor) used in manufacturing or producing the goods or the work (or labor) used in rendering the services, was work performed by members of applicant.

5 Type of commerce should be specified as "interstate," "territorial," "foreign," or other type of commerce which may lawfully be regulated by Congress. Foreign applicants relying upon use must specify commerce which Congress may regulate, using wording such as commerce with the United States or commerce between the United States and a foreign country.

6 Insert the manner or method of using the mark with the goods, i.e., "the goods," "the containers for the goods," "displays associated with the goods," "tags or labels affixed to the goods," or other method which may be in use; or state the manner or method of using the mark in the sale or advertising of the services.

7 This form should not be used for geographical terms as indications of regional origin because they are eligible for registration on the Principal Register (sec. 2(e)(2) of the act).

8 The required fee of $175.00 for each class must be submitted.

Patent and Trademark Office - U.S. DEPT. of COMMERCE

| **CERTIFICATION MARK APPLICATION, SUPPLEMENTAL REGISTER, WITH DECLARATION** (Partnership) | MARK *(identify the mark)* |
|---|---|
| | CLASS [1]: ☐ A. GOODS ☐ B. SERVICES |

TO THE COMMISSIONER OF PATENTS AND TRADEMARKS:

NAME OF PARTNERSHIP

NAMES OF PARTNERS

BUSINESS ADDRESS OF PARTNERSHIP

CITIZENSHIP OF PARTNERS

The above identified applicant has adopted and is exercising legitimate control over the use of the certification mark shown in the accompanying drawing [2] for the following goods (services)[3]:

______________________________

______________________________

and requests that said mark be registered in the United States Patent and Trademark Office on the Supplemental Register established by the Act of July 5, 1946.

The certification mark, as used by persons authorized by applicant, certifies [4] ____________________

____________________________________________;

said mark was first used on the goods (services)[3] by a person authorized by applicant on __________ *(date)*;

was first used by a person authorized by applicant on the goods (services)[3] in ______________ *(type of commerce)* commerce [5] on __________ *(date)*; and is now in use in such commerce.

*(Check one box)*

☐ The mark has been in lawful use in commerce on or in connection with the goods or services for the year preceding the filing of this application.

☐ The mark has not been in use in commerce for the full year preceding the filing of this application, but applicant requires domestic registration as a basis for foreign protection of the mark. (Applicant must submit a separate showing that domestic registration is in fact necessary for foreign protection of the mark before the full year's use will be waived.)

The mark is used by applying it to [6] ______________________________

______________________________

and five specimens showing the mark as actually used are presented herewith.

Applicant is not engaged in the production or marketing of any goods or services to which the mark is applied.

[7] [8] ______________________________ *(name of partner)*, being hereby warned that willful false statements and the like so made are punishable by fine or imprisonment, or both, under Section 1001 of Title 18 of the United States Code and that such willful false statements may jeopardize the validity of the application or any registration resulting therefrom, declares that he/she is a partner of applicant partnership; he/she believes said partnership to be the owner of the certification mark sought to be registered; to the best of his/her knowledge and belief no other person, firm, corporation or association has the right to use said mark in commerce, either in the identical form or in such near resemblance thereto as may be likely, when applied to the goods (services)[3] of such other person, to cause confusion, or to cause mistake, or to deceive; the facts set forth in this application are true; and all statements made of his/her own knowledge are true and all statements made on information and belief are believed to be true.

______________________________
*(signature of partner)*

______________________________
*(date)*

PTO-FB-TM 147 (Certification, Supp. Reg.) (Partnership) (Rev. 12-83) Patent and Trademark Office - U.S. DEPT. of COMMERCE

*(over)*

PTO-FB-TM-147 (Certification, Supp. Reg.) (Partnership) (Rev. 12-83)

REPRESENTATION

If the applicant is not domiciled in the United States, a domestic representative must be designated. See Form PTO-FB-TM 151.

If applicant wishes to furnish a power of attorney, see Form PTO-FB-TM 150. An attorney at law is not required to furnish a power.

FOOTNOTES

1 Check A or B for a single application for a single fee. (An application to register the same certification mark in Class A and in Class B may be filed, but the goods and services, and dates of use, by class, must be set out separately, and specimens and a fee for each class are required.)

2 If registration is sought for a word or numeral mark not depicted in any special form, the drawing may be the mark typed in capital letters on letter-size bond paper; otherwise, the drawing should be made with india ink on a good grade of bond paper or on bristol board.

3 Delete the word "goods" or the word "services" as appropriate.

4 Insert a statement indicating what it is that the mark certifies. The mark may, for instance, certify a particular regional origin of the goods; or the mark may certify a characteristic of material, of mode of manufacture, of quality, or accuracy, or other characteristic of the goods or services; or the mark may certify that the work (or labor) used in manufacturing or producing the goods or the work (or labor) used in rendering the services, was work performed by members of applicant.

5 Type of commerce should be specified as "interstate," "territorial," "foreign," or other type of commerce which may lawfully be regulated by Congress. Foreign applicants relying upon use must specify commerce which Congress may regulate, using wording such as commerce with the United States or commerce between the United States and a foreign country.

6 Insert the manner or method of using the mark with the goods, i.e., "the goods," "the containers for the goods," "displays associated with the goods," "tags or labels affixed to the goods," or other method which may be in use; or state the manner or method of using the mark in the sale or advertising of the services.

7 This form should not be used for geographical terms as indications of regional origin because they are eligible for registration on the Principal Register (sec. 2(e)(2) of the act).

8 The required fee of $175.00 for each class must be submitted.

Patent and Trademark Office - U.S. DEPT. of COMMERCE

| **CERTIFICATION MARK APPLICATION, SUPPLEMENTAL REGISTER, WITH OATH** (Corporation) | MARK *(identify the mark)* |
|---|---|
| | CLASS [1]: ☐ A. Goods ☐ B. Services |

TO THE COMMISSIONER OF PATENTS AND TRADEMARKS:

NAME OF CORPORATION [1]

STATE OR COUNTRY OF INCORPORATION

BUSINESS ADDRESS OF CORPORATION

The above identified applicant has adopted and is exercising legitimate control over the use of the certification mark shown in the accompanying drawing [3] for the following goods (services): [4]

______________________________________________________________

______________________________________________________________ ;

and requests that said mark be registered in the United States Patent and Trademark Office on the Supplemental Register established by the Act of July 5, 1946.

The certification mark, as used by persons authorized by applicant, certifies [5] ____________________

______________________________________________________________ ;

said mark was first used on the goods (services) [4] by person authorized by applicant on ____________ ;
*(date)*

was first used by a person authorized by applicant on the goods (services) [4] in

____________________ commerce [6] on ____________ ; and is now in use in
*(type of commerce)* *(date)*

such commerce.

*(Check one box)*

☐ The mark has been in lawful use in commerce on or in connection with the goods or services for the year preceding the filing of this application.

☐ The mark has not been in use in commerce for the full year preceding the filing of this application, but application requires domestic registration as a basis for foreign protection of the mark. (Applicant must submit a separate showing that domestic registration is in fact necessary for foreign protection of the mark before the full year's use will be waived.)

The mark is used by applying it to [7] ______________________________________

______________________________________________________________

and five specimens showing the mark as actually used are presented herewith.

Applicant is not engaged in the production or marketing of any goods or services to which the mark is applied.

8 9

State of ______________________ )
) ss.
County of ______________________ )

______________________ states that he/she is ______________________
*(name of officer of corporation)* *(official title)*

of applicant corporation and is authorized to execute this instrument on behalf of said corporation, he/she believes said corporation to be the owner of the certification mark sought to be registered; to the best of his/her knowledge and belief no other person, firm, corporation or association other than those authorized by applicant has the right to use said mark in commerce, either in the identical form or in such near resemblance thereto as to be likely, when applied to the goods (services)[4] of such other person, to cause confusion, or to cause mistake, or to deceive; and the facts set forth in this application are true.

______________________________
*(name of corporation)*

By ______________________________
*(signature of officer of corporation and official title of officer)*

JURAT:

Subscribed and sworn to before me, this ____________ day of ______________ , ____ .

______________________________
*(notary public)*

PTO-FB-TM 148 (Certification, Supp. Reg.) (Corporation) (Rev. 12-83) Patent and Trademark Office - U.S. DEPT. of COMMERCE

*(over)*

PTO–FB–TM 148 (Certification, Supp. Reg.) (Corporation) (Rev. 12-83)

## REPRESENTATION

If the applicant is not domiciled in the United States, a domestic representative must be designated. See Form PTO-FB-TM 151.

If applicant wishes to furnish a power of attorney, see Form PTO-FB-TM 150. An attorney at law is not required to furnish a power.

## JURAT

The person who signs the jurat must be authorized to administer oaths by the law of the jurisdiction where executed, and the seal or stamp of the notary, or other evidence of authority in the jurisdiction of execution, must be affixed.

## FOOTNOTES

1 Check A or B for a single application for a single fee. (An application to register the same certification mark in Class A and in Class B may be filed, but the goods and services, and dates of use, by class, must be set out separately, and specimens and a fee for each class are required.)

2 If applicant is an association or other similar type of juristic entity, change "corporation" throughout to an appropriate designation.

3 If registration is sought for a word or numeral mark not depicted in any special form, the drawing may be the mark typed in capital letters on letter-size bond paper; otherwise, the drawing should be made with india ink on a good grade of bond paper or on bristol board.

4 Delete the word "goods" or the word "services" as appropriate.

5 Insert a statement indicating what it is that the mark certifies. The mark may, for instance, certify a particular regional origin of the goods; or the mark may certify a characteristic of material, of mode of manufacture, of quality, or accuracy, or other characteristic of the goods or services; or the mark may certify that the work (or labor) used in manufacturing or producing the goods or the work (or labor) used in rendering the services, was work performed by members of applicant.

6 Type of commerce should be specified as "interstate," "territorial," "foreign," or other type of commerce which may lawfully be regulated by Congress. Foreign applicants relying upon use must specify commerce which Congress may regulate, using wording such as commerce with the United States or commerce between the United States and a foreign country.

7 Insert the manner or method of using the mark with the goods, i.e., "the goods," the containers for the goods," "displays associated with the goods," "tags or labels affixed to the goods," or other method which may be in use; or state the manner or method of using the mark in the sale or advertising of the services.

8 This form should not be used for geographical terms as indications of regional origin because they are eligible for registration on the Principal Register (sec. 2(e)(2) of the act).

9 The required fee of $175.00 for each class must be submitted.

Patent and Trademark Office - U.S. DEPT. of COMMERCE

*(Instructions on reverse side)*

**CERTIFICATION MARK APPLICATION, SUPPLEMENTAL REGISTER, WITH DECLARATION**
(Corporation)

MARK *(identify the mark)*

CLASS [1]: ☐ A. Goods ☐ B. Services

TO THE COMMISSIONER OF PATENTS AND TRADEMARKS:

NAME OF CORPORATION [2]

STATE OR COUNTRY OF INCORPORATION

BUSINESS ADDRESS OF CORPORATION

The above identified applicant has adopted and is exercising legitimate control over the use of the certification mark shown in the accompanying drawing [3] for the following goods (services): [4]

______________________________________________

______________________________________________ ;

and requests that said mark be registered in the United States Patent and Trademark Office on the Supplemental Register established by the Act of July 5, 1946.
The certification mark, as used by persons authorized by applicant, certifies [5] ____________________

______________________________________________ ;

said mark was first used on the goods (services) [4] by person authorized by applicant on ____________ ;
*(date)*
was first used by a person authorized by applicant on the goods (services) [4] in
____________________ commerce [6] on ____________ ; and is now in use in
*(type of commerce)* *(date)*
such commerce.
*(Check one box)*

☐ The mark has been in lawful use in commerce on or in connection with the goods or services for the year preceding the filing of this application.

☐ The mark has not been in use in commerce for the full year preceding the filing of this application, but application requires domestic registration as a basis for foreign protection of the mark. (Applicant must submit a separate showing that domestic registration is in fact necessary for foreign protection of the mark before the full year's use will be waived.)

The mark is used by applying it to [7] ______________________________

______________________________________________

and five specimens showing the mark as actually used are presented herewith.
Applicant is not engaged in the production or marketing of any goods or services to which the mark is applied.
8 9

______________________________
*(name of officer of corporation)*

being hereby warned that willful false statements and the like so made are punishable by fine or imprisonment, or both, under Section 1001 of Title 18 of the United States Code and that such willful false statements may jeopardize the validity of the application or any registration resulting therefrom, declares that he/she is ____________________ of applicant corporation and is authorized
*(official title)*
to execute this instrument on behalf of said corporation; he/she believes said corporation to be the owner of the certification mark sought to be registered; to the best of his/her knowledge and belief no other person, firm, corporation, or association has the right to use said mark in commerce, either in the identical form or in such near resemblance thereto as may be likely, when applied to the goods (services)[4] of such other person, to cause confusion, or to cause mistake, or to deceive; the facts set forth in this application are true; and all statements made of his/her own knowledge are true and all statements made on information and belief are believed to be true.

______________________________
*(name of corporation)*

By ______________________________
*(signature of officer of corporation and official title of officer)*

______________________________
*(date)*

PTO-FB-TM 149 (Certification, Supp. Reg.) (Corporation) (Rev. 12-83) Patent and Trademark Office - U.S. DEPT. of COMMERCE
*(over)*

PTO–FB–TM 149 (Certification, Supp. Reg.) (Corporation) (Rev. 12-83)

## REPRESENTATION

If the applicant is not domiciled in the United States, a domestic representative must be designated. See Form PTO-FB-TM 151.

If applicant wishes to furnish a power of attorney, see Form PTO-FB-TM 150. An attorney at law is not required to furnish a power.

## FOOTNOTES

1 Check A or B for a single application for a single fee. (An application to register the same certification mark in Class A and in Class B may be filed, but the goods and services, and dates of use, by class, must be set out separately, and specimens and a fee for each class are required.)

2 If applicant is an association or other similar type of juristic entity, change "corporation" throughout to an appropriate designation.

3 If registration is sought for a word or numeral mark not depicted in any special form, the drawing may be the mark typed in capital letters on letter-size bond paper; otherwise, the drawing should be made with india ink on a good grade of bond paper or on bristol board.

4 Delete the word "goods" or the word "services" as appropriate.

5 Insert a statement indicating what it is that the mark certifies. The mark may, for instance, certify a particular regional origin of the goods; or the mark may certify a characteristic of material, of mode of manufacture, of quality, or accuracy, or other characteristic of the goods or services; or the mark may certify that the work (or labor) used in manufacturing or producing the goods or the work (or labor) used in rendering the services, was work performed by members of applicant.

6 Type of commerce should be specified as "interstate," "territorial," "foreign," or other type of commerce which may lawfully be regulated by Congress. Foreign applicants relying upon use must specify commerce which Congress may regulate, using wording such as commerce with the United States or commerce between the United States and a foreign country.

7 Insert the manner or method of using the mark with the goods, i.e., "the goods," "the containers for the goods," "displays associated with the goods," "tags or labels affixed to the goods," or other method which may be in use; or state the manner or method of using the mark in the sale or advertising of the services.

8 This form should not be used for geographical terms as indications of regional origin because they are eligible for registration on the Principal Register (sec. 2(e)(2) of the act).

9 The required fee of $175.00 for each class must be submitted.

Patent and Trademark Office - U.S. DEPT. of COMMERCE

## POWER OF ATTORNEY AT LAW

When the Power is placed in the application as a paragraph thereof, use the following language:

POWER OF ATTORNEY AT LAW

Applicant hereby appoints:

______________________________

*(name(s) of Attorney(s) at Law [1])*

______________________________

*(address)*

to prosecute this application to register, to transact all business in the Patent and Trademark Office in connection therewith, and to receive the certificate of registration.

* * * * * * * *

When the Power is placed on a separate sheet, this sheet may be used by filling in the following:

POWER OF ATTORNEY AT LAW

| IDENTIFY THE MARK | SERIAL NO., IF ANY |
|---|---|
| NAME OF APPLICANT | DATE OF SIGNATURE |

Applicant hereby appoints:

______________________________

*(name(s) of Attorney(s) at Law [1])*

______________________________

*(address)*

to prosecute this application to register, to transact all business in the Patent and Trademark Office in connection therewith, and to receive the certificate of registration.

______________________________

*(signature of applicant)[2]*

* * * * * * * *

FOOTNOTES

1 Individual attorney(s) at law must be named. If the name of a law firm rather than individual attorney(s) is given, the firm name will be regarded merely as the designation of an address for sending correspondence to applicant.

2 When the power of attorney is on a separate sheet, it must be signed; however, a power of attorney which is a paragraph in the application is supported by the signature to the application and need not be signed separately.

PTO-FB-TM 150 (Power of Attorney) (Rev. 12-83)

Patent and Trademark Office - U.S. DEPT. of COMMERCE

## DESIGNATION OF DOMESTIC REPRESENTATIVE

When the Designation is placed in the application as a paragraph thereof, use the following language:

DESIGNATION OF DOMESTIC REPRESENTATIVE [1]

*(name of domestic representative)*[2]

whose postal address is ______________________________

______________________________________________

is hereby designated applicant's representative upon whom notice or process in proceedings affecting the mark may be served.

* * * * * * * *

When the Designation is placed on a separate sheet, this sheet may be used by filling in the following:

DESIGNATION OF DOMESTIC REPRESENTATIVE [1]

IDENTIFY THE MARK

NAME OF APPLICANT

SERIAL NO., IF ANY

DATE OF SIGNATURE

*(name of domestic representative)*[2]

whose postal address is ______________________________

______________________________________________

is hereby designated applicant's representative upon whom notice or process in proceedings affecting the mark may be served.

______________________________

*(signature of applicant)*[3]

* * * * * * * *

FOOTNOTES

1 The designation of the domestic representative must be separate from the appointment of an attorney.
2 A domestic representative may be a natural or a juristic person.
3 When the designation of domestic representative is on a separate sheet, it must be signed; however, a designation which is a paragraph in the application is supported by the signature to the application and need not be signed separately.

PTO-FB-TM 151 (Domestic Representative) (Rev. 12-83) Patent and Trademark Office - U.S. DEPT. of COMMERCE

**CLAIM OF PRIORITY BASED ON 15 USC 1126(d)**
**(Section 44(d) of the Trademark Act)**

If the application is based on a right of priority under 15 USC 1126(d) (Section 44(d) of the Trademark Act) the following language should be used: [1]

This application is based on 15 USC 1126(d) (Section 44(d) of the Trademark Act). The foreign application was filed ________________ in ________________________________.
*(date of filing)* *(Country)*

FOOTNOTE

1 This language may be added to the application or may be substituted for the dates of use paragraphs as appropriate.

PTO-FB-TM 152 (15 USC 1126(d)) (12-83) Patent and Trademark Office - U.S. DEPT. of COMMERCE

**CLAIM OF FOREIGN REGISTRATION BASED ON 15 USC 1126(e)**
**(Section 44(e) of the Trademark Act)**

If the application is based on a foreign registration under 15 USC 1126(e) (Section 44(e) of the Trademark Act) the following language should be used:[1]

This application is based on 15 USC 1126(e) (Section 44(e) of the Trademark Act). Submitted herewith is a certification or certified copy of Registration No. ______________________
*(Reg. No.)*

registered in ______________________________________.
*(Country)*

FOOTNOTE

1 This language may be added to the application or may be substituted for the dates of use paragraph as appropriate.

PTO-FB-TM 153 (15 USC 1126(e)) (12-83) Patent and Trademark Office - U.S. DEPT. of COMMERCE

*(Instructions on reverse side)*

| APPLICATION FOR RENEWAL OF REGISTRATION OF A MARK, WITH OATH | MARK *(Identify the mark)* |
|---|---|
| | REGISTRATION NO. |
| TO THE COMMISSIONER OF PATENTS AND TRADEMARKS: | CLASS NO.(S) |

*(check one box and fill in appropriate information [1])*

☐ NAME OF INDIVIDUAL AS RENEWAL APPLICANT, AND BUSINESS TRADE NAME, IF ANY

BUSINESS ADDRESS

RESIDENCE ADDRESS

CITIZENSHIP

☐ NAME OF PARTNERSHIP AS RENEWAL APPLICANT

NAMES OF PARTNERS

BUSINESS ADDRESS OF PARTNERSHIP

CITIZENSHIP OF PARTNERS

☐ NAME OF CORPORATION [2] AS RENEWAL APPLICANT

STATE OR COUNTRY OF INCORPORATION

BUSINESS ADDRESS OF CORPORATION

The above identified applicant for renewal requests that the above identified registration, granted to ______________ *(name of original registrant)* on ______________ *(date of issuance)* ,which applicant for renewal now owns, as shown by records in the Patent and Trademark Office, be renewed in accordance with the provisions of Section 9 of the Act of July 5, 1946.

The mark shown in said registration is still in use in ______________ *(type of commerce)* commerce [3] on or in connection with each of the following: ______________

______________
*(list the goods and/or services or insert the words "all the goods" and/or "all the services" as may be appropriate)*

which are recited in the registration, the attached specimen showing the mark as currently used.[4]

[5]

State of ______________ )
) ss.
County of ______________ )

______________
*(name of person whose signature is to be placed below [6])*

states that to the best of his/her knowledge and belief the facts set forth in this application are true.

______________
*(signature)*

JURAT:

Subscribed and sworn to before me, this ________ day of ______________ , ____ .

______________
*(notary public)*

PTO-FB-TM 200 -(Renewal) (Rev. 12-83) Patent and Trademark Office - U.S. DEPT. of COMMERCE

*(over)*

PTO–FB–TM 200 (Renewal) (Rev. 12-83)

## REPRESENTATION

If the renewal applicant is not domiciled in the United States, a domestic representative must be designated. See Form PTO-FB-TM 151. If a designation is not submitted with this form, a prior unrevoked designation will meet the requirement if such is already in the registration file.

If the renewal applicant wishes to furnish a power of attorney. Form PTO-FB-TM 150 may be modified as appropriate. An attorney at law is not required to furnish a power.

## JURAT

The person who signs the jurat must be authorized to administer oaths by the law of the jurisdiction where executed, and the seal or stamp of the notary, or other evidence of authority in the jurisdiction of execution, must be affixed.

## FOOTNOTES

1 Applicant for renewal must be the present owner of the registration.

2 If applicant for renewal is an association or other similar type of juristic entity, change "corporation" throughout to an appropriate designation.

3 Type of commerce must be specified as "interstate," "territorial," "foreign," or such other commerce as may lawfully be regulated by Congress. Foreign registrants must specify commerce which Congress may regulate, using wording such as commerce with the United States or commerce between the United States and a foreign country.

4 If the mark is not in use in commerce at the time of filing the application for renewal, but there is no intention to abandon the mark, facts must be recited to show that the nonuse is due to special circumstances. A specimen illustrating use, or facts as to nonuse, must be submitted for each class sought to be renewed.

5 The required fee for renewal sought prior to expiration is $300.00 for each class; and for delayed renewal filed within three months after expiration, an additional $100.00 for each class. If renewal is sought for less than the total number of classes in the registration, the classes for which renewal is sought should be specified.

6 Name of individual, if the applicant for renewal is an individual.
If the applicant for renewal is a partnership, the name of a partner.
If the applicant for renewal is a corporation or similar juristic entity, the name of an officer of the corporation or other juristic entity who has authority to sign for the entity, and the title of such officer.

Patent and Trademark Office - U.S. DEPT. of COMMERCE

| APPLICATION FOR RENEWAL OF REGISTRATION OF A MARK, WITH DECLARATION | MARK *(identify the mark)* |
|---|---|
| | REGISTRATION NO. |
| TO THE COMMISSIONER OF PATENTS AND TRADEMARKS: | CLASS NO.(S) |

*(check one box and fill in appropriate information [1])*

☐ NAME OF INDIVIDUAL AS RENEWAL APPLICANT, AND BUSINESS TRADE NAME, IF ANY

BUSINESS ADDRESS

RESIDENCE ADDRESS

CITIZENSHIP

☐ NAME OF PARTNERSHIP AS RENEWAL APPLICANT

NAMES OF PARTNERS

BUSINESS ADDRESS OF PARTNERSHIP

CITIZENSHIP OF PARTNERS

☐ NAME OF CORPORATION [2] AS RENEWAL APPLICANT

STATE OR COUNTRY OF INCORPORATION

BUSINESS ADDRESS OF CORPORATION

The above identified applicant for renewal requests that the above identified registration, granted to
______________________________ on ______________________,
*(name of original registrant)* *(date of issuance)*
which applicant for renewal now owns, as shown by records in the Patent and Trademark Office, be renewed in accordance with the provisions of Section 9 of the Act of July 5, 1946.
The mark shown in said registration is still in use in ______________ commerce [3] on or in
*(type of commerce)*
connection with each of the following: ______________________________
*(list the goods and/or services or insert the words "all the goods" and*
______________________________
*/or "all the services" as may be appropriate)*
which are recited in the registration, the attached specimen showing the mark as currently used.[4]
5
______________________________
*(name of person whose signature is to be placed below[4])*
being hereby warned that willful false statements and the like so made are punishable by fine or imprisonment, or both, under Section 1001 of Title 18 of the United States Code and that such willful false statements may jeopardize the validity of this application, declares that all statements made in this application of his/her knowledge are true and all statements made on information and belief are believed to be true.

______________________________
*(signature)*

______________________________
*(date)*

PTO-FB-TM 201 (Renewal) (Rev. 12-83) Patent and Trademark Office - U.S. DEPT. of COMMERCE

## REPRESENTATION

If the renewal applicant is not domiciled in the United States, a domestic representative must be designated. See Form PTO-FB-TM 151. If a designation is not submitted with this form, a prior unrevoked designation will meet the requirement if such is already in the registration file.

If the renewal applicant wishes to furnish a power of attorney, Form PTO-FB-TM 150 may be modified as appropriate. An attorney at law is not required to furnish a power.

## FOOTNOTES

1 Applicant for renewal must be the present owner of the registration.

2 If applicant for renewal is an association or other similar type of juristic entity, change "corporation" throughout to an appropriate designation.

3 Type of commerce must be specified as "interstate," "territorial," "foreign," or such other commerce as may lawfully be regulated by Congress. Foreign registrants must specify commerce which Congress may regulate, using wording such as commerce with the United States or commerce between the United States and a foreign country.

4 If the mark is not in use in commerce at the time of filing the application for renewal, but there is no intention to abandon the mark, facts must be recited to show that the nonuse is due to special circumstances. A specimen illustrating use, or facts as to nonuse, must be submitted for each class sought to be renewed.

5 The required fee for renewal sought prior to expiration is $300.00 for each class; and for delayed renewal filed within three months after expiration, an additional $100.00 for each class. If renewal is sought for less than the total number of classes in the registration, the classes for which renewal is sought should be specified.

6 Name of individual, if the applicant for renewal is an individual.

If the applicant for renewal is a partnership, the name of a partner.

If the applicant for renewal is a corporation or similar juristic entity, the name of an officer of the corporation or other juristic entity who has authority to sign for the entity, and the title of such officer.

Patent and Trademark Office - U.S. DEPT. of COMMERCE

*(Instructions below)*

| **AFFIDAVIT FOR PUBLICATION OF A MARK UNDER SECTION 12(c), WITH OATH** | MARK *(identify the mark)* |
|---|---|
| | REGISTRATION NO. |
| | DATE OF ISSUE |
| | ISSUED TO *(name of original registrant)* |

State of ______________________ )
) ss.
County of ______________________ )

______________________________________________
*(name of person whose signature is to be placed below [1])*

states that ______________________________________________
*(name of registrant[2])*

owns the above identified registration, as shown by records in the Patent and Trademark Office; that said registration is now in force; that the mark shown therein is in use in ______________
*(type of commerce)*

commerce [3] on each of the following goods stated in the registration:

______________________________________________ ;
*(list the goods or insert the words "all the goods")*

and that the benefits of the Act of July 5, 1946 are hereby claimed for said registration .
[4]

______________________
*(signature)*

JURAT:

Subscribed and sworn to before me, this ________ day of ____________ , ____ .

______________________
*(notary public)*

* * * * * * * *

## REPRESENTATION

If the registrant is not domiciled in the United States, a domestic representative must be designated. See Form PTO-FB-TM 151, changing the word "applicant" to "registrant."

If the registrant wishes to furnish a power of attorney, Form PTO-FB-TM 150 may be modified as appropriate. An attorney at law is not required to furnish a power.

## JURAT

The person who signs the jurat must be authorized to administer oaths by the law of the jurisdiction where executed, and the seal or stamp of the notary, or other evidence of authority in the jurisdiction of execution, must be affixed.

## FOOTNOTES

1 Name of individual, if the present owner of the registration is an individual.
If the present owner is a partnership, the name of a partner.
If the present owner is a corporation or similar juristic entity, the name of an officer of the corporation or other juristic entity who has authority to sign for the entity, and the title of such officer.

2 The present owner of the registration must file the affidavit. If the present owner is a successor to the original registrant, such successor is referred to as registrant.

3 Type of commerce should be specified as "interstate," "territorial," "foreign," or other type of commerce which may lawfully be regulated by Congress. Foreign registrants must specify commerce which Congress may regulate, using wording such as commerce with the United States or commerce between the United States and a foreign country.

4 The required fee of $100.00 must be submitted.

PTO-FB-TM 202 (Sec. 12c) (Rev. 12-83) Patent and Trademark Office - U.S. DEPT. of COMMERCE

*(Instructions below)*

| "AFFIDAVIT" FOR PUBLICATION OF A MARK UNDER SECTION 12(c), WITH DECLARATION | MARK *(identify the mark)* |
|---|---|
| | REGISTRATION NO. |
| | DATE OF ISSUE |
| | ISSUED TO *(name of original registrant)* |

_______________________________________________
*(name of person whose signature is to be placed below[1])*

being hereby warned that willful false statements and the like so made are punishable by fine or imprisonment, or both, under Section 1001 of Title 18 of the United States Code and that such willful false statements may jeopardize the validity of this document, declares that ______________________
*(name of registrant[2])*

owns the above identified registration, as shown by records in the Patent and Trademark Office; that said registration is now in force; that the mark shown therein is in use in ______________________
*(type of commerce)*

commerce [3] on each of the following goods stated in the registration:

_______________________________________________ ;
*(list the goods or insert the words "all the goods")*

that the benefits of the Act of July 5, 1946 are hereby claimed for said registration; and that all statements made of his/her own knowledge are true and all statements made on information and belief are believed to be true.

[4]

______________________
*(signature)*

______________________
*(date)*

* * * * * * * *

REPRESENTATION

If the registrant is not domiciled in the United States, a domestic representative must be designated. See Form PTO-FB-TM 151, changing the word "applicant" to "registrant."

If the registrant wishes to furnish a power of attorney. Form PTO-FB-TM 150 may be modified as appropriate. An attorney at law is not required to furnish a power.

FOOTNOTES

1 Name of individual, if the present owner of the registration is an individual.
If the present owner is a partnership, the name of a partner.
If the present owner is a corporation or similar juristic entity, the name of an officer of the corporation or other juristic entity who has authority to sign for the entity, and the title of such officer.

2 The present owner of the registration must file the affidavit. If the present owner is a successor to the original registrant, such successor is referred to as registrant.

3 Type of commerce should be specified as "interstate," "territorial," "foreign," or other type of commerce which may lawfully be regulated by Congress. Foreign registrants must specify commerce which Congress may regulate, using wording such as commerce with the United States or commerce between the United States and a foreign country.

4 The required fee of $100.00 must be submitted.

| AFFIDAVIT OF USE OF A MARK REQUIRED BY SECTION 8,[1] WITH OATH | MARK *(identify the mark)* |
|---|---|
| | REGISTRATION NO. |
| | CLASS NO.(S) |

State of ______________________ )
) ss.
County of ______________________ )

______________________
*(name of person whose signature is to be placed below [2])*

states that ______________________
*(name of registrant)*

owns the above identified registration, issued __________ , as shown by records in the Patent and Trademark Office. The mark shown in said registration is still in use in __________ commerce [5]
*(date [4])* *(type of commerce)*

on or in connection with the goods. The mark is still in use [6] as evidenced by [7] ______________________

______________________
8

______________________
*(signature)*

JURAT:

Subscribed and sworn to before me, this ______ day of ______________ , ______ .

______________________
*(notary public)*

* * * * * * * *

## REPRESENTATION

If the registrant is not domiciled in the United States, a domestic representative must be designated. See Form PTO-FB-TM 151, changing the word "applicant" to "registrant." If a designation is not submitted with this form, a prior unrevoked designation will meet the requirement if such is already in the registration file.

If the registrant wishes to furnish a power of attorney, Form PTO-FB-TM 150 may be modified as appropriate. An attorney at law is not required to furnish a power.

## JURAT

The person who signs the jurat must be authorized to administer oaths by the law of the jurisdiction where executed, and the seal or stamp of the notary, or other evidence of authority in the jurisdiction of execution, must be affixed.

## FOOTNOTES

1 The affidavit, of which this form is an illustration, must be filed within the sixth year after the date of registration under the Act of 1946 or after the date of publication under Section 12(c) of said Act.

2 Name of individual, if the present owner of the registration is an individual.
If the present owner is a partnership the name of a partner.
If the present owner is a corporation or similar juristic entity, the name of an officer of the corporation or other juristic entity who has authority to sign for the entity, and the title of such officer.

3 The present owner of the registration must file the affidavit. If the present owner is a successor to the original registrant, such successor is referred to as registrant.

4 If the registration issued under a prior act and has been published under Section 12(c), add: "and published under Section 12(c) on ..................."
*(date)*

5 Type of commerce should be specified as "interstate," "territorial," "foreign," or other type of commerce which may lawfully be regulated by Congress. Foreign registrants must specify commerce which Congress may regulate, using wording such as commerce with the United States or commerce between the United States and a foreign country.

6 If the mark is not in use at the time of filing the affidavit, but there is no intention to abandon the mark, facts must be recited to show that the nonuse is due to special circumstances.

7 Insert "the specimen included showing the mark as currently used," or recite facts as to sales or advertising which will show that the mark is in current use. Specimen illustrating use, or facts as to use or nonuse, are required for each class for which action is sought.

8 The required fee of $100.00 must be submitted for each class for which action is sought, and if action is sought for less than the total number of classes in the registration, the classes for which action is sought should be specified.

PTO-FB-TM 204 (Sec. 8) (Rev. 12-83) Patent and Trademark Office - U.S. DEPT. of COMMERCE

| "AFFIDAVIT" OF USE OF A MARK REQUIRED BY SECTION 8,[1] WITH DECLARATION | MARK (identify the mark) | |
|---|---|---|
| | REGISTRATION NO. | CLASS NO.(S) |

_______________________________________________
(name of person whose signature is to be placed below [2])

being hereby warned that willful false statements and the like so made are punishable by fine or imprisonment, or both, under Section 1001 of Title 18 of the United States Code and that such willful false statements may jeopardize the validity of this document, declares that ______________
(name of registrant [3])

_______________________________________________

owns the above identified registration, issued ____________ , as shown by records in the Patent and
(date [4])
Trademark Office. The mark shown in said registration is still in use in ____________ commerce [5]
(Type of Commerce)
on or in connection with the goods. The mark is still in use [6] as evidenced by [7] ______________

_______________________________________________ ;

and that all statements made of his/her own knowledge are true and all statements made on information and belief are believed to be true.
8

_______________________
(signature)

_______________________
(date)

* * * * * * * *

## REPRESENTATION

If the registrant is not domiciled in the United States, a domestic representative must be designated. See Form PTO-FB-TM 151, changing the word "applicant" to "registrant." If a designation is not submitted with this form, a prior unrevoked designation will meet the requirement if such is already in the registration file.

If the registrant wishes to furnish a power of attorney, Form PTO-FB-TM 150 may be modified as appropriate. An attorney at law is not required to furnish a power.

## FOOTNOTES

1 The affidavit, of which this form is an illustration, must be filed within the sixth year after the date of registration under the Act of 1946 or after the date of publication under Section 12(c) of said Act.

2 Name of individual, if the present owner of the registration is an individual.
If the present owner is a partnership, the name of a partner.
If the present owner is a corporation or similar juristic entity, the name of an officer of the corporation or other juristic entity who has authority to sign for the entity, and the title of such officer.

3 The present owner of the registration must file the affidavit. If the present owner is a successor to the original registrant, such successor is referred to as registrant.

4 If the registration issued under a prior act and has been published under Section 12(c), add: "and published under Section 12(c) on .................."
(date)

5 Type of commerce should be specified as "interstate," "territorial," "foreign," or other type of commerce which may lawfully be regulated by Congress. Foreign registrants must specify commerce which Congress may regulate, using wording such as commerce with the United States or commerce between the United States and a foreign country.

6 If the mark is not in use at the time of filing the affidavit, but there is no intention to abandon the mark, facts must be recited to show that the nonuse is due to special circumstances.

7 Insert "the specimen included showing the mark as currently used," or recite facts as to sales or advertising which will show that the mark is in current use. Specimen illustrating use, or facts as to use or nonuse, are required for each class for which action is sought.

8 The required fee of $100.00 must be submitted for each class for which action is sought, and if action is sought for less than the total number of classes in the registration, the classes for which action is sought should be specified.

PTO-FB-TM 205 (Sec. 8) (Rev. 12-83) Patent and Trademark Office - U.S. DEPT. of COMMERCE

*(Instructions on reverse side)*

| **AFFIDAVIT OF INCONTESTABILITY OF A MARK UNDER SECTION 15, WITH OATH** | MARK *(identify the mark)* |
|---|---|
| | REGISTRATION NO. |
| | CLASS NO.(S) |

State of ____________________ )
) ss.
County of ____________________ )

________________________________________
*(name of person whose signature is to be placed below [1])*

states that ____________________ *(name of registrant [2])* owns the above identified registration, issued ____________ *(date [3])*, as shown by records in the Patent and Trademark Office; that the mark shown therein has been in continuous use in ____________ *(type of commerce)* commerce [4] for five consecutive years from [5] ____________ *(date)* to the present, on or in connection with each of the following: ____________

________________________________________
*(list the goods and/or services or insert the words "all the goods" and/or "all the services" as may be appropriate)*

which are stated in the registration; that such mark is still in use in ____________ *(type of commerce)* commerce [4]; that there has been no final decision adverse to registrant's claim of ownership of such mark for such goods or services, or to registrant's right to register the same or to keep the same on the register; and that there is no proceeding involving said rights pending and not disposed of either in the Patent and Trademark Office or in the courts.

[6]

____________________
*(signature)*

JURAT:

Subscribed and sworn to before me, this ________ day of ____________, ____.

____________________
*(notary public)*

PTO-FB-TM 206 (Sec. 15) (Rev. 12-83) Patent and Trademark Office - U.S. DEPT. of COMMERCE

PTO–FB–TM 206 (Sec. 15) (Rev. 12-83)

## REPRESENTATION

If the registrant wishes to furnish a power of attorney, Form PTO-FB-TM 150 may be modified as appropriate. An attorney at law is not required to furnish a power.

## JURAT

The person who signs the jurat must be authorized to administer oaths by the law of the jurisdiction where executed, and the seal or stamp of the notary, or other evidence of authority in the jurisdiction of execution, must be affixed.

## FOOTNOTES

1 Name of individual, if the present owner of the registration is an individual.
If the present owner is a partnership, the name of a partner.
If the present owner is a corporation or similar juristic entity, the name of an officer of the corporation or other juristic entity who has authority to sign for the entity, and the title of such officer.

2 The present owner of the registration must file the "affidavit." If the present owner is a successor to the original registrant, such successor is referred to as registrant.

3 If the registration issued under a prior act and has been published under section 12(c), add: "and published under Section 12(c) on ____________."
*(date)*

4 Type of commerce must be specified as "interstate," "territorial," "foreign," or such other commerce as may lawfully be regulated by Congress. Foreign registrants must specify commerce which Congress may regulate, using wording such as commerce with the United States or commerce between the United States and a foreign country.

5 The date should be the beginning of a five year period of continuous use, all of which five year period falls after the date of registration under the Act of 1946 or after the date of publication under Section 12(c). A date which would produce a period of continuous use which is longer than five years may be stated provided the period indicated includes five years of continuous use after registration under the Act of 1946 or publication under Section 12(c).

6 The required fee of $100.00 must be submitted for each Class for which action is sought, and if action is sought for less than the total number of classes in the registration, the Class for which action is sought should be specified.

Patent and Trademark Office - U.S. DEPT. of COMMERCE

(nstructions on reverse side)

| "AFFIDAVIT" OF INCONTESTABILITY OF A MARK UNDER SECTION 15, WITH DECLARATION | MARK *(identify the mark)* |
|---|---|
| | REGISTRATION NO. |
| | CLASS NO.(S) |

_______________________________________________
*(name of person whose signature is to be placed below [1])*

being hereby warned that willful false statements and the like so made are punishable by fine or imprisonment, or both, under Section 1001 of Title 18 of the United States Code and that such willful false statements may jeopardize the validity of this document, declares that ____________ *(name of registrant [2])* owns the above identified registration, issued ____________ *(date [3])*, as shown by records in the Patent and Trademark Office; that the mark shown therein has been in continuous use in ____________ *(type of commerce)* commerce [4] for five consecutive years from [5] ____________ *(date)* to the present, on or in connection with each of the following: ____________ *(list the goods and/or services or insert the words "all the goods" and/or "all the services" as may be appropriate)* ____________

which are stated in the registration; that such mark is still in use in ____________ *(type of commerce)* commerce [4]; that there has been no final decision adverse to registrant's claim of ownership of such mark for such goods or services, or to registrant's right to register the same or to keep the same on the register; that there is no proceeding involving said rights pending and not disposed of either in the Patent and Trademark Office or in the courts; and that all statements made of his/her own knowledge are true and all statements made on information and belief are believed to be true.

6

_______________________
*(signature)*

_______________________
*(date)*

PTO-FB-TM 207 (Sec. 15) (Rev. 12-83)

Patent and Trademark Office - U.S. DEPT. of COMMERCE

(over)

PTO–FB–TM 207 (Sec. 15) (Rev. 12-83)

## REPRESENTATION

If the registrant wishes to furnish a power of attorney, Form PTO-FB-TM 150 may be modified as appropriate. An attorney at law is not required to furnish a power.

## FOOTNOTES

1 Name of individual, if the present owner of the registration is an individual.

If the present owner is a partnership, the name of a partner.

If the present owner is a corporation or similar juristic entity, the name of an officer of the corporation or other juristic entity who has authority to sign for the entity, and the title of such officer.

2 The present owner of the registration must file the "affidavit." If the present owner is a successor to the original registrant, such successor is referred to as registrant.

3 If the registration issued under a prior act and has been published under Section 12(c), add: "and published under Section 12(c) on __________ (date)."

4 Type of commerce must be specified as "interstate," "territorial," "foreign," or such other commerce as may lawfully be regulated by Congress. Foreign registrants must specify commerce which Congress may regulate, using wording such as commerce with the United States or commerce between the United States and a foreign country.

5 The date should be the beginning of a five year period of continuous use, all of which five year period falls after the date of registration under the Act of 1946 or after the date of publication under Section 12(c). A date which would produce a period of continuous use which is longer than five years may be stated provided the period indicated includes five years of continuous use after registration under the Act of 1946 or publication under Section 12(c).

6 The required fee of $100.00 must be submitted for each Class for which action is sought, and if action is sought for less than the total number of classes in the registration, the Class for which action is sought should be specified.

Patent and Trademark Office - U.S. DEPT. of COMMERCE

*(Instructions on reverse side)*

| **COMBINED AFFIDAVIT OF USE AND INCONTESTABILITY OF A MARK UNDER SECTIONS 8 AND 15,[1] WITH OATH** | MARK *(identify the mark)* |
|---|---|
| | REGISTRATION NO. |
| | CLASS NO.(S) |

State of ______________________ )
) ss.
County of ______________________ )

______________________________________________
*(name of person whose signature is to be placed below[2])*

states that ______________________________________________
*(name of registrant[3])*

owns the above identified registration issued __________ *(date[4])*, as shown by records in the Patent and Trademark Office; that the mark shown therein has been in continuous use in __________ *(type of commerce)* commerce[5] for five consecutive years from the date of the registration or the date of publication under Section 12(c)[6] to the present, on or in connection with each of the following:

______________________________________________

______________________________________________
*(list the goods and/or services or insert the words "all the goods" and/or "all the services" as may be appropriate)*

which are stated in the registration; that such mark is still in use in __________ *(type of commerce)* commerce[5]; that such mark is still in use as evidenced by[7] ______________________________________________

______________________________________________;

that there has been no final decision adverse to the registrant's claim of ownership of such mark for such goods or services, or to registrant's right to register the same or to keep the same on the register; and that there is no proceeding involving said rights pending and not disposed of either in the Patent and Trademark Office or in the courts.

8

______________________
*(signature)*

JURAT:

Subscribed and sworn to before me, this ________ day of ______________, ______.

______________________
*(notary public)*

PTO-FB-TM 208 (combined 8 & 15) (Rev. 12-83)

Patent and Trademark Office - U.S. DEPT. of COMMERCE

*(over)*

PTO–FB–TM 208 (combined 8 & 15) (Rev. 12-83)

## REPRESENTATION

If the registrant is not domiciled in the United States, a domestic representative must be designated for Section 8. See Form PTO-FB-TM 151, changing the word "applicant" to "registrant." If a designation is not submitted with this form, a prior unrevoked designation will meet the requirement if such is already in the registration file.

If the registrant wishes to furnish a power of attorney, Form PTO-FB-TM 150 may be modified as appropriate. An attorney at law is not required to furnish a power.

## JURAT

The person who signs the jurat must be authorized to administer oaths by the law of the jurisdiction where executed, and the seal or stamp of the notary, or other evidence of authority in the jurisdiction of execution, must be affixed.

## FOOTNOTES

1 This combined form may not be used when the Section 8 portion thereof is based on nonuse.

2 Name of individual, if the present owner of the registration is an individual.
If the present owner is a partnership, the name of a partner.
If the present owner is a corporation or similar juristic entity, the name of an officer of the corporation or other juristic entity who has authority to sign for the entity, and the title of such officer.

3 The present owner of the registration must file the affidavit. If the present owner is a successor to the original registrant, such successor is referred to as registrant.

4 If the registration issued under a prior Act and has been published under Section 12(c), add: "and published under Section 12(c) on ______________."
(date)

5 Type of commerce must be specified as "interstate," "territorial," "foreign," or such other commerce as may lawfully be regulated by Congress. Foreign registrants must specify commerce which Congress may regulate, using wording such as commerce with the United States or commerce between the United States and a foreign country.

6 This combined form is only appropriate when the five year period of continuous use which is required for Section 15 is also the first five years after registration or after publication under Section 12(c) as is required for Section 8.

7 Insert "the specimen included showing the mark as currently used," or recite facts as to sales or advertising which will show that the mark is in current use.

8 The required fee of $200.00 for each combined affidavit under Sections 8 & 15 must be submitted for each class for which action is sought, and if action is sought for less than the total number of classes in the registration, the classes for which action is sought should be specified.

Patent and Trademark Office - U.S. DEPT. of COMMERCE

*(Instructions on reverse side)*

| **COMBINED "AFFIDAVIT" OF USE AND INCONTESTABILITY OF A MARK UNDER SECTIONS 8 AND 15,[1] WITH DECLARATION** | MARK *(identify the mark)* |
|---|---|
| | REGISTRATION NO. |
| | CLASS NO.(S) |

______________________________________
*(name of person whose signature is to be placed below[a])*

being hereby warned that willful false statements and the like so made are punishable by fine or imprisonment, or both, under Section 1001 of Title 18 of the United States Code and that such willful false statements may jeopardize the validity of this document, declares that ______________ *(name of registrant[3])* owns the above identified registration issued __________ *(date[4])*, as shown by records in the Patent and Trademark Office; that the mark shown therein has been in continuous use in ______________ *(type of commerce)* __________ commerce[5] for five consecutive years from the date of the registration or the date of publication under Section 12(c)[6] to the present, on or in connection with each of the following:

______________________________________
*(list the goods and/or services or insert the words "all the goods" and/or "all the services" as may be appropriate)*

which are stated in the registration; that such mark is still in use in ______________ *(type of commerce)* commerce[5]; that such mark is still in use as evidenced by[7] ______________________________________

______________________________________,

that there has been no final decision adverse to the registrant's claim of ownership of such mark for such goods or services, or to registrant's right to register the same or to keep the same on the register; that there is no proceeding involving said rights pending and not disposed of either in the Patent and Trademark Office or in the courts; and that all statements made of his/her own knowledge are true and all statements made on information and belief are believed to be true.

8

______________________
*(signature)*

______________________
*(date)*

PTO-FB-TM 209 (combined 8 & 15) (Rev. 12-83)

Patent and Trademark Office - U.S. DEPT. of COMMERCE

PTO–FB–TM 209 (combined 8 & 15) (Rev. 12-83)

## REPRESENTATION

If the registrant is not domiciled in the United States, a domestic representative must be designated for Section 8. See Form PTO-FB-TM 151, changing the word "applicant" to "registrant." If a designation is not submitted with this form, a prior unrevoked designation will meet the requirement if such is already in the registration file.

If the registrant wishes to furnish a power of attorney, Form PTO-FB-TM 150 may be modified as appropriate. An attorney at law is not required to furnish a power.

## FOOTNOTES

1 This combined form may not be used when the Section 8 portion thereof is based on nonuse.

2 Name of individual, if the present owner of the registration is an individual.
If the present owner is a partnership, the name of a partner.
If the present owner is a corporation or similar juristic entity, the name of an officer of the corporation or other juristic entity who has authority to sign for the entity, and the title of such officer.

3 The present owner of the registration must file the affidavit. If the present owner is a successor to the original registrant, such successor is referred to as registrant.

4 If the registration issued under a prior Act and has been published under Section 12(c), add: "and published under Section 12(c) on ______________."
*(date)*

5 Type of commerce must be specified as "interstate," "territorial," "foreign," or such other commerce as may lawfully be regulated by Congress. Foreign registrants must specify commerce which Congress may regulate, using wording such as commerce with the United States or commerce between the United States and a foreign country.

6 This combined form is only appropriate when the five year period of continuous use which is required for Section 15 is also the first five years after registration or after publication under Section 12(c) as is required for Section 8.

7 Insert "the specimen included showing the mark as currently used," or recite facts as to sales or advertising which will show that the mark is in current use.

8 The required fee of $200.00 for each combined affidavit under Sections 8 & 15 must be submitted for each class for which action is sought, and if action is sought for less than the total number of classes in the registration, the classes for which action is sought should be specified.

Patent and Trademark Office - U.S. DEPT. of COMMERCE

*(Instructions on reverse side)*

**OPPOSITION TO THE REGISTRATION OF A MARK**

In the matter of trademark application Serial No. ______________________ .
Published in the *Official Gazette* on ______________________ .
*(date)*

______________________
*(name of opposer)*

v.

______________________
*(name of applicant)*

Opposition No. ______________________
*(to be inserted by Patent & Trademark Office)*

*(Check one box and fill in appropriate information)*

☐ NAME OF INDIVIDUAL AS OPPOSER, AND BUSINESS TRADE NAME, IF ANY

BUSINESS ADDRESS

☐ NAME OF PARTNERSHIP AS OPPOSER

NAMES OF PARTNERS

BUSINESS ADDRESS OF PARTNERSHIP

☐ NAME OF CORPORATION [1] AS OPPOSER

STATE OR COUNTRY OF INCORPORATION

BUSINESS ADDRESS OF CORPORATION

The above identified opposer believes that it/he/she will be damaged by registration of the mark shown in the above identified application, and hereby opposes the same.
The grounds for opposition are as follows: [2]

[3]

By ______________________
*(signature [4])*

______________________
*(identification of person signing [4])*

PTO-FB-TM 300 (Opposition) (Rev. 12-83)

Patent and Trademark Office - U.S. DEPT. of COMMERCE

*(over)*

PTO–FB–TM 300 (Opposition) (Rev. 12-83)

## REPRESENTATION

If the opposer is not domiciled in the United States, a domestic representative must be designated. See Form PTO-FB-TM 151, changing the word "applicant" to "opposer." For opposers who are foreigners, it is customary to regard a power of attorney (if one is furnished) as the equivalent of a domestic representative.

If the opposer wishes to furnish a power of attorney, Form PTO-FB-TM 150 may be modified as appropriate. An attorney at law is not required to furnish a power.

## FOOTNOTES

1 If opposer is an association or other similar type of juristic entity, change "corporation" throughout to an appropriate designation.

2 Here set forth a short and plain statement showing how the opposer would be damaged by the registration of the opposed mark, and state the grounds for opposing.

3 The required fee of $200.00 must be submitted for each party joined as opposer for each class opposed, and if less than the total number of classes in the application are opposed, the classes opposed should be specified.

4 The opposition may be signed either by counsel for opposer or by opposer himself/itself. If an opposer signing for itself is a partnership, the signature must be made by a partner; if an opposer signing for itself is a corporation or similar juristic entity, the signature must be made by an Officer of the corporation or other juristic entity who has authority to sign for the entity and whose title is given.

5 State the capacity in which the signing individual signs, e.g., attorney for opposer, opposer (if opposer is an individual), partner of opposer (if opposer is a partnership), Officer of opposer identified by title (if opposer is a corporation), etc.

Patent and Trademark Office - U.S. DEPT. of COMMERCE

*(Instructions on reverse side)*

## PETITION TO CANCEL A REGISTRATION OF A MARK

In the matter of trademark Registration No. ____________________
Date registered ____________________

____________________
*(name of petitioner)*

v.

____________________
*(name of registrant)*

Cancellation No. ____________________
*(to be inserted by Patent & Trademark Office)*

*(Check one box and fill in appropriate information)*

☐ NAME OF INDIVIDUAL AS PETITIONER, AND BUSINESS TRADE NAME, IF ANY

BUSINESS ADDRESS

☐ NAME OF PARTNERSHIP AS PETITIONER

NAMES OF PARTNERS

BUSINESS ADDRESS OF PARTNERSHIP

☐ NAME OF CORPORATION [1] AS PETITIONER

STATE OR COUNTRY OF INCORPORATION

BUSINESS ADDRESS OF CORPORATION

The above identified petitioner believes that it/he/she is or will be damaged by the above identified registration, and hereby petitions to cancel the same.
The grounds for cancellation are as follows: [2]
[3]

By ____________________
*(signature [4])*

____________________
*(identification of person signing [4])*

PTO-FB-TM 301 (Petition to Cancel) (Rev. 12-83) Patent and Trademark Office - U.S. DEPT. of COMMERCE

(over)

PTO–FB–TM 301 (Petition to Cancel) (Rev. 12-83)

## REPRESENTATION

If the petitioner is not domiciled in the United States, a domestic representative must be designated. See Form PTO-FB-TM 151, changing the word "applicant" to "petitioner." For petitioners who are foreigners, it is customary to regard a power of attorney (if one is furnished) as the equivalent of a domestic representative.

If the petitioner wishes to furnish a power of attorney, Form PTO-FB-TM 150 may be modified as appropriate. An attorney at law is not required to furnish a power.

## FOOTNOTES

1 If petitioner is an association or other similar type of juristic entity, change "corporation" throughout to an appropriate designation.

2 Here set forth a short and plain statement showing how the petitioner is or will be damaged by the registration, and state the grounds for cancellation.

3 The required fee of $200.00 must be submitted for each class sought to be cancelled, and if cancellation is sought for less than the total number of classes in the registration, the classes sought to be cancelled should be specified.

4 The opposition may be signed either by counsel for petitioner or by petitioner himself/itself. If a petitioner signing for itself is a partnership, the signature must be made by a partner; if a petitioner signing for itself is a corporation or similar juristic entity, the signature must be made by an Officer of the corporation or other juristic entity who has authority to sign for the entity and whose title is given.

5 State the capacity in which the signing individual signs, e.g., attorney for petitioner, petitioner (if petitioner is an individual), partner of petitioner (if petitioner is a partnership), Officer of petitioner identified by title (if petitioner is a corporation), etc.

Patent and Trademark Office - U.S. DEPT. of COMMERCE

| EX PARTE APPEAL FROM EXAMINER OF TRADEMARKS TO TRADEMARK TRIAL AND APPEAL BOARD | NAME OF APPLICANT |
|---|---|
| | SERIAL NO. OF APPLICATION |

TO THE TRADEMARK TRIAL AND APPEAL BOARD:

Applicant hereby appeals to the Trademark Trial and Appeal Board from the decision of the Examiner of Trademarks refusing registration.

_______________________
*(signature [1])*

FOOTNOTE

1 Signature of counsel for applicant, or
signature of individual, if the applicant is an individual;
signature of a partner, if the applicant is a partnership; or if the applicant is a corporation of similar entity, signature of an officer of the corporation or other juristic entity who has authority to sign for the entity, and the title of such officer.

PTO-FB-TM 302 (Ex parte Appeal) (Rev. 12-83) Patent and Trademark Office - U.S. DEPT. of COMMERCE

## ASSIGNMENT OF APPLICATION FOR REGISTRATION OF A MARK

Whereas ______________________________________________ ,
*(name of assignor)*

of ______________________________________________ ,
*(address)*

has adopted and is using a mark for which said assignor has filed application in the United States Patent and Trademark Office for registration, Serial No. ________________ ; and

Whereas ______________________________________________ ,
*(name of assignee)*

1

of ______________________________________________ ,
*(address)*

is desirous of acquiring said mark;

Now, therefore, for good and valuable consideration, receipt of which is hereby acknowledged, said ______________________________ does hereby assign
*(name of assignor)*

unto the said ______________________________________________
*(name of assignee)*

all right, title and interest in and to the said mark, together with the good will of the business symbolized by the mark, and the above identified application for registration of said mark.

The Commissioner of Patents and Trademarks is requested to issue the certificate of registration to said assignee.

2

______________________________________________
*(signature of assignor; if assignor is a corporation or other juristic organization, give the official title of the person who signs for assignor)*

State of ______________________ )
) ss.
County of ______________________ )

On this __________ day of ______________ , ________ , before me appeared ______________________________________ , the person who signed this instrument, who acknowledged that he/she signed it as a free act on his/her behalf (or on behalf of the identified corporation or other juristic entity with authority to do so).

*

______________________________________________
*(signature of notary public)*

* The wording of the acknowledgment may vary from this illustration but should be wording acceptable under the law of the jurisdiction where the document is executed; the person who signs the acknowledgment must be authorized to do so by the law of the jurisdiction where the document is executed, and the seal or stamp of the notary, or other evidence of authority in the jurisdiction of execution, must be affixed.

### FOOTNOTES

(1) If the postal address of the assignee is not given either in the instrument or in an accompanying paper, registration to the assignee may be delayed pending receipt of such address.

(2) If assignee is not domiciled in the United States, a domestic representative must be designated. See Form PTO-FB-TM 151, changing the word "applicant" to "assignee."

PTO-FB-TM 400 (Assignment of Application) (Rev. 12-83) — Patent and Trademark Office - U.S. DEPT. of COMMERCE

## ASSIGNMENT OF REGISTRATION OF A MARK

Whereas ______________________________________________________________,
*(name of assignor)*

of ______________________________________________________________,
*(address)*

has adopted, used and is using a mark which is registered in the United States Patent and Trademark Office, Registration No. ____________________, dated ____________________; and

Whereas ______________________________________________________________,
*(name of assignee)*

1

of ______________________________________________________________,
*(address)*

is desirous of acquiring said mark and the registration thereof;

Now, therefore, for good and valuable consideration, receipt of which is hereby acknowledged, said ________________________________ does hereby assign unto the said
*(name of assignor)*

________________________________ all right, title and interest in and to the
*(name of assignee)*

said mark, together with the good will of the business symbolized by the mark, and the above identified registration thereof.

2

________________________________________
*(signature of assignor; if assignor is a corporation or other juristic organization, give the official title of the person who signs for assignor)*

State of ______________________________ )

) ss.

County of ______________________________ )

On this __________ day of ____________________, __________, before me appeared ________________________________________, the person who signed this instrument, who acknowledged that he/she signed it as a free act on his/her own behalf (or on behalf of the identified corporation or other juristic entity with authority to do so).

*

________________________________________
*(signature of notary public)*

* The wording of the acknowledgment may vary from this illustration but should be wording acceptable under the law of the jurisdiction where the document is executed; the person who signs the acknowledgment must be authorized to do so by the law of the jurisdiction where the document is executed, and the seal or stamp of the notary, or other evidence of authority in the jurisdiction of execution, must be affixed.

FOOTNOTES

(1) If the postal address of the assignee is not given either in the instrument or in an accompanying paper, recording may be delayed pending receipt of such address.

(2) If assignee is not domiciled in the United States, a domestic representative must be designated. See Form PTO-FB-TM 151, changing the word "applicant" to "assignee."

PTO-FB-TM 401 (Assignment of Registration) (Rev. 12-83) Patent and Trademark Office - U.S. DEPT. of COMMERCE

**CERTIFICATE OF MAILING UNDER 37 CFR 1.8(a)**

When placing the Certificate directly on the correspondence,[1] use the following language:

CERTIFICATE OF MAILING UNDER 37 CFR 1.8(a).

I hereby certify that this correspondence is being deposited with the United States Postal Services as first class mail in an envelope addressed to: Commissioner of Patents and Trademarks, Washington, D. C. 20231, on ____________________ .

*(date of deposit)*

______________________________

*(print or type name of person signing Certificate)*[2]

______________________________

*(signature of person signing Certificate)*

______________________________

*(date of signature)*

* * * * * * * *

When the Certificate is to be separate,[1] fill in the following and attach this sheet securely to the correspondence:

CERTIFICATE OF MAILING UNDER 37 CFR 1.8(a).

| IDENTIFY THE MARK |
|---|
| SERIAL NO. OF APPLICATION |
| NAME OF PARTY FILING PAPER |
| IDENTIFY THE TYPE OF PAPER |

I hereby certify that the above identified correspondence, which is attached, is being deposited with the United States Postal Service as first class mail in an envelope addressed to: Commissioner of Patents and Trademarks, Washington, D. C. 20231 on ____________________

*(date of deposit)*

______________________________

*(print or type name of person signing Certificate)*[2]

______________________________

*(signature of person signing Certificate)*

______________________________

*(date of signature)*

FOOTNOTES

1 Whenever possible, the certificate of mailing should be typed or ink stamped directly on the correspondence itself. If that is not possible, fill in the second form on this sheet and attach this sheet to the correspondence securely.

2 Preferably the certificate should be signed by the applicant or other party who is filing the paper, or by such party's attorney; however, another responsible person if in position to know that the mailing was done on the date specified may sign the certificate.

PTO-FB-TM 402 (Certificate of Mailing) (Rev. 12-83) Patent and Trademark Office - U.S. DEPT. of COMMERCE

**CERTIFICATE OF EXPRESS MAIL UNDER 37 CFR 1.10**

When placing the certificate directly on the correspondence, use the following language:

"Express Mail" mailing label number ______________________________

Date of Deposit ______________________________

I hereby certify that this paper or fee is being deposited with the United States Postal Service "Express Mail Post Office to Addressee" service under 37 CFR 1.10 on the date indicated above and is addressed to the Commissioner of Patents and Trademarks, Washington, D.C. 20231.

______________________________
*(Typed or printed name of person mailing paper or fee)*

______________________________
*(Signature of person mailing paper or fee)*

PTO-FB-TM 403 (Certificate of Express Mailing) (Rev. 12-93)

# Appendix C

The international schedule of classes of goods and services adopted by the United States Patent Office on September 1, 1973, and currently in force, is as follows:

## CLASSIFICATION OF GOODS AND SERVICES UNDER THE TRADEMARK ACT

6.1 International schedule of classes of goods and services.
6.2 U.S. schedule of classes of good and services.
6.3 Schedule for certification marks.
6.4 Schedule for collective membership marks.

AUTHORITY: Rules 6.1 to 6.4 issued under sec. 41, 60 Stat. 440; 15 U.S.C. 1123. Interpret or apply sec. 30, 60 Stat. 436; 15 U.S.C. 1112.

### *6.1 International schedule of classes of goods and services.*

GOODS

1. Chemical products used in industry, science, photography, agriculture, horticulture, forestry; artificial and synthetic resins; plastics in the form of powders, liquids or pastes, for industrial use; manures (natural and artificial); fire extinguishing compositions; tempering substances and chemical preparations for soldering; chemical substances for preserving foodstuffs; tanning substances; adhesive substances used in industry.

2. Paints, varnishes, lacquers; preservatives against rust and against deterioration of wood; colouring matters, dyestuffs; mordants; natural resins; metals in foil and powder form for painters and decorators.

3. Bleaching preparations and other substances for laundry use; cleaning, polishing, scouring and abrasive preparations; soaps; perfumery, essential oils, cosmetics, hair lotions; dentifrices.

4. Industrial oils and greases (other than oils and fats and essential oils); lubricants; dust laying and absorbing compositions; fuels (including motor spirit) and illuminants; candles, tapers, night lights and wicks.

5. Pharmaceutical, veterinary, and sanitary substances; infants' and invalids' foods; plasters, material for bandaging; material for stopping teeth, dental wax, disinfectants; preparations for killing weeds and destroying vermin.

6. Unwrought and partly wrought common metals and their alloys; anchors, anvils, bells, rolled and cast building materials; rails and other metallic materials for railway tracks; chains (except driving chains for vehicles); cables and wires (nonelectric); locksmiths' work; metallic pipes and tubes; safes and cash boxes; steel balls, horseshoes; nails and screws; other goods in nonprecious metal not included in other classes; ores.

7. Machines and machine tools; motors (except for land vehicles); machine couplings and belting (except for land vehicles); large size agricultural implements; incubators.

8. Hand tools and instruments; cutlery, forks, and spoons; side arms.

9. Scientific, nautical, surveying and electrical apparatus and instruments (including wireless), photographic, cinematographic, optical, weighing, measuring, signalling, checking (supervision), life-saving and teaching apparatus and instruments; coin or counter-freed apparatus; talking machines; cash registers; calculating machines; fire extinguishing apparatus.

10. Surgical, medical, dental, and veterinary instruments and apparatus (including artificial limbs, eyes, and teeth).

11. Installations for lighting, heating, steam generating, cooking, refrigerating, drying, ventilating, water supply, and sanitary purposes.

12. Vehicles; apparatus for locomotion by land, air, or water.

13. Firearms; ammunition and projectiles; explosives substances; fireworks.

14. Precious metals and their alloys and goods in precious metals or coated therewith (except cutlery, forks and spoons); jewelry, precious stones, horological and other chronometric instruments.

15. Musical instruments (other than talking machines and wireless apparatus).

16. Paper and paper articles, cardboard and cardboard articles; printed matter, newspaper and periodicals, books; bookbinding material; photographs; stationery, adhesive materials (stationery); artists' materials; paint brushes; typewriters and office requisites (other than furniture); instructional and teaching material (other than apparatus); playing cards; printers' type and cliches (stereotype).

17. Gutta percha, india rubber, balata and substitutes, articles made from these substances and not included in other classes; plastics in the form of sheets, blocks and rods, being for use in manufacture; materials

for packing, stopping or insulating; asbestos, mica and their products; hose pipes (nonmetallic).

18. Leather and imitations of leather, and articles made from these materials and not included in other classes; skins, hides; trunks and travelling bags; umbrellas, parasols and walking sticks; whips, harness and saddlery.

19. Building materials, natural and artificial stone, cement, lime, mortar, plaster and gravel; pipes of earthenware or cement; roadmaking materials; asphalt, pitch and bitumen; portable buildings; stone monuments; chimney pots.

20. Furniture, mirrors, picture frames; articles (not included in other classes) of wood, corks, reeds, cane, wicker, horn bone, ivory, whalebone, shell, amber, mother-of-pearl, meerschaum, celluloid, substitutes for all these materials, or of plastics.

21. Small domestic utensils and containers (not of precious metals, or coated therewith) combs and sponges; brushes (other than paint brushes); brushmaking materials; instruments and material for cleaning purposes, steel wool; unworked or semi-worked glass (excluding glass used in building); glassware, porcelain and earthenware, not included in other classes.

22. Ropes, string, nets, tents, awnings, tarpaulins, sails, sacs; padding and stuffing materials (hair, kapok, feathers, seaweed, etc.); raw fibrous textile materials.

23. Yarns, threads.

24. Tissues (piece goods); bed and table covers; textile articles not included in other classes.

25. Clothing, including boots, shoes and slippers.

26. Lace and embroidery, ribands and braid; buttons, press buttons, hooks and eyes, pins and needles; artificial flowers.

27. Carpets, rugs, mats and matting; linoleums and other materials for covering existing floors; wall hangings (nontextile).

28. Games and playthings; gymnastic and sporting articles (except clothing); ornaments and decorations for Christmas trees.

29. Meats, fish, poultry and game; meat extracts; preserved, dried and cooked fruits and vegetables; jellies, jams; eggs, milk and other dairy products; edible oils and fats; preserves, pickles.

30. Coffee, tea, cocoa, sugar, rice, tapioca, sago, coffee substitutes; flour, and preparations made from cereals; bread, biscuits, cakes, pastry and confectionary, ices; honey, treacle; yeast, baking powder; salt, mustard, pepper, vinegar, sauces, spices; ice.

31. Agricultural, horticultural and forestry products and grains not included in other classes; living animals; fresh fruits and vegetables; seeds; live plants and flowers; foodstuffs for animals, malt.

32. Beer, ale and porter, mineral and aerated waters, and other non-alcoholic drinks; syrups and other preparations for making beverages.

33. Wines, spirits and liqueurs.

34. Tobacco, raw or manufactured; smokers' articles; matches.

SERVICES

35. Advertising and business.

36. Insurance and financial.

37. Construction and repair.

38. Communication.

39. Transportation and storage.

40. Material treatment.

41. Education and entertainment.

42. Miscellaneous.

The United States schedule of classes of goods and services which was followed by the Patent Office up to September 1, 1973, is as follows:

### *6.2 U.S. schedule of classes of goods and services.*

GOODS

| *Class* | *Title* |
|---|---|
| 1 | Raw or partly prepared materials. |
| 2 | Receptacles. |
| 3 | Baggage, animal equipments, portfolios, and pocketbooks. |
| 4 | Abrasives and polishing materials. |
| 5 | Adhesives. |
| 6 | Chemicals and chemical compositions. |

7 Cordage.
8 Smokers' articles, not including tobacco products.
9 Explosives, firearms, equipments, and projectiles.
10 Fertilizers.
11 Inks and inking materials.
12 Construction materials.
13 Hardware and plumbing and steam-fitting supplies.
14 Metals and metal castings and forgings.
15 Oils and greases.
16 Protective and decorative coatings.
17 Tobacco products.
18 Medicines and pharmaceutical preparations.
19 Vehicles.
20 Linoleum and oiled cloth.
21 Electrical apparatus, machines, and supplies.
22 Games, toys, and sporting goods.
23 Cutlery, machinery, and tools, and parts thereof.
24 Laundry appliances and machines.
25 Locks and safes.
26 Measuring and scientific appliances.
27 Horological instruments.
28 Jewelry and precious-metal ware.
29 Brooms, brushes, and dusters.
30 Crockery, earthenware, and porcelain.
31 Filters and refrigerators.
32 Furniture and upholstery.
33 Glassware.
34 Heating, lighting, and ventilating apparatus.
35 Belting, hose, machinery packing, and nonmetallic tires.
36 Musical instruments and supplies.
37 Paper and stationery.
38 Prints and publications.

39 Clothing.

40 Fancy goods, furnishings, and notions.

41 Canes, parasols, and umbrellas.

42 Knitted, netted, and textile fabrics, and substitutes therefor.

43 Thread and yarn.

44 Dental, medical, and surgical appliances.

45 Soft drinks and carbonated waters.

46 Foods and ingredients of foods.

47 Wines.

48 Malt beverages and liquors.

49 Distilled alcoholic liquors.

50 Merchandise not otherwise classified.

51 Cosmetics and toilet preparations.

52 Detergents and soaps.

SERVICES

| *Class* | *Title* |
|---|---|
| 100 | Miscellaneous. |
| 101 | Advertising and business. |
| 102 | Insurance and financial. |
| 103 | Construction and repair. |
| 104 | Communication. |
| 105 | Transportation and storage. |
| 106 | Material treatment. |
| 107 | Education and entertainment. |

***6.3 Schedule for certification marks.*** In the case of certification marks, all goods and services are classified in two classes as follows:

A. Goods.

B. Services.

***6.4 Schedule for collective membership marks.*** All collective membership marks are classified as follows:

200 Collective membership.

# Appendix D

## ILLUSTRATIVE FILE WRAPPER CONTENTS OF TRADEMARK REGISTRATION

The pertinent portions of the history of a trademark application to its issuance as Registration No. 1,375,136 is set forth below:

## *Trademark Application and Drawing as Filed*

IN THE UNITED STATES PATENT AND TRADEMARK OFFICE

Mark: **THE MOVIE EXCHANGE & Design**

International Class: 42

**SERVICE MARK APPLICATION**

To the Commissioner of Patents and Trademarks:

The Movie Exchange, Inc., a Delaware corporation having a place of business at 2859 Egypt Road, Audubon, Pennsylvania 19403, has adopted and is using the service mark shown in the accompanying drawing for renting video cassettes, and video cassette recorders, through retail stores, and requests that said mark be registered in the United States Patent and Trademark Office on the Principal Register established by the Act of July 5, 1946.

The service mark was first used in connection with the services on November 1, 1983; was first used in connection with the services in interstate commerce on November 1, 1983 and is now in use in such commerce.

The mark is used on promotional materials and five (5) specimens evidencing usage of the mark are annexed hereto.

Applicant disclaims the word "MOVIE" apart from the mark as shown without waiving any of its common law rights therein.

The required fee is to be charged to our Miscellaneous Account 19-1135.

Please recognize Arthur H. Seidel, a member of the bars of New York, Pennsylvania and the District of Columbia; Edward C. Gonda, a member of the bar of Pennsylvania; Joel S. Goldhammer, a member of the bars of Pennsylvania and Virginia; Michael P. Abbott, a member of the bar of Pennsylvania; and Kathleen J. Gallagher, a member of the bar of Pennsylvania; with offices at Suite 1800, Two Penn Center Plaza, Philadelphia, Pennsylvania 19102 (Tel.: 215-568-8383), as our attorneys, with full power of substitution and revocation, to prosecute this application and to transact all business in connection therewith and to receive the Certificate of Registration.

The Patent and Trademark Office is requested to direct all communications with respect to this application to the following attorneys: Arthur H. Seidel or Kathleen

J. Gallagher.

Shellie Tibbitts declares: That she is President of applicant corporation and is authorized to execute this Declaration on behalf of said corporation, that she believes said corporation to be owner of the mark sought to be registered, that to the best of her knowledge and belief no other person, firm, corporation or association has the right to use said mark in commerce, either in the identical form or in such near resemblance thereto as may be likely, when applied to the services of such other person, to cause confusion, or to cause mistake, or to deceive; that the statements made herein of her own knowledge are true and all statements made on information and belief are believed to be true; and further that these statements were made with the knowledge that willful false statements and the like so made are punishable by fine or imprisonment, or both, under Section 1001 of Title 18 of the United States Code and that such willful false statements may jeopardize the validity of the application or document or any registration resulting therefrom.

THE MOVIE EXCHANGE, INC.

Date: 7/27/84 By: ____________
SHELLIE TIBBITTS
President

THE
MOVIE
EXCHANGE
RENT
A
MOVIE
$2.95 A DAY

The Movie Exchange, Inc.

2859 Egypt Road

Audubon, Pennsylvania 19403

November 1, 1983 (first date of use)

November 1, 1983 (interstate commerce)

for renting video cassettes, and video cassette recorders, through retail stores

FORM PTO-100
(REV. 8-78)
US DEPT OF
COMM-PAT &
TM OFFICE

FILING RECEIPT
FOR TRADEMARK
APPLICATIONS
(see reverse)

No correspondence on this application should be expected before approx.

7

months from filing.

| 42 | 08/06/1984 | 73/493705 |
|---|---|---|
| CLASS | FILING DATE | SERIAL NO. |

APPLICANT
MOVIE EXCHANGE, INC., THE

MARK
THE MOVIE EXCHANGE AND DESIGN

ADDRESS
SEIDEL, GONDA & GOLDHAMMER, P.C.
SUITE 600
THREE PENN CENTER PLAZA
PHILADELPHIA, PA. 19102

ORIGINAL

## *First Office Action Rendered January 7, 1985*

IN REPLY REFER TO THE FOLLOWING AND THE FILING DATE

**U.S. DEPARTMENT OF COMMERCE**
**Patent and Trademark Office**

RECEIVED JAN 10 1985 SEIDEL, GONDA & GOLDHAMMER, P.C.

| SERIAL NO. | APPLICANT | PAPER NO. |
|---|---|---|
| 73/493705 | MOVIE EXCHANGE, INC., THE | |

MARK
THE MOVIE EXCHANGE AND DESIGN

ADDRESS
SEIDEL, GONDA & GOLDHAMMER, P.C.
SUITE 600
THREE PENN CENTER PLAZA
PHILADELPHIA, PA. 19102

EXAMINATION NO. 01

MAILING DATE 01/07/85

ADDRESS
**Commissioner of Patents and Trademarks**
**Washington, D.C. 20231**

The address of all correspondence not containing fee payments should include the words "Box 5."

Please furnish the following in all correspondence:
1. Your telephone number and zip code.
2. Mailing date of this action.
3. Examining Attorney's name and Law Office number.

FORM PTO-1525 (2-84) U.S. DEPT. OF COMM. PAT. & TM OFFICE

I have reviewed this application for trademark (and/or service mark) registration and you are advised as follows:

Registration is refused because the mark, when applied to the applicant's services, so resembles the mark(s) cited below as to be likely to cause confusion, or to cause mistake, or to deceive. (Section 2(d) of the Trademark Act, 15 U.S.C. 1052(d); TMEP section 1205.) (see attached copies):

Reg. No(s). 1,260,313

In determining the likelihood of confusion, one must consider the marks themselves for similarities in appearance, sound, connotation and commercial impression. In re E.I. DuPont de Nemours & Co., 177 USPQ 563, 567 (CCPA 1973). Applicant's mark is "The Movie Exchange" plus design and registrant's mark is "The Video Exchange." The marks generate the same commercial impression. In addition, the underlying services are identical: rental of video cassettes. Because the marks are confusingly similar and the services are identical, registration must be refused pursuant to Section 2(d) of the Act.

Although I have refused registration, you are entitled to respond to my findings by submitting evidence and arguments in support of the registrability of the mark.

If you choose to respond to my refusal to register this mark, you must also address the following informalities:

The present recitation of services is indefinite for registration purposes. You must amend the recitation. Based on the record, the following recitation is suggested and should be adopted, if accurate: Rental of video cassettes and video cassette recorders (Class 41).

**A proper response to THIS OFFICE action must be received within 6 months from the date of this action in order to avoid ABANDONMENT.**

PTOL 89 (REV 11-83)

You must disclaim the descriptive term " Exchange " apart from the mark as shown. (15 U.S.C. 1056; TMEP sections 904.02(a) and (e).) See definition attached hereto.

It is our practice to enforce Office policies to conclude examination of applications as quickly as possible. If you, in good faith, address each issue raised in this Office action but fail to resolve them satisfactorily, I will make the requirements related to any unresolved issue final in the next Office action. (See 37 CFR §2.64.) On the other hand, if you fail to address one or more of the issues raised in this Office action, I will be compelled to hold the application abandoned for failure to respond completely. (See 37 CFR §2.65.)

Cheryl M. Friedman

CMF:lmtlu

Cheryl M. Friedman
Trademark Attorney Law Ofc. 6
703 557-2937

**Int. Cls.: 41 and 42**

**Prior U.S. Cls.: 100, 101 and 107**

**Reg. No. 1,260,313**

**United States Patent and Trademark Office** **Registered Dec. 6, 1983**

**SERVICE MARK**
**Supplemental Register**

**THE VIDEO EXCHANGE**

The Video Exchange (Colorado corporation)
8040 W. Jewell Ave.
Lakewood, Colo. 80226

For: RENTAL SERVICES—NAMELY, THE RENTAL OF VIDEO TAPE CASSETTES, in CLASS 41 (U.S. Cls. 100 and 107).

First use Oct. 1, 1980; in commerce Nov. 30, 1980.

For: RETAIL STORE SERVICES—NAMELY, THE SALE OF VIDEO TAPE CASSETTES, in CLASS 42 (U.S. Cl. 101).

First use Oct. 1, 1980; in commerce Nov. 30, 1980.

Ser. No. 319,177, filed P.R. Jul. 16, 1981; Am. S.R. May 5, 1983.

KIMBERLY KREHELY, Examining Attorney

## *Amendment Filed In Patent and Trademark Office May 20, 1985*

IN THE UNITED STATES PATENT AND TRADEMARK OFFICE

| | | | |
|---|---|---|---|
| In re | : Trademark Application Of The Movie Exchange Inc. | : | |
| Serial No. | : 493,705 | : | Examiner Friedman |
| Filed | : August 6, 1984 | : | Trademark Attorney Law Office VI |
| For | : THE MOVIE EXCHANGE | : | |

**AMENDMENT**

This is in response to the Office Action dated January 7, 1985.

Please amend the above-identified application, without prejudice, as follows:

Please enter the following disclaimer:

> --Applicant disclaims "EXCHANGE" apart from the mark as shown without waiver of its common law rights therein.--

Amend the recitation of services to read:

> --Rental of video cassettes and video cassette recorders.--

**REMARKS**

Reconsideration of the refusal to register is respectfully requested in view of the following remarks. Pursuant to the request of the examining Trademark Attorney, applicant has amended the recitation of services and has entered a disclaimer of "EXCHANGE".

The Examiner has refused registration on the ground that Applicant's mark so resembles the mark identified in Registration No. 1,260,313, as to be likely to cause confusion.

Applicant submits that the mark which is identified in the cited registration "THE VIDEO EXCHANGE" is such a weak mark that it is entitled to a very narrow scope of protection and that scope of protection should not be extended to prevent registration of Applicant's mark.

The scope of protection afforded to a highly suggestive or descriptive term was stated very clearly in the case of Industrial Adhesive Company v. Borden, Inc., 218 U.S.P.Q. 945, 951 (T.T.A.B. 1983). In that case, the Board held that the use of "WONDER BOND PLUS" for cyanoacrylate adhesive was not likely to cause confusion with the use of "BOND PLUS" as used on industrial adhesives. In reaching this conclusion, the Board stated, quoting Standard Brands, Inc. v. Peters, 191 U.S.P.Q. 168, 172 (T.T.A.B. 1975):

> "It is settled that, unlike in the case of arbitrary or unique designations, suggestive or highly suggestive terms, because of their obvious connotations and possible frequent employment in a particular trade as part of trade designations, have been considered to fall within the category of 'weak' marks, and the scope of protection afforded these marks have [sic] been so limited as to permit the use and/or registration of the same mark for different goods or a composite comprising this term plus other matter, whether such matter be equally suggestive or even descriptive, for the same or similar goods."

This principle was further expounded in the case of Color Key Corp. v. Color Associates Inc., 219 U.S.P.Q. 936 (T.T.A.B. 1983). The Board determined that use of the mark "COLOR 1" for counseling services relating to wardrobe, makeup and interior design, and "COLOR KEY 1" and "KEY 1 COLORS" for instructional materials and educational services concerning color selection for home, industry, and personal fashions, was not likely to cause confusion. The rationale used for reaching this decision was stated as follows:

> "It is well established that the scope of protection afforded a merely descriptive or even highly suggestive term is less than that afforded an arbitrary or coined mark. That is, terms falling within the former category have been generally characterized as 'weak' marks, and the scope of protection extended to these marks has been limited to the substantially identical notation and/or to the subsequent use and registration thereof for substantially similar goods."

In the present case, not only is the mark identified in the cited registration a very weak mark, but it is also different in appearance and sound from Applicant's mark "THE MOVIE EXCHANGE & Design". It is submitted that because the registrant's mark is of such a non-arbitrary nature, the public could easily distinguish between the marks. This is particularly true in view of the distinctive design which is present in Applicant's mark.

Although both marks contain the term "EXCHANGE" this is an insufficient basis to hold that confusion is likely. See In re The Pelvic Anchor Corporation 166 U.S.P.Q. 217 (T.T.A.B. 1970).

In Pelvic Anchor, the Board held that the mark "PELVIC ANCHOR" does not so resemble "ANCHOR" or "ANCHOR BRAND & Design" as to be likely to cause confusion. The Board noted that the mark "PELVIC ANCHOR" incorporated the registered mark "ANCHOR" but held that that factor alone was insufficient to hold that there was a likelihood of confusion.

In a very similar fact situation, in the case of In re Lar Mor International, Inc. 221 U.S.P.Q. 180, 183 (T.T.A.B. 1983) the Board held that the mark "TRES JOLIE" for women's clothing, namely, jeans, pants, sweaters, shirts, knit tops, and skirts did not so resemble "BIEN JOLIE" for corsets, brassieres, and women's underwear of knitted or textile fabric, as to be likely to cause confusion. The Board noted that both marks may be translated to mean "very pretty" or "quite pretty". However, the highly laudatory meaning of the registered mark could not be ignored. The Board stated:

> "Aside from the inherent weakness of the registered mark, the respective marks have obvious visual and phonetic differences. As Applicant pointed out, the letters 'B' and 'J' form a prominent part of the registered mark. There are other obvious differences including the first words of the respective marks and the distinctive style of display

> of Applicant's mark. Therefore, while the marks before us are French words, we believe they are of such non-arbitrary or non-distinctive nature that the public is able to distinguish the differences between the marks as well as the differences in the goods, even though the goods may be considered 'related'."

In this case, the marks "THE VIDEO EXCHANGE" and "THE MOVIE EXCHANGE & Design" both contain the term "EXCHANGE", however, in view of the inherent weakness of the registered mark "THE VIDEO EXCHANGE" and the obvious visual and phonetic differences of the marks, it is submitted that there is no likelihood of confusion. Furthermore, it is submitted that the registered mark is so highly suggestive in nature that the public is able to distinguish the differences that exist between the mark in the cited registration and Applicant's mark. See Colgate-Palmolive Company v. Carter-Wallace, Inc. 167 U.S.P.Q. 529 (C.C.P.A 1970) ("PEAK PERIOD" for personal deodorants does not so resemble "PEAK" for dentifrice that confusion is likely). Electronic Realty Associates, Inc. v. Kayser-Roth Corporation 216 U.S.P.Q. 60 (C.C.P.A. 1982) ("GOLDEN ERA" for clothing, namely, sport shirts not likely to cause confusion with "ERA" for a variety of clothing items). Lever Brothers v. The Barcolene Company 174 U.S.P.Q. 392 (C.C.P.A 1972) ("ALL CLEAR!" for household cleaner does not so resemble 'ALL' for household cleaning products that confusion is likely). In re Reach Electronics, Inc. 175 U.S.P.Q. 734 (T.T.A.B. 1972) ("REACH" for code-signal encoders, code-signal decoders, mobile radio call indicators, radio controlled pocket pagers, code-signal memory banks, encoder-decoder combination units, adjacent channel rejector attachments, power supplies, hook-up cables, radio receivers and mobile telephone control heads not likely to cause confusion with "REAC" for amplifiers, power supplies, function generators, multipliers, dividers, recorders, servo positioning systems and coordinate converters primarily for measuring, testing and computing). Aloe Cream Laboratories, Inc. v. Helena Rubinstein, Inc. 188 U.S.P.Q. 515 (C.C.P.A 1975) ("MOISTURE ICE" for lipstick does not so resemble "MOISTURE PLUS" for skin cream and lotion as to be likely to cause confusion). In re Norfolk Wallpaper, Inc. 216 U.S.P.Q. 903 (T.T.A.B. 1983) ("THE NORFOLK PLAN" for installation of wallpaper and retail wallpaper stores services does not so resemble "NORFOLK" for interior and exterior ready made paint and varnishes, and thinners for paints and varnishes that confusion is likely).

In the present case, the fact that the mark identified in the cited registration "THE VIDEO EXCHANGE" is a weak mark is evidenced by the numerous third party registrations which contain the term "VIDEO". See Appendix 1 which contains a list of registrations that contain the term "VIDEO". Copies of the registrations listed in Appendix 1 are attached herewith.

In the case of Plus Products v. Redkin Laboratories, Inc. 199 U.S.P.Q. 111 (T.T.A.B. 1978) the Board held that the mark "pH PLUS" for facial creams and liquids, namely, deep cleansing cream, firming facial masque, toning skin freshener, moisturizing skin balancer, and night cream was not likely to cause confusion with the mark "PLUS" for the sale and distribution of cosmetics, vitamin preparations for the care of the skin and hair, vitamin and high protein products and mineral fortifiers including dietary supplements for human consumption. The Board in commenting on the thirty nine (39) third party registrations which were submitted by the Applicant stated that:

> "While the third party evidence adduced by Applicant cannot, per se, justify the registration of what may be considered to be another confusingly similar mark, it is admissible and competent to delineate opposer's rights in the term "PLUS" and thereby negate any claim of exclusivity in the cosmetic and toiletry fields as well as to suggest that purchasers would be reasonably likely, upon encountering these various marks, to attribute to the term "PLUS" its ordinary dictionary meaning. The third-party registrations as well as the history of opposer's registration efforts also reflect a

> practice on the part of the Patent and Trademark Office to register marks containing the term "PLUS" over opposer's mark "PLUS", per se, as well as over other composite marks containing "PLUS" on the basis of other matter associated therewith notwithstanding the descriptive character thereof and notwithstanding that the goods marketed or covered thereby are identical in kind or closely related and would be encountered in the same retail outlets."

The Examiner is of the opinion that the mark "THE MOVIE EXCHANGE & Design" generates the same commercial impression as the mark identified in the cited registration "THE VIDEO EXCHANGE". However, Applicant submits that the mark which is identified in the cited registration is so inherently weak that numerous marks whose connotation and commercial impression are identical to "THE VIDEO EXCHANGE" have been allowed to coexist with the cited registration. Therefore, the cited registration should not prevent the registration of Applicant's mark. See the following exhibits which are all owned by different parties:

1. Registration No. 1,130,181 for "THE VIDEO STORE" identified as Exhibit A;

2. Registration No. 1,274,658 for "VIDEO STORE GALORE & Design" identified as Exhibit B;

3. Registration No. 1,178,607 for "THE VIDEO PLACE" identified as Exhibit C;

4. Registration No. 1,209,091 for "VIDEO VILLAGE & Design" identified as Exhibit D;

5. Registration No. 1,223,252 for "VIDEO-VILLE" identified as Exhibit E;

6. Registration No. 1,230,416 for "VIDEO HEADQUARTERS" identified as Exhibit F; and

7. Registration No. 1,241,519 for "VIDEO DEPOT & Design" identified as Exhibit G.

The marks which are identified in Registration Nos. 1,130,181 "THE VIDEO STORE" and 1,178,607 "THE VIDEO PLACE", identified as Exhibit A and Exhibit C respectively, are practically identical to the mark "THE VIDEO EXCHANGE". The mark which is identified in Registration No. 1,130,181 "THE VIDEO STORE" has the same connotation as the mark which is identified in the cited registration and is for related services. The same is true for Registration No. 1,178,607 "THE VIDEO PLACE".

The term "EXCHANGE" is defined in Webster's Third New International Dictionary as a store or shop where merchandise usually of a particular type is bought, resold or repaired. See the enclosed photocopy identified as Exhibit H. Therefore, the terms "EXCHANGE" and "STORE" are synonymous. Thus, the mark which is identified in the cited registration "THE VIDEO EXCHANGE" is synonymous with the mark which is identified in Registration No. 1,130,181 "THE VIDEO STORE".

Furthermore, the mark identified in Registration No. 1,223,252 "VIDEO-VILLE" for video equipment and related merchandise, namely, prerecorded and blank video tapes and video discs and rental of video and movie equipment and accessories, was allowed to register over the mark identified in Registration No. 1,209,091 "VIDEO VILLAGE & Design" for leasing of movies recorded on video cassettes and retail store services in the field of movies, recording equipment, cameras, television and video supplies.

The only rationale perceived for the allowance of the mark identified in the cited registration "THE VIDEO EXCHANGE" over the mark identified in Registration No. 1,130,181 "THE VIDEO STORE" is that the marks are considered inherently weak as applied to the respective services. The same rationale is perceived for the allowance of the mark "VIDEO-VILLE" over "VIDEO VILLAGE and Design".

In a very similar fact situation, in the case of In re Hamilton Bank 222 U.S.P.Q. 174 (T.T.A.B. 1984) the Trademark Trial and Appeal Board held that the mark

"KEY" for banking services was not likely to cause confusion with the marks "BANKEY & Design"; "KEYCHECK"; "KEY-CARD BANK"; "KEYBANKER"; and "CB KEY". In Hamilton Bank, the Applicant made of record copies of fifteen (15) third party registrations. The Board stated:

> "Third party registrations cannot assist an Applicant in registering a mark that is likely to cause confusion with a registered mark. Such registrations are, however, competent to show that others in a particular area of commerce have adopted and registered marks incorporating a particular term. We can also note from such registrations that the term or feature common to the marks has a normally understood meaning or suggestiveness in the trade and that marks containing the term or feature have been registered for the same or closely related goods or services because the remaining portions of the marks are sufficient to distinguish the marks as a whole from one another."

The numerous similar registrations that contain the term "VIDEO" have only minor distinguishable features. For example, it appears that the mark which is identified in Registration No. 1,178,607 "THE VIDEO PLACE" was allowed over the mark identified in Registration No. 1,130,181 "THE VIDEO STORE" because the terms "place" and "store" are visually different. Furthermore, it appears that the mark which is identified in the cited registration "THE VIDEO EXCHANGE" was allowed over Registration Nos. 1,178,607 for "THE VIDEO PLACE" and 1,130,181 for "THE VIDEO STORE", although all three marks have the same connotation, because the terms "exchange", "store" and "place" are visually different.

Therefore, Applicant submits that in view of the differences that exist in Applicant's mark "THE MOVIE EXCHANGE & Design" and the mark identified in the cited registration "THE VIDEO EXCHANGE", namely, "movie" and "video" are phonetically and visually different, and Applicant's mark contains a distinctive design which is not present in registrant's mark, there does not exist a likelihood of confusion. This is particularly true in view of the very weak nature of the mark which is identified in the cited registration.

In view of the above Amendment and Remarks, Applicant respectfully requests a withdrawal of the refusal to register and an early Notice of Publication.

Respectfully submitted,

THE MOVIE EXCHANGE, INC.

BY: Arthur H. Seidel
ARTHUR H. SEIDEL
SEIDEL, GONDA & GOLDHAMMER, P.C.
Suite 1800, Two Penn Center Plaza
Philadelphia, PA 19102
Tel.: 215 568-8383
Attorneys for Applicant

I HEREBY CERTIFY THAT THIS CORRESPONDENCE IS BEING DEPOSITED WITH THE UNITED STATES POSTAL SERVICE AS FIRST CLASS MAIL IN AN ENVELOPE ADDRESSED TO: COMMISSIONER OF PATENTS AND TRADEMARKS, WASHINGTON, D.C. 20231, ON THE DATE INDICATED BELOW.

BY K Gallagher

DATE May 20, 1985

## APPENDIX 1

| Registration No. | Mark | Goods and/or Services |
|---|---|---|
| 1,323,811 | "STEREO WAREHOUSE/ RADIO WAREHOUSE & Design" | Retail store services specializing in video equipment |
| 1,317,402 | "CVN/VIDEO NETWORK & Design" | For custom assembly of video cassettes and computer components |
| 1,316,201 | "JUKEBOX VIDEO PRODUCTIONS" | For television production services |
| 1,313,999 | "VIDEOSERV" | For providing a range of electronic financial information and transaction processing services to subscribers at home by way of a series of software/ hardware systems |
| 1,312,696 | "VIDEO 2 U" | For leasing services in the area of film and discs for video players |
| 1,305,460 | "VIDEO RECALL & Design" | For providing a detailed inventory of personal and real property by means of videotape |
| 1,305,425 | "SAM THE VIDEO MAN" | For retail stores services specializing in the sale of video and sound reproduction equipment and accessories therefor |
| 1,309,416 | "STAR VIDEO MUSIC" | For producing and distributing video music programming to cable television systems |
| 1,309,409 | "VIDEOLAW" | For educational services, namely, offering videotaped continuing legal education seminars to lawyers |
| 1,305,369 | "VIDEO PARADISE" | For renting videotapes of movies and entertainment educational programs to others and retail store services in the field of video cassettes and home video equipment |
| 1,297,231 | "VIDEO UPDATE" | For retail store services in the field of video tapes, video discs and video equipment |

| | | |
|---|---|---|
| 1,297,229 | "VIDEO UPDATE & Design" | For retail store services in the field of video tapes, video discs and video equipment |
| 1,295,051 | "VIDEO VAN & Design" | For rental of motion picture video cassettes, video games, video cartridges, television sets, video cassette recorders, video cameras and video discs |
| 1,291,550 | "VIDEO-TECH" | For nightclub services |
| 1,288,113 | "AUDIO VIDEO WORLD & Design" | For rendering technical aid and assistance in the establishment and/or operation of retail audio and video stores and retail of audio and video equipment and retail audio and video store services |
| 1,286,893 | "VIDEO PUBLISHING & Design" | For pre-recorded video tapes; custom production of video tapes, rental services for video tapes; and retail mail order services for video tapes |
| 1,286,537 | "VIDEO VIBES | For amusement center services |
| 1,286,498 | "VIDEO VOID" | For production of television programs |
| 1,282,799 | "VIDEO IMAGE PRODUCTIONS" | For production of video tape commercials for advertisers, corporate programs for internal training, video tapes for medical procedures and program length features and live telecast for television stations |
| 1,280,165 | "VIDEO FUN CARD & Design" | For renting or leasing of video tapes |
| 1,277,403 | "CHANNEL 1 VIDEO TAPE, INC. MIAMI, FLORIDA & Design" | For providing television, studio and location production facilities post-production, including editing of previously recorded material |
| 1,275,651 | "VIDEO NOTARIES OF AMERICA" | For association services, namely, promoting the interest of video notaries |
| 1,274,658 | "VIDEO STORE GALORE & Design" | For retail store services in the field of video equipment |
| 1,267,412 | "VIDEO WORKS" | For retail store services in the field of pre-recorded and blank video cassettes and discs |

| | | |
|---|---|---|
| 1,263,849 | "VIDEO FUN CENTER" | For renting or leasing recorded video tapes |
| 1,263,230 | "VIDEO WORLD" | For providing video arcade entertainment services |
| 1,261,981 | "VIDEO ONE" | For video post-production services, namely, editing tapes and creating special effects for commercials and television programs |
| 1,260,668 | "NATIONAL VIDEO WHOLESALERS" | For retail store services in the field of video equipment, namely, television, video recorders, video cameras, and video cassette tapes |
| 1,260,273 | "VIDEO GRAMMY" | For association services, namely, promoting artistic progress and achievements in the field of recording arts and sciences |
| 1,249,344 | "VIDEO REPLAY & Design" | For rental of video equipment, namely, tapes, recorders, discs, televisions, cameras, wide screens, video accessories, television computers, and game computers; retail store services in the field of video equipment, namely, tapes, recorders, discs, televisions, cameras, wide screens, video accessories, television computers, and game computers |
| 1,248,736 | "VIDEO FUN CLUB" | For renting or leasing of video tapes |
| 1,246,670 | "VIDEO TRAX & Design" | For videotaping of personal property for others for insurance and security purposes, and videotaping legal depositions for others |
| 1,246,669 | "VIDEOTRAX" | For videotaping of personal property for others for insurance and security purposes and videotaping legal depositions for others |
| 1,249,524 | "INTERACTIVE VIDEO TRAINING" | For conducting classes and workshops designed to improve sales techniques |
| 1,246,672 | "VIDEOTRAX" | For videotaping of personal property for others for insurance and security purposes; and videotaping legal depositions for others |
| 1,243,196 | "VIDEO POKER CLASSIC & Design" | For promoting, arranging and conducting poker game tournaments |

| | | |
|---|---|---|
| 1,242,621 | "VIDEO JOURNAL" | For pre-recorded video cassettes containing managerial and nonmanagerial professional training courses; and educational services, namely, conducting training courses in the field of manufacturing management strategies, information technology, communications, computers in business and industry, computer data bases, computer applications, and office automation |
| 1,242,400 | "VIDEO TO-GO" | For retail store services in the field of video accessories, namely, blank and recorded video tapes and video recorder head cleaners |
| 1,241,519 | "VIDEO DEPOT & Design" | For rental services in the field of video cassettes |
| 1,236,754 | "FUTURE VIDEO & VIDEO SPECIALITY STORE & Design" | For leasing of pre-recorded video tape cassettes and video discs; and retail store services in the field of video tape cassettes, video discs and video equipment |
| 1,235,863 | "VIDEORAMA & Design" | For rental of video equipment; and retail store services specializing in video equipment |
| 1,232,551 | "VIDEO PUBLISHING & Design" | For video cassettes; rental of video tapes; and retail mail order of video tapes |
| 1,232,369 | "VIDEO POKER CLASSIC" | For promoting, arranging and conducting poker game tournaments |
| 1,231,447 | "VIDEO MAGIC INC. & Design" | For retail video cassette store services |
| 1,230,416 | "VIDEO HEADQUARTERS" | For leasing video cassettes, namely, motion pictures, television programs, and other entertainment programs, to others |
| 1,229,375 | "VIDEO TAPE ASSOCIATES" | For pre-recorded and stock video tapes; sound and pre-recorded video tape duplication services; and video taping services, namely, recording of events and productions on video tape, as well as leasing facilities for video tape recording |
| 1,227,036 | "VIDEO PROTECTION SYSTEMS & Design" | For storing identification numbers or the like of household personal property for use in the event of destruction or theft of the property |

| | | |
|---|---|---|
| 1,225,791 | "VIDEOMAGIC" | For system, channel and program identifiers and daters in the nature of video tape recordings for cable, commercial and educational television; and production of program identifiers and daters for cable, commercial and educational television |
| 1,224,597 | "VIDEOTAINERS" | For entertainment services, namely, providing customized video tape greetings for special occasions |
| 1,224,048 | "VIDEOMAGIC" | For video tape recordings, namely, system, channel and program identifiers and daters in the nature of video tape recordings for cable, commercial and educational television for sale to the cable, commercial and educational television industry for broadcast purposes; and producing animation, special effects, graphics, musical scores and titles for system, channel and identifiers and daters in the nature of video tape recordings for the cable, commercial and educational television industry for broadcast purposes |
| 1,223,252 | "VIDEO-VILLE" | For video equipment and related merchandise. namely, pre-recorded and blank video tapes and video discs; and retail of video and movie equipment and accessories |
| 1,221,229 | "THE VIDEO EMPIRE" | For rental of video cassettes, video cassette recorders or video game cassettes |
| 1,214,378 | "VIDEOSYNCRASIES" | For video recording services |
| 1,213,546 | "VIDEOTEL" | For educational services, namely, providing training in the field of sales through use of video equipment |
| 1,209,091 | "VIDEO VILLAGE & Design" | For leasing of movies recorded on video cassettes; and retail store services in the field of movies, recording equipment, cameras, television and video supplies |
| 1,204,960 | "VIDEO TREND" | For distribution services in the field of video products, namely, video tapes and discs |
| 1,201,556 | "VIDEO SOUTH" | For videotaping services for attorneys, realtors, insurance companies and special event coverage |

| | | |
|---|---|---|
| 1,201,535 | "THE VIDEO STATION & Design" | For retail store services for video cassette movies, video cassette recorders and related equipment |
| 1,200,753 | "VIDEO PLAYGROUND & Design" | For retail mail order services specializing in the sale of video apparatus and accessories |
| 1,199,086 | "VIDEO MEMORIES" | For videotaping services to the order and specification of others |
| 1,197,424 | "VIDEO VISION & Design" | For leasing video equipment and accessories therefor |
| 1,195,915 | "ABC VIDEO NEWS MAGAZINE" | For educational service, namely, providing weekly by subscription, a compilation of international and national news on videocassettes |
| 1,189,616 | "VIDEO VAULT" | For videotaping of property, documents and people to the specification of others |
| 1,181,611 | "VIDEO ENCORE" | For videotaping of people, property and documents |
| 1,178,607 | "THE VIDEO PLACE" | For retail services specializing in video equipment and accessories |
| 1,171,803 | "THE VIDEO SOCIETY" | For associations services, namely, promoting the interest of video equipment to users |
| 1,169,646 | "VIDEO-WINDOW" | For full production services of video tapes and recordings |
| 1,169,637 | "VIDEOGRAMS" | For recording electronic images on video tape to the order of others |
| 1,167,746 | "VIDEO VENTURES" | For live or video tape television program production services for others |
| 1,163,186 | "CHANNEL ONE VIDEO RECORDINGS & Design" | For mail order services in the field of movies |
| 1,154,291 | "VIDEO ONE-STOP" | For retail record, tape and film store services |
| 1,155,115 | "THE VIDEO KING" | For retail store services specializing in video equipment |

| | | |
|---|---|---|
| 1,130,181 | "THE VIDEO STORE" | For retail store services in the field of closed circuit television including security systems, and blank recording tape |
| 1,101,767 | "WESTERN VIDEOTAPE PRODUCTIONS" | For videotaping productions for others |
| 1,043,778 | "VIDEOGROUP, INC. & Design" | For television production services relating to designing and creating programs, commercials, training messages and communications that are subsequently recorded on video tape, film, slides, audio tape, books, magazines, newspapers and various other communications media; writing scripts, directing, producing, graphic design, set design, visual concept planning, cartooning, illustrating and the like |
| 1,032,552 | "VIDEOMATICS" | For preparing, advertising commercials on video tape |
| 982,351 | "VIDEO JOURNAL" | For production, duplication and distribution services for films, video tapes, video cassettes, live appearance programs and slide programs for broadcast and closed-circuit television |
| 981,463 | "VIDEO TAPE NETWORK" | For distribution of filmed and taped educational entertainment programs, the production of such programs, the training of persons in the use of video equipment and the training of persons in the programming and use of closed circuit video equipment |
| 955,420 | "VIDEOVOICE" | For leasing of equipment for use in connection with the transmission of visual information in voice communication |
| 888,478 | "VIDEOMAGINATION" | For production of television commercials |

**Int. Cl.: 42**

**U.S. Cl.: 101**

**Reg. No. 1,130,181**

**U.S. Patent and Trademark Office** **Reg. Jan. 29, 1980**

---

## SERVICE MARK
**Supplemental Register**

# THE VIDEO STORE

Ted Easterling (U.S.A. citizen) d.b.a. Videomed
7738 Clairemont Mesa Blvd.
San Diego, Calif. 92111

For: Retail Store Services in the Field of Closed Circuit Television Including Security Systems, and Blank Recording Tape—in Class 42. (U.S. Cl. 101)

First use Aug. 1976, in commerce Nov. 3, 1976.

Ser. No. 123,281. Filed Apr. 18, 1977.

MARK HARRISON, Examiner

EXHIBIT A

**Prior U.S. Cl.: 101**

**Reg. No. 1,274,658**
**Registered Apr. 17, 1984**

## United States Patent and Trademark Office

### SERVICE MARK
**Principal Register**

Video Productions of Lafayette, Inc. (Louisiana corporation)
4652 Johnston St.
Lafayette, La. 70503

For: RETAIL STORE SERVICES IN THE FIELD OF VIDEO EQUIPMENT, in CLASS 42 (U.S. Cl. 101)

First use Jan. 1, 1982; in commerce Jan. 1, 1982.

No claim is made to the exclusive right to use "Video Store", apart from the mark as shown.

Ser. No. 407,580, filed Dec. 29, 1982.

RUSS HERMAN, Examining Attorney

EXHIBIT B

**Int. Cl.: 42**

**Prior U.S. Cl.: 101**

**Reg. No. 1,178,607**

**United States Patent and Trademark Office** **Registered Nov. 17, 1981**

**SERVICE MARK**
**Principal Register**

**THE VIDEO PLACE**

Home Video Outlet Corporation (Virginia corporation)
9700 Beach Mill Rd.
Great Falls, Va. 22066

For: RETAIL STORE SERVICES SPECIALIZING IN VIDEO EQUIPMENT AND ACCESSORIES, in CLASS 42 (U.S. Cl. 101).

First use May 1979; in commerce May 1979.

Without waiving any of its common law rights therein, applicant disclaims the word "Video" apart from the mark as shown.

Ser. No. 236,383, filed Oct. 23, 1979.

MARTIN MARKS, Primary Examiner

EXHIBIT C

**Prior U.S. Cls.: 101 and 107**

**Reg. No. 1,209,091**
**Registered Sep. 14, 1982**

## United States Patent and Trademark Office

### SERVICE MARK
### Principal Register

Video Village, Inc. (Kentucky corporation)
423 Southland Dr.
Lexington, Ky. 40503

For: LEASING OF MOVIES RECORDED ON VIDEO CASSETTES, in CLASS 41 (U.S. Cl. 107).
First use Aug. 1, 1979; in commerce Sep. 5, 1980.
For: RETAIL STORE SERVICES IN THE FIELD OF MOVIES, RECORDING EQUIPMENT, CAMERAS, TELEVISION AND VIDEO SUPPLIES, in CLASS 42 (U.S. Cl. 101).
First use Aug. 1, 1979; in commerce Sep. 5, 1980.

No registration rights are claimed for the word "Video" apart from the mark as shown; however, the applicant waives none of its common law rights in the mark as shown or any feature thereof.

Ser. No. 279,843, filed Sep. 29, 1980.

B. H. VERTIZ, Primary Examiner

ROBERT J. CROWE, Examiner

EXHIBIT D

Prior U.S. Cls.: 21 and 101

Reg. No. 1,223,252

United States Patent and Trademark Office

Registered Jan. 11, 1983

TRADEMARK
SERVICE MARK
Principal Register

VIDEO-VILLE

Video Future 21 Inc. (Canada corporation)
Suite 1090, Mississauga Executive Centre
Two Robert Speck Pkwy.
Mississauga, Ontario, Canada L4Z 1H8

For: VIDEO EQUIPMENT AND RELATED MERCHANDISE—NAMELY, PRE-RECORDED AND BLANK VIDEO TAPES AND VIDEO DISCS, in CLASS 9 (U.S. Cl. 21).

For: RENTAL OF VIDEO AND MOVIE EQUIPMENT AND ACCESSORIES, in CLASS 41 (U.S. Cl. 101).

Priority claimed under Sec. 44(d) on Canada application No. 467,319, filed Mar. 23, 1981, Reg. No. 269,147, dated May 14, 1982, expires May 14, 1997.

Ser. No. 329,222, filed Sep. 22, 1981.

J. TINGLEY, Examining Attorney

EXHIBIT E

Prior U.S. Cl.: 107

Reg. No. 1,230,416

United States Patent and Trademark Office

Registered Mar. 8, 1983

SERVICE MARK
Principal Register

VIDEO HEADQUARTERS

MBS Studios, Inc. (Illinois corporation)
5685 N. Lincoln Ave.
Chicago, Ill. 60659

For: LEASING VIDEO CASSETTES—NAMELY, MOTION PICTURES, TELEVISION PROGRAMS, AND OTHER ENTERTAINMENT PROGRAMS, TO OTHERS, in CLASS 41 (U.S. Cl. 107).

First use May 15, 1980; in commerce May 15, 1980.

No claim is made to the exclusive right to use "Video", apart from the mark as shown.

Ser. No. 289,186, filed Dec. 10, 1980.

KIMBERLY KREHELY, Examining Attorney

EXHIBIT F

Cl.: 107

**United States Patent and Trademark Office** — **Reg. No. 1,241,519**
Registered Jun. 7, 1983

## SERVICE MARK
### Principal Register

The Video Depot, Inc. (Ohio corporation)
7690 Bond St.
Glenwillow, Ohio 44139

For: RENTAL SERVICES IN THE FIELD OF VIDEO CASSETTES, in CLASS 41 (U.S. Cl. 107).

First use Apr. 4, 1981; in commerce May 14, 1981.

No claim is made to the exclusive right to use the word "Video", apart from the mark as shown.

Ser. No. 319,263, filed Jul. 17, 1981.

STEVEN R. FOSTER, Examining Attorney

EXHIBIT G

# Webster's Third New International Dictionary

## OF THE ENGLISH LANGUAGE UNABRIDGED

A Merriam-Webster

REG. U.S. PAT. OFF.

*Utilizing all the experience and resources of more than one hundred years of Merriam-Webster dictionaries*

EDITOR IN CHIEF

PHILIP BABCOCK GOVE, Ph.D.

AND

THE MERRIAM-WEBSTER

EDITORIAL STAFF

G. & C. MERRIAM COMPANY, *Publishers*

SPRINGFIELD, MASSACHUSETTS, U.S.A.

EXHIBIT H

[1]**ex·change** \iks'chānj, eks'ch *also* 'eks,ch-\ *n, often attrib* [ME *eschaunge, exchaunge,* fr. MF *eschange,* fr. *eschangier*] **1 :** the act of giving or taking one thing in return for another as if equivalent: as **a :** the restoration to their fellows of persons captured during military action usu. by each contesting side in equivalent numbers **b :** the process of reciprocal transfer of ownership (as between persons) **:** TRADE, BARTER; *broadly* **:** a complex of transactions that results in the actual interchange of goods and services (as among primitive peoples) even though any one transfer may be widely separated in space and time from another and may take place under the guise of presenting gifts or in consequence of traditional ceremonies — compare KULA **c :** a mutual grant under the law of equal interests one being in consideration of the other **d :** reciprocal transfer (as of military or naval commissions) between individuals usu. with some added gratuity to the individual accepting the less desirable **2 a :** the act of substituting one thing in the place of another ⟨the gradual ~ of her grief for quiet peace⟩ ⟨the startling transformation wrought by the ~ of his rags for royal raiment⟩ **b :** reciprocal giving and receiving (as of courtesies, blows, or words) **c :** a mutual capture of men in chess or checkers **d :** reciprocal interchange of sisters or daughters whereby two men in certain primitive societies obtain wives for themselves or for their brothers or sons ⟨the custom of marriage by ~⟩ **e :** a chemical reaction or process in which one atom, ion, or group changes places with another ⟨isotopic ~⟩ — see ION EXCHANGE; compare DOUBLE DECOMPOSITION, SUBSTITUTION 1d **3 :** something offered, given, or received in an exchange (as goods, blows, or words): as **a :** a usu. brief and often heated, acrid, or witty dialogue **b :** a publication (as a periodical) given (as by a publisher or author) in return for another publication; *also* **:** an item or article reprinted from a newspaper **4 a :** funds (as drafts, checks, or bills of exchange) payable currently at a distant point either in (1) a foreign currency or (2) in domestic currency — called also respectively (1) *foreign exchange,* (2) *domestic exchange* **b :** the amount paid for the collection (as of a draft, bill of exchange, or check drawn in one place upon another) **c** (1) **:** interchange or conversion of the money of two countries or of current and uncurrent money with allowance for difference in value (2) **:** RATE OF EXCHANGE (3) **:** the amount of the difference in value between two currencies or between values at two places — compare ARBITRAGE **d exchanges** *pl* **:** the items (as drafts, checks) that are presented in a clearinghouse for settlement by mutual interchange of credits and debits and payment of balances **5 :** a place where things or services are exchanged: as **a** *obs* **:** a money changer's place of business **b :** a place devoted to the transaction (as between merchants, bankers, and brokers) of business usu. at the professional level — often used in combination ⟨the grain ~⟩ ⟨a southern stock ~⟩ **c :** an organized market or center for trading in certain commodities at wholesale or on contracts calling for future delivery ⟨a produce ~⟩ **d :** a store or shop where merchandise usu. of a particular type is bought, resold, or repaired ⟨a typewriter ~⟩ **e :** a cooperative store or society ⟨a farmers' ~⟩ **f** *archaic* **:** BARROOM, SALOON **g :** TELEPHONE EXCHANGE **h :** POST EXCHANGE — **in exchange** *adv* **:** as a substitute ⟨what will you give me *in exchange*⟩; *sometimes* **:** as payment ⟨he received $10 *in exchange* for a couple of hours of work⟩

***Notice of Publication Received September 9, 1985***

UNITED STATES DEPARTMENT OF COMMERCE
Patent and Trademark Office
Address: COMMISSIONER OF PATENTS AND TRADEMARKS
Washington, D.C. 20231

RECEIVED
SEP 9 1985
SEIDEL, GONDA, GOLDHAMMER & ABBOTT P.C.

NOTICE OF PUBLICATION UNDER 12(a)

1. Serial No.:
73/493,705

2. Mark:
THE MOVIE EXCHANGE
and design

3. Applicant.
MOVIE EXCHANGE, INC., THE

4. Publication Date:
OCT. 1, 1985

The mark of the application above identified appears to be entitled to registration The mark will, in accordance with Section 12(a) of the Trademark Act of 1946, be published in the Official Gazette on the date indicated above for the purpose of opposition by any person who believes he will be damaged by the registration of the mark. If no opposition is filed within the time specified by Section 13 of the Statute or by rules 2.101 and 2.102 of the Trademark Rules, the Commissioner of Patents and Trademarks may issue a certificate of registration.

Copies of the trademark portion of the Official Gazette containing the publication of the mark may be obtained at $5.00 each for domestic orders, or at $6.25 each for foreign orders from:

The Superintendent of Documents
U.S. Government Printing Office
Washington,D.C 20402

By direction of the Commissioner.

5. Send correspondence to:

ARTHUR H. SEIDEL
SEIDEL, GONDA & GOLDHAMMER
SUITE 600
THREE PENN CENTER PLAZA
PHILADELPHIA, PA 19102

**Int. Cl.: 41**

**Prior U.S. Cls.: 100 and 107**

**Reg. No. 1,375,136**

**United States Patent and Trademark Office** **Registered Dec. 10, 1985**

**SERVICE MARK**
**PRINCIPAL REGISTER**

MOVIE EXCHANGE, INC., THE (DELAWARE CORPORATION)
2859 EGYPT ROAD
AUDUBON, PA 19403

FOR: RENTAL OF VIDEO CASSETTES AND VIDEO CASSETTE RECORDERS, IN CLASS 41 (U.S. CLS. 100 AND 107).

FIRST USE 11-1-1983; IN COMMERCE 11-1-1983.

NO CLAIM IS MADE TO THE EXCLUSIVE RIGHT TO USE "MOVIE EXCHANGE", APART FROM THE MARK AS SHOWN.

SER. NO. 493,705, FILED 8-6-1984.

C. A. SIDOTI, EXAMINING ATTORNEY

# Appendix E

## COPYRIGHT OFFICE APPLICATION FORMS, REGULATIONS, AND CIRCULARS (REVISED JANUARY 1985)

The following illustrate some of the most common types of forms for copyright registrations—Form CA, supplementary copyright registration; Form GR/CP, adjunct application for a group of contributions to periodicals; Form IS, request for issuance of an import statement; Form JB, recordation of coin operated phonorecord players; Form MW, a claim for protection in a mask work; Form PA, work of the performing arts; Form RE, renewal registration; Form SE, registration of each individual issue of a serial; Form SR, sound recordings; Form TX, nondramatic literary work; Form VA, works of the visual arts; and a form requesting special handling. Also included in the Appendix is a listing of Copyright Office Circulars.

**USE THIS FORM WHEN:**

- An earlier registration has been made in the Copyright Office; and
- Some of the facts given in that registration are incorrect or incomplete; and
- You want to place the correct or complete facts on record.

**FORM CA**

UNITED STATES COPYRIGHT OFFICE
LIBRARY OF CONGRESS
WASHINGTON, D.C. 20559

# Application for Supplementary Copyright Registration

To Correct or Amplify Information Given in the Copyright Office Record of an Earlier Registration

**What is "Supplementary Copyright Registration"?** Supplementary registration is a special type of copyright registration provided for in section 408(d) of the copyright law.

**Purpose of Supplementary Registration.** As a rule, only one basic copyright registration can be made for the same work. To take care of cases where information in the basic registration turns out to be incorrect or incomplete, the law provides for "the filing of an application for supplementary registration, to correct an error in a copyright registration or to amplify the information given in a registration."

**Earlier Registration Necessary.** Supplementary registration can be made only if a basic copyright registration for the same work has already been completed.

**Who May File.** Once basic registration has been made for a work, any author or other copyright claimant, or owner of any exclusive right in the work, who wishes to correct or amplify the information given in the basic registration, may submit Form CA.

**Please Note:**

- Do not use Form CA to correct errors in statements on the copies or phonorecords of the work in question, or to reflect changes in the content of the work. If the work has been changed substantially, you should consider making an entirely new registration for the revised version to cover the additions or revisions.
- Do not use Form CA as a substitute for renewal registration. For works originally copyrighted between January 1, 1950 and December 31, 1977, registration of a renewal claim within strict time limits is necessary to extend the first 28-year copyright term to the full term of 75 years. This cannot be done by filing Form CA.
- Do not use Form CA as a substitute for recording a transfer of copyright or other document pertaining to rights under a copyright. Recording a document under section 205 of the statute gives all persons constructive notice of the facts stated in the document and may have other important consequences in cases of infringement or conflicting transfers. Supplementary registration does not have that legal effect.

**How to Apply for Supplementary Registration:**

***First:*** Study the information on this page to make sure that filing an application on Form CA is the best procedure to follow in your case.

***Second:*** Turn this page over and read through the specific instructions for filling out Form CA. Make sure, before starting to complete the form, that you have all of the detailed information about the basic registration you will need.

***Third:*** Complete all applicable spaces on this form, following the line-by-line instructions on the back of this page. Use typewriter, or print the information in dark ink.

***Fourth:*** Detach this sheet and send your completed Form CA to: Register of Copyrights, Library of Congress, Washington, D.C. 20559. Unless you have a Deposit Account in the Copyright Office, your application must be accompanied by a non-refundable filing fee in the form of a check or money order for $10 payable to: *Register of Copyrights.* Do not send copies, phonorecords, or supporting documents with your application, since they cannot be made part of the record of a supplementary registration.

**What Happens When a Supplementary Registration is Made?** When a supplementary registration is completed, the Copyright Office will assign it a new registration number in the appropriate registration category, and issue a certificate of supplementary registration under that number. The basic registration will not be expunged or cancelled, and the two registrations will both stand in the Copyright Office records. The supplementary registration will have the effect of calling the public's attention to a possible error or omission in the basic registration, and of placing the correct facts or the additional information on official record. Moreover, if the person on whose behalf Form CA is submitted is the same as the person identified as copyright claimant in the basic registration, the Copyright Office will place a note referring to the supplementary registration in its records of the basic registration.

PLEASE READ DETAILED INSTRUCTIONS ON REVERSE

Please read the following line-by-line instructions carefully and refer to them while completing Form CA.

# INSTRUCTIONS

For Completing FORM CA (Supplementary Registration)

**PART A: BASIC INSTRUCTIONS**

• ***General Instructions:*** The information in this part identifies the basic registration to be corrected or amplified. Each item must agree exactly with the information as it already appears in the basic registration (even if the purpose of filing Form CA is to change one of these items).

• ***Title of Work:*** Give the title as it appears in the basic registration, including previous or alternative titles if they appear.

• ***Registration Number:*** This is a series of numerical digits, preceded by one or more letters. The registration number appears in the upper right hand corner of the certificate of registration.

• ***Registration Date:*** Give the year when the basic registration was completed.

• ***Name(s) of Author(s) and Name(s) of Copyright Claimant(s):*** Give all of the names as they appear in the basic registration.

**PART B: CORRECTION**

• ***General Instructions:*** Complete this part **only** if information in the basic registration was incorrect at the time that basic registration was made. Leave this part blank and complete Part C, instead, if your purpose is to add, update, or clarify information rather than to rectify an actual error.

• ***Location and Nature of Incorrect Information:*** Give the line number and the heading or description of the space in the basic registration where the error occurs (for example: "Line number 3 . . . Citizenship of author").

• ***Incorrect Information as It Appears in Basic Registration:*** Transcribe the erroneous statement exactly as it appears in the basic registration.

• ***Corrected Information:*** Give the statement as it should have appeared.

• ***Explanation of Correction (Optional):*** If you wish, you may add an explanation of the error or its correction.

**PART C: AMPLIFICATION**

• ***General Instructions:*** Complete this part if you want to provide any of the following: (1) additional information that could have been given but was omitted at the time of basic registration; (2) changes in facts, such as changes of title or address of claimant, that have occurred since the basic registration; or (3) explanations clarifying information in the basic registration.

• ***Location and Nature of Information to be Amplified:*** Give the line number and the heading or description of the space in the basic registration where the information to be amplified appears.

• ***Amplified Information:*** Give a statement of the added, updated, or explanatory information as clearly and succinctly as possible.

• ***Explanation of Amplification (Optional):*** If you wish, you may add an explanation of the amplification.

**PARTS D, E, F, G: CONTINUATION, FEE, MAILING INSTRUCTIONS AND CERTIFICATION**

• ***Continuation (Part D):*** Use this space if you do not have enough room in Parts B or C.

• ***Deposit Account and Mailing Instructions (Part E):*** If you maintain a Deposit Account in the Copyright Office, identify it in Part E. Otherwise, you will need to send the non-refundable filing fee of $10 with your form. The space headed "Correspondence" should contain the name and address of the person to be consulted if correspondence about the form becomes necessary.

• ***Certification (Part F):*** The application is not acceptable unless it bears the handwritten signature of the author, or other copyright claimant, or of the owner of exclusive right(s), or of the duly authorized agent of such author, claimant, or owner.

• ***Address for Return of Certificate (Part G):*** The address box must be completed legibly, since the certificate will be returned in a window envelope.

**PRIVACY ACT ADVISORY STATEMENT**
**Required by the Privacy Act of 1974 (Public Law 93-579)**

AUTHORITY FOR REQUESTING THIS INFORMATION
- Title 17, U.S.C., Sec. 408 (d)

FURNISHING THE REQUESTED INFORMATION IS
- Voluntary

BUT IF THE INFORMATION IS NOT PROVIDED
- It may be necessary to delay or refuse supplementary registration

PRINCIPAL USES OF REQUESTED INFORMATION
- Establishment and maintenance of a public record
- Evaluation for compliance with legal requirements

OTHER ROUTINE USES
- Public inspection and copying
- Preparation of public indexes
- Preparation of public catalogs of copyright registrations
- Preparation of search reports upon request

NOTE
- No other Advisory Statement will be given you in connection with the application
- Please retain this statement and refer to it if we communicate with you regarding this application

**FORM CA**
UNITED STATES COPYRIGHT OFFICE

REGISTRATION NUMBER

| TX | TXU | PA | PAU | VA | VAU | SR | SRU | RE |
|---|---|---|---|---|---|---|---|---|

Effective Date of Supplementary Registration

MONTH DAY YEAR

**DO NOT WRITE ABOVE THIS LINE. FOR COPYRIGHT OFFICE USE ONLY**

**(A) Basic Instructions**

**TITLE OF WORK:**

**REGISTRATION NUMBER OF BASIC REGISTRATION:**

**YEAR OF BASIC REGISTRATION:**

**NAME(S) OF AUTHOR(S):**

**NAME(S) OF COPYRIGHT CLAIMANT(S):**

**(B) Correction**

**LOCATION AND NATURE OF INCORRECT INFORMATION IN BASIC REGISTRATION:**

Line Number ............ Line Heading or Description ............

**INCORRECT INFORMATION AS IT APPEARS IN BASIC REGISTRATION:**

**CORRECTED INFORMATION:**

**EXPLANATION OF CORRECTION:** (Optional)

**(C) Amplification**

**LOCATION AND NATURE OF INFORMATION IN BASIC REGISTRATION TO BE AMPLIFIED:**

Line Number ............ Line Heading or Description ............

**AMPLIFIED INFORMATION:**

**EXPLANATION OF AMPLIFIED INFORMATION:** (Optional)

| | EXAMINED BY<br>CHECKED BY | FORM CA RECEIVED: | FOR COPYRIGHT OFFICE USE ONLY |
|---|---|---|---|
| | CORRESPONDENCE:<br>☐ YES | REMITTANCE NUMBER AND DATE: | |
| | REFERENCE TO THIS REGISTRATION ADDED TO BASIC REGISTRATION:<br>☐ YES ☐ NO | DEPOSIT ACCOUNT FUNDS USED: ☐ | |

**DO NOT WRITE ABOVE THIS LINE. FOR COPYRIGHT OFFICE USE ONLY**

**CONTINUATION OF:** (Check which) ☐ PART B OR ☐ PART C

**D** **Continuation**

**DEPOSIT ACCOUNT:** If the registration fee is to be charged to a Deposit Account established in the Copyright Office, give name and number of Account:

Name ............................................ Account Number ....................

**CORRESPONDENCE:** Give name and address to which correspondence should be sent:

Name ............................................ Apt. No. ....................

Address ............................................
(Number and Street) (City) (State) (ZIP Code)

**E** **Deposit Account and Mailing Instructions**

**CERTIFICATION** ✱ I, the undersigned, hereby certify that I am the: (Check one)

☐ author ☐ other copyright claimant ☐ owner of exclusive right(s) ☐ authorized agent of: ............................................
(Name of author or other copyright claimant, or owner of exclusive right(s))

of the work identified in this application and that the statements made by me in this application are correct to the best of my knowledge.

☞ Handwritten signature: (X) ............................................

Typed or printed name ............................................

Date: ............................................

✱ 17 USC §506(e): FALSE REPRESENTATION—Any person who knowingly makes a false representation of a material fact in the application for copyright registration provided for by section 409, or in any written statement filed in connection with the application, shall be fined not more than $2,500.

**F** **Certification (Application must be signed)**

............................................
(Name)

............................................
(Number, Street and Apartment Number)

............................................
(City) (State) (ZIP code)

**MAIL CERTIFICATE TO**

**(Certificate will be mailed in window envelope)**

**G** **Address for Return of Certificate**

January 1984—60,000

☆ U.S. GOVERNMENT PRINTING OFFICE 1984—421-278 510

**THIS FORM:**

- Can be used solely as an adjunct to a basic application for copyright registration.
- Is not acceptable unless submitted together with Form TX, Form PA, or Form VA.
- Is acceptable only if the group of works listed on it all qualify for a single copyright registration under 17 U.S.C. § 408 (c)(2).

**FORM GR/CP**

UNITED STATES COPYRIGHT OFFICE
LIBRARY OF CONGRESS
WASHINGTON, D.C. 20559

# ADJUNCT APPLICATION
## *for Copyright Registration for a Group of Contributions to Periodicals*

**WHEN TO USE FORM GR/CP:** Form GR/CP is the appropriate adjunct application form to use when you are submitting a basic application on Form TX, Form PA, or Form VA, for a group of works that qualify for a single registration under section 408(c)(2) of the copyright statute.

**WHEN DOES A GROUP OF WORKS QUALIFY FOR A SINGLE REGISTRATION UNDER 17 U.S.C. §408 (c)(2)?** The statute provides that a single copyright registration for a group of works can be made if **all** of the following conditions are met:

(1) All of the works are by the same author, who is an individual (not an employer for hire); and

(2) All of the works were first published as contributions to periodicals (including newspapers) within a twelve-month period; and

(3) Each of the contributions as first published bore a separate copyright notice, and the name of the owner of copyright in the work (or an abbreviation or alternative designation of the owner) was the same in each notice; and

(4) One copy of the entire periodical issue or newspaper section in which each contribution was first published must be deposited with the application; and

(5) The application must identify each contribution separately, including the periodical containing it and the date of its first publication.

**How to Apply for Group Registration:**

***First:*** Study the information on this page to make sure that all of the works you want to register together as a group qualify for a single registration.

***Second:*** Turn this page over and read through the detailed instructions for group registration. Decide which form you should use for the basic registration (Form TX for nondramatic literary works; or Form PA for musical, dramatic, and other works of the performing arts; or Form VA for pictorial and graphic works). Be sure that you have all of the information you need before you start filling out both the basic and the adjunct application forms.

***Third:*** Complete the basic application form, following the detailed instructions accompanying it **and the special instructions on the reverse of this page**.

***Fourth:*** Complete the adjunct application on Form GR/CP and mail it, together with the basic application form and the required copy of each contribution, to: Register of Copyrights, Library of Congress, Washington, D.C. 20559. Unless you have a Deposit Account in the Copyright Office, your application and copies must be accompanied by a check or money order for $10, payable to: *Register of Copyrights.*

# PROCEDURE FOR GROUP REGISTRATION

### TWO APPLICATION FORMS MUST BE FILED

When you apply for a single registration to cover a group of contributions to periodicals, you must submit two application forms:

(1) A basic application on either Form TX, or Form PA, or Form VA. It must contain all of the information required for copyright registration except the titles and information concerning publication of the contributions.

(2) An adjunct application on Form GR/CP. The purpose of this form is to provide separate identification for each of the contributions and to give information about their first publication, as required by the statute.

### WHICH BASIC APPLICATION FORM TO USE

The basic application form you choose to submit should be determined by the nature of the contributions you are registering. As long as they meet the statutory qualifications for group registration (outlined on the reverse of this page), the contributions can be registered together even if they are entirely different in nature, type, or content. However, you must choose which of three forms is generally the most appropriate on which to submit your basic application:

***Form TX:*** for nondramatic literary works consisting primarily of text. Examples are fiction, verse, articles, news stories, features, essays, reviews, editorials, columns, quizzes, puzzles, and advertising copy.

***Form PA:*** for works of the performing arts. Examples are music, drama, choreography, and pantomimes.

***Form VA:*** for works of the visual arts. Examples are photographs, drawings, paintings, prints, art reproductions, cartoons, comic strips, charts, diagrams, maps, pictorial ornamentation, and pictorial or graphic material published as advertising.

If your contributions differ in nature, choose the form most suitable for the majority of them. However, if any of the contributions consists preponderantly of nondramatic text matter in English, you should file Form TX for the entire group. This is because Form TX is the only form containing spaces for information about the manufacture of copies, which the statute requires to be given for certain works.

### REGISTRATION FEE FOR GROUP REGISTRATION

The fee for registration of a group of contributions to periodicals is $10, no matter how many contributions are listed on Form GR/CP. Unless you maintain a Deposit Account in the Copyright Office, the registration fee must accompany your application forms and copies. Make your remittance payable to: *Register of Copyrights.*

### WHAT COPIES SHOULD BE DEPOSITED FOR GROUP REGISTRATION?

The application forms you file for group registration must be accompanied by one complete copy of each contribution listed in Form GR/CP, exactly as the contribution was first published in a periodical. The deposit must consist of the entire issue of the periodical containing the contribution; or, if the contribution was first published in a newspaper, the deposit should consist of the entire section in which the contribution appeared. Tear sheets or proof copies are not acceptable for deposit.

### COPYRIGHT NOTICE REQUIREMENTS

For published works, the law provides that a copyright notice in a specified form "shall be placed on all publicly distributed copies from which the work can be visually perceived." The required form of the notice generally consists of three elements: (1) the symbol "©", or the word "Copyright", or the abbreviation "Copr.", (2) the year of first publication of the work; and (3) the name of the owner of copyright in the work, or an abbreviation or alternative form of the name. For example: "© 1978 Samuel Craig".

Among the conditions for group registration of contributions to periodicals, the statute establishes two requirements involving the copyright notice:

(1) Each of the contributions as first published must have borne a separate copyright notice; and

(2) "The name of the owner of copyright in the work, or an abbreviation by which the name can be recognized, or a generally known alternative designation of the owner" must have been the same in each notice.

### HOW TO FILL OUT THE BASIC APPLICATION FORM WHEN APPLYING FOR GROUP REGISTRATION

In general, the instructions for filling out the basic application (Form TX, Form PA, or Form VA) apply to group registrations. In addition, please observe the following specific instructions:

***Space 1 (Title):*** Do not give information concerning any of the contributions in space 1 of the basic application. Instead, in the block headed "Title of this Work", state: "See Form GR/CP, attached". Leave the other blocks in space 1 blank.

***Space 2 (Author):*** Give the name and other information concerning the author of all of the contributions listed in Form GR/CP. To qualify for group registration, all of the contributions must have been written by the same individual author.

***Space 3 (Creation and Publication):*** In the block calling for the year of creation, give the year of creation of the last of the contributions to be completed. Leave the block calling for the date and nation of first publication blank.

***Space 4 (Claimant):*** Give all of the requested information, which must be the same for all of the contributions listed on Form GR/CP.

***Other spaces:*** Complete all of the applicable spaces, and be sure that the form is signed in the certification space.

### HOW TO FILL OUT FORM GR/CP

#### PART A: IDENTIFICATION OF APPLICATION

• ***Identification of Basic Application:*** Indicate, by checking one of the boxes, which of the basic application forms (Form TX, or Form PA, or Form VA) you are filing for registration.

• ***Identification of Author and Claimant:*** Give the name of the individual author exactly as it appears in line 2 of the basic application, and give the name of the copyright claimant exactly as it appears in line 4. These must be the same for all of the contributions listed in Part B of Form GR/CP.

#### PART B: REGISTRATION FOR GROUP OF CONTRIBUTIONS

• ***General Instructions:*** Under the statute, a group of contributions to periodicals will qualify for a single registration only if the application "identifies each work separately, including the periodical containing it and its date of first publication." Part B of the Form GR/CP provides lines enough to list 19 separate contributions; if you need more space, use additional Forms GR/CP. If possible, list the contributions in the order of their publication, giving the earliest first. Number each line consecutively.

• ***Important:*** All of the contributions listed on Form GR/CP must have been published within a single twelve-month period. This does not mean that all of the contributions must have been published during the same calendar year, but it does mean that, to be grouped in a single application, the earliest and latest contributions must not have been published more than twelve months apart. Example: Contributions published on April 1, 1978, July 1, 1978, and March 1, 1979, could be grouped together, but a contribution published on April 15, 1979, could not be registered with them as part of the group.

• ***Title of Contribution:*** Each contribution must be given a title that is capable of identifying that particular work and of distinguishing it from others. If the contribution as published in the periodical bears a title (or an identifying phrase that could serve as a title), transcribe its wording completely and exactly.

• ***Identification of Periodical:*** Give the over-all title of the periodical in which the contribution was first published, together with the volume and issue number (if any) and the issue date.

• ***Pages:*** Give the number of the page of the periodical issue on which the contribution appeared. If the contribution covered more than one page, give the inclusive pages, if possible.

• ***First Publication:*** The statute defines "publication" as "the distribution of copies or phonorecords of a work to the public by sale or other transfer of ownership, or by rental, lease, or lending"; a work is also "published" if there has been an "offering to distribute copies or phonorecords to a group of persons for purposes of further distribution, public performance, or public display." Give the full date (month, day, and year) when, and the country where, publication of the periodical issue containing the contribution first occurred. If first publication took place simultaneously in the United States and other countries, it is sufficient to state "U.S.A."

**NOTE:** The advantage of group registration is that it allows any number of works published within a twelve-month period to be registered "on the basis of a single deposit, application, and registration fee." On the other hand, group registration may also have disadvantages under certain circumstances. If infringement of a published work begins before the work has been registered, the copyright owner can still obtain the ordinary remedies for copyright infringement (including injunctions, actual damages and profits, and impounding and disposition of infringing articles). However, in that situation—where the copyright in a published work is infringed before registration is made—the owner cannot obtain special remedies (statutory damages and attorney's fees) unless registration was made within three months after first publication of the work.

# ADJUNCT APPLICATION
## *for*
## *Copyright Registration for a Group of Contributions to Periodicals*

**FORM GR/CP**

UNITED STATES COPYRIGHT OFFICE

| REGISTRATION NUMBER | | |
|---|---|---|
| TX | PA | VA |
| EFFECTIVE DATE OF REGISTRATION | | |
| (Month) | (Day) | (Year) |
| FORM GR/CP RECEIVED | | |
| Page ____ of ____ pages | | |

- Use this adjunct form only if your are making a single registration for a group of contributions to periodicals, and you are also filing a basic application on Form TX, Form PA, or Form VA. Follow the instructions, attached.
- Number each line in Part B consecutively. Use additional Forms GR/CP if you need more space.
- Submit this adjunct form with the basic application form. Clip (do not tape or staple) and fold all sheets together before submitting them.

**DO NOT WRITE ABOVE THIS LINE. FOR COPYRIGHT OFFICE USE ONLY**

**(A) Identification of Application**

**IDENTIFICATION OF BASIC APPLICATION:**
- This application for copyright registration for a group of contributions to periodicals is submitted as an adjunct to an application filed on: (Check which)

☐Form TX ☐Form PA ☐Form VA

**IDENTIFICATION OF AUTHOR AND CLAIMANT:** (Give the name of the author and the name of the copyright claimant in all of the contributions listed in Part B of this form. The names should be the same as the names given in spaces 2 and 4 of the basic application.)

Name of Author: ..........

Name of Copyright Claimant: ..........

**(B) Registration For Group of Contributions**

**COPYRIGHT REGISTRATION FOR A GROUP OF CONTRIBUTIONS TO PERIODICALS:** (To make a single registration for a group of works by the same individual author, all first published as contributions to periodicals within a 12-month period (see instructions), give full information about each contribution. If more space is needed, use additional Forms GR/CP.)

☐ Title of Contribution: ..........
Title of Periodical: .......... Vol. ...... No. ...... Issue Date .......... Pages ..........
Date of First Publication: .......... (Month) (Day) (Year) Nation of First Publication .......... (Country)

☐ Title of Contribution: ..........
Title of Periodical: .......... Vol. ...... No. ...... Issue Date .......... Pages ..........
Date of First Publication: .......... (Month) (Day) (Year) Nation of First Publication .......... (Country)

☐ Title of Contribution: ..........
Title of Periodical: .......... Vol. ...... No. ...... Issue Date .......... Pages ..........
Date of First Publication: .......... (Month) (Day) (Year) Nation of First Publication .......... (Country)

☐ Title of Contribution: ..........
Title of Periodical: .......... Vol. ...... No. ...... Issue Date .......... Pages ..........
Date of First Publication: .......... (Month) (Day) (Year) Nation of First Publication .......... (Country)

☐ Title of Contribution: ..........
Title of Periodical: .......... Vol. ...... No. ...... Issue Date .......... Pages ..........
Date of First Publication: .......... (Month) (Day) (Year) Nation of First Publication .......... (Country)

☐ Title of Contribution: ..........
Title of Periodical: .......... Vol. ...... No. ...... Issue Date .......... Pages ..........
Date of First Publication: .......... (Month) (Day) (Year) Nation of First Publication .......... (Country)

☐ Title of Contribution: ..........
Title of Periodical: .......... Vol. ...... No. ...... Issue Date .......... Pages ..........
Date of First Publication: .......... (Month) (Day) (Year) Nation of First Publication .......... (Country)

FOR COPYRIGHT OFFICE USE ONLY

DO NOT WRITE ABOVE THIS LINE. FOR COPYRIGHT OFFICE USE ONLY

**B** Continued

☐ Title of Contribution: ..........
Title of Periodical: .......... Vol. ..... No. ..... Issue Date .......... Pages ..........
Date of First Publication: .......... (Month) (Day) (Year) Nation of First Publication .......... (Country)

☐ Title of Contribution: ..........
Title of Periodical: .......... Vol. ..... No. ..... Issue Date .......... Pages ..........
Date of First Publication: .......... (Month) (Day) (Year) Nation of First Publication .......... (Country)

☐ Title of Contribution: ..........
Title of Periodical: .......... Vol. ..... No. ..... Issue Date .......... Pages ..........
Date of First Publication: .......... (Month) (Day) (Year) Nation of First Publication .......... (Country)

☐ Title of Contribution: ..........
Title of Periodical: .......... Vol. ..... No. ..... Issue Date .......... Pages ..........
Date of First Publication: .......... (Month) (Day) (Year) Nation of First Publication .......... (Country)

☐ Title of Contribution: ..........
Title of Periodical: .......... Vol. ..... No. ..... Issue Date .......... Pages ..........
Date of First Publication: .......... (Month) (Day) (Year) Nation of First Publication .......... (Country)

☐ Title of Contribution: ..........
Title of Periodical: .......... Vol. ..... No. ..... Issue Date .......... Pages ..........
Date of First Publication: .......... (Month) (Day) (Year) Nation of First Publication .......... (Country)

☐ Title of Contribution: ..........
Title of Periodical: .......... Vol. ..... No. ..... Issue Date .......... Pages ..........
Date of First Publication: .......... (Month) (Day) (Year) Nation of First Publication .......... (Country)

☐ Title of Contribution: ..........
Title of Periodical: .......... Vol. ..... No. ..... Issue Date .......... Pages ..........
Date of First Publication: .......... (Month) (Day) (Year) Nation of First Publication .......... (Country)

☐ Title of Contribution: ..........
Title of Periodical: .......... Vol. ..... No. ..... Issue Date .......... Pages ..........
Date of First Publication: .......... (Month) (Day) (Year) Nation of First Publication .......... (Country)

☐ Title of Contribution: ..........
Title of Periodical: .......... Vol. ..... No. ..... Issue Date .......... Pages ..........
Date of First Publication: .......... (Month) (Day) (Year) Nation of First Publication .......... (Country)

☐ Title of Contribution: ..........
Title of Periodical: .......... Vol. ..... No. ..... Issue Date .......... Pages ..........
Date of First Publication: .......... (Month) (Day) (Year) Nation of First Publication .......... (Country)

☐ Title of Contribution: ..........
Title of Periodical: .......... Vol. ..... No. ..... Issue Date .......... Pages ..........
Date of First Publication: .......... (Month) (Day) (Year) Nation of First Publication .......... (Country)

U S GOVERNMENT PRINTING OFFICE 1978—261-022/12 Apr. 1978—300,000

**FORM IS**
UNITED STATES COPYRIGHT OFFICE
LIBRARY OF CONGRESS
WASHINGTON, D.C. 20559

# REQUEST FOR ISSUANCE OF AN IMPORT STATEMENT

*under §601 of the U.S. Copyright Law*

**Use the request form on the next page (Form IS) when:**

- You are the copyright owner of a nondramatic literary work that is subject to the manufacturing provisions of §601 of the copyright law (see below); and
- Registration for the work has already been made, or is being made now; and
- Copies of the work have been manufactured outside the United States or Canada, and you want to import up to 2,000 copies of the foreign edition into the United States under the exception in 17 U.S.C. §601(b)(2).

**WHEN TO USE THE REQUEST FORM:** Submit the form on the next page (Form IS) if you wish to import copies of a work and, because of the manufacturing provisions of the copyright law, you need an Import Statement from the Copyright Office to present to officials of the United States Customs Service.

**WHAT ARE THE "MANUFACTURING PROVISIONS"?** The copyright statute currently provides that, as a general rule, the copies of a work "consisting preponderantly of nondramatic literary material that is in the English language" be manufactured in the United States or Canada in order to be lawfully imported and publicly distributed in the United States. There are a number of exceptions to this provision, and these exceptions fall into three general categories deriving from: (1) the nature of the work; or (2) the processes used to manufacture the copies; or (3) certain facts existing at the time of importation or distribution of copies in the United States. One of the exceptions of the third type provides for the issuance of an Import Statement which will permit the importation of up to 2,000 copies of a foreign edition.

**WHAT IS AN "IMPORT STATEMENT"?** Under section 601(b)(2) of the copyright law, the manufacturing provisions do not apply "where the United States Customs Service is presented with an Import Statement issued under the seal of the Copyright Office, in which case a total of no more than 2,000 copies of any one such work shall be allowed entry." Thus, by presenting a valid Import Statement to the U.S. Customs Service, you can lawfully import a maximum of 2,000 copies of a work manufactured abroad, and distribute them publicly in the United States, without affecting any rights under the copyright.

**WHEN AN IMPORT STATEMENT IS NOT NECESSARY:** An Import Statement is **not** needed as a condition for importation of copies of a foreign edition in the following cases:

(1) Where the work does not consist "preponderantly of nondramatic literary material that is in the English language"; or

(2) Where none of the processes used to manufacture the copies are covered by the manufacturing provisions. In general, the processes covered by section 601 are: (1) typesetting and plate-making (where a typographic process preceded the actual printing); (2) the making of plates by a lithographic or photoengraving process (where this was a final or intermediate step before printing); and (3) the final printing and binding processes (in all cases); or

(3) Where, in general, the author is not a U.S. citizen or domiciliary (there are some limitations and qualifications on this general exception); or

(4) Where one of the other specific exceptions in section 601(b) applies.

In all other cases, if you want to import copies of a foreign edition, you will need an Import Statement.

**HOW TO REQUEST ISSUANCE OF AN IMPORT STATEMENT:**

- ***First:*** Study the information given here to make sure that obtaining an Import Statement is the appropriate procedure to follow in your case.
- ***Second:*** Complete all applicable spaces on the request form (Form IS), following the line-by-line instructions. Use typewriter or print in dark ink. Be sure to sign the form at space D.
- ***Third:*** Detach your completed request form and send it to: Register of Copyrights, Library of Congress, Washington, D.C. 20559. Unless you have a Deposit Account in the Copyright Office, your request must be accompanied by a check or money order for $3, payable to: Register of Copyrights.

**REGISTRATION REQUIRED:** The statute provides that the Import Statement shall be issued "at the time of registration for the work under section 408 or at any time thereafter." Thus, an Import Statement can be issued only if:

- Registration for the work has already been made; or
- An application for copyright registration (on Form TX), with the necessary deposit and fee, are submitted at the same time as the request for an Import Statement. Write to the Copyright Office if you need forms and information about copyright registration.

**WHO CAN OBTAIN AN IMPORT STATEMENT:** Under the statute, the Copyright Office is authorized to issue an Import Statement to "the copyright owner or to a person designated by such owner." The "copyright owner" for this purpose is either: (1) the author of the work (including, in the case of a work made for hire, the employer or other person for whom the work was prepared), or (2) the copyright claimant identified in the registration for the work, or (3) a person or organization that has obtained ownership of one or more exclusive rights initially owned by the author, including the exclusive right to import copies of the work into the United States. The request form must be signed by the copyright owner as shown in the records of the Copyright Office (or by that owner's duly authorized agent), and must designate the person or organization to whom the statement is to be issued.

**WHAT TO DO WITH THE IMPORT STATEMENT:** A certified Import Statement will be issued for 2,000 copies, the maximum number importable under the law. The Import Statement is a valuable document, and you should take care to preserve it from loss until you need it. The Statement should be presented to the officials of the U.S. Customs Service at the appropriate port of entry at the time of importation. If the total number of copies actually imported is less than the 2,000-copy maximum, the Customs officials will notify the Copyright Office, which will issue another Import Statement for the balance. There is no need to request an additional Import Statement in this situation, and there is no additional charge for the service.

**HOW TO FILL OUT THE REQUEST FORM (FORM IS)**

**SPACE A: IDENTIFICATION OF WORK**

***General Instructions:*** The information in this space identifies the work of which copies are to be imported under the Import Statement. If registration has already been made for the work, each item in Space A should agree with the information in the certificate of registration; the registration number and effective date of registration appearing on the certificate should be transcribed in the boxes in the upper right hand corner of Form IS. If you are applying for registration at the same time you are submitting your request for issuance of an Import Statement, make sure that the information on Form IS agrees exactly with the information in your application on Form TX; in that case the Copyright Office will supply the registration number and date when it issues the Import Statement.

***Title, Author(s), Claimant(s):*** Give the title (including any previous or alternative titles) and all names as they appear in your application or certificate covering the work.

**SPACE B: PERSON DESIGNATED TO RECEIVE IMPORT STATEMENT**

Give the full name and complete mailing address of the person or organization to whom the Copyright Office will issue the certified Import Statement. This space should be completed even if the same name and address appear elsewhere on the form.

**SPACE C: FEE AND CONTACT**

***Deposit Account:*** If you maintain a Deposit Account in the Copyright Office, identify it in Space C. Otherwise you will need to send a fee of $3 with your request.

***Person to Contact:*** Identify an individual person whom we can write to about this request, if necessary. Include that person's full address and telephone number, including area code.

**SPACE D: CERTIFICATION**

The Import Statement will not be issued unless this space includes the handwritten signature of the copyright owner of the work as shown in the records of the Copyright Office (or of that owner's duly authorized agent), and includes the other identifying information called for.

**PRIVACY ACT ADVISORY STATEMENT**

**Required by the Privacy Act of 1974 (Public Law 93-579)**

AUTHORITY FOR REQUESTING THIS INFORMATION:
- Title 17 U.S.C., Sec. 601

FURNISHING THE REQUESTED INFORMATION IS:
- Voluntary

BUT IF THE INFORMATION IS NOT FURNISHED:
- It may be necessary to delay or refuse the issuance of an Import Statement
- You may be prevented from importing copies of your work under 17 U.S.C. Sec., 601(b)
- If you try to import copies without an Import Statement, they may be subject to seizure and forfeiture under 17 U.S.C. Sec., 603(c)

PRINCIPAL USES OF REQUESTED INFORMATION:
- Preparation of Import Statement
- Establishment and maintenance of a public record
- Examination of the statement for compliance with legal requirements

OTHER ROUTINE USES:
- Preparation of duplicate Import Statements, if necessary
- Public inspection and copying
- Preparation of public indexes
- Preparation of search reports upon request

# REQUEST FOR ISSUANCE OF AN IMPORT STATEMENT

*under §601 of the U.S. Copyright Law*

**FORM IS**

UNITED STATES COPYRIGHT OFFICE
LIBRARY OF CONGRESS
WASHINGTON, D.C. 20559

REGISTRATION NUMBER:

EFFECTIVE DATE OF REGISTRATION:
(Month) (Day) (Year)

DATE OF ISSUE OF IMPORT STATEMENT:
(Month) (Day) (Year)

**(A) Identification of Work**

**TITLE OF WORK:**

**NAME(S) OF AUTHOR(S):**

**NAME(S) OF COPYRIGHT CLAIMANT(S):**

**NOTE:** If registration has already been made for this work, give the registration number and the effective date of registration in the boxes in the upper right hand corner of this form.

**(B) Designee**

**ISSUE IMPORT STATEMENT TO:** (Give full name and mailing address)

Name: .......... Apt. No. ..........

Address: ..........
(Number and Street) (City) (State) (ZIP Code)

**(C) Fee and Contact**

**DEPOSIT ACCOUNT:** (If the fee for issuing the Import Statement is to be charged to a Deposit Account established in the Copyright Office, give name and number of Account.)

Name: ..........

Account Number: ..........

**PERSON TO CONTACT:** (Give name, address, and telephone number of individual who can be contacted if further information is needed.)

Name: ..........

Telephone ( ) ..........
(Area Code)

Address ..........
(Apt)
(City) (State) (ZIP Code)

**(D) Certification (Request must be signed)**

**CERTIFICATION OF REQUEST BY COPYRIGHT OWNER (OR AGENT OF OWNER):**

✱ By signing this request form I certify that I am the:
☐ copyright owner (as shown in the records of the Copyright Office) of the work identified in Space A
☐ duly authorized agent of the copyright owner of the work identified in Space A, whose name as shown in the records of the Copyright Office is: ..........

(Name of Copyright Owner)

and that the Copyright Office is hereby authorized to issue an Import Statement to the name and address given in Space B.

Handwritten signature: (X) ..........
Typewritten or printed name: ..........
Address: ..........
Date: ..........

**DO NOT WRITE BELOW THIS LINE. FOR COPYRIGHT OFFICE USE ONLY**

EXAMINED BY
CHECKED BY
CORRESPONDENCE
☐ Yes
DEPOSIT ACCOUNT FUNDS USED ☐
REQUEST RECEIVED:
REMITTANCE NUMBER AND DATE:

✱ 17 U.S.C. §506(e) FALSE REPRESENTATION – Any person who knowingly makes a false representation of a material fact in the application for copyright registration provided for by section 409, or in any written statement filed in connection with the application, shall be fined not more than $2,500.

☆U.S. GOVERNMENT PRINTING OFFICE: 1982-361-278/61

Sept. 1982—20,000

# APPLICATION FOR RECORDATION OF *Coin-Operated Phonorecord Players*

**FORM JB**
LICENSING DIVISION
COPYRIGHT OFFICE
LIBRARY OF CONGRESS
WASHINGTON, D.C. 20557

**USE THIS FORM WHEN:**

- You are the operator of one or more coin-operated phonorecord players (jukeboxes); and
- You want to obtain a compulsory license to cover public performances of copyrighted music on your jukeboxes, as provided by the new copyright law; and
- You are also sending to the Licensing Division of the Copyright Office the statutory royalty fee for each jukebox listed on the form.

**Copyright Law on Jukebox Performances:** As of January 1, 1978, public performances of recorded music on jukeboxes were no longer free from copyright liability. In general, the Copyright Act gives the owner of copyright in a "nondramatic musical work embodied in a phonorecord" the exclusive right "to perform the work publicly by means of a coin-operated phonorecord player." However, there is an important limitation on this exclusive right: instead of requiring negotiated licenses for jukebox performances in all cases, the statute (17 U.S.C. §116) establishes an annual royalty fee and sets out a procedure for obtaining compulsory licenses covering performances on particular jukeboxes.

**General Requirements for Compulsory Licenses:** Obtaining a compulsory license for jukebox performances generally requires the "operator" to do three things:

(1) File an application on Form JB, identifying each jukebox to be covered;

(2) Pay into the Copyright Office a royalty fee for each jukebox identified on the application.

(3) Affix a certificate issued by the Copyright Office to each licensed jukebox.

There are strict time limits for each of these requirements. To remain valid, a compulsory license must be obtained annually. Detailed information and instructions concerning these requirements appear on the back of this page.

**Effect of Having (Or Not Having) a Compulsory License:** As long as a compulsory license is in effect for a particular coin-operated phonorecord player (jukebox), the performances of nondramatic music on that player are free from further copyright liability. On the other hand, if an operator fails to comply with the compulsory licensing requirements with respect to a particular jukebox, every unauthorized public performance of a copyrighted musical work on that machine will be a separate act of copyright infringement under the statute. This means that one or more civil (or, in some cases, criminal) actions for damages and other remedies could be brought against the operator in the federal courts.

**How to Obtain a Compulsory License:**

***First:*** Study the general information on this page, then turn the page over and read through the detailed information and specific instructions for filling out Form JB. Make sure, before starting to complete the form, that you have all of the information you will need to identify the phonorecord players in space **E.**

***Second:*** Complete all applicable spaces on the form, following the detailed instructions. To list more than 15 phonorecord players, use as many continuation sheets (Form JB/CON) as you need; supplies can be obtained from the Licensing Division of the Copyright Office. Use typewriter, or print the information in dark ink. **Be sure to sign the form at space C.**

***Third:*** Compute the total royalty fee, following the detailed instructions on the back of this page, and obtain a certified check, cashier's check, or money order in the full amount. It should be payable to: *Register of Copyrights.*

***Fourth:*** Detach this sheet and send your completed application (including any continuation sheets), **together with the royalty fee,** to: Licensing Division, Copyright Office, Library of Congress, Washington, D.C. 20557. Take special care to observe the statutory time limits described on the back of this page.

***Fifth:*** As soon as possible after receiving your certificates from the Copyright Office, and no later than the statutory deadline, affix the correct certificate to each phonorecord player, in accordance with the requirements outlined on the next page.

**PRIVACY ACT ADVISORY STATEMENT**

Required by the Privacy Act of 1974 (Public Law 93-579)

AUTHORITY FOR REQUESTING THIS INFORMATION
- Title 17, U.S.C., §116

FURNISHING THE REQUESTED INFORMATION IS
- Voluntary

BUT IF THE INFORMATION IS NOT FURNISHED
- It may be necessary to delay or refuse issuance of the certificate
- You may be liable for civil or criminal penalties for copyright infringement with respect to public performance of nondramatic musical works on a coin-operated phonorecord player (17 U.S.C. §§502-506, 509)

PRINCIPAL USES OF REQUESTED INFORMATION
- Preparation of detailed statements of account for the Copyright Royalty Tribunal
- Establishment and maintenance of a public record
- Examination of the application for compliance with legal requirements before issuance of a certificate

OTHER ROUTINE USES
- Public inspection and copying
- Preparation of public indexes
- Publication and sale of listings
- Preparation of search reports upon request

NOTE
- No other advisory statement will be given you in connection with this application
- Please retain this statement and refer to it if we communicate with you regarding this application

# More Information About Compulsory Licenses For Jukebox Performances

## WHO CAN OBTAIN A COMPULSORY LICENSE?

Under the law the right to obtain a compulsory license belongs to the "operator" of a "coin-operated phonorecord player."

• An "*operator*" is any person who, alone or jointly with others: (1) owns the player; or (2) has the power to make the player "available for placement in an establishment for purposes of public performance"; or (3) "has the power to exercise primary control over the selection of the musical works made available for public performance" on the player.

• A "*coin-operated phonorecord player*" is a machine or device (usually called a "jukebox") that: (1) is used solely for performing nondramatic music; (2) is activated by inserting coins, tokens, or currency; (3) allows patrons to select the works to be played from a list of titles; and (4) is located in an establishment making no admission charge.

## WHEN TO FILE FOR A COMPULSORY LICENSE:

Submit a Form JB application identifying each jukebox to be covered before or within one month after the date performances were first made available on that player. NOTE: The operator will need to renew the certificates for the next year. The Licensing Division will mail the renewal application Form JB/R to the operator.

Payment of the total royalty fee for all of the coin-operated phonorecord players listed on the application must accompany Form JB. Your remittance must be in the form of a certified check, cashier's check, or money order, payable to: Register of Copyrights.

## CERTIFICATE OF RECORDATION:

• ***Issuance of Certificate:*** After receiving an acceptable application and fee, the Copyright Office is given 20 days in which to issue a separate certificate for each phonorecord player. The certificates will be given a "date of issue" and will be mailed to the operator at the address given in space **A** on Form JB.

• ***Affixing the Certificate:*** The statute requires the operator to affix the certificate to the phonorecord player "in a position where it ca. be readily examined by the public," and it provides strict time limits for doing so. The certificate must be affixed "on or before March 1" of the year in which it is issued, or "within 10 days after the date of issue of the certificate," whichever is later.

*IMPORTANT:* The Copyright Office will not issue a certificate for any jukebox listed on the application until it has received the required information and an acceptable remittance covering the total royalty fee for that application.

# HOW TO FILL OUT FORM JB

## Specific Instructions for Spaces A thru E

### SPACE A: OPERATOR OF PHONORECORD PLAYER

• **General Instructions:** Make sure that the person or organization identified in this space is the "operator" of all of the "coin-operated phonorecord players" identified on the form. The meaning of these terms is explained in the column to the left.

• ***Name of Operator:*** Give the full legal name of the operator, followed by any fictitious or assumed name or names that are used for conducting business. If the operator is a partnership, give the name of the partnership followed by the name of at least one individual partner.

• ***Address of Operator:*** Give the full address at which the operator actually conducts business. A post office box or similar designation will not generally be accepted.

### SPACE B: SUMMARY OF APPLICATION

• ***Licensing Year:*** Give the calendar year that this application covers. The licensing year covers January 1 through December 31.

• ***Royalty Rate:*** Locate the statutory royalty rate that corresponds to the licensing year covered by this application.

1982—$25.00  1985—$50.00
1983—$25.00  1986—$50.00
1984—$50.00

• ***Number of Players:*** Count the number of coin-operated phonorecord players (jukeboxes) identified on the application (including all continuation sheets), and give the total. Multiply the total number of players by the statutory royalty rate.

• ***Provision for Half-year Certificates:*** The statute provides that, if performances "are made available on a particular phonorecord player for the first time after July 1 of any year, the royalty fee" is one half the statutory royalty rate. *Do not mix* jukeboxes paid at the full year rate with jukeboxes paid at the half-year rate on the same application; file separate applications.

### SPACE C: CERTIFICATION

The application is not acceptable unless it bears the handwritten signature of the operator of the coin-operated phonorecord players, or of the duly authorized agent of the operator. If a business entity is identified as the operator in space **A**, the signature should be that of a corporate officer (if the entity is a corporation), or that of a partner (if the entity is a partnership).

### SPACE D: INDIVIDUAL TO BE CONTACTED IF FURTHER INFORMATION IS NEEDED

Identify an individual person whom we can call or write to about this application. Include that person's full address and telephone number, including area code.

### SPACE E: IDENTIFICATION OF COIN-OPERATED PHONORECORD PLAYERS

• ***General Instructions:*** Each phonorecord player must be listed separately; do not combine information about different machines in the same line. You do not need to list the players in any particular order, but it will help us in issuing certificates if you bring together machines made by the same manufacturer on consecutive lines.

• ***Manufacturer:*** The manufacturer must be identified separately for each coin-operated phonorecord player listed on the application. Give the full name except for the following: For Rock-Ola Manufacturing Corp. give RKA; for Rowe International, Inc. give RWE; for Seeburg Corp. give SE; for Wurlitzer Co. give WR.

• ***Serial Number:*** If there is a serial number on the machine, it must be given on the application. If the machine never had a serial number, or if its number has been removed or defaced, the space can be left blank, but in that case the other identifying information must be given.

• ***Other Identifying Information:*** You may leave the spaces in the right hand column of a particular line blank if you have given the serial number for the player.

# APPLICATION FOR RECORDATION OF COIN-OPERATED PHONORECORD PLAYERS

| FOR COPYRIGHT OFFICE USE ONLY | |
|---|---|
| AMOUNT | REMITTANCE NUMBER |
| | |
| APPLICATION RECEIVED | |
| CERTIFICATE(S) ISSUED | |
| CERTIFICATE(S) MAILED | |

**FORM JB**
COPYRIGHT OFFICE

**A Operator**

**NAME AND ADDRESS OF OPERATOR:**

Name:
Address: (Number and Street)
(City or Town) (State) (Zip Code)

**B Summary of Application**

**LICENSING YEAR:** (Give the calendar year covered by this application.)
Year 19

**ROYALTY RATE:** (Locate the statutory rate that corresponds to the licensing year, as explained in the instructions.)
$

**NUMBER OF PLAYERS:** (Give the total number of players listed in this application including continuation sheets.) Multiply this number by the royalty rate
X =

**TOTAL ROYALTY FEE:**
$ *

***Royalty fee must be paid by certified check, cashier's check or money order, payable to Register of Copyrights before certificates can be issued.**

**C Certification**

**CERTIFICATION *** I, the undersigned, hereby certify that I am the: (Check one)

☐ operator ☐ duly authorized agent of operator (Name of operator)

of the phonorecord players identified in this application, and that the statements made by me are correct to the best of my knowledge.

Handwritten signature: (X)
Typed or printed name
Title (Corporate officer or partner — See instructions)
Date

**D Contact**

**INDIVIDUAL TO BE CONTACTED IF FURTHER INFORMATION IS NEEDED:**

Name Telephone ( ) (Area Code)
Address (Number, Street, Rural Route, Apt. No.)
(City, Town, State, Zip Code)

**E Identification**

**IDENTIFICATION OF COIN-OPERATED PHONORECORD PLAYERS:** Full name or abbreviation of manufacturer *must* be given in all cases. Serial number must be given if available. Other information must be given if serial number is lacking. See instructions.

| | | |
|---|---|---|
| 1 | Manufacturer<br>Serial Number<br>FOR COPYRIGHT OFFICE USE ONLY | Other identifying information:<br>Model No. Model Year<br>Type of Sound: ☐ Mono ☐ Stereo ☐ Quadraphonic ☐ Other<br>Record Capacity Charge per play<br>Model Name |
| 2 | Manufacturer<br>Serial Number<br>FOR COPYRIGHT OFFICE USE ONLY | Other identifying information:<br>Model No. Model Year<br>Type of Sound: ☐ Mono ☐ Stereo ☐ Quadraphonic ☐ Other<br>Record Capacity Charge per play<br>Model Name |
| 3 | Manufacturer<br>Serial Number<br>FOR COPYRIGHT OFFICE USE ONLY | Other identifying information:<br>Model No. Model Year<br>Type of Sound: ☐ Mono ☐ Stereo ☐ Quadraphonic ☐ Other<br>Record Capacity Charge per play<br>Model Name |

U.S. GOVERNMENT PRINTING OFFICE: 1983 421-279 1039 December 1980 100,000

| | | | |
|---|---|---|---|
| 4 | Manufacturer<br>Serial Number<br>FOR COPYRIGHT OFFICE USE ONLY | Other identifying information:<br>Model No. Model Year<br>Type of Sound: ☐ Mono ☐ Stereo ☐ Quadraphonic ☐ Other<br>Record Capacity Charge per play<br>Model Name | **E** (Continued) |
| 5 | Manufacturer<br>Serial Number<br>FOR COPYRIGHT OFFICE USE ONLY | Other identifying information:<br>Model No. Model Year<br>Type of Sound: ☐ Mono ☐ Stereo ☐ Quadraphonic ☐ Other<br>Record Capacity Charge per play<br>Model Name | |
| 6 | Manufacturer<br>Serial Number<br>FOR COPYRIGHT OFFICE USE ONLY | Other identifying information:<br>Model No. Model Year<br>Type of Sound: ☐ Mono ☐ Stereo ☐ Quadraphonic ☐ Other<br>Record Capacity Charge per play<br>Model Name | |
| 7 | Manufacturer<br>Serial Number<br>FOR COPYRIGHT OFFICE USE ONLY | Other identifying information:<br>Model No. Model Year<br>Type of Sound: ☐ Mono ☐ Stereo ☐ Quadraphonic ☐ Other<br>Record Capacity Charge per play<br>Model Name | |
| 8 | Manufacturer<br>Serial Number<br>FOR COPYRIGHT OFFICE USE ONLY | Other identifying information:<br>Model No. Model Year<br>Type of Sound: ☐ Mono ☐ Stereo ☐ Quadraphonic ☐ Other<br>Record Capacity Charge per play<br>Model Name | |
| 9 | Manufacturer<br>Serial Number<br>FOR COPYRIGHT OFFICE USE ONLY | Other identifying information:<br>Model No. Model Year<br>Type of Sound: ☐ Mono ☐ Stereo ☐ Quadraphonic ☐ Other<br>Record Capacity Charge per play<br>Model Name | |
| 10 | Manufacturer<br>Serial Number<br>FOR COPYRIGHT OFFICE USE ONLY | Other identifying information:<br>Model No. Model Year<br>Type of Sound: ☐ Mono ☐ Stereo ☐ Quadraphonic ☐ Other<br>Record Capacity Charge per play<br>Model Name | |
| 11 | Manufacturer<br>Serial Number<br>FOR COPYRIGHT OFFICE USE ONLY | Other identifying information:<br>Model No. Model Year<br>Type of Sound: ☐ Mono ☐ Stereo ☐ Quadraphonic ☐ Other<br>Record Capacity Charge per play<br>Model Name | |
| 12 | Manufacturer<br>Serial Number<br>FOR COPYRIGHT OFFICE USE ONLY | Other identifying information:<br>Model No. Model Year<br>Type of Sound: ☐ Mono ☐ Stereo ☐ Quadraphonic ☐ Other<br>Record Capacity Charge per play<br>Model Name | |
| 13 | Manufacturer<br>Serial Number<br>FOR COPYRIGHT OFFICE USE ONLY | Other identifying information:<br>Model No. Model Year<br>Type of Sound: ☐ Mono ☐ Stereo ☐ Quadraphonic ☐ Other<br>Record Capacity Charge per play<br>Model Name | |
| 14 | Manufacturer<br>Serial Number<br>FOR COPYRIGHT OFFICE USE ONLY | Other identifying information:<br>Model No. Model Year<br>Type of Sound: ☐ Mono ☐ Stereo ☐ Quadraphonic ☐ Other<br>Record Capacity Charge per play<br>Model Name | |
| 15 | Manufacturer<br>Serial Number<br>FOR COPYRIGHT OFFICE USE ONLY | Other identifying information:<br>Model No. Model Year<br>Type of Sound: ☐ Mono ☐ Stereo ☐ Quadraphonic ☐ Other<br>Record Capacity Charge per play<br>Model Name | |

**FORM MW**
UNITED STATES COPYRIGHT OFFICE

REGISTRATION NUMBER
**MW**

EFFECTIVE DATE OF REGISTRATION

Month Day Year

APPLICATION RECEIVED

DEPOSIT RECEIVED

REMITTANCE NUMBER AND DATE

DO NOT WRITE ABOVE THIS LINE. IF YOU NEED MORE SPACE, USE A SEPARATE CONTINUATION SHEET.

**1.** TITLE OF THIS WORK ______

**2.** NATURE OF DEPOSIT ______

**3.** NAME AND ADDRESS OF CURRENT OWNER(S) ______

**4.** CITIZENSHIP OR DOMICILE OF CURRENT OWNER(S)
Citizen of: ______
or
Domiciled in: ______

**5.** DERIVATION OF OWNERSHIP: If the person who created the mask work which is subject matter of this application is NOT named as the owner, check one:

☐ a. The owner is the employer of a person who created such mask work within the scope of his/her employment.
☐ b. The owner has acquired the rights by transfer from the creator, employer or representative.
☐ c. The owner is the legal representative of the deceased or legally incapacitated creator.

**6.** DATE AND NATION OF FIRST COMMERCIAL EXPLOITATION
Month ______ Day ______ Year ______
Nation ______

**7.** CITIZENSHIP OR DOMICILE OF OWNER AT THE TIME OF FIRST COMMERCIAL EXPLOITATION (See instructions)
Citizen of: ______
Domiciled in: ______

**8.** NATURE OF CONTRIBUTION: Mask works generally contain designs that are staple, commonplace, or familiar in the semiconductor industry, or are variations of such designs, or are designs which have been previously commercially exploited or previously registered for protection.

Describe the new, original contribution in this mask work for which statutory protection is sought: ______

**9.** CONTACT PERSON FOR CORRESPONDENCE ABOUT THIS CLAIM
Name: ______
Daytime telephone number: ( ) ______
Address (if other than given at space 12): ______

**10.** DEPOSIT ACCOUNT
Name of Account: ______
Account Number: ______

**11.** CERTIFICATION: I, the undersigned, hereby certify that I have the authority to submit this application and that the statements made herein are correct to the best of my knowledge.*

HANDWRITTEN SIGNATURE (X) ______
(This application MUST be signed.)

TYPED SIGNATURE ______

**12.** MAIL CERTIFICATE TO

Name

Number Street Apartment Number

City State ZIP

Certificate will be mailed in window envelope

PLEASE BE SURE THAT YOU HAVE:
- Signed the application at space 11
- Enclosed a check or money order for $20, payable to **Register of Copyrights.**
- Enclosed deposit, application, and fee

MAIL TO:
Library of Congress
Department MW
Washington, DC 20540

*Any person who knowingly makes a false representation of a material fact in the application for registration as provided in 18 USC 1001 shall be fined not more than $10,000

# GENERAL INFORMATION

Form MW should be used for registration of a claim for protection in a mask work which is fixed in a semiconductor chip product, by or under the authority of the owner of the mask work.

A "mask work" is a series of related images, however fixed or encoded, having or representing the predetermined, three-dimensional pattern of metallic, insulating, or semiconductor material present or removed from the layers of a semiconductor chip product, and in which the relation of the images to one another is such that each image has the pattern of the surface of one form of the semiconductor chip product. To be protected, a mask work must be original. If the mask work consists of designs that are staple, commonplace or familiar in the semiconductor industry, any variation or combination of such designs must, considered as a whole, be original to be protected. In no case does protection for a mask work extend to any idea, procedure, process, system, method of operation, concept, discovery, or the like embodied or illustrated in a mask work. Nor is a design protectible if it is dictated by a particular electronic function or is one of only a few available design choices that will accomplish that function.

Protection for a mask work begins on the date on which the mask work is registered, or the date of first commercial exploitation anywhere in the world, whichever occurs first, and lasts for a term of 10 years. During such time, the owner has the exclusive rights to: 1) reproduce the mask work by any means; 2) import or distribute semiconductor chip products embodying the mask work; and 3) authorize or induce others to reproduce, to import, or to distribute.

Statutory protection for a mask work which has been commercially exploited anywhere in the world is terminated if application for registration of a claim for protection is not made within 2 years after the date of first commercial exploitation.

**DEPOSIT TO ACCOMPANY APPLICATION:** The Act requires the deposit of identifying material as specified in the Copyright Office Regulations.

**MASK WORK PROTECTION DIFFERENT FROM COPYRIGHT:** Both the Copyright Law and the Semiconductor Chip Protection Law are administered by the Copyright Office and involve protection for intellectual property. However, they differ from each other in most respects, including term, ownership, eligibility, scope of exclusive rights, limitations on exclusive rights, remedies, and registration procedures.

**FOR FORMS OR INFORMATION:** For information, write or call the Copyright Office, Library of Congress, Washington, D.C. 20559, (202) 287-8700. For forms call (202) 287-9100.

**PRIVACY ACT ADVISORY STATEMENT**
**Required by the Privacy Act of 1974 (P.L. 93-579):**

The authority for requesting this information is title 17 U.S.C., sec. 908, which provides for mandatory registration of claims to mask work protection. Furnishing of the information is voluntary, but if the information is not furnished, it is probable that registration will be refused. Unless a judicial appeal should result in an order compelling registration, any inchoate rights in the mask work would be forfeited at the expiration of 2 years from first commercial exploitation.

The principal uses of the requested information are the examination of the application for registration to determine compliance with legal requirements and the establishment and maintenance of a public record of claims of protection.

Other routine uses include public inspection and copying, preparation of public indexes, preparation of public catalogs of mask work registrations, and preparation of search reports upon request.

NOTE: No other advisory statement will be given in connection with this application. Please keep this statement and refer to it if we communicate with you regarding this application.

**MASK WORK NOTICE:** The owner of a protected mask work may affix a notice to the mask work or to the semiconductor chip product embodying the mask work in such a way as to give reasonable notice of such protection. The notice consists of two elements: 1) the words "mask work," the symbol *M*, or the letter M in a circle Ⓜ; and 2) the name of the owner or owners of the mask work or an abbreviation by which the name is recognized or is generally known. The affixation of a notice is not a condition of protection under the law, but it constitutes prima facie evidence of notice of protection.

# SPACE BY SPACE INSTRUCTIONS

Use an original Form MW from the Copyright Office. DO NOT SEND PHOTOCOPIED FORMS

**Space 1:** TITLE.
Every work submitted for registration must be given a title for purposes of cataloging and identification. This title may include the name of the semiconductor chip product in which the mask work is embodied, e.g., "ASTRA 2014," "Mask work as contained in ASTRA 2014," "Modification of ASTRA 2014," "Memory Cell 5522," or "Register X22."

**Space 2:** NATURE OF DEPOSIT.
Give a short description of the object deposited as identifying material, e.g., "chips plus seven of nine acetate layers," "acetate color overlay sheets," or "composite plot."

**Spaces 3, 4, and 5:** INFORMATION ABOUT CURRENT OWNER(S).
The owner of a mask work is: 1) the person who created the mask work; 2) the legal representative of that person if that person is deceased or under a legal incapacity; 3) the employer for whom a person created the mask work within the scope of his or her employment; or 4) the party to whom all the rights of such a person, employer or representative are transferred. Give the name(s) and address(es) of the current owner(s) of the mask work which is the subject matter of this application. Use a continuation sheet if additional space is needed.

Give the citizenship or domicile of the current owner in space 4.

If the current owner is not the person who created the mask work which is the subject matter of this application, check the appropriate box in space 5 to explain how the owner acquired the right to claim protection in this mask work.

**Space 6:** DATE AND NATION OF FIRST COMMERCIAL EXPLOITATION.
To "commercially exploit" a mask work is to distribute to the public for commercial purposes, a semiconductor chip product embodying the mask work. The offering to sell or transfer a semiconductor chip product is a commercial exploitation only when the offer is in writing and occurs after the fixation of a mask work in a semiconductor chip product.

If this mask work has been commercially exploited anywhere in the world, give the exact date (month, day and year) and the nation of first commercial exploitation. If the work has not yet been commercially exploited, leave this space blank.

**Space 7:** CITIZENSHIP OR DOMICILE OF OWNER AT TIME OF FIRST COMMERCIAL EXPLOITATION.
When a work has been commercially exploited, eligibility for protection may depend upon the nationality or domicile of whoever owned the work at the time of first commercial exploitation. If the mask work which is the subject of this application was commercially exploited, and if the nationality or domicile of the owner at the time of first commercial exploitation is different from that given in space 4, then complete this space.

**Space 8:** NATURE OF CONTRIBUTION.
Mask works generally contain preexisting material which is common in the semiconductor industry. Such material is not protectible. However, if staple designs are combined in a way that is original, the new authorship may be protected. Further, portions of a work which may have been previously commercially exploited or previously registered for protection may not be included in the claim.

Give a brief, general statement that describes the new protectible contribution that is the basis of this claim. This statement may, if appropriate, refer to any previous mask work upon which the mask work being registered is based, as an aid in distinguishing the new contribution from the preexisting material.

**Spaces 9, 10, 11, and 12:**
CORRESPONDENCE. In space 9, give the name, address, and daytime telephone number of the person to contact if further information about this claim is needed.

DEPOSIT ACCOUNT. Complete space 10 if an existing deposit account is to be charged for the filing fee.

CERTIFICATION. Give the handwritten signature of a person authorized to certify the facts asserted in this application. **The application must be signed.**

ADDRESS FOR RETURN OF CERTIFICATE. The name and address must be completed legibly; the certificate will be mailed in a window envelope.

December 1984—25,000

☆ U.S. GOVERNMENT PRINTING OFFICE: 1984-461-585/10,040

**FORM PA**
UNITED STATES COPYRIGHT OFFICE

REGISTRATION NUMBER

PA PAU

EFFECTIVE DATE OF REGISTRATION

Month Day Year

DO NOT WRITE ABOVE THIS LINE. IF YOU NEED MORE SPACE, USE A SEPARATE CONTINUATION SHEET.

**1**

**TITLE OF THIS WORK ▼**

**PREVIOUS OR ALTERNATIVE TITLES ▼**

**NATURE OF THIS WORK ▼** See instructions

**2**

**a** **NAME OF AUTHOR ▼** | **DATES OF BIRTH AND DEATH** Year Born ▼ Year Died ▼

Was this contribution to the work a "work made for hire"? ☐ Yes ☐ No

**AUTHOR'S NATIONALITY OR DOMICILE** Name of Country OR { Citizen of ▶ / Domiciled in ▶

**WAS THIS AUTHOR'S CONTRIBUTION TO THE WORK** Anonymous? ☐ Yes ☐ No Pseudonymous? ☐ Yes ☐ No — If the answer to either of these questions is "Yes," see detailed instructions.

**NATURE OF AUTHORSHIP** Briefly describe nature of the material created by this author in which copyright is claimed. ▼

**b** **NAME OF AUTHOR ▼** | **DATES OF BIRTH AND DEATH** Year Born ▼ Year Died ▼

Was this contribution to the work a "work made for hire"? ☐ Yes ☐ No

**AUTHOR'S NATIONALITY OR DOMICILE** Name of country OR { Citizen of ▶ / Domiciled in ▶

**WAS THIS AUTHOR'S CONTRIBUTION TO THE WORK** Anonymous? ☐ Yes ☐ No Pseudonymous? ☐ Yes ☐ No — If the answer to either of these questions is "Yes," see detailed instructions.

**NATURE OF AUTHORSHIP** Briefly describe nature of the material created by this author in which copyright is claimed. ▼

**c** **NAME OF AUTHOR ▼** | **DATES OF BIRTH AND DEATH** Year Born ▼ Year Died ▼

Was this contribution to the work a "work made for hire"? ☐ Yes ☐ No

**AUTHOR'S NATIONALITY OR DOMICILE** Name of Country OR { Citizen of ▶ / Domiciled in ▶

**WAS THIS AUTHOR'S CONTRIBUTION TO THE WORK** Anonymous? ☐ Yes ☐ No Pseudonymous? ☐ Yes ☐ No — If the answer to either of these questions is "Yes," see detailed instructions.

**NATURE OF AUTHORSHIP** Briefly describe nature of the material created by this author in which copyright is claimed. ▼

**NOTE**
Under the law, the "author" of a "work made for hire" is generally the employer, not the employee (see instructions). For any part of this work that was "made for hire" check "Yes" in the space provided, give the employer (or other person for whom the work was prepared) as "Author" of that part, and leave the space for dates of birth and death blank.

**3**

**YEAR IN WHICH CREATION OF THIS WORK WAS COMPLETED** This information must be given in all cases. ◀ Year

**DATE AND NATION OF FIRST PUBLICATION OF THIS PARTICULAR WORK** Complete this information ONLY if this work has been published. Month ▶ Day ▶ Year ▶ ◀ Nation

**4**

**COPYRIGHT CLAIMANT(S)** Name and address must be given even if the claimant is the same as the author given in space 2.▼

See instructions before completing this space

**TRANSFER** If the claimant(s) named here in space 4 are different from the author(s) named in space 2, give a brief statement of how the claimant(s) obtained ownership of the copyright.▼

DO NOT WRITE HERE / OFFICE USE ONLY:
APPLICATION RECEIVED
ONE DEPOSIT RECEIVED
TWO DEPOSITS RECEIVED
REMITTANCE NUMBER AND DATE

**MORE ON BACK ▶** • Complete all applicable spaces (numbers 5-9) on the reverse side of this page • See detailed instructions. • Sign the form at line 8

DO NOT WRITE HERE

Page 1 of ______ pages

EXAMINED BY

FORM PA

CHECKED BY

☐ CORRESPONDENCE Yes

☐ DEPOSIT ACCOUNT FUNDS USED

FOR COPYRIGHT OFFICE USE ONLY

**DO NOT WRITE ABOVE THIS LINE. IF YOU NEED MORE SPACE, USE A SEPARATE CONTINUATION SHEET.**

**5**

**PREVIOUS REGISTRATION** Has registration for this work, or for an earlier version of this work, already been made in the Copyright Office?
☐ **Yes** ☐ **No** If your answer is "Yes," why is another registration being sought? (Check appropriate box) ▼
☐ This is the first published edition of a work previously registered in unpublished form.
☐ This is the first application submitted by this author as copyright claimant.
☐ This is a changed version of the work, as shown by space 6 on this application.
If your answer is "Yes," give: **Previous Registration Number** ▼ **Year of Registration** ▼

**6**

**DERIVATIVE WORK OR COMPILATION** Complete both space 6a & 6b for a derivative work; complete only 6b for a compilation.
a. **Preexisting Material** Identify any preexisting work or works that this work is based on or incorporates. ▼

See instructions before completing this space.

b. **Material Added to This Work** Give a brief, general statement of the material that has been added to this work and in which copyright is claimed. ▼

**7**

**DEPOSIT ACCOUNT** If the registration fee is to be charged to a Deposit Account established in the Copyright Office, give name and number of Account.
**Name** ▼ **Account Number** ▼

**CORRESPONDENCE** Give name and address to which correspondence about this application should be sent. Name/Address/Apt/City/State/Zip ▼

Area Code & Telephone Number ▶

Be sure to give your daytime phone ◀ number.

**8**

**CERTIFICATION*** I, the undersigned, hereby certify that I am the
Check only one ▼
☐ author
☐ other copyright claimant
☐ owner of exclusive right(s)
☐ authorized agent of ____________________
Name of author or other copyright claimant, or owner of exclusive right(s) ▲

of the work identified in this application and that the statements made by me in this application are correct to the best of my knowledge.

**Typed or printed name and date** ▼ If this is a published work, this date must be the same as or later than the date of publication given in space 3.

______________________________ **date** ▶ __________

**Handwritten signature (X)** ▼

**9**

**MAIL CERTIFICATE TO**

**Certificate will be mailed in window envelope**

| Name ▼ |
|---|
| Number/Street/Apartment Number ▼ |
| City/State/ZIP ▼ |

**Have you:**
- Completed all necessary spaces?
- Signed your application in space 8?
- Enclosed check or money order for $10 payable to *Register of Copyrights*?
- Enclosed your deposit material with the application and fee?

**MAIL TO:** Register of Copyrights, Library of Congress, Washington, D.C. 20559

* 17 U.S.C. § 506(e): Any person who knowingly makes a false representation of a material fact in the application for copyright registration provided for by section 409, or in any written statement filed in connection with the application, shall be fined not more than $2,500.

☆U.S. GOVERNMENT PRINTING OFFICE: 1984—461-584/10,008

October 1984—200,000

**FORM RE**
UNITED STATES COPYRIGHT OFFICE
LIBRARY OF CONGRESS
WASHINGTON, D.C. 20559

# APPLICATION FOR *Renewal Registration*

## HOW TO REGISTER A RENEWAL CLAIM:

- ***First:*** Study the information on this page and make sure you know the answers to two questions:
  (1) What are the renewal time limits in your case?
  (2) Who can claim the renewal?
- ***Second:*** Turn this page over and read through the specific instructions for filling out Form RE. Make sure, before starting to complete the form, that the copyright is now eligible for renewal, that you are authorized to file a renewal claim, and that you have all of the information about the copyright you will need.
- ***Third:*** Complete all applicable spaces on Form RE, following the line-by-line instructions on the back of this page. Use typewriter, or print the information in dark ink.
- ***Fourth:*** Detach this sheet and send your completed Form RE to: Register of Copyrights, Library of Congress, Washington, D.C. 20559. Unless you have a Deposit Account in the Copyright Office, your application must be accompanied by a check or money order for $6, payable to: *Register of Copyrights*. Do not send copies, phonorecords, or supporting documents with your renewal application.

**WHAT IS RENEWAL OF COPYRIGHT?** For works originally copyrighted between January 1, 1950 and December 31, 1977, the statute now in effect provides for a first term of copyright protection lasting for 28 years, with the possibility of renewal for a second term of 47 years. If a valid renewal registration is made for a work, its total copyright term is 75 years (a first term of 28 years, plus a renewal term of 47 years). Example: For a work copyrighted in 1960, the first term will expire in 1988, but if renewed at the proper time the copyright will last through the end of 2035.

**SOME BASIC POINTS ABOUT RENEWAL:**

(1) There are strict time limits and deadlines for renewing a copyright.

(2) Only certain persons who fall into specific categories named in the law can claim renewal.

(3) The new copyright law does away with renewal requirements for works first copyrighted after 1977. However, copyrights that were already in their first copyright term on January 1, 1978 (that is, works originally copyrighted between January 1, 1950 and December 31, 1977) **still have to be renewed** in order to be protected for a second term.

**TIME LIMITS FOR RENEWAL REGISTRATION:** The new copyright statute provides that, in order to renew a copyright, the renewal application and fee must be received in the Copyright Office "within one year prior to the expiration of the copyright." It also provides that all terms of copyright will run through the end of the year in which they would otherwise expire. Since all copyright terms will expire on December 31st of their last year, all periods for renewal registration will run from December 31st of the 27th year of the copyright, and will end on December 31st of the following year.

To determine the time limits for renewal in your case:

(1) First, find out the date of original copyright for the work. (In the case of works originally registered in unpublished form, the date of copyright is the date of registration; for published works, copyright begins on the date of first publication.)

(2) Then add 28 years to the year the work was originally copyrighted.

Your answer will be the calendar year during which the copyright will be eligible for renewal, and December 31st of that year will be the renewal deadline. Example: a work originally copyrighted on April 19, 1957, will be eligible for renewal between December 31, 1984, and December 31, 1985.

**WHO MAY CLAIM RENEWAL:** Renewal copyright may be claimed only by those persons specified in the law. Except in the case of four specific types of works, the law gives the right to claim renewal to the individual author of the work, regardless of who owned the copyright during the original term. If the author is dead, the statute gives the right to claim renewal to certain of the author's beneficiaries (widow and children, executors, or next of kin, depending on the circumstances). The present owner (proprietor) of the copyright is entitled to claim renewal only in four specified cases, as explained in more detail on the reverse of this page.

**CAUTION:** Renewal registration is possible only if an acceptable application and fee are **received** in the Copyright Office during the renewal period and before the renewal deadline. If an acceptable application and fee are not received before the renewal deadline, the work falls into the public domain and the copyright cannot be renewed. The Copyright Office has no discretion to extend the renewal time limits.

**PRIVACY ACT ADVISORY STATEMENT**
**Required by the Privacy Act of 1974 (Public Law 93-579)**

AUTHORITY FOR REQUESTING THIS INFORMATION:
- Title 17, U.S.C., Sec. 304

FURNISHING THE REQUESTED INFORMATION IS:
- Voluntary

BUT IF THE INFORMATION IS NOT FURNISHED:
- It may be necessary to delay or refuse renewal registration
- If renewal registration is not made, the copyright will expire at the end of its 28th year

PRINCIPAL USES OF REQUESTED INFORMATION:
- Establishment and maintenance of a public record
- Examination of the application for compliance with legal requirements

OTHER ROUTINE USES:
- Public inspection and copying
- Preparation of public indexes
- Preparation of public catalogs of copyright registrations
- Preparation of search reports upon request

NOTE:
- No other advisory statement will be given you in connection with this application
- Please retain this statement and refer to it if we communicate with you regarding this application

# INSTRUCTIONS FOR COMPLETING FORM RE

**SPACE 1: RENEWAL CLAIM(S)**

• ***General Instructions:*** In order for this application to result in a valid renewal, space 1 must identify one or more of the persons who are entitled to renew the copyright under the statute. Give the full name and address of each claimant, with a statement of the basis of each claim, using the wording given in these instructions.

• ***Persons Entitled to Renew:***

A. The following persons may claim renewal in all types of works except those enumerated in Paragraph B, below:

1. The author, if living. State the claim as: *the author.*
2. The widow, widower, and/or children of the author, if the author is not living. State the claim as: *the widow (widower) of the author* . . . . . . . . . . . . . (Name of author) and/or *the child (children) of the deceased author* . . . . . . . . . . . . . (Name of author)
3. The author's executor(s), if the author left a will and if there is no surviving widow, widower, or child. State the claim as: *the executor(s) of the author* . . . . . . . . . . . . . (Name of author)
4. The next of kin of the author, if the author left no will and if there is no surviving widow, widower, or child. State the claim as: *the next of kin of the deceased author* . . . . . . . . . . . . . (Name of author) *there being no will.*

B. In the case of the following four types of works, the proprietor (owner of the copyright at the time of renewal registration) may claim renewal:

1. Posthumous work (a work as to which no copyright assignment or other contract for exploitation has occurred during the author's lifetime). State the claim as: *proprietor of copyright in a posthumous work.*
2. Periodical, cyclopedic, or other composite work. State the claim as: *proprietor of copyright in a composite work.*
3. "Work copyrighted by a corporate body otherwise than as assignee or licensee of the individual author." State the claim as: *proprietor of copyright in a work copyrighted by a corporate body otherwise than as assignee or licensee of the individual author.* (This type of claim is considered appropriate in relatively few cases.)
4. Work copyrighted by an employer for whom such work was made for hire. State the claim as: *proprietor of copyright in a work made for hire.*

**SPACE 2: WORK RENEWED**

• ***General Instructions:*** This space is to identify the particular work being renewed. The information given here should agree with that appearing in the certificate of original registration.

• ***Title:*** Give the full title of the work, together with any subtitles or descriptive wording included with the title in the original registration. In the case of a musical composition, give the specific instrumentation of the work.

• ***Renewable Matter:*** Copyright in a new version of a previous work (such as an arrangement, translation, dramatization, compilation, or work republished with new matter) covers only the additions, changes, or other new material appearing for the first time in that version. If this work was a new version, state in general the new matter upon which copyright was claimed.

• ***Contribution to Periodical, Serial, or other Composite Work:*** Separate renewal registration is possible for a work published as a contribution to a periodical, serial, or other composite work, whether the contribution was copyrighted independently or as part of the larger work in which it appeared. Each contribution published in a separate issue ordinarily requires a separate renewal registration. However, the new law provides an alternative, permitting groups of periodical contributions by the same individual author to be combined under a single renewal application and fee in certain cases.

If this renewal application covers a single contribution, give all of the requested information in space 2. If you are seeking to renew a group of contributions, include a reference such as "See space 5" in space 2 and give the requested information about all of the contributions in space 5.

**SPACE 3: AUTHOR(S)**

• ***General Instructions:*** The copyright secured in a new version of a work is independent of any copyright protection in material published earlier. The only "authors" of a new version are those who contributed copyrightable matter to it. Thus, for renewal purposes, the person who wrote the original version on which the new work is based cannot be regarded as an "author" of the new version, unless that person also contributed to the new matter.

• ***Authors of Renewable Matter:*** Give the full names of all authors who contributed copyrightable matter to this particular version of the work.

**SPACE 4: FACTS OF ORIGINAL REGISTRATION**

• ***General Instructions:*** Each item in space 4 should agree with the information appearing in the original registration for the work. If the work being renewed is a single contribution to a periodical or composite work that was not separately registered, give information about the particular issue in which the contribution appeared. You may leave this space blank if you are completing space 5.

• ***Original Registration Number:*** Give the full registration number, which is a series of numerical digits, preceded by one or more letters. The registration number appears in the upper right hand corner of the certificate of registration.

• ***Original Copyright Claimant:*** Give the name in which ownership of the copyright was claimed in the original registration.

• ***Date of Publication or Registration:*** Give only one date. If the original registration gave a publication date, it should be transcribed here; otherwise the registration was for an unpublished work, and the date of registration should be given.

**SPACE 5: GROUP RENEWALS**

• ***General Instructions:*** A single renewal registration can be made for a group of works if **all** of the following statutory conditions are met: (1) all of the works were written by the same author, who is named in space 3 and who is or was an individual (not an employer for hire); (2) all of the works were first published as contributions to periodicals (including newspapers) and were copyrighted on their first publication; (3) the renewal claimant or claimants, and the basis of claim or claims, as stated in space 1, is the same for all of the works; (4) the renewal application and fee are "received not more than 28 or less than 27 years after the 31st day of December of the calendar year in which all of the works were first published"; and (5) the renewal application identifies each work separately, including the periodical containing it and the date of first publication.

***Time Limits for Group Renewals:*** To be renewed as a group, all of the contributions must have been first published during the same calendar year. For example, suppose six contributions by the same author were published on April 1, 1960, July 1, 1960, November 1, 1960, February 1, 1961, July 1, 1961, and March 1, 1962. The three 1960 copyrights can be combined and renewed at any time during 1988, and the two 1961 copyrights can be renewed as a group during 1989, but the 1962 copyright must be renewed by itself, in 1990.

***Identification of Each Work:*** Give all of the requested information for each contribution. The registration number should be that for the contribution itself if it was separately registered, and the registration number for the periodical issue if it was not.

**SPACES 6, 7 AND 8: FEE, MAILING INSTRUCTIONS, AND CERTIFICATION**

• ***Deposit Account and Mailing Instructions (Space 6):*** If you maintain a Deposit Account in the Copyright Office, identify it in space 6. Otherwise, you will need to send the renewal registration fee of $6 with your form. The space headed "Correspondence" should contain the name and address of the person to be consulted if correspondence about the form becomes necessary.

• ***Certification (Space 7):*** The renewal application is not acceptable unless it bears the handwritten signature of the renewal claimant or the duly authorized agent of the renewal claimant.

• ***Address for Return of Certificate (Space 8):*** The address box must be completed legibly, since the certificate will be returned in a window envelope.

# FORM RE

UNITED STATES COPYRIGHT OFFICE

REGISTRATION NUMBER

EFFECTIVE DATE OF RENEWAL REGISTRATION

(Month) (Day) (Year)

DO NOT WRITE ABOVE THIS LINE. FOR COPYRIGHT OFFICE USE ONLY

**1 Renewal Claimant(s)**

**RENEWAL CLAIMANT(S), ADDRESS(ES), AND STATEMENT OF CLAIM:** (See Instructions)

1 Name ..........
Address ..........
Claiming as .......... (Use appropriate statement from instructions)

2 Name ..........
Address ..........
Claiming as .......... (Use appropriate statement from instructions)

3 Name ..........
Address ..........
Claiming as .......... (Use appropriate statement from instructions)

**2 Work Renewed**

**TITLE OF WORK IN WHICH RENEWAL IS CLAIMED:**

**RENEWABLE MATTER:**

**CONTRIBUTION TO PERIODICAL OR COMPOSITE WORK:**

Title of periodical or composite work: ..........

If a periodical or other serial, give: Vol. .......... No. .......... Issue Date ..........

**3 Author(s)**

**AUTHOR(S) OF RENEWABLE MATTER:**

**4 Facts of Original Registration**

**ORIGINAL REGISTRATION NUMBER:** ..........

**ORIGINAL COPYRIGHT CLAIMANT:**

**ORIGINAL DATE OF COPYRIGHT:**

- If the original registration for this work was made in published form, give:
  DATE OF PUBLICATION: .......... (Month) (Day) (Year)

OR

- If the original registration for this work was made in unpublished form, give:
  DATE OF REGISTRATION: .......... (Month) (Day) (Year)

| | EXAMINED BY: ........<br>CHECKED BY: ......... | RENEWAL APPLICATION RECEIVED: | FOR COPYRIGHT OFFICE USE ONLY |
|---|---|---|---|
| | DEPOSIT ACCOUNT FUNDS USED:<br>☐ | REMITTANCE NUMBER AND DATE: | |

**DO NOT WRITE ABOVE THIS LINE. FOR COPYRIGHT OFFICE USE ONLY**

**RENEWAL FOR GROUP OF WORKS BY SAME AUTHOR:** To make a single registration for a group of works by the same individual author published as contributions to periodicals (see instructions), give full information about each contribution. If more space is needed, request continuation sheet (Form RE/CON).

**(5) Renewal for Group of Works**

1 Title of Contribution: ..........
Title of Periodical: .......... Vol. ...... No. ...... Issue Date ..........
Date of Publication: .......... (Month) (Day) (Year) Registration Number: ..........

2 Title of Contribution: ..........
Title of Periodical: .......... Vol. ...... No. ...... Issue Date ..........
Date of Publication: .......... (Month) (Day) (Year) Registration Number: ..........

3 Title of Contribution: ..........
Title of Periodical: .......... Vol. ...... No. ...... Issue Date ..........
Date of Publication: .......... (Month) (Day) (Year) Registration Number: ..........

4 Title of Contribution: ..........
Title of Periodical: .......... Vol. ...... No. ...... Issue Date ..........
Date of Publication: .......... (Month) (Day) (Year) Registration Number: ..........

5 Title of Contribution: ..........
Title of Periodical: .......... Vol. ...... No. ...... Issue Date ..........
Date of Publication: .......... (Month) (Day) (Year) Registration Number: ..........

6 Title of Contribution: ..........
Title of Periodical: .......... Vol. ...... No. ...... Issue Date ..........
Date of Publication: .......... (Month) (Day) (Year) Registration Number: ..........

7 Title of Contribution: ..........
Title of Periodical: .......... Vol. ...... No. ...... Issue Date ..........
Date of Publication: .......... (Month) (Day) (Year) Registration Number: ..........

**DEPOSIT ACCOUNT:** (If the registration fee is to be charged to a Deposit Account established in the Copyright Office, give name and number of Account.)

Name: ..........
Account Number: ..........

**CORRESPONDENCE:** (Give name and address to which correspondence about this application should be sent.)

Name: ..........
Address: .......... (Apt.)
.......... (City) (State) (ZIP)

**(6) Fee and Correspondence**

**CERTIFICATION:** I, the undersigned, hereby certify that I am the: (Check one)
☐ renewal claimant ☐ duly authorized agent of: .......... (Name of renewal claimant)
of the work identified in this application, and that the statements made by me in this application are correct to the best of my knowledge.

Handwritten signature: (X) ..........
Typed or printed name: ..........
Date: ..........

**(7) Certification (Application must be signed)**

.......... (Name)
.......... (Number, Street and Apartment Number)
.......... (City) (State) (ZIP code)

**MAIL CERTIFICATE TO**

**(Certificate will be mailed in window envelope)**

**(8) Address for Return of Certificate**

U S GOVERNMENT PRINTING OFFICE 1978—261-022/10 Apr. 1978 500,000

# Filling Out Application Form SE

*Detach and read these instructions before completing this form. Make sure all applicable spaces have been filled in before you return this form.*

## BASIC INFORMATION

**When To Use This Form:** Use a separate Form SE for registration of each individual issue of a serial, Class SE. A serial is defined as a work issued or intended to be issued in successive parts bearing numerical or chronological designations and intended to be continued indefinitely. This class includes a variety of works: periodicals; newspapers; annuals; the journals, proceedings, transactions, etc., of societies. Do not use Form SE to register an individual contribution to a serial. Request Form TX for such contributions.

**Deposit to Accompany Application:** An application for copyright registration must be accompanied by a deposit consisting of copies or phonorecords representing the entire work for which registration is to be made. The following are the general deposit requirements as set forth in the statute:

**Unpublished Work:** Deposit one complete copy (or phonorecord).

**Published Work:** Deposit two complete copies (or phonorecords) of the best edition.

**Work First Published Outside the United States:** Deposit one complete copy (or phonorecord) of the first foreign edition.

**Mailing Requirements:** It is important that you send the application, the deposit copy or copies, and the $10 fee together in the same envelope or package. The Copyright Office cannot process them unless they are received together. Send to: *Register of Copyrights, Library of Congress, Washington, D.C. 20559.*

**The Copyright Notice:** For published works, the law provides that a copyright notice in a specified form "shall be placed on all publicly distributed copies from which the work can be visually perceived." Use of the copyright notice is the responsibility of the copyright owner and does not require advance permission from the Copyright Office. The required form of the notice for copies generally consists of three elements: (1) the symbol "©"; or the word "Copyright," or the abbreviation "Copr."; (2) the year of first publication; and (3) the name of the owner of copyright. For example: "© 1981 National News Publishers, Inc." The notice is to be affixed to the copies "in such manner and location as to give reasonable notice of the claim of copyright." For further information about copyright registration, notice, or special questions relating to copyright problems, write:

Information and Publications Section, LM-455
Copyright Office, Library of Congress, Washington, D.C. 20559

**PRIVACY ACT ADVISORY STATEMENT Required by the Privacy Act of 1974 (P.L. 93-579)**
The authority for requesting this information is title 17, U.S.C., secs. 409 and 410. Furnishing the requested information is voluntary. But if the information is not furnished, it may be necessary to delay or refuse registration and you may not be entitled to certain relief, remedies, and benefits provided in chapters 4 and 5 of title 17, U.S.C.

The principal uses of the requested information are the establishment and maintenance of a public record and the examination of the application for compliance with legal requirements.

Other routine uses include public inspection and copying, preparation of public indexes, preparation of public catalogs of copyright registrations, and preparation of search reports upon request.

NOTE: No other advisory statement will be given in connection with this application. Please keep this statement and refer to it if we communicate with you regarding this application.

## LINE-BY-LINE INSTRUCTIONS

### 1 SPACE 1: Title

**Title of This Serial:** Every work submitted for copyright registration must be given a title to identify that particular work. If the copies or phonorecords of the work bear a title (or an identifying phrase that could serve as a title), copy that wording *completely* and *exactly* on the application. Give the volume and number of the periodical issue for which you are seeking registration. The "Date on copies" in space 1 should be the date appearing on the actual copies (for example: "June 1981," "Winter 1981"). Indexing of the registration and future identification of the work will depend on the information you give here.

**Previous or Alternative Titles:** Complete this space only if there are any additional titles for the serial under which someone searching for the registration might be likely to look, or under which a document pertaining to the work might be recorded.

### 2 SPACE 2: Author(s)

**General Instructions:** After reading these instructions, decide who are the "authors" of this work for copyright purposes. In the case of a serial issue, the organization which directs the creation of the serial issue as a whole is generally considered the author of the "collective work" (see "Nature of Authorship") whether it employs a staff or uses the efforts of volunteers. Where, however, an individual is independently responsible for the serial issue, name that person as author of the "collective work."

**Name of Author:** The fullest form of the author's name should be given. In the case of a "work made for hire," the statute provides that "the employer or other person for whom the work was prepared is considered the author." If this issue is a "work made for hire," the author's name will be the full legal name of the hiring organization, corporation, or individual. The title of the periodical should not ordinarily be listed as "author" because the title itself does not usually correspond to a legal entity capable of authorship. When an individual creates an issue of a serial independently and not as an "employee" of an organization or corporation, that individual should be listed as the "author."

**Author's Nationality or Domicile:** Give the country of which the author is a citizen, or the country in which the author is domiciled. Nationality or domicile **must** be given in all cases. The citizenship of an organization formed under United States Federal or state law should be stated as "U.S.A."

**What is a "Work Made for Hire"?** A "work made for hire" is defined as: (1) "a work prepared by an employee within the scope of his or her employment"; or (2) "a work specially ordered or commissioned for use as a contribution to a collective work, as a part of a motion picture or other audiovisual work, as a translation, as a supplementary work, as a compilation, as an instructional text, as a test, as answer material for a test, or as an atlas, if the parties expressly agree in a written instrument signed by them that the work shall be considered a work made for hire." An organization that uses the efforts of volunteers in the creation of a "collective work" (see "Nature of Authorship") may also be considered the author of a "work made for hire" even though those volunteers were not specifically paid by the organization. In the case of a "work made for hire," give the full legal name of the employer and check "Yes" to indicate that the work was made for hire. You may also include the name of the employee along with the name of the employer (for example: "Elster Publishing Co., employer for hire of John Ferguson").

**"Anonymous" or "Pseudonymous" Work:** Leave this space **blank** if the serial is a "work made for hire." An author's contribution to a work is "anonymous" if that author is not identified on the copies or phonorecords of the work. An author's contribution to a work is "pseudonymous" if that author is identified on the copies or phonorecords under a fictitious name. If the work is "anonymous" you may: (1) leave the line blank; or (2) state "anonymous" on the line; or (3) reveal the author's identity. If the work is "pseudonymous" you may: (1) leave the line blank; or (2) give the pseudonym and identify it as such (for example: "Huntley Haverstock, pseudonym"); or (3) reveal the author's name, making clear which is the real name and which is the pseudonym (for example: "Judith Barton, whose pseudonym is Madeline Elster"). However, the citizenship or domicile of the author **must** be given in all cases.

**Dates of Birth and Death:** Leave this space blank if the author's contribution was a "work made for hire." If the author is dead, the statute requires that the year of death be included in the application unless the work is anonymous or pseudonymous. The author's birth date is optional, but is useful as a form of identification.

**Nature of Authorship:** Give a brief statement of the nature of the particular author's contribution to the work. If an organization directed, controlled, and supervised the creation of the serial issue as a whole, check the box "collective work." The term "collective work" means that the author is responsible for compilation and editorial revision, and may also be responsible for certain individual contributions to the serial issue. Further examples of "Authorship" which may apply both to organizational and to individual authors are "Entire text"; "Entire text and/or illustrations"; "Editorial revision, compilation, plus additional new material."

## 3 SPACE 3: Creation and Publication

**General Instructions:** Do not confuse "creation" with "publication." Every application for copyright registration must state "the year in which creation of the work was completed." Give the date and nation of first publication only if the work has been published.

**Creation:** Under the statute, a work is "created" when it is fixed in a copy or phonorecord for the first time. Where a work has been prepared over a period of time, the part of the work existing in fixed form on a particular date constitutes the created work on that date. The date you give here should be the year in which this particular issue was completed.

**Publication:** The statute defines "publication" as "the distribution of copies or phonorecords of a work to the public by sale or other transfer of ownership, or by rental, lease, or lending"; a work is also "published" if there has been an "offering to distribute copies or phonorecords to a group of persons for purposes of further distribution, public performance, or public display." Give the full date (month, day, year) when, and the country where, publication of this particular issue first occurred. If first publication took place simultaneously in the United States and other countries, it is sufficient to state "U.S.A."

## 4 SPACE 4: Claimant(s)

**Name(s) and Address(es) of Copyright Claimant(s):** This space must be completed. Give the name(s) and address(es) of the copyright claimant(s) of this work even if the claimant is the same as the author named in space 2. Copyright in a work belongs initially to the author of the work (including, in the case of a work made for hire, the employer or other person for whom the work was prepared). The copyright claimant is either the author of the work or a person or organization to whom the copyright initially belonging to the author has been transferred.

**Transfer:** The statute provides that, if the copyright claimant is not the author, the application for registration must contain "a brief statement of how the claimant obtained ownership of the copyright." A transfer of copyright ownership (other than one brought about by operation of law) must be in writing. If any copyright claimant named in space 4 is not an author named in space 2, give a brief, general statement describing the means by which that claimant obtained ownership of the copyright from the original author. Examples: "By written contract"; "Written transfer of all rights by author"; "Assignment"; "Inherited by will." Do not attach the actual document of transfer or other attachments or riders.

## 5 SPACE 5: Previous Registration

**General Instructions:** This space applies only rarely to serials. Complete space 5 if this particular issue has been registered earlier or if it contains a substantial amount of material that has been previously registered. Do not complete this space if the previous registrations are simply those made for earlier issues.

**Previous Registration:**

a. **Check this box** if this issue has been registered in unpublished form and a second registration is now sought to cover the first published edition.

b. **Check this box** if someone other than the author is identified as copyright claimant in the earlier registration and the author is now seeking registration in his or her own name. If the work in question is a contribution to a collective work, as opposed to the issue as a whole, file Form TX, not Form SE.

c. **Check this box** (and complete space 6) if this particular issue, or a substantial portion of the material in it, has been previously registered and you are now seeking registration for the additions and revisions which appear in this issue for the first time.

**Previous Registration Number and Date:** Complete this line if you checked one of the boxes above. If more than one previous registration has been made for the issue or for material in it, give only the number and year date for the latest registration.

## 6 SPACE 6: Derivative Work or Compilation

**General Instructions:** Complete space 6 if this issue is a "changed version," "compilation," or "derivative work," which incorporates one or more earlier works that have already been published or registered for copyright, or that have fallen into the public domain. Do not complete space 6 for an issue consisting of entirely new material appearing for the first time, such as a new issue of a continuing serial. A "compilation" is defined as "a work formed by the collection and assembling of preexisting materials or of data that are selected, coordinated, or arranged in such a way that the resulting work as a whole constitutes an original work of authorship." A "derivative work" is "a work based on one or more preexisting works." Examples of derivative works include translations, fictionalizations, abridgments, condensations, or "any other form in which a work may be recast, transformed, or adapted." Derivative works also include works "consisting of editorial revisions, annotations, or other modifications" if these changes, as a whole, represent an original work of authorship.

**Preexisting Material (space 6a):** For derivative works, complete this space and space 6b. In space 6a identify the preexisting work that has been recast, transformed, adapted, or updated. Example: "1978 Morgan Co. Sales Catalog." Do not complete space 6a for compilations.

**Material Added to This Work (space 6b):** Give a brief, general statement of the new material covered by the copyright claim for which registration is sought. **Derivative work** examples include: "Editorial revisions and additions to the Catalog"; "Translation"; "Additional material." If a periodical issue is a **compilation**, describe both the compilation itself and the material that has been compiled. Examples: "Compilation of previously published journal articles"; "Compilation of previously published data." An issue may be both a derivative work and a compilation, in which case a sample statement might be: "Compilation of [describe] and additional new material."

## 7 SPACE 7: Manufacturing Provisions

**General Instructions:** The copyright statute currently provides, as a general rule, that the copies of a published work "consisting preponderantly of nondramatic literary material in the English language" be manufactured in the United States or Canada in order to be lawfully imported and publicly distributed in the United States. If the work being registered is unpublished or not in English, leave this space blank. Complete this space if registration is sought for a published work "consisting preponderantly of nondramatic literary material that is in the English language." Identify those who manufactured the copies and where those manufacturing processes were performed. As an exception to the manufacturing provisions, the statute prescribes that, where manufacture has taken place outside the United States or Canada, a maximum of 2000 copies of the foreign edition may be imported into the United States without affecting the copyright owners' rights. For this purpose, the Copyright Office will issue an Import Statement upon request and payment of a fee of $3 at the time of registration or at any later time. For further information about import statements, write for Form IS.

## 8 SPACE 8: Reproduction for Use of Blind or Physically Handicapped Individuals

**General Instructions:** One of the major programs of the Library of Congress is to provide Braille editions and special recordings of works for the exclusive use of the blind and physically handicapped. In an effort to simplify and speed up the copyright licensing procedures that are a necessary part of this program, section 710 of the copyright statute provides for the establishment of a voluntary licensing system to be tied in with copyright registration. Copyright Office regulations provide that you may grant a license for such reproduction and distribution solely for the use of persons who are certified by competent authority as unable to read normal printed material as a result of physical limitations. The license is entirely voluntary, nonexclusive, and may be terminated upon 90 days notice.

**How to Grant the License:** If you wish to grant it, check one of the three boxes in space 8. Your check in one of these boxes, together with your signature in space 10, will mean that the Library of Congress can proceed to reproduce and distribute under the license without further paperwork. For further information, write for Circular R63.

## 9,10,11 SPACE 9, 10, 11: Fee, Correspondence, Certification, Return Address

**Deposit Account:** If you maintain a Deposit Account in the Copyright Office, identify it in space 9. Otherwise leave the space blank and send the fee of $10 with your application and deposit.

**Correspondence** (space 9): This space should contain the name, address, area code, and telephone number of the person to be consulted if correspondence about this application becomes necessary.

**Certification** (space 10): The application cannot be accepted unless it bears the date and the **handwritten signature** of the author or other copyright claimant, or of the owner of exclusive right(s), or of the duly authorized agent of the author, claimant, or owner of exclusive right(s).

**Address for Return of Certificate** (space 11): The address box must be completed legibly since the certificate will be returned in a window envelope.

**FORM SE**
UNITED STATES COPYRIGHT OFFICE

REGISTRATION NUMBER

U

EFFECTIVE DATE OF REGISTRATION

Month Day Year

**DO NOT WRITE ABOVE THIS LINE. IF YOU NEED MORE SPACE, USE A SEPARATE CONTINUATION SHEET.**

**1**

**TITLE OF THIS SERIAL ▼**

**Volume ▼** **Number ▼** **Date on Copies ▼** **Frequency of Publication ▼**

**PREVIOUS OR ALTERNATIVE TITLES ▼**

**2**

**a**

**NAME OF AUTHOR ▼**

**DATES OF BIRTH AND DEATH**
Year Born ▼ Year Died ▼

Was this contribution to the work a "work made for hire"?
☐ Yes
☐ No

**AUTHOR'S NATIONALITY OR DOMICILE**
Name of Country
OR { Citizen of ▶ ______ / Domiciled in ▶ ______

**WAS THIS AUTHOR'S CONTRIBUTION TO THE WORK**
Anonymous? ☐ Yes ☐ No
Pseudonymous? ☐ Yes ☐ No
If the answer to either of these questions is "Yes," see detailed instructions.

**NATURE OF AUTHORSHIP** Briefly describe nature of the material created by this author in which copyright is claimed. ▼
☐ **Collective Work** Other:

**b**

**NAME OF AUTHOR ▼**

**DATES OF BIRTH AND DEATH**
Year Born ▼ Year Died ▼

Was this contribution to the work a "work made for hire"?
☐ Yes
☐ No

**AUTHOR'S NATIONALITY OR DOMICILE**
Name of country
OR { Citizen of ▶ ______ / Domiciled in ▶ ______

**WAS THIS AUTHOR'S CONTRIBUTION TO THE WORK**
Anonymous? ☐ Yes ☐ No
Pseudonymous? ☐ Yes ☐ No
If the answer to either of these questions is "Yes," see detailed instructions.

**NATURE OF AUTHORSHIP** Briefly describe nature of the material created by this author in which copyright is claimed. ▼
☐ **Collective Work** Other:

**c**

**NAME OF AUTHOR ▼**

**DATES OF BIRTH AND DEATH**
Year Born ▼ Year Died ▼

Was this contribution to the work a "work made for hire"?
☐ Yes
☐ No

**AUTHOR'S NATIONALITY OR DOMICILE**
Name of Country
OR { Citizen of ▶ ______ / Domiciled in ▶ ______

**WAS THIS AUTHOR'S CONTRIBUTION TO THE WORK**
Anonymous? ☐ Yes ☐ No
Pseudonymous? ☐ Yes ☐ No
If the answer to either of these questions is "Yes," see detailed instructions.

**NATURE OF AUTHORSHIP** Briefly describe nature of the material created by this author in which copyright is claimed. ▼
☐ **Collective Work** Other:

**NOTE**
Under the law, the "author" of a "work made for hire" is generally the employer, not the employee (see instructions). For any part of this work that was "made for hire" check "Yes" in the space provided, give the employer (or other person for whom the work was prepared) as "Author" of that part, and leave the space for dates of birth and death blank.

**3**

**YEAR IN WHICH CREATION OF THIS ISSUE WAS COMPLETED** **This information must be given in all cases.**
______ ◀ Year

**DATE AND NATION OF FIRST PUBLICATION OF THIS PARTICULAR ISSUE**
**Complete this information ONLY if this work has been published.** Month ▶ ______ Day ▶ ______ Year ▶ ______
______ ◀ Nation

**4**

See instructions before completing this space.

**COPYRIGHT CLAIMANT(S)** Name and address must be given even if the claimant is the same as the author given in space 2.▼

**TRANSFER** If the claimant(s) named here in space 4 are different from the author(s) named in space 2, give a brief statement of how the claimant(s) obtained ownership of the copyright.▼

DO NOT WRITE HERE / OFFICE USE ONLY
APPLICATION RECEIVED
ONE DEPOSIT RECEIVED
TWO DEPOSITS RECEIVED
REMITTANCE NUMBER AND DATE

**MORE ON BACK ▶**
• Complete all applicable spaces (numbers 5-11) on the reverse side of this page
• See detailed instructions.
• Sign the form at line 10

**DO NOT WRITE HERE**

Page 1 of ______ pages

EXAMINED BY | FORM SE

CHECKED BY

☐ CORRESPONDENCE Yes

☐ DEPOSIT ACCOUNT FUNDS USED

FOR COPYRIGHT OFFICE USE ONLY

**DO NOT WRITE ABOVE THIS LINE. IF YOU NEED MORE SPACE, USE A SEPARATE CONTINUATION SHEET.**

**5**

**PREVIOUS REGISTRATION** Has registration for this issue, or for an earlier version of this particular issue, already been made in the Copyright Office?

☐ **Yes** ☐ **No** If your answer is "Yes," why is another registration being sought? (Check appropriate box) ▼

**a.** ☐ This is the first published version of an issue previously registered in unpublished form.

**b.** ☐ This is the first application submitted by this author as copyright claimant.

**c.** ☐ This is a changed version of this issue, as shown by space 6 on this application.

If your answer is "Yes," give: **Previous Registration Number** ▼ **Year of Registration** ▼

**6**

**DERIVATIVE WORK OR COMPILATION** Complete both space 6a & 6b for a derivative work; complete only 6b for a compilation.

**a. Preexisting Material** Identify any preexisting work or works that this work is based on or incorporates. ▼

**b. Material Added to This Work** Give a brief, general statement of the material that has been added to this work and in which copyright is claimed. ▼

See instructions before completing this space.

**7**

**MANUFACTURERS AND LOCATIONS** If this is a published work consisting preponderantly of nondramatic literary material in English, the law may require that the copies be manufactured in the United States or Canada for full protection. If so, the names of the manufacturers who performed certain processes, and the places where these processes were performed **must** be given. See instructions for details.

**Names of Manufacturers** ▼ **Places of Manufacture** ▼

**8**

**REPRODUCTION FOR USE OF BLIND OR PHYSICALLY HANDICAPPED INDIVIDUALS** A signature on this form at space 10, and a check in one of the boxes here in space 8, constitutes a non-exclusive grant of permission to the Library of Congress to reproduce and distribute solely for the blind and physically handicapped and under the conditions and limitations prescribed by the regulations of the Copyright Office: (1) copies of the work identified in space 1 of this application in Braille (or similar tactile symbols); or (2) phonorecords embodying a fixation of a reading of that work; or (3) both.

**a** ☐ Copies and Phonorecords **b** ☐ Copies Only **c** ☐ Phonorecords Only

See instructions.

**9**

**DEPOSIT ACCOUNT** If the registration fee is to be charged to a Deposit Account established in the Copyright Office, give name and number of Account.

**Name** ▼ **Account Number** ▼

**CORRESPONDENCE** Give name and address to which correspondence about this application should be sent. Name/Address/Apt/City/State/Zip ▼

Area Code & Telephone Number ▶

Be sure to give your daytime phone ◀ number.

**10**

**CERTIFICATION*** I, the undersigned, hereby certify that I am the

Check one ▶
☐ author
☐ other copyright claimant
☐ owner of exclusive right(s)
☐ authorized agent of ______

Name of author or other copyright claimant, or owner of exclusive right(s) ▲

of the work identified in this application and that the statements made by me in this application are correct to the best of my knowledge.

**Typed or printed name and date** ▼ If this is a published work, this date must be the same as or later than the date of publication given in space 3.

**date** ▶

**Handwritten signature (X)** ▼

**11**

**MAIL CERTIFICATE TO**

**Certificate will be mailed in window envelope**

Name ▼

Number/Street/Apartment Number ▼

City/State/ZIP ▼

**Have you:**

- Completed all necessary spaces?
- Signed your application in space 10?
- Enclosed check or money order for $10 payable to *Register of Copyrights*?
- Enclosed your deposit material with the application and fee?

**MAIL TO:** Register of Copyrights, Library of Congress, Washington, D.C. 20559

* 17 U.S.C. § 506(e): Any person who knowingly makes a false representation of a material fact in the application for copyright registration provided for by section 409, or in any written statement filed in connection with the application, shall be fined not more than $2,500.

☆U.S. GOVERNMENT PRINTING OFFICE: 1982-361-278/59 Sept. 1982—210,000

# Filling Out Application Form SR

*Detach and read these instructions before completing this form. Make sure all applicable spaces have been filled in before you return this form.*

## BASIC INFORMATION

**When to Use This Form:** Use Form SR for copyright registration of published or unpublished sound recordings. It should be used where the copyright claim is limited to the sound recording itself, and it may also be used where the same copyright claimant is seeking simultaneous registration of the underlying musical, dramatic, or literary work embodied in the phonorecord.

With one exception, "sound recordings" are works that result from the fixation of a series of musical, spoken, or other sounds. The exception is for the audio portions of audiovisual works, such as a motion picture soundtrack or an audio cassette accompanying a filmstrip; these are considered a part of the audiovisual work as a whole.

**Deposit to Accompany Application:** An application for copyright registration of a sound recording must be accompanied by a deposit consisting of phonorecords representing the entire work for which registration is to be made.

**Unpublished Work:** Deposit one complete phonorecord.

**Published Work:** Deposit two complete phonorecords of the best edition, together with "any printed or other visually perceptible material" published with the phonorecords.

**Work First Published Outside the United States:** Deposit one complete phonorecord of the first foreign edition.

**Contribution to a Collective Work:** Deposit one complete phonorecord of the best edition of the collective work.

**The Copyright Notice:** For published sound recordings, the law provides that a copyright notice in a specified form "shall be placed on all publicly distributed phonorecords of the sound recording." Use of the copyright notice is the responsibility of the copyright owner and does not require advance permission from the Copyright Office. The required form of the notice for phonorecords of sound recordings consists of three elements: (1) the symbol "℗" (the letter "P" in a circle); (2) the year of first publication of the sound recording; and (3) the name of the owner of copyright. For example: "℗ 1981 Rittenhouse Record Co." The notice is to be "placed on the surface of the phonorecord, or on the label or container, in such manner and location as to give reasonable notice of the claim of copyright." For further information about copyright, write:

Information and Publications Section, LM-455
Copyright Office, Library of Congress, Washington, D.C. 20559

**PRIVACY ACT ADVISORY STATEMENT Required by the Privacy Act of 1974 (P.L. 93-579)**

The authority for requesting this information is title 17, U.S.C., secs. 409 and 410. Furnishing the requested information is voluntary. But if the information is not furnished, it may be necessary to delay or refuse registration and you may not be entitled to certain relief, remedies, and benefits provided in chapters 4 and 5 of title 17, U.S.C.

The principal uses of the requested information are the establishment and maintenance of a public record and the examination of the application for compliance with legal requirements.

Other routine uses include public inspection and copying, preparation of public indexes, preparation of public catalogs of copyright registrations, and preparation of search reports upon request.

NOTE: No other advisory statement will be given in connection with this application. Please keep this statement and refer to it if we communicate with you regarding this application.

## LINE-BY-LINE INSTRUCTIONS

### 1 SPACE 1: Title

**Title of This Work:** Every work submitted for copyright registration must be given a title to identify that particular work. If the phonorecords or any accompanying printed material bear a title (or an identifying phrase that could serve as a title), transcribe that wording completely and exactly on the application. Indexing of the registration and future identification of the work may depend on the information you give here.

**Nature of Material Recorded:** Indicate the general type or character of the works or other material embodied in the recording. The box marked "Literary" should be checked for nondramatic spoken material of all sorts, including narration, interviews, panel discussions, and training material. If the material recorded is not musical, dramatic, or literary in nature, check "Other" and briefly describe the type of sounds fixed in the recording. For example: "Sound Effects", "Bird Calls"; "Crowd Noises."

**Previous or Alternative Titles:** Complete this space if there are any additional titles for the work under which someone searching for the registration might be likely to look, or under which a document pertaining to the work might be recorded.

### 2 SPACE 2: Author(s)

**General Instructions:** After reading these instructions, decide who are the "authors" of this work for copyright purposes. Then, unless the work is a "collective work," give the requested information about every "author" who contributed any appreciable amount of copyrightable matter to this version of the work. If you need further space, request additional Continuation Sheets. In the case of a collective work, such as a collection of previously published or registered sound recordings, give information about the author of the collective work as a whole. If you are submitting this Form SR to cover the recorded musical, dramatic, or literary work as well as the sound recording itself, it is important for space 2 to include full information about the various authors of all of the material covered by the copyright claim, making clear the nature of each author's contribution.

**Name of Author:** The fullest form of the author's name should be given. Unless the work was "made for hire," the individual who actually created the work is its "author." In the case of a work made for hire, the statute provides that "the employer or other person for whom the work was prepared is considered the author."

**What is a "Work Made for Hire"?** A "work made for hire" is defined as: (1) "a work prepared by an employee within the scope of his or her employment"; or (2) "a work specially ordered or commissioned for use as a contribution to a collective work, as a part of a motion picture or other audiovisual work, as a translation, as a supplementary work, as a compilation, as an instructional text, as a test, as answer material for a test, or as an atlas, if the parties expressly agree in a written instrument signed by them that the work shall be considered a work made for hire." If you have checked "Yes" to indicate that the work was "made for hire," you must give the full legal name of the employer (or other person for whom the work was prepared). You may also include the name of the employee along with the name of the employer (for example: "Elster Record Co., employer for hire of John Ferguson").

**"Anonymous" or "Pseudonymous" Work:** An author's contribution to a work is "anonymous" if that author is not identified on the copies or phonorecords of the work. An author's contribution to a work is "pseudonymous" if that author is identified on the copies or phonorecords under a fictitious name. If the work is "anonymous" you may: (1) leave the line blank; or (2) state "anonymous" on the line; or (3) reveal the author's identity. If the work is "pseudonymous" you may: (1) leave the line blank; or (2) give the pseudonym and identify it as such (for example: "Huntley Haverstock, pseudonym"); or (3) reveal the author's name, making clear which is the real name and which is the pseudonym (for example: "Judith Barton, whose pseudonym is Madeline Elster"). However, the citizenship or domicile of the author **must** be given in all cases.

**Dates of Birth and Death:** If the author is dead, the statute requires that the year of death be included in the application unless the work is anonymous or pseudonymous. The author's birth date is optional, but is useful as a form of identification. Leave this space blank if the author's contribution was a "work made for hire."

**Author's Nationality or Domicile:** Give the country of which the author is a citizen, or the country in which the author is domiciled. Nationality or domicile **must** be given in all cases.

**Nature of Authorship:** Give a brief general statement of the nature of this particular author's contribution to the work. If you are submitting this Form SR to cover both the sound recording and the underlying musical, dramatic, or literary work, make sure that the precise nature of each author's contribution is reflected here. Examples where the authorship pertains to the recording: "Sound Recording"; "Performance and Recording"; "Compilation and Remixing of Sounds." Examples where the authorship pertains to both the recording and the underlying work: "Words, Music, Performance, Recording"; "Arrangement of Music and Recording"; "Compilation of Poems and Reading."

## 3 SPACE 3: Creation and Publication

**General Instructions:** Do not confuse "creation" with "publication." Every application for copyright registration must state "the year in which creation of the work was completed." Give the date and nation of first publication only if the work has been published.

**Creation:** Under the statute, a work is "created" when it is fixed in a copy or phonorecord for the first time. Where a work has been prepared over a period of time, the part of the work existing in fixed form on a particular date constitutes the created work on that date. The date you give here should be the year in which the author completed the particular version for which registration is now being sought, even if other versions exist or if further changes or additions are planned.

**Publication:** The statute defines "publication" as "the distribution of copies or phonorecords of a work to the public by sale or other transfer of ownership, or by rental, lease, or lending"; a work is also "published" if there has been an "offering to distribute copies or phonorecords to a group of persons for purposes of further distribution, public performance, or public display." Give the full date (month, day, year) when, and the country where, publication first occurred. If first publication took place simultaneously in the United States and other countries, it is sufficient to state "U.S.A."

## 4 SPACE 4: Claimant(s)

**Name(s) and Address(es) of Copyright Claimant(s):** Give the name(s) and address(es) of the copyright claimant(s) in this work even if the claimant is the same as the author. Copyright in a work belongs initially to the author of the work (including, in the case of a work made for hire, the employer or other person for whom the work was prepared). The copyright claimant is either the author of the work or a person or organization to whom the copyright initially belonging to the author has been transferred.

**Transfer:** The statute provides that, if the copyright claimant is not the author, the application for registration must contain "a brief statement of how the claimant obtained ownership of the copyright." If any copyright claimant named in space 4 is not an author named in space 2, give a brief, general statement summarizing the means by which that claimant obtained ownership of the copyright. Examples: "By written contract"; "Transfer of all rights by author"; "Assignment"; "By will." Do not attach transfer documents or other attachments or riders.

## 5 SPACE 5: Previous Registration

**General Instructions:** The questions in space 5 are intended to find out whether an earlier registration has been made for this work and, if so, whether there is any basis for a new registration. As a rule, only one basic copyright registration can be made for the same version of a particular work.

**Same Version:** If this version is substantially the same as the work covered by a previous registration, a second registration is not generally possible unless: (1) the work has been registered in unpublished form and a second registration is now being sought to cover this first published edition; or (2) someone other than the author is identified as copyright claimant in the earlier registration, and the author is now seeking registration in his or her own name. If either of these two exceptions apply, check the appropriate box and give the earlier registration number and date. Otherwise, do not submit Form SR; instead, write the Copyright Office for information about supplementary registration or recordation of transfers of copyright ownership.

**Changed Version:** If the work has been changed, and you are now seeking registration to cover the additions or revisions, check the last box in space 5, give the earlier registration number and date, and complete both parts of space 6 in accordance with the instructions below.

**Previous Registration Number and Date:** If more than one previous registration has been made for the work, give the number and date of the latest registration.

## 6 SPACE 6: Derivative Work or Compilation

**General Instructions:** Complete space 6 if this work is a "changed version," "compilation," or "derivative work," and if it incorporates one or more earlier works that have already been published or registered for copyright, or that have fallen into the public domain, or sound recordings that were fixed before February 15, 1972. A "compilation" is defined as "a work formed by the collection and assembling of preexisting materials or of data that are selected, coordinated, or arranged in such a way that the resulting work as a whole constitutes an original work of authorship." A "derivative work" is "a work based on one or more preexisting works." Examples of derivative works include recordings reissued with substantial editorial revisions or abridgments of the recorded sounds, and recordings republished with new recorded material, or "any other form in which a work may be recast, transformed, or adapted." Derivative works also include works "consisting of editorial revisions, annotations, or other modifications" if these changes, as a whole, represent an original work of authorship.

**Preexisting Material (space 6a):** Complete this space and space 6b for derivative works. In this space identify the preexisting work that has been recast, transformed, or adapted. For example, the preexisting material might be: "1970 recording by Sperryville Symphony of Bach Double Concerto." Do not complete this space for compilations.

**Material Added to This Work (space 6b):** Give a brief, general statement of the **additional** new material covered by the copyright claim for which registration is sought. In the case of a derivative work, identify this new material. Examples: "Recorded performances on bands 1 and 3"; "Remixed sounds from original multitrack sound sources"; "New words, arrangement, and additional sounds." If the work is a compilation, give a brief, general statement describing both the material that has been compiled **and** the compilation itself. Example: "Compilation of 1938 Recordings by various swing bands."

## 7,8,9 SPACE 7, 8, 9: Fee, Correspondence, Certification, Return Address

**Deposit Account:** If you maintain a Deposit Account in the Copyright Office, identify it in space 7. Otherwise leave the space blank and send the fee of $10 with your application and deposit.

**Correspondence** (space 7): This space should contain the name, address, area code, and telephone number of the person to be consulted if correspondence about this application becomes necessary.

**Certification** (space 8): The application cannot be accepted unless it bears the date and the **handwritten signature** of the author or other copyright claimant, or of the owner of exclusive right(s), or of the duly authorized agent of the author, claimant, or owner of exclusive right(s).

**Address for Return of Certificate** (space 9): The address box must be completed legibly since the certificate will be returned in a window envelope.

# MORE INFORMATION

**"Works":** "Works" are the basic subject matter of copyright; they are what authors create and copyright protects. The statute draws a sharp distinction between the "work" and "any material object in which the work is embodied."

**"Copies" and "Phonorecords":** These are the two types of material objects in which "works" are embodied. In general, **"copies"** are objects from which a work can be read or visually perceived, directly or with the aid of a machine or device, such as manuscripts, books, sheet music, film, and videotape. **"Phonorecords"** are objects embodying fixations of sounds, such as audio tapes and phonograph disks. For example, a song (the "work") can be reproduced in sheet music ("copies") or phonograph disks ("phonorecords"), or both.

**"Sound Recordings":** These are "works," not "copies" or "phonorecords." "Sound recordings" are "works that result from the fixation of a series of musical, spoken, or other sounds, but not including the sounds accompanying a motion picture or other audiovisual work." Example: When a record company issues a new release, the release will typically involve two distinct "works": the "musical work" that has been recorded, and the "sound recording" as a separate work in itself. The material objects that the record company sends out are "phonorecords": physical reproductions of both the "musical work" and the "sound recording."

## Should You File More Than One Application?

If your work consists of a recorded musical, dramatic, or literary work, and both that "work," and the sound recording as a separate "work," are eligible for registration, the application form you should file depends on the following:

**File Only Form SR if:** The copyright claimant is the same for both the musical, dramatic, or literary work and for the sound recording, and you are seeking a single registration to cover both of these "works."

**File Only Form PA (or Form TX) if:** You are seeking to register only the musical, dramatic, or literary work, not the sound recording. Form PA is appropriate for works of the performing arts; Form TX is for nondramatic literary works.

**Separate Applications Should Be Filed on Form PA (or Form TX) and on Form SR if:** (1) The copyright claimant for the musical, dramatic, or literary work is different from the copyright claimant for the sound recording; or (2) You prefer to have separate registrations for the musical, dramatic, or literary work and for the sound recording.

**FORM SR**
UNITED STATES COPYRIGHT OFFICE

REGISTRATION NUMBER

SR SRU

EFFECTIVE DATE OF REGISTRATION

Month Day Year

**DO NOT WRITE ABOVE THIS LINE. IF YOU NEED MORE SPACE, USE A SEPARATE CONTINUATION SHEET.**

**1**

**TITLE OF THIS WORK ▼**

**PREVIOUS OR ALTERNATIVE TITLES ▼**

**NATURE OF MATERIAL RECORDED ▼** See instructions

☐ Musical ☐ Musical-Dramatic
☐ Dramatic ☐ Literary
☐ Other ______

**2**

**a** **NAME OF AUTHOR ▼**

**DATES OF BIRTH AND DEATH** Year Born ▼ Year Died ▼

Was this contribution to the work a "work made for hire"? ☐ Yes ☐ No

**AUTHOR'S NATIONALITY OR DOMICILE** Name of Country OR { Citizen of ▶ ______ Domiciled in ▶ ______

**WAS THIS AUTHOR'S CONTRIBUTION TO THE WORK** Anonymous? ☐ Yes ☐ No Pseudonymous? ☐ Yes ☐ No — If the answer to either of these questions is "Yes," see detailed instructions.

**NATURE OF AUTHORSHIP** Briefly describe nature of the material created by this author in which copyright is claimed. ▼

**b** **NAME OF AUTHOR ▼**

**DATES OF BIRTH AND DEATH** Year Born ▼ Year Died ▼

Was this contribution to the work a "work made for hire"? ☐ Yes ☐ No

**AUTHOR'S NATIONALITY OR DOMICILE** Name of country OR { Citizen of ▶ ______ Domiciled in ▶ ______

**WAS THIS AUTHOR'S CONTRIBUTION TO THE WORK** Anonymous? ☐ Yes ☐ No Pseudonymous? ☐ Yes ☐ No — If the answer to either of these questions is "Yes," see detailed instructions.

**NATURE OF AUTHORSHIP** Briefly describe nature of the material created by this author in which copyright is claimed. ▼

**c** **NAME OF AUTHOR ▼**

**DATES OF BIRTH AND DEATH** Year Born ▼ Year Died ▼

Was this contribution to the work a "work made for hire"? ☐ Yes ☐ No

**AUTHOR'S NATIONALITY OR DOMICILE** Name of Country OR { Citizen of ▶ ______ Domiciled in ▶ ______

**WAS THIS AUTHOR'S CONTRIBUTION TO THE WORK** Anonymous? ☐ Yes ☐ No Pseudonymous? ☐ Yes ☐ No — If the answer to either of these questions is "Yes," see detailed instructions.

**NATURE OF AUTHORSHIP** Briefly describe nature of the material created by this author in which copyright is claimed. ▼

**NOTE**

Under the law, the "author" of a "work made for hire" is generally the employer, not the employee (see instructions). For any part of this work that was "made for hire" check "Yes" in the space provided, give the employer (or other person for whom the work was prepared) as "Author" of that part, and leave the space for dates of birth and death blank.

**3**

**YEAR IN WHICH CREATION OF THIS WORK WAS COMPLETED** **This information must be given in all cases.** ______ ◀ Year

**DATE AND NATION OF FIRST PUBLICATION OF THIS PARTICULAR WORK** **Complete this information ONLY if this work has been published.** Month ▶ ______ Day ▶ ______ Year ▶ ______ ______ ◀ Nation

**4**

See instructions before completing this space.

**COPYRIGHT CLAIMANT(S)** Name and address must be given even if the claimant is the same as the author given in space 2.▼

**TRANSFER** If the claimant(s) named here in space 4 are different from the author(s) named in space 2, give a brief statement of how the claimant(s) obtained ownership of the copyright.▼

DO NOT WRITE HERE OFFICE USE ONLY

APPLICATION RECEIVED

ONE DEPOSIT RECEIVED

TWO DEPOSITS RECEIVED

REMITTANCE NUMBER AND DATE

**MORE ON BACK ▶** • Complete all applicable spaces (numbers 5-9) on the reverse side of this page. • See detailed instructions. • Sign the form at line 8.

**DO NOT WRITE HERE**

Page 1 of ______ pages

EXAMINED BY

CHECKED BY

☐ CORRESPONDENCE Yes

☐ DEPOSIT ACCOUNT FUNDS USED

**FORM SR**

FOR COPYRIGHT OFFICE USE ONLY

**DO NOT WRITE ABOVE THIS LINE. IF YOU NEED MORE SPACE, USE A SEPARATE CONTINUATION SHEET.**

**PREVIOUS REGISTRATION** Has registration for this work, or for an earlier version of this work, already been made in the Copyright Office? **5**

☐ **Yes** ☐ **No** If your answer is "Yes," why is another registration being sought? (Check appropriate box) ▼

☐ This is the first published edition of a work previously registered in unpublished form.

☐ This is the first application submitted by this author as copyright claimant.

☐ This is a changed version of the work, as shown by space 6 on this application.

If your answer is "Yes," give: **Previous Registration Number** ▼ **Year of Registration** ▼

**DERIVATIVE WORK OR COMPILATION** Complete both space 6a & 6b for a derivative work; complete only 6b for a compilation. **6**

**a. Preexisting Material** Identify any preexisting work or works that this work is based on or incorporates. ▼

See instructions before completing this space.

**b. Material Added to This Work** Give a brief, general statement of the material that has been added to this work and in which copyright is claimed. ▼

**DEPOSIT ACCOUNT** If the registration fee is to be charged to a Deposit Account established in the Copyright Office, give name and number of Account. **7**

**Name** ▼ **Account Number** ▼

**CORRESPONDENCE** Give name and address to which correspondence about this application should be sent. Name/Address/Apt/City/State/Zip ▼

Area Code & Telephone Number ▶

Be sure to give your daytime phone ◀ number.

**CERTIFICATION*** I, the undersigned, hereby certify that I am the **8**

Check one ▼

☐ author

☐ other copyright claimant

☐ owner of exclusive right(s)

☐ authorized agent of ____________________

Name of author or other copyright claimant, or owner of exclusive right(s) ▲

of the work identified in this application and that the statements made by me in this application are correct to the best of my knowledge.

**Typed or printed name and date** ▼ If this is a published work, this date must be the same as or later than the date of publication given in space 3.

date ▶

**Handwritten signature (X)** ▼

**MAIL CERTIFICATE TO** **9**

Name ▼

Number/Street/Apartment Number ▼

City/State/ZIP ▼

**Certificate will be mailed in window envelope**

**Have you:**

- Completed all necessary spaces?
- Signed your application in space 8?
- Enclosed check or money order for $10 payable to *Register of Copyrights*?
- Enclosed your deposit material with the application and fee?

**MAIL TO:** Register of Copyrights, Library of Congress, Washington, D.C. 20559

* 17 U.S.C. § 506(e): Any person who knowingly makes a false representation of a material fact in the application for copyright registration provided for by section 409, or in any written statement filed in connection with the application, shall be fined not more than $2,500.

☆U.S. GOVERNMENT PRINTING OFFICE: 1982-361-278/63

Sept. 1982—210,000

# Filling Out Application Form TX

*Detach and read these instructions before completing this form. Make sure all applicable spaces have been filled in before you return this form.*

## BASIC INFORMATION

**When to Use This Form:** Use Form TX for registration of published or unpublished non-dramatic literary works, excluding periodicals or serial issues. This class includes a wide variety of works: fiction, non-fiction, poetry, textbooks, reference works, directories, catalogs, advertising copy, compilations of information, and computer programs. For periodicals and serials, use Form SE.

**Deposit to Accompany Application:** An application for copyright registration must be accompanied by a deposit consisting of copies or phonorecords representing the entire work for which registration is to be made. The following are the general deposit requirements as set forth in the statute:

**Unpublished Work:** Deposit one complete copy (or phonorecord).

**Published Work:** Deposit two complete copies (or phonorecords) of the best edition.

**Work First Published Outside the United States:** Deposit one complete copy (or phonorecord) of the first foreign edition.

**Contribution to a Collective Work:** Deposit one complete copy (or phonorecord) of the best edition of the collective work.

**The Copyright Notice:** For published works, the law provides that a copyright notice in a specified form "shall be placed on all publicly distributed copies from which the work can be visually perceived." Use of the copyright notice is the responsibility of the copyright owner and does not require advance permission from the Copyright Office. The required form of the notice for copies generally consists of three elements: (1) the symbol "©", or the word "Copyright," or the abbreviation "Copr."; (2) the year of first publication; and (3) the name of the owner of copyright. For example: "© 1981 Constance Porter." The notice is to be affixed to the copies "in such manner and location as to give reasonable notice of the claim of copyright."

For further information about copyright registration, notice, or special questions relating to copyright problems, write:

Information and Publications Section, LM-455
Copyright Office
Library of Congress
Washington, D.C. 20559

**PRIVACY ACT ADVISORY STATEMENT**
**Required by the Privacy Act of 1974 (Public Law 93-579)**

AUTHORITY FOR REQUESTING THIS INFORMATION:
- Title 17, U.S.C., Secs. 409 and 410

FURNISHING THE REQUESTED INFORMATION IS:
- Voluntary

BUT IF THE INFORMATION IS NOT FURNISHED:
- It may be necessary to delay or refuse registration
- You may not be entitled to certain relief, remedies, and benefits provided in chapters 4 and 5 of title 17, U.S.C.

PRINCIPAL USES OF REQUESTED INFORMATION:
- Establishment and maintenance of a public record
- Examination of the application for compliance with legal requirements

OTHER ROUTINE USES:
- Public inspection and copying
- Preparation of public indexes
- Preparation of public catalogs of copyright registrations
- Preparation of search reports upon request

NOTE:
- No other advisory statement will be given you in connection with this application
- Please keep this statement and refer to it if we communicate with you regarding this application

## LINE-BY-LINE INSTRUCTIONS

### 1 SPACE 1: Title

**Title of This Work:** Every work submitted for copyright registration must be given a title to identify that particular work. If the copies or phonorecords of the work bear a title (or an identifying phrase that could serve as a title), transcribe that wording *completely* and *exactly* on the application. Indexing of the registration and future identification of the work will depend on the information you give here.

**Previous or Alternative Titles:** Complete this space if there are any additional titles for the work under which someone searching for the registration might be likely to look, or under which a document pertaining to the work might be recorded.

**Publication as a Contribution:** If the work being registered is a contribution to a periodical, serial, or collection, give the title of the contribution in the "Title of this Work" space. Then, in the line headed "Publication as a Contribution," give information about the collective work in which the contribution appeared.

### 2 SPACE 2: Author(s)

**General Instructions:** After reading these instructions, decide who are the "authors" of this work for copyright purposes. Then, unless the work is a "collective work," give the requested information about every "author" who contributed any appreciable amount of copyrightable matter to this version of the work. If you need further space, request additional Continuation sheets. In the case of a collective work, such as an anthology, collection of essays, or encyclopedia, give information about the author of the collective work as a whole.

**Name of Author:** The fullest form of the author's name should be given. Unless the work was "made for hire," the individual who actually created the work is its "author." In the case of a work made for hire, the statute provides that "the employer or other person for whom the work was prepared is considered the author."

**What is a "Work Made for Hire"?** A "work made for hire" is defined as: (1) "a work prepared by an employee within the scope of his or her employment"; or (2) "a work specially ordered or commissioned for use as a contribution to a collective work, as a part of a motion picture or other audiovisual work, as a translation, as a supplementary work, as a compilation, as an instructional text, as a test, as answer material for a test, or as an atlas, if the parties expressly agree in a written instrument signed by them that the work shall be considered a work made for hire." If you have checked "Yes" to indicate that the work was "made for hire," you must give the full legal name of the employer (or other person for whom the work was prepared). You may also include the name of the employee along with the name of the employer (for example: "Elster Publishing Co , employer for hire of John Ferguson").

**"Anonymous" or "Pseudonymous" Work:** An author's contribution to a work is "anonymous" if that author is not identified on the copies or phonorecords of the work. An author's contribution to a work is "pseudonymous" if that author is identified on the copies or phonorecords under a fictitious name. If the work is "anonymous" you may: (1) leave the line blank; or (2) state " anonymous" on the line; or (3) reveal the author's identity. If the work is "pseudonymous" you may : (1) leave the line blank; or (2) give the pseudonym and identify it as such (for example: "Huntley Haverstock, pseudonym"); or (3) reveal the author's name, making clear which is the real name and which is the pseudonym (for example: "Judith Barton, whose pseudonym is Madeline Elster"). However, the citizenship or domicile of the author **must** be given in all cases.

**Dates of Birth and Death:** If the author is dead, the statute requires that the year of death be included in the application unless the work is anonymous or pseudonymous. The author's birth date is optional, but is useful as a form of identification. Leave this space blank if the author's contribution was a "work made for hire."

**Author's Nationality or Domicile:** Give the country of which the author is a citizen, or the country in which the author is domiciled. Nationality or domicile **must** be given in all cases.

**Nature of Authorship:** After the words "Nature of Authorship" give a brief general statement of the nature of this particular author's contribution to the work. Examples: "Entire text"; "Coauthor of entire text"; "Chapters 11-14"; "Editorial revisions"; "Compilation and English translation"; "New text."

## 3 SPACE 3: Creation and Publication

**General Instructions:** Do not confuse "creation" with "publication." Every application for copyright registration must state "the year in which creation of the work was completed." Give the date and nation of first publication only if the work has been published.

**Creation:** Under the statute, a work is "created" when it is fixed in a copy or phonorecord for the first time. Where a work has been prepared over a period of time, the part of the work existing in fixed form on a particular date constitutes the created work on that date. The date you give here should be the year in which the author completed the particular version for which registration is now being sought, even if other versions exist or if further changes or additions are planned.

**Publication:** The statute defines "publication" as "the distribution of copies or phonorecords of a work to the public by sale or other transfer of ownership, or by rental, lease, or lending"; a work is also "published" if there has been an "offering to distribute copies or phonorecords to a group of persons for purposes of further distribution, public performance, or public display." Give the full date (month, day, year) when, and the country where, publication first occurred. If first publication took place simultaneously in the United States and other countries, it is sufficient to state "U.S.A."

## 4 SPACE 4: Claimant(s)

**Name(s) and Address(es) of Copyright Claimant(s):** Give the name(s) and address(es) of the copyright claimant(s) in this work even if the claimant is the same as the author. Copyright in a work belongs initially to the author of the work (including, in the case of a work made for hire, the employer or other person for whom the work was prepared). The copyright claimant is either the author of the work or a person or organization to whom the copyright initially belonging to the author has been transferred.

**Transfer:** The statute provides that, if the copyright claimant is not the author, the application for registration must contain "a brief statement of how the claimant obtained ownership of the copyright." If any copyright claimant named in space 4 is not an author named in space 2, give a brief, general statement summarizing the means by which that claimant obtained ownership of the copyright. Examples: "By written contract"; "Transfer of all rights by author"; "Assignment"; "By will." Do not attach transfer documents or other attachments or riders.

## 5 SPACE 5: Previous Registration

**General Instructions:** The questions in space 5 are intended to find out whether an earlier registration has been made for this work and, if so, whether there is any basis for a new registration. As a general rule, only one basic copyright registration can be made for the same version of a particular work.

**Same Version:** If this version is substantially the same as the work covered by a previous registration, a second registration is not generally possible unless: (1) the work has been registered in unpublished form and a second registration is now being sought to cover this first published edition; or (2) someone other than the author is identified as copyright claimant in the earlier registration, and the author is now seeking registration in his or her own name. If either of these two exceptions apply, check the appropriate box and give the earlier registration number and date. Otherwise, do not submit Form TX; instead, write the Copyright Office for information about supplementary registration or recordation of transfers of copyright ownership.

**Changed Version:** If the work has been changed, and you are now seeking registration to cover the additions or revisions, check the last box in space 5, give the earlier registration number and date, and complete both parts of space 6 in accordance with the instructions below.

**Previous Registration Number and Date:** If more than one previous registration has been made for the work, give the number and date of the latest registration.

## 6 SPACE 6: Derivative Work or Compilation

**General Instructions:** Complete space 6 if this work is a "changed version," "compilation," or "derivative work," and if it incorporates one or more earlier works that have already been published or registered for copyright, or that have fallen into the public domain. A "compilation" is defined as "a work formed by the collection and assembling of preexisting materials or of data that are selected, coordinated, or arranged in such a way that the resulting work as a whole constitutes an original work of authorship." A "derivative work" is "a work based on one or more preexisting works." Examples of derivative works include translations, fictionalizations, abridgments, condensations, or "any other form in which a work may be recast, transformed, or adapted." Derivative works also include works "consisting of editorial revisions, annotations, or other modifications" if these changes, as a whole, represent an original work of authorship.

**Preexisting Material (space 6a):** For derivative works, complete this space and space 6b. In space 6a identify the preexisting work that has been recast, transformed, or adapted. An example of preexisting material might be: "Russian version of Goncharov's 'Oblomov'." Do not complete space 6a for compilations.

**Material Added to This Work (space 6b):** Give a brief, general statement of the new material covered by the copyright claim for which registration is sought. **Derivative work** examples include: "Foreword, editing, critical annotations"; "Translation"; "Chapters 11-17." If the work is a **compilation**, describe both the compilation itself and the material that has been compiled. Example: "Compilation of certain 1917 Speeches by Woodrow Wilson." A work may be both a derivative work and compilation, in which case a sample statement might be: "Compilation and additional new material."

## 7 SPACE 7: Manufacturing Provisions

**General Instructions:** The copyright statute currently provides, as a general rule, that the copies of a published work "consisting preponderantly of nondramatic literary material in the English language" be manufactured in the United States or Canada in order to be lawfully imported and publicly distributed in the United States. If the work being registered is unpublished or not in English, leave this space blank. Complete this space if registration is sought for a published work "consisting preponderantly of nondramatic literary material that is in the English language." Identify those who manufactured the copies and where those manufacturing processes were performed. As an exception to the manufacturing provisions, the statute prescribes that, where manufacture has taken place outside the United States or Canada, a maximum of 2000 copies of the foreign edition may be imported into the United States without affecting the copyright owners' rights. For this purpose, the Copyright Office will issue an Import Statement upon request and payment of a fee of $3 at the time of registration or at any later time. For further information about import statements, write for Form IS.

## 8 SPACE 8: Reproduction for Use of Blind or Physically Handicapped Individuals

**General Instructions:** One of the major programs of the Library of Congress is to provide Braille editions and special recordings of works for the exclusive use of the blind and physically handicapped. In an effort to simplify and speed up the copyright licensing procedures that are a necessary part of this program, section 710 of the copyright statute provides for the establishment of a voluntary licensing system to be tied in with copyright registration. Copyright Office regulations provide that you may grant a license for such reproduction and distribution solely for the use of persons who are certified by competent authority as unable to read normal printed material as a result of physical limitations. The license is entirely voluntary, nonexclusive, and may be terminated upon 90 days notice.

**How to Grant the License:** If you wish to grant it, check one of the three boxes in space 8. Your check in one of these boxes, together with your signature in space 10, will mean that the Library of Congress can proceed to reproduce and distribute under the license without further paperwork. For further information, write for Circular R63.

## 9,10,11 SPACE 9, 10, 11: Fee, Correspondence, Certification, Return Address

**Deposit Account:** If you maintain a Deposit Account in the Copyright Office, identify it in space 9. Otherwise leave the space blank and send the fee of $10 with your application and deposit.

**Correspondence** (space 9): This space should contain the name, address, area code, and telephone number of the person to be consulted if correspondence about this application becomes necessary.

**Certification** (space 10): The application can not be accepted unless it bears the date and the **handwritten signature** of the author or other copyright claimant, or of the owner of exclusive right(s), or of the duly authorized agent of author, claimant, or owner of exclusive right(s).

**Address for Return of Certificate** (space 11): The address box must be completed legibly since the certificate will be returned in a window envelope.

# FORM TX
UNITED STATES COPYRIGHT OFFICE

REGISTRATION NUMBER

TX TXU

EFFECTIVE DATE OF REGISTRATION

Month Day Year

**DO NOT WRITE ABOVE THIS LINE. IF YOU NEED MORE SPACE, USE A SEPARATE CONTINUATION SHEET.**

## 1

**TITLE OF THIS WORK ▼**

**PREVIOUS OR ALTERNATIVE TITLES ▼**

**PUBLICATION AS A CONTRIBUTION** If this work was published as a contribution to a periodical, serial, or collection, give information about the collective work in which the contribution appeared. **Title of Collective Work ▼**

If published in a periodical or serial give: **Volume ▼** **Number ▼** **Issue Date ▼** **On Pages ▼**

## 2

a **NAME OF AUTHOR ▼** **DATES OF BIRTH AND DEATH** Year Born ▼ Year Died ▼

Was this contribution to the work a "work made for hire"? ☐ Yes ☐ No

**AUTHOR'S NATIONALITY OR DOMICILE** Name of Country OR { Citizen of ▶ Domiciled in ▶

**WAS THIS AUTHOR'S CONTRIBUTION TO THE WORK** Anonymous? ☐ Yes ☐ No Pseudonymous? ☐ Yes ☐ No — If the answer to either of these questions is "Yes," see detailed instructions.

**NATURE OF AUTHORSHIP** Briefly describe nature of the material created by this author in which copyright is claimed. ▼

**NOTE**

Under the law, the "author" of a "work made for hire" is generally the employer, not the employee (see instructions). For any part of this work that was "made for hire" check "Yes" in the space provided, give the employer (or other person for whom the work was prepared) as "Author" of that part, and leave the space for dates of birth and death blank.

b **NAME OF AUTHOR ▼** **DATES OF BIRTH AND DEATH** Year Born ▼ Year Died ▼

Was this contribution to the work a "work made for hire"? ☐ Yes ☐ No

**AUTHOR'S NATIONALITY OR DOMICILE** Name of country OR { Citizen of ▶ Domiciled in ▶

**WAS THIS AUTHOR'S CONTRIBUTION TO THE WORK** Anonymous? ☐ Yes ☐ No Pseudonymous? ☐ Yes ☐ No — If the answer to either of these questions is "Yes," see detailed instructions.

**NATURE OF AUTHORSHIP** Briefly describe nature of the material created by this author in which copyright is claimed. ▼

c **NAME OF AUTHOR ▼** **DATES OF BIRTH AND DEATH** Year Born ▼ Year Died ▼

Was this contribution to the work a "work made for hire"? ☐ Yes ☐ No

**AUTHOR'S NATIONALITY OR DOMICILE** Name of Country OR { Citizen of ▶ Domiciled in ▶

**WAS THIS AUTHOR'S CONTRIBUTION TO THE WORK** Anonymous? ☐ Yes ☐ No Pseudonymous? ☐ Yes ☐ No — If the answer to either of these questions is "Yes," see detailed instructions.

**NATURE OF AUTHORSHIP** Briefly describe nature of the material created by this author in which copyright is claimed. ▼

## 3

**YEAR IN WHICH CREATION OF THIS WORK WAS COMPLETED** **This information must be given in all cases.** ◀ Year

**DATE AND NATION OF FIRST PUBLICATION OF THIS PARTICULAR WORK** **Complete this information ONLY if this work has been published.** Month ▶ Day ▶ Year ▶ ◀ Nation

## 4

**COPYRIGHT CLAIMANT(S)** Name and address must be given even if the claimant is the same as the author given in space 2.▼

See instructions before completing this space.

**TRANSFER** If the claimant(s) named here in space 4 are different from the author(s) named in space 2, give a brief statement of how the claimant(s) obtained ownership of the copyright.▼

DO NOT WRITE HERE — OFFICE USE ONLY

APPLICATION RECEIVED

ONE DEPOSIT RECEIVED

TWO DEPOSITS RECEIVED

REMITTANCE NUMBER AND DATE

**MORE ON BACK ▶** • Complete all applicable spaces (numbers 5-11) on the reverse side of this page. • See detailed instructions. • Sign the form at line 10.

**DO NOT WRITE HERE**

Page 1 of_______pages

EXAMINED BY

FORM TX

CHECKED BY

☐ CORRESPONDENCE Yes

☐ DEPOSIT ACCOUNT FUNDS USED

FOR COPYRIGHT OFFICE USE ONLY

**DO NOT WRITE ABOVE THIS LINE. IF YOU NEED MORE SPACE, USE A SEPARATE CONTINUATION SHEET.**

**5**

**PREVIOUS REGISTRATION** Has registration for this work, or for an earlier version of this work, already been made in the Copyright Office?
☐ Yes ☐ No If your answer is "Yes," why is another registration being sought? (Check appropriate box) ▼
☐ This is the first published edition of a work previously registered in unpublished form.
☐ This is the first application submitted by this author as copyright claimant.
☐ This is a changed version of the work, as shown by space 6 on this application.
If your answer is "Yes," give: **Previous Registration Number ▼** **Year of Registration ▼**

**6**

**DERIVATIVE WORK OR COMPILATION** Complete both space 6a & 6b for a derivative work; complete only 6b for a compilation.
**a. Preexisting Material** Identify any preexisting work or works that this work is based on or incorporates. ▼

**b. Material Added to This Work** Give a brief, general statement of the material that has been added to this work and in which copyright is claimed. ▼

See instructions before completing this space.

**7**

**MANUFACTURERS AND LOCATIONS** If this is a published work consisting preponderantly of nondramatic literary material in English, the law may require that the copies be manufactured in the United States or Canada for full protection. If so, the names of the manufacturers who performed certain processes, and the places where these processes were performed **must** be given. See instructions for details.
**Names of Manufacturers ▼** **Places of Manufacture ▼**

**8**

**REPRODUCTION FOR USE OF BLIND OR PHYSICALLY HANDICAPPED INDIVIDUALS** A signature on this form at space 10, and a check in one of the boxes here in space 8, constitutes a non-exclusive grant of permission to the Library of Congress to reproduce and distribute solely for the blind and physically handicapped and under the conditions and limitations prescribed by the regulations of the Copyright Office: (1) copies of the work identified in space 1 of this application in Braille (or similar tactile symbols); or (2) phonorecords embodying a fixation of a reading of that work; or (3) both.
a ☐ Copies and Phonorecords b ☐ Copies Only c ☐ Phonorecords Only

See instructions.

**9**

**DEPOSIT ACCOUNT** If the registration fee is to be charged to a Deposit Account established in the Copyright Office, give name and number of Account.
**Name ▼** **Account Number ▼**

**CORRESPONDENCE** Give name and address to which correspondence about this application should be sent. Name/Address/Apt/City/State/Zip ▼

Area Code & Telephone Number ▶

Be sure to give your daytime phone ◀ number.

**10**

**CERTIFICATION*** I, the undersigned, hereby certify that I am the
Check one ▶
☐ author
☐ other copyright claimant
☐ owner of exclusive right(s)
☐ authorized agent of ______
Name of author or other copyright claimant, or owner of exclusive right(s) ▲

of the work identified in this application and that the statements made by me in this application are correct to the best of my knowledge.

**Typed or printed name and date ▼** If this is a published work, this date must be the same as or later than the date of publication given in space 3.

**date ▶**

**Handwritten signature (X) ▼**

**11**

**MAIL CERTIFICATE TO**

Name ▼

Number/Street/Apartment Number ▼

City/State/ZIP ▼

**Certificate will be mailed in window envelope**

**Have you:**
- Completed all necessary spaces?
- Signed your application in space 10?
- Enclosed check or money order for $10 payable to *Register of Copyrights*?
- Enclosed your deposit material with the application and fee?

**MAIL TO:** Register of Copyrights, Library of Congress, Washington, D.C. 20559

* 17 U.S.C. § 506(e): Any person who knowingly makes a false representation of a material fact in the application for copyright registration provided for by section 409, or in any written statement filed in connection with the application, shall be fined not more than $2,500.

☆ U.S. GOVERNMENT PRINTING OFFICE: 1983: 381-278/507

Sept. 1983—600,000

# Filling Out Application Form VA

*Detach and read these instructions before completing this form. Make sure all applicable spaces have been filled in before you return this form.*

## BASIC INFORMATION

**When to Use This Form:** Use Form VA for copyright registration of published or unpublished works of the visual arts. This category consists of "pictorial, graphic, or sculptural works," including two-dimensional and three-dimensional works of fine, graphic, and applied art, photographs, prints and art reproductions, maps, globes, charts, technical drawings, diagrams, and models.

**What Does Copyright Protect?** Copyright in a work of the visual arts protects those pictorial, graphic, or sculptural elements that, either alone or in combination, represent an "original work of authorship." The statute declares: "In no case does copyright protection for an original work of authorship extend to any idea, procedure, process, system, method of operation, concept, principle, or discovery, regardless of the form in which it is described, explained, illustrated, or embodied in such work."

**Works of Artistic Craftsmanship and Designs:** "Works of artistic craftsmanship" are registrable on Form VA, but the statute makes clear that protection extends to "their form" and not to "their mechanical or utilitarian aspects." The "design of a useful article" is considered copyrightable "only if, and only to the extent that, such design incorporates pictorial, graphic, or sculptural features that can be identified separately from, and are capable of existing independently of, the utilitarian aspects of the article."

**Labels and Advertisements:** Works prepared for use in connection with the sale or advertisement of goods and services are registrable if they contain "original work of authorship." Use Form VA if the copyrightable material in the work you are registering is mainly pictorial or graphic; use Form TX if it consists mainly of text. **NOTE:** Words and short phrases such as names, titles, and slogans cannot be protected by copyright, and the same is true of standard symbols, emblems, and other commonly used graphic designs that are in the public domain. When used commercially, material of that sort can sometimes be protected under state laws of unfair competition or under the Federal trademark laws. For information about trademark registration, write to the Commissioner of Patents and Trademarks, Washington, D.C. 20231.

**Deposit to Accompany Application:** An application for copyright registration must be accompanied by a deposit consisting of copies representing the entire work for which registration is to be made.

**Unpublished Work:** Deposit one complete copy.

**Published Work:** Deposit two complete copies of the best edition.

**Work First Published Outside the United States:** Deposit one complete copy of the first foreign edition.

**Contribution to a Collective Work:** Deposit one complete copy of the best edition of the collective work.

**The Copyright Notice:** For published works, the law provides that a copyright notice in a specified form "shall be placed on all publicly distributed copies from which the work can be visually perceived." Use of the copyright notice is the responsibility of the copyright owner and does not require advance permission from the Copyright Office. The required form of the notice for copies generally consists of three elements: (1) the symbol "©", or the word "Copyright," or the abbreviation "Copr."; (2) the year of first publication; and (3) the name of the owner of copyright. For example: "© 1981 Constance Porter." The notice is to be affixed to the copies "in such manner and location as to give reasonable notice of the claim of copyright."

For further information about copyright registration, notice, or special questions relating to copyright problems, write:

Information and Publications Section, LM-455
Copyright Office, Library of Congress, Washington, D.C. 20559

**PRIVACY ACT ADVISORY STATEMENT Required by the Privacy Act of 1974 (P.L. 93-579)**

The authority for requesting this information is title 17, U.S.C., secs. 409 and 410. Furnishing the requested information is voluntary. But if the information is not furnished, it may be necessary to delay or refuse registration and you may not be entitled to certain relief, remedies, and benefits provided in chapters 4 and 5 of title 17, U.S.C.

The principal uses of the requested information are the establishment and maintenance of a public record and the examination of the application for compliance with legal requirements.

Other routine uses include public inspection and copying, preparation of public indexes, preparation of public catalogs of copyright registrations, and preparation of search reports upon request.

NOTE: No other advisory statement will be given in connection with this application. Please keep this statement and refer to it if we communicate with you regarding this application.

## LINE-BY-LINE INSTRUCTIONS

### 1 SPACE 1: Title

**Title of This Work:** Every work submitted for copyright registration must be given a title to identify that particular work. If the copies of the work bear a title (or an identifying phrase that could serve as a title), transcribe that wording *completely* and *exactly* on the application. Indexing of the registration and future identification of the work will depend on the information you give here.

**Previous or Alternative Titles:** Complete this space if there are any additional titles for the work under which someone searching for the registration might be likely to look, or under which a document pertaining to the work might be recorded.

**Publication as a Contribution:** If the work being registered is a contribution to a perodical, serial, or collection, give the title of the contribution in the "Title of This Work"space. Then, in the line headed "Publication as a Contribution," give information about the collective work in which the contribution appeared.

**Nature of This Work:** Briefly describe the general nature or character of the pictorial, graphic, or sculptural work being registered for copyright. Examples: "Oil Painting"; "Charcoal Drawing"; "Etching"; "Sculpture"; "Map"; "Photograph"; "Scale Model"; "Lithographic Print"; "Jewelry Design"; "Fabric Design."

### 2 SPACE 2: Author(s)

**General Instructions:** After reading these instructions, decide who are the "authors" of this work for copyright purposes. Then, unless the work is a "collective work," give the requested information about every "author" who contributed any appreciable amount of copyrightable matter to this version of the work. If you need further space, request additional Continuation Sheets. In the case of a collective work, such as a catalog of paintings or collection of cartoons by various authors, give information about the author of the collective work as a whole.

**Name of Author:** The fullest form of the author's name should be given. Unless the work was "made for hire," the individual who actually created the work is its "author." In the case of a work made for hire, the statute provides that "the employer or other person for whom the work was prepared is considered the author."

**What is a "Work Made for Hire"?** A "work made for hire" is defined as: (1) "a work prepared by an employee within the scope of his or her employment"; or (2) "a work specially ordered or commissioned for use as a contribution to a collective work, as a part of a motion picture or other audiovisual work, as a translation, as a supplementary work, as a compilation, as an instructional text, as a test, as answer material for a test, or as an atlas, if the parties expressly agree in a written instrument signed by them that the work shall be considered a work made for hire." If you have checked "Yes" to indicate that the work was "made for hire," you must give the full legal name of the employer (or other person for whom the work was prepared). You may also include the name of the employee along with the name of the employer (for example: "Elster Publishing Co., employer for hire of John Ferguson").

**"Anonymous" or "Pseudonymous" Work:** An author's contribution to a work is "anonymous" if that author is not identified on the copies or phonorecords of the work. An author's contribution to a work is "pseudonymous" if that author is identified on the copies or phonorecords under a fictitious name. If the work is "anonymous" you may: (1) leave the line blank; or (2) state "anonymous" on the line; or (3) reveal the author's identity. If the work is "pseudonymous" you may: (1) leave the line blank; or (2) give the pseudonym and identify it as such (for example: "Huntley Haverstock, pseudonym"); or (3) reveal the author's name, making clear which is the real name and which is the pseudonym (for example: "Henry Leek, whose pseudonym is Priam Farrel"). However, the citizenship or domicile of the author **must** be given in all cases.

**Dates of Birth and Death:** If the author is dead, the statute requires that the year of death be included in the application unless the work is anonymous or pseudonymous. The author's birth date is optional, but is useful as a form of identification. Leave this space blank if the author's contribution was a "work made for hire."

**Author's Nationality or Domicile:** Give the country of which the author is a citizen, or the country in which the author is domiciled. Nationality or domicile **must** be given in all cases.

**Nature of Authorship:** Give a brief general statement of the nature of this particular author's contribution to the work. Examples: "Painting"; "Photograph"; "Silk Screen Reproduction"; "Co-author of Cartographic Material"; "Technical Drawing"; "Text and Artwork."

## 3 SPACE 3: Creation and Publication

**General Instructions:** Do not confuse "creation" with "publication." Every application for copyright registration must state "the year in which creation of the work was completed." Give the date and nation of first publication only if the work has been published.

**Creation:** Under the statute, a work is "created" when it is fixed in a copy or phonorecord for the first time. Where a work has been prepared over a period of time, the part of the work existing in fixed form on a particular date constitutes the created work on that date. The date you give here should be the year in which the author completed the particular version for which registration is now being sought, even if other versions exist or if further changes or additions are planned.

**Publication:** The statute defines "publication" as "the distribution of copies or phonorecords of a work to the public by sale or other transfer of ownership, or by rental, lease, or lending"; a work is also "published" if there has been an "offering to distribute copies or phonorecords to a group of persons for purposes of further distribution, public performance, or public display." Give the full date (month, day, year) when, and the country where, publication first occurred. If first publication took place simultaneously in the United States and other countries, it is sufficient to state "U.S.A."

## 4 SPACE 4: Claimant(s)

**Name(s) and Address(es) of Copyright Claimant(s):** Give the name(s) and address(es) of the copyright claimant(s) in this work even if the claimant is the same as the author. Copyright in a work belongs initially to the author of the work (including, in the case of a work made for hire, the employer or other person for whom the work was prepared). The copyright claimant is either the author of the work or a person or organization to whom the copyright initially belonging to the author has been transferred.

**Transfer:** The statute provides that, if the copyright claimant is not the author, the application for registration must contain "a brief statement of how the claimant obtained ownership of the copyright." If any copyright claimant named in space 4 is not an author named in space 2, give a brief, general statement summarizing the means by which that claimant obtained ownership of the copyright. Examples: "By written contract"; "Transfer of all rights by author"; "Assignment"; "By will." Do not attach transfer documents or other attachments or riders.

## 5 SPACE 5: Previous Registration

**General Instructions:** The questions in space 5 are intended to find out whether an earlier registration has been made for this work and, if so, whether there is any basis for a new registration. As a rule, only one basic copyright registration can be made for the same version of a particular work.

**Same Version:** If this version is substantially the same as the work covered by a previous registration, a second registration is not generally possible unless: (1) the work has been registered in unpublished form and a second registration is now being sought to cover this first published edition; or (2) someone other than the author is identified as copyright claimant in the earlier registration, and the author is now seeking registration in his or her own name. If either of these two exceptions apply, check the appropriate box and give the earlier registration number and date. Otherwise, do not submit Form VA; instead, write the Copyright Office for information about supplementary registration or recordation of transfers of copyright ownership.

**Changed Version:** If the work has been changed, and you are now seeking registration to cover the additions or revisions, check the last box in space 5, give the earlier registration number and date, and complete both parts of space 6 in accordance with the instructions below.

**Previous Registration Number and Date:** If more than one previous registration has been made for the work, give the number and date of the latest registration.

## 6 SPACE 6: Derivative Work or Compilation

**General Instructions:** Complete space 6 if this work is a "changed version," "compilation," or "derivative work," and if it incorporates one or more earlier works that have already been published or registered for copyright, or that have fallen into the public domain. A "compilation" is defined as "a work formed by the collection and assembling of preexisting materials or of data that are selected, coordinated, or arranged in such a way that the resulting work as a whole constitutes an original work of authorship." A "derivative work" is "a work based on one or more preexisting works." Examples of derivative works include reproductions of works of art, sculptures based on drawings, lithographs based on paintings, maps based on previously published sources, or "any other form in which a work may be recast, transformed, or adapted." Derivative works also include works "consisting of editorial revisions, annotations, or other modifications" if these changes, as a whole, represent an original work of authorship.

**Preexisting Material (space 6a):** Complete this space **and** space 6b for derivative works. In this space identify the preexisting work that has been recast, transformed, or adapted. Examples of preexisting material might be "Grunewald Altarpiece"; or "19th century quilt design." Do not complete this space for compilations.

**Material Added to This Work (space 6b):** Give a brief, general statement of the **additional** new material covered by the copyright claim for which registration is sought. In the case of a derivative work, identify this new material. Examples: "Adaptation of design and additional artistic work"; "Reproduction of painting by photolithography"; "Additional cartographic material"; "Compilation of photographs." If the work is a compilation, give a brief, general statement describing both the material that has been compiled **and** the compilation itself. Example: "Compilation of 19th Century Political Cartoons."

## 7,8,9 SPACE 7, 8, 9: Fee, Correspondence, Certification, Return Address

**Deposit Account:** If you maintain a Deposit Account in the Copyright Office, identify it in space 7. Otherwise leave the space blank and send the fee of $10 with your application and deposit.

**Correspondence** (space 7): This space should contain the name, address, area code, and telephone number of the person to be consulted if correspondence about this application becomes necessary.

**Certification** (space 8): The application cannot be accepted unless it bears the date and the **handwritten signature** of the author or other copyright claimant, or of the owner of exclusive right(s), or of the duly authorized agent of the author, claimant, or owner of exclusive right(s).

**Address for Return of Certificate** (space 9): The address box must be completed legibly since the certificate will be returned in a window envelope.

# MORE INFORMATION

## Form of Deposit for Works of the Visual Arts

**Exceptions to General Deposit Requirements:** As explained on the reverse side of this page, the statutory deposit requirements (generally one copy for unpublished works and two copies for published works) will vary for particular kinds of works of the visual arts. The copyright law authorizes the Register of Copyrights to issue regulations specifying "the administrative classes into which works are to be placed for purposes of deposit and registration, and the nature of the copies or phonorecords to be deposited in the various classes specified." For particular classes, the regulations may require or permit "the deposit of identifying material instead of copies or phonorecords," or "the deposit of only one copy or phonorecord where two would normally be required."

## What Should You Deposit?

The detailed requirements with respect to the kind of deposit to accompany an application on Form VA are contained in the Copyright Office Regulations. The following does not cover all of the deposit requirements, but is intended to give you some general guidance.

**For an Unpublished Work,** the material deposited should represent the entire copyrightable content of the work for which registration is being sought.

**For a Published Work,** the material deposited should generally consist of two complete copies of the best edition. Exceptions: (1) For certain types of works, one complete copy may be deposited instead of two. These include greeting cards, postcards, stationery, labels, advertisements, scientific drawings, and globes; (2) For most three-dimensional sculptural works, and for certain two-dimensional works, the Copyright Office Regulations require deposit of identifying material (photographs or drawings in a specified form) rather than copies; and (3) Under certain circumstances, for works published in five copies or less or in limited, numbered editions, the deposit may consist of one copy or of identifying reproductions.

# FORM VA

UNITED STATES COPYRIGHT OFFICE

REGISTRATION NUMBER

VA VAU

EFFECTIVE DATE OF REGISTRATION

Month Day Year

DO NOT WRITE ABOVE THIS LINE. IF YOU NEED MORE SPACE, USE A SEPARATE CONTINUATION SHEET.

**1**

**TITLE OF THIS WORK ▼** **NATURE OF THIS WORK ▼** See instructions

**PREVIOUS OR ALTERNATIVE TITLES ▼**

**PUBLICATION AS A CONTRIBUTION** If this work was published as a contribution to a periodical, serial, or collection, give information about the collective work in which the contribution appeared. **Title of Collective Work ▼**

If published in a periodical or serial give: **Volume ▼** **Number ▼** **Issue Date ▼** **On Pages ▼**

**2**

**a** **NAME OF AUTHOR ▼** **DATES OF BIRTH AND DEATH** Year Born ▼ Year Died ▼

Was this contribution to the work a "work made for hire"? ☐ Yes ☐ No

**AUTHOR'S NATIONALITY OR DOMICILE** Name of Country OR { Citizen of ▶ / Domiciled in ▶

**WAS THIS AUTHOR'S CONTRIBUTION TO THE WORK** Anonymous? ☐ Yes ☐ No Pseudonymous? ☐ Yes ☐ No — If the answer to either of these questions is "Yes," see detailed instructions.

**NATURE OF AUTHORSHIP** Briefly describe nature of the material created by this author in which copyright is claimed. ▼

**NOTE**

Under the law, the "author" of a "work made for hire" is generally the employer, not the employee (see instructions). For any part of this work that was "made for hire" check "Yes" in the space provided, give the employer (or other person for whom the work was prepared) as "Author" of that part, and leave the space for dates of birth and death blank.

**b** **NAME OF AUTHOR ▼** **DATES OF BIRTH AND DEATH** Year Born ▼ Year Died ▼

Was this contribution to the work a "work made for hire"? ☐ Yes ☐ No

**AUTHOR'S NATIONALITY OR DOMICILE** Name of country OR { Citizen of ▶ / Domiciled in ▶

**WAS THIS AUTHOR'S CONTRIBUTION TO THE WORK** Anonymous? ☐ Yes ☐ No Pseudonymous? ☐ Yes ☐ No — If the answer to either of these questions is "Yes," see detailed instructions.

**NATURE OF AUTHORSHIP** Briefly describe nature of the material created by this author in which copyright is claimed. ▼

**c** **NAME OF AUTHOR ▼** **DATES OF BIRTH AND DEATH** Year Born ▼ Year Died ▼

Was this contribution to the work a "work made for hire"? ☐ Yes ☐ No

**AUTHOR'S NATIONALITY OR DOMICILE** Name of Country OR { Citizen of ▶ / Domiciled in ▶

**WAS THIS AUTHOR'S CONTRIBUTION TO THE WORK** Anonymous? ☐ Yes ☐ No Pseudonymous? ☐ Yes ☐ No — If the answer to either of these questions is "Yes," see detailed instructions.

**NATURE OF AUTHORSHIP** Briefly describe nature of the material created by this author in which copyright is claimed. ▼

**3**

**YEAR IN WHICH CREATION OF THIS WORK WAS COMPLETED** **This information must be given in all cases.** ◀ Year

**DATE AND NATION OF FIRST PUBLICATION OF THIS PARTICULAR WORK** **Complete this information ONLY if this work has been published.** Month ▶ Day ▶ Year ▶ ◀ Nation

**4**

**COPYRIGHT CLAIMANT(S)** Name and address must be given even if the claimant is the same as the author given in space 2.▼

See instructions before completing this space.

**TRANSFER** If the claimant(s) named here in space 4 are different from the author(s) named in space 2, give a brief statement of how the claimant(s) obtained ownership of the copyright.▼

DO NOT WRITE HERE OFFICE USE ONLY

APPLICATION RECEIVED

ONE DEPOSIT RECEIVED

TWO DEPOSITS RECEIVED

REMITTANCE NUMBER AND DATE

**MORE ON BACK ▶** • Complete all applicable spaces (numbers 5-9) on the reverse side of this page • See detailed instructions. • Sign the form at line 8.

DO NOT WRITE HERE

Page 1 of ______ pages

EXAMINED BY

**FORM VA**

CHECKED BY

☐ CORRESPONDENCE Yes

☐ DEPOSIT ACCOUNT FUNDS USED

FOR COPYRIGHT OFFICE USE ONLY

**DO NOT WRITE ABOVE THIS LINE. IF YOU NEED MORE SPACE, USE A SEPARATE CONTINUATION SHEET.**

## 5

**PREVIOUS REGISTRATION** Has registration for this work, or for an earlier version of this work, already been made in the Copyright Office?

☐ **Yes** ☐ **No** If your answer is "Yes," why is another registration being sought? (Check appropriate box) ▼

☐ This is the first published edition of a work previously registered in unpublished form.

☐ This is the first application submitted by this author as copyright claimant.

☐ This is a changed version of the work, as shown by space 6 on this application.

If your answer is "Yes," give: **Previous Registration Number ▼** **Year of Registration ▼**

## 6

**DERIVATIVE WORK OR COMPILATION** Complete both space 6a & 6b for a derivative work; complete only 6b for a compilation.

a. **Preexisting Material** Identify any preexisting work or works that this work is based on or incorporates. ▼

See instructions before completing this space.

b. **Material Added to This Work** Give a brief, general statement of the material that has been added to this work and in which copyright is claimed. ▼

## 7

**DEPOSIT ACCOUNT** If the registration fee is to be charged to a Deposit Account established in the Copyright Office, give name and number of Account.

**Name ▼** **Account Number ▼**

**CORRESPONDENCE** Give name and address to which correspondence about this application should be sent. Name/Address/Apt/City/State/Zip ▼

Area Code & Telephone Number ▶

Be sure to give your daytime phone ◀ number.

## 8

**CERTIFICATION*** I, the undersigned, hereby certify that I am the

Check only one ▼

☐ author

☐ other copyright claimant

☐ owner of exclusive right(s)

☐ authorized agent of ______________________

Name of author or other copyright claimant, or owner of exclusive right(s) ▲

of the work identified in this application and that the statements made by me in this application are correct to the best of my knowledge.

**Typed or printed name and date ▼** If this is a published work, this date must be the same as or later than the date of publication given in space 3.

**date ▶**

**Handwritten signature (X) ▼**

## 9

**MAIL CERTIFICATE TO**

Name ▼

Number/Street/Apartment Number ▼

City/State/ZIP ▼

**Certificate will be mailed in window envelope**

**Have you:**

- Completed all necessary spaces?
- Signed your application in space 8?
- Enclosed check or money order for $10 payable to *Register of Copyrights*?
- Enclosed your deposit material with the application and fee?

**MAIL TO:** Register of Copyrights, Library of Congress, Washington, D.C. 20559

* 17 U.S.C. § 506(e): Any person who knowingly makes a false representation of a material fact in the application for copyright registration provided for by section 409, or in any written statement filed in connection with the application, shall be fined not more than $2,500.

☆ U.S. GOVERNMENT PRINTING OFFICE: 1981: 355-312

Nov. 1981-600,000

Copyright Office • The Library of Congress • Washington, D.C. 20559

# request for special handling

1 *NOTE: The special handling of a claim severely disrupts the entire registration process. It is, therefore, granted only in the most urgent of cases. A request for special handling is subject to the approval of the Chief of the Acquisitions and Processing Division, who takes into account the workload situation of the office at the time the request is made. A minimum period of five working days is required to process a claim under our special handling procedures.*

Why is there an urgent need for special handling?

2 If special handling is needed because of litigation, please answer the following questions:

a. Is the litigation actual or prospective?

b. Are you (or your client) the plaintiff or defendant in the action? Please specify.

c. What are the names of the parties and what is the name of the court where the action is pending or expected?

d. What is the latest date on which the certificate(s) or other requested item(s) could be furnished to you and still be of use in this matter?

I certify that the statements made above are correct to the best of my knowledge.

(Signature)

(Address)

(Phone) (Date)

FOR COPYRIGHT OFFICE USE ONLY Information Specialist handling matter

## remarks

C-2 - December 1978 - 500

## CIRCULARS

| | |
|---|---|
| R1. | Copyright Basics |
| R1b. | Limitations on the Information Furnished by the Copyright Office |
| R1c. | Copyright Registration Procedures |
| R1d. | New Copyright Registration Procedures |
| R1e. | The Certification Space of The Application Form |
| R1f. | Before You Submit an Application for Registration of a Claim to Copyright |
| R2. | Publications on Copyright |
| R2b. | Selected Bibliographies |
| R4. | Copyright Fees Effective January 1, 1978 |
| R5. | How To Open and Maintain a Deposit Account in the Copyright Office |
| R5a. | Requirements for Maintaining a Deposit Account in the Copyright Office |
| R6. | Obtaining Copies of Copyright Office Records and Deposits |
| R7a. | Simultaneous Deposit of the Elements for Registration |
| R7b. | "Best Edition" of Published Works for The Collections of the Library of Congress |
| R7c. | The Effects of Not Replying Promptly to Copyright Office Correspondence |
| R7d. | Mandatory Deposit of Copies or Phonorecords for the Library of Congress |
| R8. | Supplementary Copyright Registration |
| R8a. | The Effective Date of Registration |
| R12. | Recordation of Transfers & Other Documents |
| R13. | Trademarks |
| R15. | Renewal of Copyright |

R15a. Duration of Copyright

R15T. Extention of Copyright Terms

R21. Reproduction of Copyrighted Works by Educators and Librarians

R22. How to Investigate the Copyright Status of a Work

R30. Special Postage Rates for Deposit Copies Mailed to the Copyright Office

R31. Ideas, Methods or Systems

R32. Blank Forms and Other Work Not Protected by Copyright

R33. Computing and Measuring Devices

R34. Copyright Protection Not Available for Names, Titles, or Short Phrases

R38a. International Copyright Relations of The United States.

R38c. International Copyright Conventions

R40a. Specifications for Visual Arts Identifying Material

R40b. Deposit Requirements for Registration of Claims to Copyright in Visual Arts Material

R44. Cartoons and Comic Strips

R45. Copyright Registration for Motion Pictures Including Video Recordings

R47e. Radio and Television Programs

R50. Copyright Registration for Musical Compositions

R51. Repeal of Notice of Use Requirement

R56a. Copyright Registration of Musical Compositions and Sound Recordings

R60a. Registration for Periodicals on Form TX

R61. Copyright Registration for Computer Programs

R62. Copyright Registration for Serials on Forms SE

| | |
|---|---|
| R63. | Reproductions of Copyrighted Works for Blind and Physically Handicapped Individuals |
| R70. | Performances of Music on Coin-Operated Phonorecord Players |
| R71. | Replacement Certificates for Coin-Operated Phonorecord Players |
| R72. | Correcting Errors in Juke Box Certificates and Securing Appropriate Refunds |
| R73. | Compulsory License for Making and Distributing Phonorecords |
| R75. | The Licensing Division of The Copyright Office |
| R96. Section 201.4 | Recordation of Transfers and Certain Other Documents |
| R96. Section 201.6 | Payment and Refund of Copyright Office Fees |
| R96. Section 201.8 | Import Statements |
| R96. Section 201.10 | Notices of Termination of Transfers and Licenses Covering Extended Renewal Term |
| R96. Section 201.13 | Notices of Objection to Certain Noncommercial Performances Of Nondramatic Literary or Musical Works |
| R96. Section | Warnings of Copyright for Use by Certain Libraries and Archives |
| R96. Section 201.15 | Voluntary License to Permit Reproduction of Nondramatic Literary Works Solely for Use of the Blind and Physically Handicapped |
| R96. Section 201.20 | Methods of Affixation and Positions of the Copyright Notice on Various Types of Works |
| R96. Section 201.22 | Advance Notices of Potential Infringement of Works Consisting of Sounds, Images, or Both |

| | |
|---|---|
| R96. Section 201.23 | Transfer of Unpublished Copyright Deposits to the Library of Congress |
| R96. Section 202.17 | Renewals |
| R96h. | Section 202.1 of The Regulations of the Copyright Office |
| R99. | Highlights of The New Copyright Law |
| R100. | Federal Statutory Protection for Mask Works |

# Table of Cases

# Table of Statutes, Rules, and Regulations

## United States Code



## Code of Federal Regulations



## Federal Register



## Federal Rules of Evidence



## Copyright Office Letters



## Copyright Revision Act of 1978

## Trademark Act of 1905



## Trademark Act of 1946

# Index of Subjects